The Eagle in the Desert

The Gulf Region

THE EAGLE IN THE DESERT

Looking Back on U.S. Involvement in the Persian Gulf War

Edited by
William Head and Earl H. Tilford, Jr.

PRAEGER

Westport, Connecticut
London

Library of Congress Cataloging-in-Publication Data

The eagle in the desert : looking back on U.S.
involvement in the Persian Gulf War / edited by William Head and
Earl H. Tilford, Jr.
    p. cm.
    Includes bibliographical references (p.   ) and index.
    ISBN 0-275-95025-5 (alk. paper).—ISBN 0-275-95397-1
(pbk.)
    1. Persian Gulf War, 1991—Participation, American. I. Head,
William P., 1949- . II. Tilford, Earl H.
DS79.724.U6E2   1996
956.7044'2373—dc20   95-30699

British Library Cataloguing in Publication Data is available.

Copyright © 1996 by William Head and Earl H. Tilford, Jr.

All rights reserved. No portion of this book may be
reproduced, by any process or technique, without the
express written consent of the publisher.

Library of Congress Catalog Card Number: 95-30699
ISBN: 0-275-95025-5
      0-275-95397-1 (pbk.)

First published in 1996

Praeger Publishers, 88 Post Road West, Westport, CT 06881
An imprint of Greenwood Publishing Group, Inc.

Printed in the United States of America

The paper used in this book complies with the
Permanent Paper Standard issued by the National
Information Standards Organization (Z39.48-1984).

P

> In order to keep this title in print and available to the academic community, this edition was produced using digital reprint technology in a relatively short print run. This would not have been attainable using traditional methods. Although the cover has been changed from its original appearance, the text remains the same and all materials and methods used still conform to the highest book-making standards.

Contents

Illustrations	vii
Preface *William Head*	ix
Abbreviations and Acronyms	xiii
Introduction *William Head*	1
Part I: Politics, Alliances, and Regional Views	17
1. The Gulf War Coalition: The Politics and Economics of a Most Unusual Alliance *Daniel S. Papp*	21
2. But Was It *Jihad?*: Islam and the Ethics of the Persian Gulf War *Sohail H. Hashmi*	47
Part II: Bringing the Eagle to the Gulf Desert: Airlift, Supplies, and Logistics	65
3. Air Mobility in Operations Desert Shield and Desert Storm: An Assessment *John W. Leland*	67

4. Sustaining the War Machine: U.S. Air Force Logistics
   Support during the Gulf War — 87
   William Suit

Part III: The Air War: Planning and Combat — 107

5. Thunder and Storm: Strategic Air Operations in the Gulf
   War — 111
   Daniel T. Kuehl

6. Parallel Warfare: What Is It? Where Did It Come From?
   Why Is It Important? — 127
   David A. Deptula

7. Command and Control in the Gulf War: A Military
   Revolution in Airpower? — 157
   Mark D. Mandeles

Part IV: The Ground War: The Army and the Marines — 173

8. Playing in the Sandbox: Doctrine, Combat, and Outcome on
   the Ground — 175
   Larry E. Cable

9. U.S. Marine Operations in the Persian Gulf War, 1990–1991 — 201
   John T. Quinn and Jack Shulimson

Part V: The Navy's Role in the Gulf War — 223

10. On the Storm's Outer Edge: U.S. Navy Operations in the
    Persian Gulf War — 225
    Robert J. Schneller, Jr.

11. Sailing in the Sand: The U.S. Navy's Role in the Gulf War — 251
    Norman Friedman

Part VI: Reexamining the Allied "Victory" in the Gulf War — 267

12. Clausewitz's *On War* and the Gulf War — 269
    Michael T. Corgan

13. A New Covenant?: The Apostles of Douhet and the Persian
    Gulf War — 290
    Caroline F. Ziemke

Selected Bibliography — 311

Index — 323

About the Editors and Contributors — 347

Illustrations

TABLES

1.1	Coalition Military Forces Deployed against Iraq	22
1.2	Desert Shield and Desert Storm Strategic Airlift and Sealift: August 1990–March 1991	25
1.3	Major Financial Contributors to the Coalition	26
4.1	Aircraft Mission Capable Rates	100
10.1	NAVCENT Command Structure	231

FIGURES

6.1	Basic Electric Circuits	131
6.2	Series versus Parallel Warfare	132
6.3	Air Campaign Attack Schemes	144
7.1	Map of Assigned Targets	160
7.2	The Planning Cycle	161
8.1	Map Showing the Coalition Offensive	186
9.1	Map Showing the Order of Battle, February 23, 1991	215

Preface

In the much ballyhooed motion picture *MacArthur*, the renowned actor Gregory Peck has one particularly poignant moment in the middle of the movie. It is near dawn off the Inchon coast. He is on the bridge of the invasion forces' flagship peering through his high-powered binoculars. One of his senior aides joins him as the first glint of sunlight crosses the skyline behind them. MacArthur looks at his aide and launches into a woeful stream of verbal doubts about the success of the daring Inchon Landing. "Colonel, this could be the shortest landing on record. What if the tides are too high, what if they have found out we're coming and are sitting out there waiting for us? Thousands of our boys will die, the Communists will win, and my career will be ruined!"

The aide, mouth gaping, is incredulous and amazed. After a long pause he declares, "General are you serious?" MacArthur replies, "Why, didn't you know that even I have doubts?" Relieved, the colonel smiles, and the general returns to his inspection of the landing. Of course, this was a movie. The scene is apocryphal. Although it could have happened, and to some degree is very truthful, it is one more case of Hollywood taking literary license to heighten the drama of a defining theatrical moment and an important historical event.

There are times when real life is even more dramatic than the movies. In September 1991, while at an Army War College–Georgia Tech Conference entitled "Strategic Mobility, Forward Presence, and the Defense of American Interests," at Georgia Tech, then Brigadier General Richard Larson (later Major General), who had been General H. Norman Schwarzkopf's senior in-theater Army Supply and Logistics Officer, told a real-life story of equal poignancy.

It seems that one particularly dark desert night, not long before the opening of the ground campaign, General Schwarzkopf, in a rather agitated mood, collected Larson and several other senior officers, put them in some "Humvees," and drove everyone out to the forward areas. Once at the front lines, he peered through some high-resolution night vision binoculars at the enemy defenses. He then bade the remaining members of his group to do the same. After the last person had done so, he turned and declared to the gathered company, "Do you see those fortifications . . . that barbed wire . . . those tank traps? Two, three, four, ten thousand, maybe more of our boys could die taking those positions! I'll be responsible! How can I face their mothers and fathers? How can I face the American people?" Everyone present stood dumbfounded. After a tense moment of silence, the general turned and walked to the vehicles and everyone drove back to headquarters. No one spoke of the incident again.

A few days later, Allied troops swept through the fearsome Iraqi defenses and, within ten days, had won a smashing military victory with a loss of less than 300 lives. General Schwarzkopf not only could face the U.S. public, but also became one of its most celebrated military heroes of the post–World War II era. Knowing what we know now, we realize that Iraq was a fifth-rate Third World regional military force. Nonetheless, current realities beg for further investigation, including an examination of the human factors that lurk behind every military adventure. Many know of other poignant anecdotes such as the aforementioned—stories of fear and heroism, humor and tragedy, life and death. Popular wisdom says that the Allies won a spectacular victory. After all, didn't the general's book, CNN's videotape (for $29.95), and the myriad of other popular books frantically produced in 1991 and 1992 tell us just that? President George Bush officially declared that the Gulf victory had "kicked the hell out of the Vietnam Syndrome."

However, as time has passed and critical analyses have provided a more sober perspective, it seems that there are still many more stories to tell than have been told; there are a vast number of critical military lessons begging to be learned, and there are reams and reams of documents, letters, diaries, memoirs, and so forth which still need to be researched. So the study of the Persian Gulf War has only just begun. Because Saddam Hussein still rules Iraq, tensions are still keenly felt in the region, and the potential for nuclear terrorism grows every day. The study of the Gulf War needs to continue until all the stories are told and all the lessons are learned—good or bad, happy or sad. The 300 Allied soldiers, along with the thousands of Iraqis who did die, deserve at least that much.

The Eagle in the Desert proposes to begin this new era of reexamination. Although it does not presume to be the only definitive work, it does seek to break significant new ground using the reams of new research and several fresh approaches to the analysis of the story. In the end, it will try to begin the process of placing the Gulf War in its true historical perspective.

In any work of this magnitude, there are many people who need to be thanked for their effort and support. Obviously, the authors' chapters and their cooperation were essential to the creation of this book. In addition, my friend and co-editor Earl H. Tilford, Jr.'s professional skills, intellectual ability, and total dedication were indispensable to the completion of our work. In addition, I want to thank my friend and colleague, Dick Iobst, who provided much moral and editorial support. Finally, I must reserve a special thanks to my friend Phil Booth, who provided vital technical and computer support without which the project would have been impossible. Ultimately, we wish to dedicate this book to those who served their country, especially to those who made the supreme sacrifice.

—William Head

Abbreviations and Acronyms

AAA	Antiaircraft Artillery
AAV	Assault Amphibian Vehicle
AB	Air Base
ABCCC	Airborne Command and Control Center
ABDR	Aircraft Battle Damage Repair
ACTS	Air Corps Tactical School
AFB	Air Force Base
AFLC	Air Force Logistics Command
AFLIF	Air Force Logistics Information File
AFLMC	Air Force Logistics Management Center
AFRES	Air Force Reserve
AFSC	Air Force Systems Command
AHIP	Army Helicopter Improvement Program
AIS	Avionics Intermediate Station
AMC	Air Mobility Command
ANG	Air National Guard
AOR	Area of Responsibility
ARAMCO	Arabian American Oil Company

ARC	Air Reserve Component
ARG	Amphibious Ready Group
ASARS	Airborne Strategic Attack Radar System
ATE	Automatic Test Equipment
ATO	Air Tasking Order
AWACS	Airborne Warning and Control System
BDA	Battle Damage Assessment
BEEF	(Prime) Base Engineering Emergency Force
BH	"Black Hole"
BLSS	Base Level Self-Sufficiency
BSSG	Brigade Service Support Group
BW	Biological Warfare
CAFMS	Computer Aided Flight Management System
CAFMS	Computer Assisted Force Management System
CAG	Command Assessment Group
CALCM	Conventional Air Launched Cruise Missile
CAP	Civil Air Patrol
CAS	Close Air Support
CAT	Crisis Action Team
CENTCOM	Central Command
CENTAF	Central Air Forces
CEP	Circular Error Probable
CHOP	Change of Operation Control
CIA	Central Intelligence Agency
CINC	Commander-in-Chief
CINCENT	Commander-in-Chief, Central Command
CINCMAC	Commander-in-Chief, Military Airlift Command
CINCUSTRANSCOM	Commander-in-Chief, U.S. Transportation Command
CLSS	Combat Logistics Support Squadron
CMH	Center for Military History (U.S. Army)
COMALF	Commander, Airlift Forces
ComdC	Command Chronologies, USMC
COMUSMARCENT	Commander, U.S. Marine Central Command
COMUSMIF	Commander, U.S. Maritime Interception Force
COMUSNAVCENT	Commander, U.S. Naval Forces Central Command
CONOPS	Concept of Operations
CONUS	Continental United States
CRAF	Commercial Reserve Air Fleet

Abbreviations and Acronyms

CRC	Control Reporting Center
CSCE	Conference on Security and Cooperation in Europe
CSE	Command Support Equipment
CSS	Combat Supply System
CSSA	CENTAF Supply Support Activity
C3	Command, Control, and Communications
CTF	Central Task Force
CTF	Commander, Task Force
CTF	Command Task Force
CW	Chemical Warfare
DASC	Direct Air Support Center
DCS	Deputy Chief of Staff
DLA	Defense Logistics Agency
DOD	Department of Defense
DSB	Defense Science Board
ECM	Electronic Countermeasures
EMP	Electromagnetic Pulse
EOQ	Economic Order Quantity
EPW	Enemy Prisoners of War
EST	Eastern Standard Time
FAA	Federal Aviation Authority
FAC	Forward Air Controller
FBIS	Foreign Broadcast Information Service
FM	Financial Management Directorate
FMF	Fleet Marine Force
FOSK	Follow on Spares Kit
FOUO	For Official Use Only
FSSG	Force Service Support Group
GAT	Guidance, Appointment, and Targeting Cell (USAF)
GCC	Gulf Cooperation Council
GMT	Greenwich Mean Time
GPO	Government Printing Office
GWAPS	Gulf War Air Power Survey
HFDF	High-Frequency Radio Direction Finders
HIDACZ	High-Density Air Control Zone
HMLA	Helicopter, Marine Light Attack Squadron
HMMV	High Mobility Multi-Wheel Vehicle

HNS	Host Nation Support
HO	History Office (USAF)
HPMSK	High Priority Mission Support Kit
HQMAC	Headquarters, Military Airlift Command
IADS	Integrated Air Defense System
ILC	International Logistics Command
ILM	Intermediate Level Maintenance
IOC	Interceptor Operations Center
IRR	Individual Ready Reserve
ISO	International Standards Organization
JCS	Joint Chiefs of Staff
JEIM	Jet Engine Intermediate Maintenance
JFACC	Joint Forces Air Component Commander
JFC-E	Joint Forces Command–East
JFC-N	Joint Forces Command–North
JOPES	Joint Operation Planning and Execution System
JOTS	Joint Operational Tactical System
JSTARS	Joint Strategic Target Attack Radar System
JTFME	Joint Task Force, Middle East
JULLS	Joint Universal Lessons Learned System
KIA	Killed In Action
KTO	Kuwaiti Theater of Operations
LAI Bn	Light Armored Infantry Battalion
LAMPS	Light Airborne Multi-Purpose System
LANTIRN	Low Altitude Navigation Target Infrared Radar for Night
LAV	Light Armored Vehicle
LGB	Laser Guided Bomb
LOGAIR	Logistics Airlift
LRI	Long-Range International Cargo Aircraft
LRU	Line Replaceable Unit
MAC	Military Airlift Command
MAG	Marine Aircraft Group
MAJCOM	Major Command
MAP	Master Attack Plan
MARCENT	Marine Central Command
MAW	Marine Air Wing
MAW	Military Airlift Wing
MC	Mission Capable

Abbreviations and Acronyms

MCHC	Marine Corps Historical Center
MCM	Mine Countermeasures
MEB	Marine Expeditionary Brigade
MEF	Marine Expeditionary Force
MEU	Marine Expeditionary Unit
MICAP	Mission Incapable
MIF	Maritime Interception Force
MISREP	Mission Report
MIT	Massachusetts Institute of Technology
MPF	Marine Prepositioning Forces
MPS	Marine Prepositioning Ships
MPSRons	Marine Prepositioning Ship Squadrons
MRC	Major Regional Contingency
MSB	Minesweeping Boat
MSC	Minesweeper, Coastal
MTL	Master Target List
MTMC	Military Traffic Management Command (U.S. Army)
NATO	North Atlantic Treaty Organization
NAVCENT	Naval Forces Central Command
NBC	Nuclear, Biological, and Chemical
NGFS	Naval Gunfire Support (Task Force)
NSC	National Security Council
NVA	North Vietnamese Army
OI	Office of Information (U.S. Navy)
OIC	Organization of the Islamic Conference
OPEC	Organization of Petroleum Exporting Countries
PACAF	Pacific Air Forces
PAT	Process Action Team
PAVN	Peoples' Army of Vietnam
PDM	Programmed Depot Maintenance
PGM	Precision Guided Missile
PLO	Palestine Liberation Organization
PMEL	Precision Measurement Equipment Laboratory
POL	Petroleum, Oil, Lubricants
POMCUS	Prepositioning of Materiel Configured to Unit Sets
PRC	People's Republic of China
RADS	Rapid Area Distribution Support
RCT	Regimental Combat Team

RED HORSE	Rapid Engineering Deployable Heavy Operations Repair Squadron Engineering
RIBS	(Prime) Readiness in Base Services
RMA	Revolution in Military Affairs
RO/RO	Roll On/Roll Off Ship (Merchantman)
RORSAT	Recoverable Orbital Satellite
RPV	Remotely Piloted Vehicle
RRF	Ready Reserve Force
SAAWC	Sector Antiair Warfare Commander
SAC	Strategic Air Command
SAMs	Surface-to-Air Missiles
SAT	Site Activation Team
Scud	NATO code name for medium-range missiles (others include such terms as Slug)
SEAD	Suppression of Enemy Air Defenses
SMCR	Selected Marine Corps Reserve
SOC	Sector Operations Centers
SOC	Special Operations Capable
SOCOM	Southern Command
SOSS	Soviet Ocean Surveillance System
SRU	Shop Replaceable Unit
SSI	Strategic Studies Institute (U.S. Army)
STAMP	Standard Air Munitions Package
STRAPP	Standard Tank, Rack, Adapter, and Pylon Package
STU-III	Secure Telephone Unit—III
TAC	Tactical Air Command
TACC	Tactical Air Control Center
TACS	Tactical Air Control System
TAOC	Tactical Air Operations Center
TAW	Tactical Air Wing
TDY	Temporary Duty
TFW	Tactical Fighter Wing
TLAM	Tomahawk Land Attack (Cruise) Missile
TOT	Time on Target
TOW Missile	Tube-Launched Optically Cited Wire-Guided Missile
TPFDD	Time-Phased Force Deployment Data
TPFDDL	Time-Phased Force Deployment Data List
TPM	Technical Performance Measurement
TPW	Target Planning Worksheet

TRADOC	Training and Doctrine Command (U.S. Army)
21AF	Twenty First Air Force
UAE	United Arab Emirates
U.K.	United Kingdom
UN	United Nations
U.S.	United States
USAF	United States Air Force
USAFE	United States Air Forces, Europe
USCENTCOM	United States Central Command
USMC	United States Marine Corps
USSBS	United States Strategic Bombing Survey
USSR	Union of Soviet Socialist Republics
USTRANSCOM	United States Transportation Command
WRM	Wartime Readiness Materiel
WRSK	War Readiness Spares Kit

The Eagle
in
the Desert

Introduction
William Head

According to some American leaders in 1991 and even some historians today, in early 1991 the United States and its Allies won a smashing victory over the evil forces of Saddam Hussein. An enormous Iraqi land army, bristling with tanks, artillery, chemical weapons, and Scuds, was expelled from Kuwait with staggering losses through a combination of superior modern automated tactical air power and well-trained, well-equipped, and well-led ground forces. It was a victory so complete and so decisive that U.S. political and military leaders declared that it was a complete vindication for the defeat in Vietnam. It was, these leaders proclaimed, a war won because of the American military's ability to learn from its mistakes in Vietnam. Even the American news media fell into line quickly, comparing the two wars at every turn and using mostly old retired Vietnam era officers as analysts. As one old hand declared publicly on CNN, "The Gulf War has sponged away all the stigma of Vietnam. Never again will the American military make the mistakes of Southeast Asia."

But now, nearly half a decade after the fact, several questions from the Gulf War still beg to be answered: Why did the war happen? Was the Gulf War a vindication for Vietnam? Did the American military really learn anything from the war in Vietnam? Did they really adapt? What did the Allies actually win in the Gulf War, if anything? Finally, have we learned anything from the Gulf War (that is, anything worth learning)?

In seeking answers to these questions, it seems that there are far more differences between the wars than similarities. Moreover, there is growing evidence to suggest that the United States learned little of value from Vietnam to help it win a battlefield victory against a fifth-rate Third World power in 1991. In retrospect, many analysts are becoming increasingly convinced that despite its military successes, the United States garnered little of worth from the Gulf War. Indeed, the Iraqi Army is still regionally strong. It still has 2,500 battle tanks and 400 to 600 modern tactical aircraft, and its nuclear and chemical capabilities may or may not still exist. In more general terms, the entire effort to find lessons to learn, something which has always pervaded the U.S. military, is fraught with important and dangerous pitfalls, especially in light of even more recent experiences in Bosnia, Somalia, Haiti, and Kuwait again.

The supposedly defeated Iraqi military moved several tens of thousands of troops within striking distance of the Kuwaiti border in late September and early October 1994. In response, President Bill Clinton, acting with UN Security Council authority, ordered 4,000 American troops to the Gulf on October 8, 1994. Three days later, the president ordered several tens of thousands of additional troops to the region in support of a general Allied buildup. Although on October 14 Iraqi troops pulled back following negotiations with Russian diplomats, on October 17 the Iraqi Parliament passed a resolution declaring that they would never give up their claims on Kuwait. At the time this volume went to press, even though the immediate crisis seemed to be in abeyance, clearly Saddam Hussein was far from defeated. These events simply further validate the aforementioned questions.

In the end, although reexamination and asking "what if" questions are excellent historical exercises, comparing wars and attempting to learn lessons to create hard-and-fast military doctrine and eternal foreign policies is a risky business full of potentially dire consequences. We are all familiar with the old axiom that armies and leaders always prepare to fight the last war. Indeed, a brief recall of American and European strategic and tactical planning and training suggests just such a pattern.

In the Civil War, the major senior commanders, such as Lee and Grant, had studied extensively the battles and wars of the Napoleonic era as well as the resulting doctrinal writings of the Baron Antoine Henri de Jomini. As a result, these leaders used offensive tactics which focused on massed infantry attacks, ignoring such technological advances as breach loading rifles and larger artillery pieces. The result was dozens of Waterloo-style battles that cost 686,000 American lives (including deaths from wounds and disease).

In World War I, all the belligerents, having studied the Crimean War, Civil War, and Franco–Prussian War, misunderstood or ignored such technological advances as machine guns, airplanes, tanks, and even larger artillery. When Maxim invented the machine gun, he argued that it would surely end wars of mass slaughter since no commander would ever make another frontal assault. They did, and 12 million died in World War I.

Prior to World War II, the French Maginot Line presupposed a World War I–style German assault. Instead, they were overrun by blitzkrieg. In Vietnam, the United States, ignoring the examples of the Philippine Huk Insurrection in the early twentieth century and the French failures in the first Indochina War, clung to the "lessons" of massive mechanized armies employing massive firepower "learned" in World War II and Korea. In fact, America's Vietnam experience was replete with a myriad of misconceptions, arrogant assumptions, and doctrinal paralysis from the president to every squad leader, from ill-conceived foreign policy decisions to tactical blunders.

Now flush with victory in the Gulf, what lessons will we learn to prepare us for the next war? Because of the seeming ease of the victory, will historians gloss over this conflict? The danger of the Gulf War is that, unlike Vietnam, which has been analyzed in minute detail and provided valuable political, diplomatic, and military truths, analysts will fail to examine critically the war that went so well and leave us to draw the wrong conclusions for the next war.

Even after the Gulf victory, the ghosts of the Vietnam War still stalk the American national psyche. They remain so haunting and so debilitating that in the effort to exorcise these specters, to purge past failures, the United States and its leaders over the past decade have embraced a series of hollow military victories over fifth-rate troops in Third World countries. In an effort to reaffirm our national honor and our moral purpose and restore our self-worth so tainted by the defeat in Vietnam, we have altered history, in literature and films, and overcelebrated military victories undertaken for dubious purposes.

In this regard, the Gulf War has been portrayed as an end, "Rambo" Schwarzkopf making right the political and media betrayal of the military in Southeast Asia. This has led too many Americans to view the Persian Gulf War as some sort of vindication for Vietnam. President George Bush, from the outset of the air war, established this tone for the general public when he declared, "I instructed our military commanders to take every necessary step to prevail as quickly as possible. . . . I've told the American people before that this will not be another Vietnam, and I repeat this here tonight. Our troops . . . will not be asked to fight with one arm tied behind their back."[1]

Such sentiments struck a cord with the most senior military commanders. This was not surprising since the vast majority had spent their formative years in Vietnam and had bitter memories of what they believed were the shortsighted war policies of Presidents Lyndon B. Johnson and Richard M. Nixon. In a series of October 1990 interviews with Chairman of the Joint Chiefs of Staff (JCS), General Colin Powell; Lieutenant General Walter E.

Boomer, Commander of U.S. Marine forces in the Gulf; Admiral Frank B. Kelso II, JCS Naval Chief; and General Carl E. Vuono, Army Chief of Staff, in *U.S. News & World Report,* the latter summed up his comrade's feelings when he noted that "the group of leaders who are in the key positions, we were all about the same rank during Vietnam days, majors and lieutenant colonels, and I think all of us were shaped by the low point in the military in the early 70's."[2]

In December, General Powell once again alluded to military leaderships' concern about the ghost of Vietnam. During a final inspection tour of the Gulf Theater, the general declared that once diplomacy fails, "you go in to win decisively, not to force people to the negotiating table." The statement was an obvious referral to what he believed to be the mistaken policies of Vietnam.[3]

The American public embraced these same concerns and was also firmly convinced of the need to fight a different war in the Persian Gulf. Understandably, even Saddam Hussein attempted to take advantage of America's Vietnam phobia. During and after the fall hostage crisis, Saddam took every opportunity to warn the American public that a war with Iraq might be another long, bloody, and divisive struggle "like Vietnam."[4]

In spite of politically popular notions that a disloyal press, the antiwar movement, and civilian political restriction on the U.S. military cost the United States the war in Southeast Asia and the general public determination to avoid another Vietnam, most analysts agree that these two wars, even though comparisons can be made, were very different.

The most critical difference is that although the Vietnam conflict occurred at the height of the Cold War, the struggle in the Persian Gulf is the first major post–Cold War conflict. In Vietnam, U.S. political leaders always had to be concerned with widening the war into a Third World war with the Soviet Union and/or the People's Republic of China (PRC). A Cold War mindset compelled the United States to pour hundreds of billions of dollars into a war effort in which 58,000 Americans died. East–West rivalries motivated the USSR and PRC to supply a constant stream of arms, materiel, and spare parts to their client ally. From the standpoint of American air power, one of the most significant items the Soviets supplied North Vietnam in abundant quantities were surface-to-air missiles, or SAMs, which wrought heavy losses on U.S. aircraft by forcing the crews to fly into the teeth of a heavy antiaircraft artillery (AAA) defense.[5]

After initial Allied air attacks destroyed almost all of Iraq's considerably more advanced SAMs, their antiaircraft capability was very limited because air operations were conducted at high altitude. This was even more significant since the Soviet Union, Iraq's primary supplier of these sophisticated weapons, was ostensibly part of the thirty-five-nation Coalition and did not provide replacements. China stayed out, as did most of the other major arms suppliers, due, at least in part, to the UN embargo. Although Iraqi nighttime AAA fire was spectacular to see on the CNN evening news, its effectiveness was minimal compared to what the SAMs might have done.

Other critical variations range from the obvious contrasts of weather, climate, and terrain to the technological advances which exceeded the predictions of even the most optimistic Allied avionics advocates. From an air power standpoint, operations in Vietnam posed the most difficult challenges of jungle terrains and tropical climates. Bombing, locating enemy targets, and wear and tear on aircraft were only a few of the difficulties faced by U.S. air forces. On the other hand, in the Iraqi and Kuwaiti Theater, Allied aircraft (attrition notwithstanding) provided Coalition air forces with one of the best sets of natural circumstances available in air war history. It is also worth mentioning that aircraft damage and fatigue problems unique to the area were effectively remedied by well-trained Air Force field repair teams used for training exercises conducted in the Nevada desert.

New electronic warfare, avionics, and weapon system packages have also made fighting an effective conventional air war easier. In addition, the structural toughness of these modern jets is remarkable considering the numerous minor hits they took without crashing. Similar structural and engine damage would have downed many of America's World War II, Korean, or Vietnam vintage aircraft.

In a brief quantitative comparison, one can immediately note fundamental differences. By the end of Allied operations on February 27, 1991, their air forces had flown over 110,000 combat sorties and nearly 125,000 overall sorties, losing only fifty-one planes and thirty-eight combat aircraft, with twenty-nine of those being American. The enormity of this effort can be appreciated when compared to similar numbers from the air war in Vietnam. From June 1965 to August 1973, B-52s flew 125,479 sorties, while tactical aircraft flew over 2 million sorties during the same time.

During the Vietnam conflict, two of the most significant air campaigns were the Linebacker I (May 10–October 23) and II (December 18–29) campaigns of 1972. In the first, "155,548 tons of bombs fell on North Vietnam, one-fourth the tonnage dropped during Rolling Thunder" (1965–1968). In the second, U.S. Air Force B-52s flew 729 sorties, dropping 15,237 tons of bombs. Over the six months of the Linebacker campaigns, the numbers of bomber sorties and tons of bombs dropped were essentially the same as in the six weeks of the Persian Gulf War. With the use of "smart bombs" and superior targeting technology raids by the Allies, tactical aircraft were far more proficient than similar attacks had been in Vietnam; fewer bombs did more damage per sortie in the Gulf War than in Vietnam.[6]

The Gulf War, although waged against a Third World country, was a classic conventional war fought along the lines of strategies and tactics developed in World War II, Korea, and the Arab–Israeli Wars of the previous four decades, and America's military is very good at conventional combat. However, as Douglas Pike explains in his books on the Viet Cong and People's Army of North Vietnam (PAVN), the nature of the Vietnam conflict was not, for the most part, conventional. Even when it did finally take on more characteristics of a conventional war, it did so at the choosing of the enemy and not the Americans.

Pike argues convincingly that the Vietnamese Communist leaders conceived of their struggle, or *dau tranh minh,* on two levels—one a sociopolitical and economic struggle (political, or *dau tranh chinh tri*) and the other a military or armed struggle (armed, or *dau tranh vu trang*). In this regard, they undertook action against the Allies in three ways: *dich van*—action among the enemy; *dan van*—action among the people; and *binh van*—action against the enemy. Pike makes a powerful argument that American leadership never grasped the true reality of the war. Thus, the U.S. public viewed the war as a painful social necessity, whereas to the Communist Vietnamese it was a total commitment to struggle. Pike provides compelling evidence that the North Vietnamese Communists' resolution was almost inexhaustible and that they were willing and able to absorb large numbers of casualties. From the military standpoint, this was largely due to the previously mentioned Soviet resupply of critical weapons. With these advantages they could, and did, carry on the war at both *dau tranh* levels, alternating one to the other as circumstances necessitated.[7]

George Herring, in his well-respected book *America's Longest War* and his 1990 Harmon Memorial Lecture at the Air Force Academy entitled "The Johnson Administration's Conduct of Limited War in Vietnam," points out that U.S. perceptions of the conflict changed too late and too little, thus so did American policies. Kennedy, and especially Johnson, tried to dictate what the character and nature of the struggle would be and how the results would be formed. Instead, as Herring and Douglas Pike both argue, the enemy dictated the nature and results of the war in Indochina because, in the end, it meant more to them.[8]

As Herring notes, U.S. goals—that is, Johnson's—were ill conceived and based on tenuous Johnsonian notions of limited war.[9] Worst of all, in trying to help the South, American leaders sublimated South Vietnamese leadership structure, ultimately eliminating—via lack of experience and training, as well as death, or loss of power through incessant coups—most of those necessary for the South eventually to protect and defend itself.[10]

Certainly, this is easily contrasted with the circumstances in the Gulf conflict. Saddam Hussein, as President Bush suggested, compared more with Benito Mussolini or Adolf Hitler than Ho Chi-minh. Iraq's invasion of a weaker neighbor compares more with the German invasion of Poland in 1939 or the Italian invasion of Ethiopia in 1935 than any military action taken by the Vietminh, Viet Cong, or regular North Vietnamese Army (NVA) until after 1975. In addition, Iraqi tactics more closely resembled those employed in World War I by both sides or by the French at the Maginot Line in 1940, rather than PAVN or Viet Cong insurgency tactics.

Iraq had no military strategy worthy of the word, whereas the Communist Vietnamese strategies articulated through time were consistently superior to any strategy attempted by the Americans. The comparison goes even deeper when one examines the Germans' strategies of blitzkrieg and their right-end run through the low countries in 1940 with General Schwarzkopf's "Hail Mary" end run around the Iraqi forces in southern Kuwait.[11]

Moreover, the tactics used by the Vietnamese and the ones which should have been used by the Americans were completely foreign to the U.S. establishment, which was incapable of adjusting. In the Gulf War, the U.S. military fought using tactics it had developed to fight the Soviets in Europe. Fortunately for the United States, the Iraqi Army was trained and equipped by the Soviet Union.

On the other hand, the advances and improvements in the U.S. military since 1975 are not because of specific lessons from the war in Southeast Asia but because the character and opinions of present-day leaders were formed by that war; they were determined not to lose again.

Although it is evident to me that Vietnam furnished few specific military lessons for U.S. and Allied combat planners in the Persian Gulf, the policies developed after 1975 out of the aura of defeat, combined with basic common sense and professional expertise, led to an Allied military victory in the Persian Gulf War. But to proclaim that Coalition forces did nothing wrong in the Gulf is a disservice that may be perpetrated on a grand scale since these forces performed so well in the Persian Gulf. It is a mistake derived from the sensitivity of defeat and now compounded by an apparently total victory.

Indeed, the numbers from the Gulf War are also remarkable. For example, during the strategic airlift of August 17, 1990 to March 1, 1991, U.S. cargo transport aircraft flew 15,317 sorties with 519,458 tons of supplies and 482,997 passengers. Overall it was, in seven months, the greatest American airlift in total numbers since the eight-year effort of U.S. airlift during the Vietnam conflict.[12] To quote General Hansford T. Johnson, Commander, U.S. Transport Command, "We moved more tons more miles in the first six weeks of Desert Shield than in 65 weeks of the Berlin Airlift."[13]

However, ultimately this momentous effort was capably executed because of the innovation of airlift experts in the Air Force. To get the job done, some C-141s arrived in Saudi Arabia without their paint scheme. Several KC-10 and KC-135R refuelers were temporarily converted into cargo haulers, and the Commercial Reserve Air Fleet (CRAF) was activated on August 17, 1990 to assure the rapid deployment of adequate soldiers and supplies to the Gulf region.[14] Of course, as many experts have noted, the buildup could never have proceeded effectively if Saddam Hussein had used his air force early on to harass transports or to bomb Saudi airfields.

Another important aspect of the Gulf War was the heavy-handed method of executive control over the powers of the government and military to make war. In examining President Bush's policy-making style and the role of his advisers in Robert Woodward's book *The Commanders,* it is worth noting the many similarities in the civilian leadership and the contrast in the military leaders during the two wars.[15]

In this regard, one is also struck by the declining role of Congress beginning in the Vietnam era. In its patriotic but misguided desire to support President Johnson's policies, especially during the Gulf of Tonkin resolution, even long-time "hawks" like Senators J. William Fulbright and Richard B. Russell unwittingly abdicated their constitutional authority to wage war. This grew to such an extent that, despite later efforts to the contrary by senators like Sam Nunn, Congress was all but completely circumvented by President Bush during preparations for the Persian Gulf War.[16]

In retrospect, thoughtful scholars should also ask, What if the war had not gone so well? After all, "what ifs" are important in the historical scheme of things since things like war are so full of risk and should be analyzed fully. What if Iraqi tanks had crossed into Saudi Arabia immediately after securing Kuwait? What if their air force had been used properly from the outset? What if the war had lasted for a year or two or three? Or what would have happened even if the war had gone "less well"—as it surely would have if Iraqi forces had operated properly? If any of these caveats had been factored in, the president and Congress surely would have come to blows. Would this have meant the curtailment of presidential power under the War Powers Act? Indeed, we all need to ask these questions, especially from the perspective of these two conflicts.

But the Gulf War is more than merely an event to be compared to the Vietnam conflict. Such myopia on the part of far too many writers only proves that the Vietnam syndrome is still alive. The Gulf War was the product of Persian Gulf regional and international rivalries, failed diplomacy, egomaniacal dictators, international oil concerns, and so forth. *The Eagle in the Desert* thus attempts to view the Gulf War in this broader context. Even in terms of the military operations themselves, the authors and editors attempt to cover all the aspects of the campaign on both sides, not only the glamorous parts such as the air war and General Schwarzkopf's end run. Only a reexamination of all the aspects of the Gulf War can help prevent popular and politically expedient misconceptions and misrepresentations from allowing the truth to fade into a cozy notion of a perfect victory.

In the end, each war is, of course, distinct. In Clausewitzian terms, warfare is a clash of societies defined by political objectives and conducted according to cultural determinants with diplomatic, political, economic, and military means operating concurrently. Thus, engaging in an honest debate of historical facts (i.e., scholarship), not seeking lessons learned, produces educated officers and policy makers who are capable of developing flexible and intelligent doctrine. Lessons learned have always doomed us to fight the last war. They create doctrine that works only if we fight the same enemy, in the same place, with the same weapons, and with the same leaders. To quote Loren Baritz of the University of Rochester, in his book on American involvement in Vietnam, "Our National Myth showed us we were good, our technology made us strong, and our bureaucracy gave us standard operating procedures. It was not a winning combination."[17] It never is.

For most Americans, the Persian Gulf War began on August 2, 1990, when Iraqi troops invaded Kuwait, initiating a series of events which would culminate in a war between Iraq and a thirty-five-nation international Coalition led by the United States.[18] The goal of this anthology is to elaborate on both the history and scope of this conflict. It begins with background chapters and carries through the military operations to place the war in better historical perspective. This having been said, the focus of the book goes from August 1990 to March 1991.

In *Eagle in the Desert,* Daniel S. Papp and Sohail H. Hashmi open by analyzing the background of the Iraq–Kuwait conflict and how the United States pulled together the vast coalition that fought the Iraqis. In his article "But Was It Jihad?: Islam and the Ethics of the Persian Gulf War," Hashmi discusses the sociopolitical, cultural, and religious nuances of the region and how they confronted the ethics of the West. He uses this as a baseline from which he explains the defining factors that led the leaders of the Arab and Muslim world to react the way they did to Saddam Hussein's invasion of Kuwait. It also examines the moral context within which these decisions were made.

In "The Gulf War Coalition: The Politics and Economics of a Most Unusual Alliance," Papp follows with an expert analysis of how President Bush not only orchestrated the formation of the vast Allied Coalition, but also manipulated the American and international political arena to gain general UN and limited congressional backing in order to commit nearly half a million U.S. and 700,000 international forces to fight Iraq.

In the aftermath of the Persian Gulf War, many military, political, and geopolitical analysts have sought to place this conflict into a historical context. Some, like Richard P. Hallion in his expert 1992 work *Storm Over Iraq: Air Power and the Gulf War,* have suggested that in spite of the exhaustive work already done, much more time needs to transpire before a complete history of the Persian Gulf War can be written.[19]

In this book, Mark D. Mandeles, in "Command and Control in the Gulf War: A Military Revolution in Airpower?" and Michael T. Corgan, in "Clausewitz's *On War* and the Gulf War," both attempt to place the war into historical perspective in terms of the advance of military technology and military theory and doctrine, respectively. They, like Caroline F. Ziemke in her chapter "A New Covenant?: The Apostles of Douhet and the

Persian Gulf War," seek to reevaluate and reexamine the Gulf conflict in the light of new evidence they claim should change the way Americans look at the outcome of the war.

Mandeles, using conventional analysis, tries to focus on how technological advances in weaponry helped the Allies defeat the Iraqis. In this regard, his work takes a similar tack to Hallion's aforementioned larger work. However, the two come to somewhat different conclusions—Hallion finds such advances (especially in the air war) decisive, whereas Mandeles is less enthusiastic about the effects of these new weapons. He even goes so far as to ask if there really was a military or technological revolution, as suggested by many in the popular press.

Corgan, on the other hand, employees classic Clausewitzian terms not only to place the war in historical context, but also to discover if there were any universal military truths derived which might be converted into modern military doctrine.

Although Hallion is no doubt correct that only the passage of time can provide better historical perspective, analysts of every hue have literally produced dozens of books and articles on almost every aspect of the Gulf War since it ended in March 1991. As noted earlier, many have determined to seek lessons to learn from the conflict based on the unparalleled amount of declassified data already available to researchers. Among the most controversial is Harry G. Summer, Jr.'s *On Strategy II,* and one of the most popular is General Schwarzkopf's *It Doesn't Take a Hero.*[20]

Of course, this much literature has meant that in the years since the war ended, many questions have been raised about the conduct of the conflict and its results. If anything, the issues raised seem to grow with each passing month and debate seems to intensify. Even senior U.S. military leaders appeared to contribute to this discussion during Senate hearings held in mid-April 1994, when they admitted that Coalition forces made some mistakes. They suggested that they had not carried out as perfect or "clean" a campaign as first indicated in sanitized press releases provided to the news media during and just after the war. As a result, they opened themselves and their performance to renewed scrutiny from all directions.

Such is the case in Larry E. Cable's look at the Army's role in the war and the general ground campaign entitled, "Playing in the Sandbox: Doctrine, Combat, and Outcome on the Ground." Although Cable gives the "devil" his due—in this case, General Schwarzkopf—he takes to task the claims that they won a perfect, clean, and/or a well-managed military victory. Although this book includes others who are more certain of the excellence of the U.S. and Allied military, Cable's chapter provides readers with an alternative view of several key issues so they can draw their own conclusions.

In the end, this kind of intensive examination should prove valuable since it should provide a more historical view of this important moment in world and U.S. history. As the English political philosopher John Stuart Mill suggested, the essence of the democratic process is free debate and the search for compromise and solution.

Although the resulting consensus of this debate may not portray the U.S. military as perfect or any service's role as decisive, it provides us with a more objective view of the entire conflict. Furthermore, it may go far in supporting the currently prevailing military convictions, which suggest that coalition forces fought well and demonstrated the essential viability of modern U.S. military technology and training.

Indeed, there are many views on the war and many conflicting arguments. In the initial period after the war, and even today, many military leaders have described the war as an exoneration of the U.S. defeat in Vietnam. As the ground war unfolded, President George Bush declared, "By God, we've kicked the Vietnam Syndrome once and for all."[21] As noted earlier, senior military leaders like Generals Colin Powell and H. Norman Schwarzkopf, as well as analysts like Harry Summers, Jr., agreed with the president.[22]

In this regard, these Gulf War enthusiasts also see the conflict as a watershed event in American history. Some historians concurred. One such article in *Air Power Journal,* written by Lieutenant Colonel Price T. Bingham and entitled "Air Power in Desert Storm and the Need for Doctrinal Change," argues, "perhaps the most important lesson the U.S. military could learn from Desert Storm is that it needs to change its doctrine to recognize the reality that air power can dominate modern conventional war."[23]

In the work in Part III of this book on the air campaign, Colonel David A. Deptula, in his chapter "Parallel Warfare: What Is It? Where Did It Come From? Why Is It Important?", and Lieutenant Colonel Daniel T. Kuehl, in his article "Thunder and Storm: Strategic Air Operations in the Gulf War," both seek to flesh out the details of the air war from its planning stages through the operations stage to the creation of no-fly zones. They circumvent the overexuberant platitudes about airpower winning the war alone or being overrated, and they place the campaign in a more proper historical perspective. Also in Part III is Mark D. Mandeles's earlier mentioned chapter, which takes an opposing view of the air war, if only by degrees. Not only does this chapter provide an alternative vision of airpower and technology, but it bridges this section and the final section, which is even more critical of the entire Allied effort in the Gulf War.

These chapters are neatly supported in Part II by William Suit's "Sustaining the War Machine: U.S. Air Force Logistics Support during the Gulf War," and John W. Leland's expert chapter on airlift entitled, "Air Mobility in Operation Desert Shield/Desert Storm: An Assessment." Both pieces demonstrate the breadth of the role airpower played in the Gulf

War—from rapid deployment, to airlift of war supplies and personnel, to strategic and tactical combat operations, to humanitarian relief.

In spite of Bingham's arguments, there are a growing number of people who believe that the Persian Gulf War did not end the Vietnam syndrome, that it will ultimately be no more significant than any of the other brushfire wars of the post–World War II era, and that although airpower was impressive it did not prove to be decisive for all wars and against all opponents. These so-called radicals argue that airpower is not likely to be decisive in most future conflicts simply because it has never been the decisive factor in warfare.

Caroline F. Ziemke, in "A New Covenant: The Apostles of Douhet and the Persian Gulf War," takes exception with the sanguine assessment of Summers and Bingham. She decries the use of high-sounding military and technological terms and jargon for a substantive and critical analysis of the key events of the Gulf War. She, like Corgan, Mandeles, and Cable, asks us to consider important questions which, despite the popular acclaim provided the Allied performance in the Gulf War, have not, she believes, yet been answered. They take many of the aforementioned sympathetic viewpoints to task in a stinging plea for historians and analysts to avoid the euphoric clichés of leaders like George Bush and undertake a truly critical review of every aspect of the Gulf War.

Still others fall in between these opposing views. They concede that this war, although fought against a fifth-rate Third World dictatorship, was handled well by both the Coalition's civilian and military leaders. The moderates also argue that although airpower may not have fulfilled its eternal goal of achieving total and decisive victory with little or no ground/naval support, at least one can say that it was the centerpiece of the tactical military victory. These historians are reluctant to draw lessons learned from what they believe was an important Third World conflict—but one not as significant as Vietnam or Korea. They also remind us all that even though he lost the war, Saddam Hussein still holds a firm grip on power in Iraq and has great influence in the region.

In the end, all these groups and those in between have been left with the difficult task of trying to seek the consensus that will form the historical mainstream. This book attempts to provide the reader with not only the breadth of these aforementioned viewpoints, but also with fresh analysis derived from the most current research. In this regard, the editors have sought to cover as many aspects of the war as possible.

Besides those chapters already mentioned, *The Eagle in the Desert* includes an analysis of the Navy's role by Norman Friedman entitled, "Sailing in the Sand: The U.S. Navy's Role in the Gulf War" and Robert J. Schneller, Jr., entitled, "On the Storm's Outer Edge: U.S. Navy Operations in the Persian Gulf War"; as well as a look at Marine operations by John T.

Quinn and Jack Shulimson entitled "U.S. Marine Operations in the Persian Gulf War."

Ultimately, no matter what the topic or the viewpoint, this book is not designed to be the final word on the Persian Gulf War, but a means to continue the search for meaning from the conflict and to place it, as close as humanly possible, in its proper historical perspective.

NOTES

1. Transcript, "Nationwide Television Broadcast of a Speech by President George Bush on the Beginning of the Air War in the Persian Gulf," 9:00 P.M. EST, January 16, 1991. This copy found in *Facts on File* 51, no. 2617 (January 17, 1991): 28.

2. "Lines in the Sand," *U.S. News & World Report* 109, no. 13 (October 1, 1990): 29–34. Following along with this theme, one of the most popular and compelling revisionist (nonscholarly) books written on Vietnam was by Admiral Ulysses Simpson Grant Sharp, *Strategy for Defeat: Vietnam in Retrospect* (Novato, Calif.: Presidio Press, 1986) [hereafter *Strategy for Defeat*]. Admiral Sharp blames the U.S. defeat on U.S. political leaders, who he claims had a lack of resolve.

3. "You Go in to Win Decisively," *U.S. News & World Report* 109, no. 25 (December 24, 1990): 26; Speech, George Herring, "The Johnson Administration's Conduct of Limited War in Vietnam," U.S. Air Force Academy Harmon Memorial Lecture, October 14, 1990 [hereafter Harmon Lecture].

4. Editorial, "Why Hussein Smells Victory," *U.S. News & World Report* 109, no. 25 (December 24, 1990): 67.

5. For a further examination of this issue, see George Herring, *America's Longest War* (New York: John Wiley & Sons, 1979), 130–31, 147–51 [hereafter *America's Longest War*]; Mark Clodfelter, *The Limits of Air Power: The American Bombing of North Vietnam* (New York: The Free Press, 1989), 137, 188–93 [hereafter *Limits of Air Power*]; Carl Berger, ed., *The United States Air Force in Southeast Asia, 1961–1973: An Illustrated Account* (Washington, D.C.: Office of Air Force History, 1984), 70–79, 166–67, 219–21 [hereafter *The USAF in S.E. Asia*]; Earl H. Tilford, Jr., *Setup: What the Air Force Did in Vietnam and Why* (Maxwell AFB, Ala.: Air University Press, 1991) [hereafter *Setup*]. The best chapter for this issue is chapter 3 on Rolling Thunder, 89–163. Those who read Tilford and Clodfelter's books after reading Admiral Sharp's work will observe that these historians disagree with the admiral on the potentially decisive nature of airpower in Vietnam.

6. Berger, *The USAF in S.E. Asia*, 95–99, 166–67; Clodfelter, *Limits of Air Power*, 166, 194. For details on Linebacker, see Clodfelter, 156–72, 181–202; Briefing Transcript, by Pentagon spokesperson Peter Williams, January 27, 1991, section 1, 6. The differences in sortie numbers provided by different sources is that helicopter sorties were often not included. However, during the February 28, 1991, Theater Briefing, the Allied spokesperson placed the official number of sorties at 106,000 for forty-three days of combat. See *Facts on File* 51, no. 2623 (February 28, 1991): 129. In addition, sortie numbers in Vietnam also vary. For example, the *Washington Post*, in a January 31, 1991 article, placed the total aforementioned, Vietnam B-52 sorties at 126,615. However, in reviewing USAF figures, this number

was the total of planned sorties. The B-52 sortie is the number actually flown. See *Facts on File* 51, no. 2619 (January 31, 1991): 60.

7. For details of PAVN and Viet Cong strategies, see Douglas Pike, *PAVN: People's Army of North Vietnam* (Novato, Calif.: Presidio Press, 1986). Chapter 1 and the Conclusion express the aforementioned thesis effectively [hereafter *PAVN*]. See also Douglas Pike, *Vietcong: The Organization and Techniques of the National Liberation Front of South Vietnam* (Cambridge, Mass.: MIT Press, 1966), 85–105 [hereafter *Vietcong*].

8. Herring, *America's Longest War*, 43–107; Herring, Harmon Lecture. Pike, *PAVN*, see chapters 2–4. These pages examine, through exhaustive primary research, the civil and colonial nature of the struggle and how U.S. entry tried to change it but failed. This issue is also dealt with throughout Pike's *Vietcong*. Another more conservative work which generally agrees with the aforementioned notion is David Chanoff and Van Toai Doan, *Portrait of the Enemy* (New York: Random House, 1986).

9. Herring, Harmon Lecture.

10. For an excellent and remarkably balanced account of problems experienced by South Vietnamese leaders and their problems with decision making due to the U.S. presence, see Bui Diem and David Chanoff, *In the Jaws of History* (Boston: Houghton Mifflin, 1987).

11. Anthony Kemp, *The Maginot Line, Myth and Reality* (New York: Military Heritage Press, 1988), 84–92.

12. Message, U.S. Central Command to Military Airlift Command, Report, "Desert Storm Airlift Figures," Feb. 282134Z; MAC News Service, "CNC MAC Discusses the Past Year—Part I," *End of Year Report*, Dec. 90 [hereafter "CNC MAC"]; John Berry, "How Much Is Enough," *Newsweek* 66, no. 19 (November 5, 1990): 16–17; SMSgt. Douglas I. Gilbert, "Logistics Lifeline: Sustaining Desert Shield," *Airman* 34, no. 11 (November 1990): 22–23.

13. "CNC MAC."

14. For three excellent articles discussing the problems of massive airlift, the lessons of the past, and the solutions used in the Persian Gulf, see Major Donald E. Hamblin, "Distribution Priority System: Time for a Change?" *Air Force Journal of Logistics* 14, no. 4 (Fall 1990): 17–21; Major Benjamin L. Dilla, "Logistics Support Limitations in the Vietnam War: Lessons for Today's Logisticians," in *ibid.*, 35–38; SSgt. James C. Mesco, "Airlifting Logistics: Warner Robins Air Logistics Center's Support of 'Desert Shield' Airlift Operations," *Air Force Journal of Logistics* 15, no. 2 (Summer 1991): 6–10.

15. Robert Woodward, *The Commanders* (New York: Simon & Schuster, 1991).

16. Caroline Ziemke, "From the Tonkin Gulf to the Persian Gulf: Richard B. Russell, Sam Nunn and the Senate's Role in War Making," unpublished article presented at a conference entitled "Vietnam: Impact and Legacy." Co-sponsored by Association of Third World Studies and Georgia Tech's School of International Affairs at Georgia Institute of Technology, Atlanta, Georgia, February 7–8, 1991. Also see Herring, Harmon Lecture.

17. Loren Baritz, *Backfire: A History of How American Culture Led Us into Vietnam and Made Us Fight the Way We Did* (New York: Ballantine, 1986), 40.

18. Roger Cohen and Claudio Gatti, *In the Eye of the Storm: The Life of General H. Norman Schwarzkopf* (New York: Farrar, Straus and Giroux, 1991), 218

[hereafter *Eye of the Storm*]. The Coalition included Afghanistan, Argentina, Australia, Bahrain, Bangladesh, Belgium, Britain, Canada, China, Czechoslovakia, Denmark, Egypt, France, Germany, Greece, Italy, Kuwait, Morocco, The Netherlands, New Zealand, Niger, Norway, Oman, Pakistan, Poland, Qatar, Saudi Arabia, Senegal, Soviet Union, Spain, Syria, The Republic of Korea (South), Turkey, United Arab Emirates, and the United States.

19. Richard P. Hallion, *Storm Over Iraq: Air Power and the Gulf War* (Washington, D.C.: Smithsonian Institution Press, 1992), ix–x [hereafter *Storm Over Iraq*].

20. Three examples of articles written on lessons from the Gulf War are Mark Clodfelter, "Of Demons, Storms, and Thunder: A Preliminary Look at Vietnam's Impact on the Persian Gulf Air Campaign," *Air Power Journal* (Winter 1991): 17–32; Price T. Bingham, "Air Power in Desert Storm and the Need for Doctrinal Change," *Air Power Journal* (Winter 1991): 33–46; and William Head, "Air Power in the Persian Gulf: An Initial Search for the Right Lessons" (Winter 1992): 10–19. One of the best books on the general topic is Lawrence Freedman and Efraim Karsh, *The Gulf Conflict 1990–1991: Diplomacy and War in the New World Order* (Princeton, N.J.: Princeton University Press, 1993) [hereafter *Gulf Conflict*]. Also see Harry G. Summers, Jr., *On Strategy II: A Critical Analysis of the Gulf War* (New York: Dell, 1992) [hereafter *On Strategy II*]; and H. Norman Schwarzkopf, *It Doesn't Take a Hero* (New York: Henry Holt, 1992) [hereafter *Hero*].

21. Stanley W. Cloud, "Exorcising the Old Demon," *Time*, March 11, 1991, p. 52. For an interesting look at George Bush's role in the war, see Jean Edward Smith, *George Bush's War* (New York: Henry Holt, 1992).

22. For Schwarzkopf's view of this issue, see Cohen and Gatti, *Eye of the Storm*, 212–14. These pages also discuss the views of others like Powell, Boomer, etc. Also see H. Norman Schwarzkopf's autobiography, *It Doesn't Take a Hero*. For more on Harry Summers's thesis, see his introductory chapter in *On Strategy II*.

23. Bingham, "Air Power in Desert Storm," 33. For two publications which view the war, especially the air campaign, from the opposing points of view mentioned in the text, see Hallion, *Storm Over Iraq* and Eliot Cohen et al., *Gulf War Air Power Survey* (Washington, D.C.: USAF Office of History, 1993). Hallion's expertise as an airpower theorist was best demonstrated in a 1994 presentation entitled "The Future of Air Power." In it he became the first thinker to examine the long- or short-term ramifications of the Gulf War not only on airpower, but on the Air Force and the military aeronautical operations, theory, doctrine, and implementation of new technologies. Filled with pertinent facts and efficient and aesthetic logic, it carries the analysis of airpower to the next level.

Part I
POLITICS, ALLIANCES, AND REGIONAL VIEWS

This first part opens with a chapter by Daniel S. Papp entitled, "The Gulf War Coalition: The Politics and Economics of a Most Unusual Alliance." Papp seeks to explain the inner workings of the Bush administration's efforts to convince a hesitant Arab world to oppose the Iraqi invasion of Kuwait. He also explores the means by which this "most unusual coalition" was formed and the reasons it was able to hold together.

Of course, as Papp also notes, the United States took the leadership of the anti-Iraq Coalition beginning in early August 1990, following the Iraqi invasion and occupation of its tiny neighbor Kuwait. With strong support from British Prime Minister Margaret Thatcher and later the entire Western alliance, the United States successfully convinced thirty-five nations, under UN auspices, to formally support the initiative to defend Saudi Arabia, then isolate Iraq, and finally liberate Kuwait.

Certainly, the Coalition partners all had their own reasons for taking up this cause, even though some, like China and the Soviet Union, did so reluctantly. The United States for its part, concerned over a disruption of the balance of power and a destabilization of the region, moved to supply the bulk of fighting forces in Operations Desert Shield and Desert Storm. Of course, the United States also feared a reduction in the flow of oil from Kuwait, especially for its Allies in Europe.

Moreover, American leaders were fearful of an invasion of their long-time Persian Gulf ally, Saudi Arabia, as well as the involvement and harm of America's primary Middle Eastern ally, Israel. Perhaps equally significant was President George Bush's desire to improve his less than stalwart image within the international community. Certainly, whether justified or not, we can all remember the media term *wimp factor* used in relationship with the president's actions regarding the Persian Gulf conflict.

Nearly all European nations were involved. No doubt Britain's historic support of Kuwait, and the key role it had played in the tiny principality's establishment in the late nineteenth century and its survival in the first half of the twentieth century, had a great deal to do with Great Britain's eagerness to oppose the Iraqi invasion. All the West European states and Japan depended heavily on moderately priced Kuwaiti oil supplies and could ill afford to risk Iraqi price increases, which would be reflected at their gas pumps for all their citizens and voters to see.

Most significantly, as Papp points out, the inclusion of Saudi Arabia in the Coalition was critical for gaining support from the Arab world and for providing the United States and its Allies with forward operating bases to carry the military operations of early 1991. Saudi reluctance stemmed from its concerns over past demonstrations of a lack of U.S. resolve in such matters, U.S. support of Israel, hints of the colonial past, and the unsettling influence of U.S. and Western culture on Saudi society. In the late 1970s, President Jimmy Carter had sent unarmed F-15s to "protect" Saudi Arabia during the Iranian Revolution, and President Ronald Reagan had pulled U.S. forces out of Lebanon in 1983 on the heels of the Marine barracks attack. In addition, most Arab states despised the wealthy and often arrogant Kuwaitis. Many moderate Arab states wondered why they should risk war with the powerful Iraqi armed forces over such an anathema as Kuwait.

Finally, Papp discusses the important role that President Bush's personal touch played in influencing not only Arab support and cooperation, but Chinese moderation and Soviet acquiescence to the Coalition.

Sohail H. Hashmi's chapter, "But Was It *Jihad?*: Islam and the Ethics of the Persian Gulf War," examines the debate over the moral nature of the war, especially from the viewpoint of Muslims. Although he focuses on this debate by looking into current writings and traditional Arab arguments from the Koran, he also provides the reader with an insight into the temper of the Arab and Muslim worlds just before and during the Gulf War. In this regard, he deals not only with the theoretical realm of the conflict, but also with the reality of why so many Arab states were, ultimately, willing to engage Saddam Hussein and support the United States. His explanation of terms and concepts like *jihad* and *'ulama* provide the Western reader with a better grasp of what people in the Middle East believed to be the true essence of the Persian Gulf conflict. Indeed, all of us would do well to remember the old military axiom, "Know your enemy." In this case, we should know more about the region with which we are dealing to understand what effect the eagle's (America's) presence had on the people and nations of the Persian Gulf desert.

—William Head

1

The Gulf War Coalition: The Politics and Economics of a Most Unusual Alliance

Daniel S. Papp

Behind the military successes that were Operations Desert Shield and Desert Storm lay a most unusual Coalition. In a formal sense not an alliance, this Coalition brought together erstwhile friends and foes, democrats and dictators, Christians and Muslims, and rich and poor in opposition to the Iraqi invasion and occupation of Kuwait.

The core of the Coalition was the thirty-five states from within and beyond the Middle East that contributed over a quarter million troops, almost 4,000 tanks, more than 2,100 aircraft, and at least 219 ships to the military effort against Iraq. A few states provided large numbers of troops, tanks, planes, and ships to the anti-Iraq effort, as Table 1.1 shows.[1] Others provided only token forces. Regardless of the size of the armed forces that they contributed to the anti-Iraq coalition, these states are usually considered the alliance that won the Persian Gulf War.

But other states also made major contributions to the anti-Iraq effort, even though their armed forces were not deployed in the Persian Gulf area during Operations Desert Shield and Desert Storm. Some, such as Japan and South Korea, helped fund the Coalition's military efforts.[2] Others, such as China, made political contributions by supporting, or at least not opposing, economic, military, and other sanctions against Iraq. The contributions of these states to the anti-Iraq effort were not as direct as those of the Coalition's core, but their contributions nevertheless helped make Operations Desert Shield and Desert Storm possible.

Table 1.1
Coalition Military Forces Deployed against Iraq

Country	Troops	Tanks	Planes	Ships
Afghanistan[1]	300	---	---	---
Argentina	450	---	---	2
Australia	---	---	---	3
Bahrain	3,500	---	---	---
Bangladesh	2,000	---	---	---
Belgium[2]	---	---	18	2
Canada	1,700	---	30	2
Czechoslovakia	350	---	---	---
Denmark	---	---	---	1
Egypt	40,000	400	---	---
France	20,000	350	75	14
Germany[2]	---	---	18	---
Greece	---	---	---	1
Hungary	40	---	---	---
Honduras	150	---	---	---
Italy[2]	---	---	26	4
Kuwait	11,500	---	35	---
Morocco	2,000	---	---	---
Netherlands[2]	---	---	18	2
Niger[3]	480	---	---	---
Norway	---	---	---	2
New Zealand	---	---	2	---
Oman	25,500	75	50	12
Pakistan	10,000	---	---	---
Poland	100	---	---	2
Portugal	---	---	---	1
Qatar	7,000	24	19	9
Saudi Arabia	110,000	550	180	8
Senegal	500	---	---	---
(Soviet Union)[4]	---	---	---	(2)
Spain	---	---	---	3
Syria[5]	71,000	300	---	---
Turkey[6]	120,000	???	???	2
UAE	40,000	200	80	15
United Kingdom	42,000	???	58	16
United States	532,000	2,000	1,800	120

Source: Developed from Joseph P. Englehardt, "Desert Shield and Desert Storm: A Chronology and Troop List for the 1990–1991 Persian Gulf Crisis," *SSI Special Report* (Carlisle, Pa.: Strategic Studies Institute, March 1991).

1. Afghan *mujahadeen* forces, not Afghan government forces.
2. Each deployed one squadron of approximately eighteen aircraft to Turkey.
3. Deployed in Medina and Mecca to guard Islamic shrines.
4. Two ships operating in the Gulf area were not part of Coalition forces.
5. Includes 50,000 in Syria on Iraqi border and 2,000 in UAE.
6. No commitment of involvement unless attacked. Troops shown deployed in Turkey near the Iraqi border.

The United States spearheaded the creation and maintenance of this diverse and ill-defined Coalition. This was an impressive achievement. In many respects, creating and maintaining the Coalition was as stunning a success as Operations Desert Shield and Desert Storm.

Given how critical the Coalition was to Operations Desert Shield and Desert Storm, it is extremely important that we understand how and why this most unusual alliance came about, and how and why it stayed together. This chapter will undertake these tasks.

WHY THE COALITION WAS IMPORTANT

In the absence of this most unusual alliance, it is highly unlikely that either Operation Desert Shield or Operation Desert Storm would have been as successful as they were. Indeed, there is even room to question whether either operation would have occurred if the Coalition had not been formed or if it had not been as large and multifaceted as it was. The Coalition was critically important for four primary reasons.

International Political Legitimacy

First, the existence of the Coalition provided international political legitimacy to the effort to deter further Iraqi aggression and to expel Iraq from Kuwait. Despite Iraq's blatant violation of Kuwaiti sovereignty, many states that eventually sent armed forces to the Persian Gulf area as part of the Coalition had no intention of undertaking a deployment on their own and were even hesitant to undertake a deployment as part of a small coalition. For example, on August 4, 1990, two days after the Iraqi invasion, U.S. National Security Adviser Brent Scowcroft stated that he saw "a strong impulse on the part of many Arabs to think that they can put Saddam back in his cage by tossing him Kuwait as a bone."[3]

Indeed, even in the United States, existence of a broad, multifaceted Coalition helped legitimize first the U.S. military buildup in Saudi Arabia and then the use of armed force to expel Iraq from Kuwait. Although it may be argued accurately that U.S. forces by themselves could have both deterred and defeated Iraq, thereby obviating the need for a Coalition, it is not certain that in the absence of a large anti-Iraqi Coalition the United States could have deployed so sizable a force to the Middle East. The existence of a sizable Coalition permitted the U.S. government to argue that it was acting in concert with international public opinion in the United States and in the U.S. Congress to support a large military deployment and the eventual use of military force.[4]

Armed Forces

Second, and more obviously, the members of the Coalition provided the armed forces that deterred further Iraqi aggression and eventually expelled Iraq from Kuwait. Had no Coalition been formed, deterrence would have been more uncertain and the expulsion of Iraq from Kuwait would have been rendered virtually impossible.

Here, the central roles that the United States and Saudi Arabia played in the alliance must be addressed. In the United States' case, Table 1.1 illustrated that the preponderance of military might in the alliance was provided by the United States. More need not be said in this chapter about the centrality of U.S. armed forces to the deterrence of possible Iraqi aggression against Saudi Arabia and the expulsion of Iraq from Kuwait.

But it is often overlooked that had Saudi Arabia decided not to participate in the alliance, neither Desert Shield nor Desert Storm would have been possible. Virtually every Coalition soldier, tank, and artillery piece deployed for Operations Desert Shield and Desert Storm operated out of Saudi Arabia. So, too, did most Coalition aircraft. Indeed, Saudi Arabia served not only as the base of operations for Coalition armed forces, but it was the only possible base of operations for Coalition forces if further Iraqi aggression was to be deterred and if Kuwait was to be liberated.

Table 1.2 makes this reality clear by detailing the size and scope of the U.S. airlift and sealift operations that made Desert Shield and Desert Storm possible. Virtually every flight and voyage shown in Table 1.2 ended at a Saudi airfield or port. This leads to a simple and obvious but often overlooked conclusion: Had Saudi Arabia opted not to accept U.S. armed forces, neither Desert Shield nor Desert Storm would have occurred.

Financial Support

Third, the Coalition was also important because several of its members helped pay for the costs of deploying military forces to the Gulf and fighting the war against Iraq. Several Coalition members also helped defray the financial losses of Middle Eastern states that participated in the economic embargo against Iraq. The financial contributions of Coalition members to other Coalition states involved in the anti-Iraq effort are shown in Table 1.3.

Several of the financial contributors to the anti-Iraq effort, most notably Japan, were not members of the Coalition's core (i.e., they did not deploy armed forces to the Persian Gulf). Nevertheless, their financial support contributed to the eventual successes of Desert Shield and Desert Storm.

Table 1.2
Desert Shield and Desert Storm Strategic Airlift and Sealift: August 1990–March 1991

Aircraft Type	Flights	Passengers	Tons of Cargo
C-141	8,537	93,126	155,955
C-5	3,770	84,385	222,024
C-9	209	NA	NA
KC-10	379	1,111	12,129
Commercial	3,309	321,005	145,225
Other	NA	1,093	10,219
Total	16,204	500,720	543,552

Ship Type	Voyages	Passengers	Tons of Cargo
Fast Sealift	33	NA	321,941
Prepositioning	46	NA	464,289
Ready Reserve	131	NA	691,048
U.S. Flag	65	NA	317,193
Allied	206	NA	646,315
Total	481	NA	2,440,786

Source: Developed by the author from statistics provided by James Matthews, USTRANSCOM Historian, at the Georgia Tech–U.S. Army War College Conference, "Strategic Mobility, Forward Presence, and the Defense of American Interests," Atlanta, Georgia, September 6–7, 1991.

Isolating and Pressuring Iraq

It may also be argued that the Coalition was important for a fourth reason: because it increased Iraq's international isolation and heightened pressure on Iraq to change its policies toward Kuwait. This argument is especially important in regard to the Soviet Union and China's role in the anti-Iraq effort. Although neither were members of the Coalition's core, their willingness to cooperate with the Coalition played a critical role in the Persian Gulf conflict.

Indeed, U.S. policy makers recognized this from the beginning of the crisis. For example, in the Soviet case, Bush immediately sought to align U.S. and Soviet positions on the Iraqi invasion. Thus, U.S. Secretary of State James Baker, who had been in the USSR meeting with Soviet Foreign Minister Shevardnadze at Irkutsk on August 1–2 discussing the Afghanistan situation, cut short his post-Irkutsk visit to Mongolia and hurried to Moscow. On August 3, the two foreign secretaries issued a joint U.S.–Soviet statement condemning the "flagrant unlawful invasion of Kuwait by the armed forces of Iraq." The two superpowers also "jointly urge[d] the entire international community to join [them] and suspend all supplies of arms to Iraq on an international scale."[5]

Table 1.3

Major Financial Contributors to the Coalition (Financial Aid in $ Billions Received by)

Pledged by	US	UK	Turkey/Egypt	Other	Aid in Kind
Saudi Arabia	16.80	.56	2.85	1.77	6.0
Kuwait	16.01	1.32	2.50	2.18	--
UAE	3.50	.50	.85	.62	.14
EC	--	--	.80	--	--
France	--	.18	.20	.03	--
Germany	6.57	.60	1.19	.94	.53
Italy	.45	--	.65	--	--
Other EC	--	.02	.19	--	--
Japan	10.74	--	2.13	.10	.46
South Korea	.37	--	.10	.02	.02
Norway	--	--	.02	.08	--
Switzerland	--	--	.12	--	--
Other	--	--	.17	--	--

Notes: Figures for Egypt do not include $7 billion in debt forgiveness from the United States and $7 billion in debt forgiveness from Arab States. EC stands for European Community.

Source: International Institute for Strategic Studies, *The Military Balance, 1991-1992* (London: International Institute for Strategic Studies, 1991), 242.

After Washington and Moscow issued the joint statement, it was clear that Saddam Hussein could not look to the USSR for support in the gathering conflict.[6] This was an immense success for U.S. policy. Indeed, throughout Operations Desert Shield and Desert Storm, the United States was careful to include the Soviet Union in policy considerations and attempted to convince the USSR to support Coalition positions whenever possible. U.S. attempts to convince other states to join the Coalition were driven in part by these objectives, but in none of the other U.S. attempts to enlist allies were the objectives behind the effort as apparent as they were with the USSR.

However, too much stock must not be placed in the impact that isolation and pressure had on Iraqi policy, despite the importance the United States attached to it. In the final analysis, Iraq never changed its intention to retain control of Kuwait until it was expelled from Kuwait by military force. Thus, it was not clear that isolating Iraq or increasing pressure on Iraq had any positive impact on how the Gulf crisis unfolded.

At a minimum, then, the Coalition was important because it enhanced the political legitimacy, provided the military forces, and paid the costs of the effort to deter possible Iraqi aggression against Saudi Arabia and to expel Iraq from Kuwait. In the absence of the Coalition, the outcome of the Persian Gulf crisis undoubtedly would have been considerably different.

CREATING THE COALITION

After Iraq invaded Kuwait at about 7:00 P.M. Washington time on August 1, 1990, most members of the international community quickly condemned the Iraqi aggression. However, since the invasion came as a complete surprise to virtually everyone, no country had a strategy or plan in place to expel Iraq from Kuwait. Similarly, no one had a strategy or plan in place to assemble a coalition either to defend Saudi Arabia against possible Iraqi aggression or to liberate Kuwait.

The United States was the first country to react to the Iraqi invasion with concrete actions. Within hours of the Iraqi assault, the United States froze all Iraqi and Kuwaiti assets in the United States and prohibited all trade with Iraq. The United States also asked North Atlantic Treaty Organization (NATO) states to consider similar actions. In addition, the United States quickly offered to deploy a squadron of F-15 fighters to Saudi Arabia if the kingdom wished to bolster its defenses.[7]

The United States and Great Britain

However, this did not mean that the United States had decided to create and lead an alliance or to counter the Iraqi invasion with armed force. Indeed, President George Bush appeared on television the morning of August 2 and dismissed military action, declaring that "we're not discussing intervention." Bush declared that he "intended to have this invasion be reversed and have [Iraq] get out of Kuwait," but he stressed diplomacy, not military force. He even responded to a question about whether he was considering military intervention or sending troops by specifically rejecting such policy courses, stating that he was "not contemplating such action."[8] With the United States leaning away from a military response, there was reason to wonder whether any state would step forward to lead more than declaratory opposition to the invasion.

From the U.S. perspective, there were many reasons for inaction. Kuwait was a small country that was far away. It had an autocratic government. It had been invaded by a powerful military force. The United States had few identifiable interests there aside from oil. The United States was reducing the size of its armed forces. Arab resolve to oppose Iraq was uncertain at best. More important, few Americans looked favorably on new foreign military action. All of these points were discussed at a National Security Council (NSC) meeting on the morning of August 2. Some attendees even dismissed Kuwait as only "a filling station." Although attendees agreed that Iraq's aggression could not be ignored, the meeting ended inconclusively.[9]

After the NSC meeting, Bush flew to Colorado to attend an Aspen Institute conference, at which he and British Prime Minister Margaret Thatcher were keynote speakers. During the flight, Bush telephoned King Fahd of Saudi Arabia, King Hussein of Jordan, and President Mubarak of Egypt. Fahd was not available, but Bush talked with Hussein and Mubarak, who were together in Alexandria. Both urged Bush to allow Arab states to find a solution to what they considered an inter-Arab problem. Hussein noted that Saddam had told him earlier that day that Iraq would withdraw from Kuwait within a week. Bush agreed to give Hussein forty-eight hours to obtain a formal promise from Saddam to withdraw.[10]

When *Air Force 1* landed in Colorado, no concrete movement to counter Iraq's invasion of Kuwait or to create a coalition to counter the invasion of Kuwait had yet occurred. It even appeared that Saddam might be provided a brief breathing period so that he could clarify his intentions. If there was to be an anti-Iraq coalition, it still had no leader.

This soon changed. When Bush arrived in Aspen, he met with Margaret Thatcher. The two leaders discussed what might be done to expel Saddam from Kuwait. Thatcher stressed that Saddam "must be stopped" and pledged British forces to help any U.S. military effort to liberate Kuwait. She also opined that France would contribute forces. Bush's discussions with Thatcher had a clear impact on the U.S. president. At an afternoon press conference, Bush stressed that he was "not ruling any options in" concerning the Iraqi aggression, nor was he "ruling any options out." This was a significantly different position from the one he had expressed earlier in the day. The president also observed that it was important that "the international community act together to ensure that Iraqi forces leave Kuwait immediately."[11] Senior British officials later asserted that the British prime minister had "performed a successful backbone transplant" on Bush.[12]

There is no doubt that Thatcher strengthened Bush's resolve to oppose Saddam. But another factor also probably contributed to the president's changed position. As early as the morning NSC meeting, the Central Intelligence Agency (CIA) reported that Iraqi forces were being resupplied and beginning to mass near the Saudi border.[13] This continued throughout the day. Bush was probably notified of this while he was at Aspen. Thus, even as Thatcher was strengthening his resolve, Bush was probably cognizant of a growing Iraqi threat to Saudi Arabia.

The combination of his discussions with Thatcher and his probable awareness of the Iraqi buildup proved decisive. On the return trip to Washington, Bush finally contacted King Fahd. During a thirty-minute conversation, Bush told Fahd that Saddam "won't stop" and that the United States and Great Britain were "willing to offer air support and more" to help Saudi Arabia defend itself. Fahd was noncommittal.[14]

Bush arrived back in Washington on the evening of August 2. The NSC met the following morning, again examining the threat the Iraqi invasion presented to U.S. interests as well as possible U.S. responses. But this time, the meeting ended with Bush ordering National Security Adviser Brent Scowcroft; Secretary of Defense Dick Cheney; Chairman of the Joint Chiefs of Staff (JCS) General Colin Powell; Commander-in-Chief (CINC), U.S. Central Command (USCENTCOM) General H. Norman Schwarzkopf; and several others to assemble at Camp David the following morning to brief him on possible military options.[15]

No decisions had been made to form a coalition or to send U.S. armed forces to the Middle East, but it was clear that Bush had decided that the United States would take the leadership role in opposing Iraq's invasion.

The Key Recruit: Saudi Arabia

Scowcroft also began laying the foundation for U.S.–Saudi cooperation. After the August 3 NSC meeting, Scowcroft met with Saudi Arabia's ambassador to the United States, Prince Bandar bin Sultan. Scowcroft told Bandar that the United States was "inclined" to help in any way possible. The prince thanked Scowcroft, but reminded him that during the Iranian revolution the United States had prevailed on Saudi Arabia to allow the United States to deploy two squadrons of F-15s to his country as a gesture of support. Saudi Arabia agreed, but when the planes were halfway to the desert kingdom, U.S. President Jimmy Carter revealed that they were unarmed. Scowcroft assured Bandar that that would not happen again.[16]

George Bush stopped by Scowcroft's office during the meeting. The U.S. president and the Saudi ambassador were close friends, and Bush gave Bandar his "word of honor" that the United States would "see this through with you." The prince took this as a serious commitment. Bush ordered Scowcroft to arrange a briefing for Bandar on Operations Plan 1002-90 (a USCENTCOM plan to deploy 250,000 U.S. troops to the Persian Gulf for the defense of the Saudi peninsula) and on the latest satellite reconnaissance pictures of the Iraqi buildup on the Saudi–Kuwaiti border.

Bandar received his briefing at the Pentagon later on August 3. Bandar told Secretary Cheney, who gave much of the briefing, that the briefing had sobered him and that he now advocated deploying U.S. air and ground forces to Saudi Arabia. Cheney told Bandar that if Saudi Arabia invited U.S. forces to deploy and Bush approved, General Schwarzkopf or someone else could go to the Gulf to coordinate the deployment. Bandar promised to present the message to King Fahd.[17]

On August 4, senior administration officials, including Bush, Cheney, Powell, Vice President Dan Quayle, Secretary of State James Baker, White House Chief of Staff John Sununu, and several others received a briefing at Camp David from Schwarzkopf on CENTCOM Operations Plan 1002-90. The general told his listeners that Plan 1002 had a "deterrence piece" designed to protect Saudi Arabia and a "war-fighting piece" requiring a much larger force deployment. It would take seventeen weeks to get the full deterrence piece in place and eight to twelve months to deploy the warfighting piece.

When Schwarzkopf finished the briefing, the senior political officials remained behind to hear additional sensitive intelligence about Saudi Arabia and to reach a decision on what to do. What they heard was not reassuring. Some Saudi leaders saw no evidence of a threat from Iraq. Others favored offering Iraq billions of oil revenue dollars in the hopes of preventing an attack. In addition, Saudi Arabia had not yet responded to the earlier U.S. offer to send a squadron of F-15s (to Saudi Arabia) and had turned down a request for military overflights and augmented reconnaissance flights. Nevertheless, after considerable discussion, consensus was reached that President Bush should call King Fahd to gauge his thinking on the invasion and to offer Saudi Arabia assistance.

Bush called Fahd, telling him that the Iraqi threat was real and urging him to act. Fahd responded that Saudi Arabia had no need for ground troops, but might need assistance with airpower and equipment. The king also inquired about the low-level briefing team Bush was sending to Saudi Arabia with the latest satellite pictures of Iraqi forces in Kuwait. Even though no one on the U.S. side recalled making such an offer, Bush promised to put a team together. What apparently had happened was that Prince Bandar either misunderstood what Cheney told him during the August 3 Pentagon briefing or intentionally misconstrued to his king the nature of the team the United States would be willing to send to Saudi Arabia.[18]

Bush, however, wanted to send a high-level team to assure that decisions would be made. After considerable uncertainty, King Fahd on August 5 finally agreed to accept a high-level team. Secretary Cheney led the team, which left for Saudi Arabia later that day with the specific objective, as outlined by Bush, of convincing Saudi Arabia to accept U.S. forces.[19]

Arriving in Saudi Arabia on August 6, Cheney, Schwarzkopf, and the rest of the Americans showed Fahd and his advisers satellite pictures of the Iraqi buildup on the Saudi–Kuwait border, briefed them on Plan 1002, and urged them to allow the United States to deploy forces to their country. After considerable discussion among himself and his advisers, the Saudi king agreed to allow the deployment. Cheney called Bush with the news, and U.S. forces began moving to Saudi Arabia later that same day.[20]

Important Regional Support: Other Arab States

With Saudi Arabia agreeing to accept U.S. forces, it became critically important for both countries to include more Arab countries in the anti-Iraq effort. However, despite the flagrancy of Iraq's aggression against Kuwait, this was not necessarily an easy task. Within the Arab world, Kuwaitis were not well liked. Many Arabs also disliked the United States. Nor could it be overlooked that Iraq had a powerful military force and that Saddam had proven himself willing to use that force against those who disagreed with him.

Indeed, in the first two days after the Iraqi invasion of Kuwait, most Middle Eastern states refrained from commenting on the Iraqi invasion. As previously recounted, Egypt's President Hossni Mubarak and Jordan's King Hussein even counseled President Bush to use restraint and allow Arab states to find an Arab solution to the problem. The two men, along with King Fahd, were also trying to arrange an Arab summit meeting for Sunday, August 5, in Jeddah, Saudi Arabia. By Friday, August 3, Syrian President Hafaz Assad, who had long despised Saddam, was the only Arab head of state to publicly decry Iraq's aggression.[21]

Meanwhile, Arab League foreign ministers were meeting in Cairo. Immediately after the Iraqi invasion, the Arab League did nothing. But in a meeting on Saturday, August 4, it voted 14 to 7 to "condemn Iraqi aggression against Kuwait." Egypt led the effort to pass the resolution. Jordan opposed it.[22]

Egypt's action fit within the context of an Arab solution to the Kuwaiti crisis, but it was evident that Egypt had moved to the front of Arab opposition to the Iraqi invasion of Kuwait. There were five reasons for Egypt to do this. First, Mubarak received a barrage of phone calls from Bush, Cheney, and U.S. ambassador to Egypt Frank Wisner underlining the seriousness of the Iraqi threat and requesting Egyptian opposition to Iraq. Second, Mubarak and Bush had a close personal relationship. This added weight to Bush's requests. Third, the United States provided over $2 billion of economic assistance to Egypt each year. This too added weight to U.S. requests. Fourth, despite his appeals for an Arab solution to the problem, Mubarak was convinced that Saddam had not been honest in late July when Mubarak attempted to mediate the Iraqi dispute with Kuwait. Finally, although it is not clear when Egypt received its first promises of additional economic aid, such promises may have been made early in the effort to create the Coalition.[23]

Egypt played an equally important role in abetting the early stages of the U.S. force buildup in the region. After his August 6 meeting with King Fahd, Secretary of Defense Cheney flew to Egypt to see Mubarak. Although on this visit he did not convince the Egyptian president to send troops to Saudi Arabia, Cheney did get Mubarak's permission to allow the USS *Eisenhower* aircraft carrier battle group to transit the Suez Canal.[24] After his stopover in Egypt, Cheney flew on to Morocco to meet with King Hassan, who had also been called by Bush. Hassan immediately offered to send troops to Saudi Arabia.[25] The Coalition was already beginning to gain both tacit and concrete Arab support.

But the Coalition's real breakthrough in the Arab world took place on August 10, when a hastily convened Arab League summit meeting voted to denounce Iraq, support Saudi self-defense measures, and send troops to support the Saudi effort. Of the Arab League's twenty-one members, only Tunisia was absent. Twelve states supported the resolution, three opposed it (Iraq, Libya, and the Palestine Liberation Organization, or PLO), two abstained (Algeria and Yemen), and three did not vote (Jordan, Sudan, and Mauritania).[26] The first contingent of Egyptian troops landed in Saudi Arabia the next day. They were soon joined by troops from Bahrain, Morocco, Oman, Qatar, Syria, and the United Arab Emirates.[27] The Coalition's Arab leg was in place.

Quiet Collaborators: China and the Soviet Union

As major international actors that had friendly relations with Iraq, sold arms to Iraq, and were members of the United Nations Security Council, China and the Soviet Union both had potential to help or hinder Coalition efforts to counter Iraq's invasion of Kuwait. The United States, therefore, paid significant attention to both states throughout the Persian Gulf crisis.

The U.S. effort paid off. Although neither China nor the Soviet Union became active members of the Coalition, both terminated their military and economic contacts with Iraq, and both either supported or refrained from opposing U.S. and Coalition resolutions at the United Nations.

China's case was particularly interesting. On August 4, China declared that it would not support United Nations sanctions against Iraq. But on August 6, China joined with twelve other states on the UN Security Council to pass Resolution 661, which imposed economic sanctions on Iraq. China also agreed to stop shipping arms to Iraq.[28] What had happened?

Put simply, the United States had contacted China through the State Department and National Security Adviser Scowcroft to request China's support (or at least lack of opposition) for U.S. positions. The United States also pointed out that it had been restrained in its criticism of the June 1989 Tiananmen Square massacre, and that Chinese support of U.S. positions might help China regain acceptance in the international community. In addition, George Bush had been U.S. ambassador to China and had a web of personal contacts at senior levels in the Chinese government.[29] Although it is impossible to weigh the relative importance of each of these factors, together they were sufficient to convince China to support the August 6 UN resolution. China also either supported or abstained from voting on subsequent UN resolutions on the Gulf crisis.

The Coalition also needed Soviet support, or at least the absence of opposition. Once again, the Bush administration succeeded admirably even though the USSR never joined the core of the Coalition. Throughout Operations Desert Storm and Desert Shield, the United States paid close attention to Soviet attitudes on the Gulf crisis, seeking continually to have the United States and USSR present a united front.

For example, after the August 3 joint U.S.–Soviet declaration on the Iraqi invasion, Bush met with Gorbachev on two separate occasions to discuss the Gulf crisis. On September 9, the two presidents met in Helsinki, issuing a joint statement that declared that they were "united in the belief that Iraq's aggression must not be tolerated."[30] The two leaders met privately again in Paris on November 19 during a meeting of the Conference on Security and Cooperation in Europe (CSCE), and once again they discussed the Persian Gulf situation. This time, Bush failed to win Gorbachev's support for the use of force to expel Iraq from Kuwait, but he did obtain his agreement that force could not be ruled out.[31] Nevertheless, the Soviet Union on November 29 supported UN Resolution 678, which authorized coalition states to use "all necessary means" against Iraq to force it to withdraw from Kuwait if it had not done so by January 15, 1991.

It is clearly evident that skillful U.S. diplomacy and shared interests influenced China and the Soviet Union quietly to collaborate with the Coalition. Both states stopped arms sales to Iraq, participated in the economic sanctions against Iraq, and either supported or abstained on the twelve UN resolutions relating to Iraq's invasion of its neighbor. Without Chinese and Soviet collaboration, the course of the Persian Gulf crisis undoubtedly would have been considerably different.

The Western Alliance

Member states of the Western alliance, including Japan, also played important roles in the anti-Iraq coalition. Indeed, fifteen of the thirty-five core states in the Coalition were members of the Western alliance. Every NATO state except Iceland and Luxembourg contributed armed forces. Most sent forces either to defend Saudi Arabia or to liberate Kuwait. Germany, constitutionally proscribed from sending combat forces abroad, sent planes to help defend NATO ally Turkey, which shared a border with Iraq and feared an Iraqi assault. Several other states followed Germany's example even though they had no constitutional limitations on sending armed forces abroad. Australia and New Zealand also sent military units. Japan, also constitutionally proscribed from sending combat units abroad, was the single largest non-Middle Eastern contributor of funds to cover the cost of military operations.

For the most part, these states joined the Coalition with little or no urging. In one case, Great Britain, a West European leader, even appeared to be more upset about the Iraqi aggression than did the United States. British and French naval vessels began steaming toward the Persian Gulf as early as August 4. The Western European Union signed on with the Coalition on August 21.[32]

Well before the end of August 1990, then, the Coalition that countered the Iraqi invasion of Kuwait was formed and operational. But questions remained. The Coalition had been assembled, but could it stay together?

And if it stayed together, could it deter further Iraqi aggression and expel Iraq from Kuwait?

STRAINS ON THE COALITION

Based primarily on the states of the Western alliance and moderate to conservative Arab states, the Coalition was nevertheless diverse. Not surprisingly, then, it was subject to serious internal strains that had the potential to disrupt it. Each will be discussed separately.

Arab Uncertainty about the U.S. Commitment

Although many Arab states opposed Iraq's invasion of Kuwait and believed themselves to be threatened by Iraq's military power and its proven willingness to use it, most were also uncertain about whether they should oppose Iraq's aggression. There was a basic reason for this. Given Iraq's military power and its proven willingness to use it, any Arab state that opposed Saddam too ardently risked the Iraqi leader's wrath and perhaps opened his country to a fate similar to that of Kuwait. For many Arab leaders, and for King Fahd in particular, assurances had to exist that if they opposed Saddam, the United States would commit itself fully to the anti-Iraqi operation. At least at first, they were not certain about the degree to which the United States was willing to commit itself to Persian Gulf affairs. For example, Fahd and other Arab leaders remembered that when the United States suffered casualties in Lebanon in 1983, the Reagan administration quickly found a way to withdraw.[33]

Arab uncertainty over the U.S. willingness to commit itself waned and then disappeared, first as George Bush gave his word of honor that the United States intended to see the situation through to a successful resolution and then as the U.S. military buildup proceeded. Nevertheless, at the outset of Operation Desert Shield, this was a real Arab concern.

Arab Discomfort with Kuwait

In addition, many Arab leaders wondered why they should risk the wrath of Saddam Hussein to help Kuwait. Kuwait as a state and Kuwaitis as a people were little liked and less respected in the Arab world. This too was a powerful disincentive for Arab states to oppose Iraq's invasion.

The Clash of Religion and Cultures

Another disincentive was Arab discomfort with U.S. and Western culture. As an open and liberal society, the United States was anathema in much of the Arab world, especially among radical Arab leaders, religious fundamentalists, and many ordinary men and women in the streets.

In addition, the clash of cultures between conservative Islamic society and open Western societies, which would almost certainly accompany any extended deployment of non-Arab forces in Saudi Arabia, further reduced the attractiveness of such a deployment. Indeed, just before Secretary Cheney met with King Fahd on August 6, Fahd checked with Islamic religious leaders to obtain a reading on their views of the possible presence of large numbers of U.S. troops in Saudi Arabia. They acquiesced to the U.S. deployment, but not without misgivings.[34]

Even more forebodingly, the clash of cultures had the potential to increase as a threat to the Coalition the longer U.S. and Western troops were deployed in Saudi Arabia. Civilian and military leaders in all states were well aware of this danger and worked to prevent it from becoming a problem. Nevertheless, the possibility that the clash of cultures would worsen over time and undermine the Coalition was one factor that led to the decision to resolve the Gulf crisis as quickly as possible once it became clear that Saddam Hussein did not intend to withdraw from Kuwait.

The Israeli Factor

Beyond the strains imposed by the clash of cultures, the United States was also Israel's closest ally. This both reduced the attractiveness of the United States as an ally to some Arab states and had the potential to increase tensions between the United States and Arab states once the Coalition was formed.

Understandably, it also led Iraq to attempt to draw Israel into the conflict once fighting started. Had Iraq's Scud attacks against Israel been successful in drawing the Jewish state into the war, the Coalition may well have unraveled. Keeping Israel out of the conflict consequently was a major U.S. policy objective throughout the crisis.[35]

History and the Specter of Colonialism

Similarly, the burden of history lay heavily on the Coalition. The Arab world's colonial experience with the West had not been a happy one, and allowing large numbers of non-Arab troops to enter Arab lands once again raised the specter of renewed colonialism in the minds of many Middle Eastern leaders and people.

This led to a paradoxical concern even among many Arabs who supported the Coalition. As already discussed, many Middle Easterners who opposed Iraq's invasion of Kuwait were concerned that non-Arab Coalition members would not stay the course against Iraq. Conversely, many were also concerned that non-Arab Coalition forces would stay too long. Many retained this concern even after the United States promised that troops would stay no longer than Saudi Arabia wanted them to.

Arab Unity

The issue of Arab unity also raised doubts and uncertainties in many Arab states about the wisdom of opposing Iraq. The effort to obtain Arab unity was one reason why the Arab League had always sought unanimity in its decisions. Even though in reality Arab unity was more fiction than fact, many Arab leaders considered it an ideal to be sought and obtained. Thus, especially given the low regard in which Kuwait was held in much of the Arab world, the desire to obtain Arab unity even at the price of concessions to Iraq remained a concern that had the potential to weaken the Coalition.

Iraqi Propaganda

Iraqi propaganda also had the potential to weaken the Coalition. Saddam Hussein used many tactics in his propaganda effort, appealing for Arab unity, calling for a *jihad* against the United States and the West, stressing economic inequities and class conflict within moderate and conservative Arab Coalition members, and calling on Arabs throughout the region to rise up against their governments. Although in the final analysis Iraq's propaganda efforts had little or no impact on the Coalition's unity, many Coalition governments were exceedingly concerned that Saddam Hussein's propaganda efforts would fall on receptive ears.

Soviet Uncertainty

Finally, despite its willingness to support Coalition positions in general terms, the USSR on occasion evidenced discomfort with the Coalition's policy directions and threatened to break ranks with the United States and other Coalition members. For example, Gorbachev's reluctance during the November 1990 Paris CSCE meeting to support the use of military force against Iraq had the potential to derail the effort to expel Iraq from Kuwait militarily. This episode has already been discussed and will not be repeated here.

This was not the only time that the USSR undertook an initiative on its own in seeming opposition to Coalition policies. On February 9, 1991, Gorbachev announced that he believed that the Coalition's air attacks against Iraq had gone beyond the UN's mandate and that he was therefore sending a special representative, Evgeny Primakov, to Baghdad with a peace proposal. The Iraqis accepted Primakov's proposal, presenting Bush and the rest of the Coalition with the "nightmare scenario" of the Coalition unraveling in the middle of the war effort. However, President Bush called Gorbachev, and the two presidents spoke for over a half hour. In the end, the USSR maintained solidarity with the Coalition.[36] Nevertheless, at least for a short time, the USSR's initiative jeopardized the Coalition's ability to attain its war objectives.

KEEPING THE COALITION TOGETHER: TOOLS OF MANAGEMENT

Once the Coalition was assembled, keeping it together required a skillful and subtle management effort. The United States and George Bush led that effort, using a variety of political and economic tools sometimes openly, sometimes subtly.

There is no evidence that Bush had a game plan about how to manage the Coalition. Rather, he managed the Coalition on an ad hoc basis, using the tools that were available as they became necessary and useful. Just as the Coalition itself was diverse, so too were the tools that Bush and the United States used to keep it together.

U.S. Leadership

American leadership was the central factor in drawing the Coalition together and keeping it together. There is little doubt that in the absence of this leadership, the Coalition never would have been assembled and the Iraqi occupation and annexation of Kuwait would have become an accepted part of the international scene.

The willingness of the United States to form and lead a Coalition, aided and abetted by Margaret Thatcher, developed the day after Iraq invaded Kuwait and escalated rapidly. Indeed, by August 5, President Bush was so strongly committed to the objectives of deterring Iraqi aggression against Saudi Arabia and expelling Iraq from Kuwait that he had already given his word of honor to Saudi Arabia's ambassador to the United States, Bandar bin Sultan, that the United States would not abandon Saudi Arabia; promised Sheikh Jabir al Ahmed al Sabah of Kuwait that the United States would liberate his country and restore him to power; and told the world via CNN News that Iraqi aggression "will not stand."[37] American leadership of the alliance did not flag throughout the months that Iraqi forces occupied Kuwait.

The importance of U.S. leadership was well recognized in the Bush administration and elsewhere as well. As National Security Adviser Brent Scowcroft observed on August 4, the Saudis could "not go out front [in opposition to Iraq] until they know whether we can be counted on."[38] The leadership of the United States was requisite.

But the challenge of leadership is not just leading. Especially with a coalition as diverse as that which opposed Iraq, the challenge is also to lead without moving so far in advance of the views of other coalition states that the Coalition is undermined and weakened. Throughout Operations Desert Shield and Desert Storm, the Bush administration proved equally adept at this requirement of leadership.

Personal Diplomacy

Personal diplomacy was also an immensely important tool used to create and maintain the Coalition. Personal diplomacy had four separate and distinct aspects.

The first was personal friendships. During his prepresidential years of government service and business, George Bush had met and nurtured relationships with heads of state and other senior leaders throughout the world. He continued to do this after assuming the presidency. Bush's efforts to develop personal relationships paid off during Operations Desert Shield and Desert Storm.

Phone calls were a second central part of personal diplomacy. Bush personally called over sixty heads of state and government leaders requesting support for U.S. and international efforts to deter Iraqi aggression and expel Iraq from Kuwait. Bush began his barrage of phone calls on August 2. Three days later, before he left Camp David on Sunday, August 5, he had talked to King Fahd at least five times and had called President Turgut Ozal of Turkey several times. Bush had also phoned Prime Minister Brian Mulroney of Canada; Emir Sheikh Jabir al Ahmed al Sabah of Kuwait; and leaders in France, Germany, Japan, and other countries as well. By the time Secretary of State James Baker traveled to Damascus in mid-September to meet with Syrian President Hafez Assad, Bush had already spoken to the leader of the one-time pariah state at least three times. In these and other phone calls, Bush often "mustered all his finesse on the telephone" to persuade foreign leaders of the wisdom of his views.[39]

Personal diplomacy also included foreign trips by virtually every senior U.S. administration official to guarantee support for the anti-Iraq effort. Bush took three foreign trips during late 1990 to help line up support, going to Helsinki in September to meet with Gorbachev, to Europe and the Middle East in November, and to Latin America in December.[40] Secretary of Defense Cheney concentrated on trips to the Middle East to discuss military issues. Treasury Secretary Nicholas Brady was dispatched to Germany, Japan, South Korea, Saudi Arabia, and the Gulf states to "twist their arms a little bit," in Bush's words, to fund the Coalition's activities.[41] But the real champion of travel was Secretary of State James Baker, who between early August and late November traveled at least 100,000 miles and held over 200 meetings with foreign ministers and heads of state.[42] Baker later estimated that he traveled another 50,000 miles and held another 100 meetings with foreign leaders between late November and the beginning of Operation Desert Storm.[43]

The fourth aspect of personal diplomacy was nurturing relationships with foreign diplomats in Washington. For example, from the outset Saudi Ambassador Bandar was kept abreast of the administration's plans and thinking on a regular basis, even being told during the week of December 17 that Bush had basically made up his mind that war with Iraq was inevitable and that ongoing diplomatic activities were mere exercises.[44] Similarly, on December 21, Bush invited the ambassadors from twenty-eight core Coalition countries to the White House for a meeting on Coalition plans.[45]

Tactical, Political, and Diplomatic Skill

In addition to leadership and personal diplomacy, the Bush administration also used excellent political and diplomatic skill in managing the Coalition. Thus, when new policy departures were contemplated, the ground was usually well prepared beforehand or as the policy unfolded. For example, when, on October 31, Bush decided to double the size of the U.S. force deployed in Saudi Arabia to give the Coalition an offensive option, he quickly dispatched Secretary of State Baker to other states to inform them of the decision and win their approval.[46]

In another striking case of tactical diplomatic and political skill, the day after the United Nations voted on Resolution 678, authorizing states to use "all necessary means" to drive Iraq from Kuwait, Bush declared that he was sending Baker to Baghdad to find a peaceful solution to the building crisis and was willing to meet with Iraq's foreign minister Tariq Aziz in Washington. Although neither visit ever took place, Bush's offer succeeded in emphasizing that the Coalition would use force unwillingly and only as a last resort. Politically, at least within the United States, this was exactly the image that Bush wanted the Coalition to have.[47]

The United States also frequently used diplomatic carrots and sticks. The actions of the United States in regard to China, the Soviet Union, and Jordan provide examples. In China's case, the week before the UN voted on Resolution 678, the United States invited Beijing to send a trade delegation to Washington to improve trade relations and expand U.S.-Chinese trade.[48] China abstained on the resolution, and the trade delegation visited Washington. In the Soviet case, the U.S. effort to gain Soviet support for the Coalition led the United States to refuse to support the Baltic states' request to attend the 1990 CSCE meeting and to cancel Assistant Secretary of the Treasury Bruce Bartlett's visit to Lithuania.[49] In Jordan's case, Bush sent Deputy National Security Adviser Robert Gates to Jordan in August to warn King Hussein that if Jordan did not condemn Iraq's invasion of

Kuwait, the United States would significantly slow economic aid to Jordan.[50]

Money

Money also played an important role in the formation and maintenance of the Coalition. As Table 1.3 shows, Saudi Arabia, Kuwait, the UAE, Japan, and Germany bankrolled the coalition, with the United States and several Arab states also forgiving approximately $14 billion in debts owed by Egypt.

The United States received over $50 billion of funds to pay for its costs in Operations Desert Shield and Desert Storm, and Great Britain received over $2 billion. In addition, Syria, Turkey, Egypt, and several other states received compensation from Saudi Arabia and other states for trade revenues lost as a result of their joining the embargo against Iraqi trade.[51]

The United States played a major role in convincing donor states to provide funds. Had the United States failed, money may not have been available to pay for the costs of Operations Desert Shield and Desert Storm. It is not certain that the U.S. body politic would have supported the war effort under such conditions. Beyond the United States, had money not been available to pay for lost trade revenues and other costs of the war effort, the Coalition may never have formed. Had the Coalition formed in the absence of money, it would not have been as effective as it was.

Saddam Hussein's Blunders

Efforts to form and maintain the Coalition were also aided and abetted by Saddam Hussein's own blunders. On several occasions, Saddam undertook actions that directly influenced Coalition states to strengthen the forces that they had deployed in and around Saudi Arabia.

France provides the best example. French destroyers headed for the Persian Gulf the day after Iraq invaded Kuwait, but France did not send a sizable naval force to the Gulf until August 19, the day after Saddam announced he was detaining Westerners, including French citizens, in Iraq and Kuwait.[52] Slightly less than a month later, Saddam repeated his blunder by sending Iraqi troops into the French Embassy in Kuwait. France responded this time by sending 4,000 more soldiers to Saudi Arabia.[53]

Similarly, British resolve was strengthened when Iraq took British citizens hostage and when Saddam appeared on television with them. Nor did Iraq's pillage of Kuwait and Saddam's statements that Iraq refused to give up "one square inch" of Kuwait enhance the Coalition's willingness to negotiate with Iraq.[54]

The United Nations

The willingness of the United States to work through the UN also enhanced the legitimacy of the anti-Iraq effort and helped create and maintain the Coalition. As shown in the following chart, the UN passed twelve separate resolutions pertaining to the Iraqi invasion of Kuwait, all of which passed with significant majorities. As already discussed, the United States expended considerable effort to assure support for these resolutions, especially among the permanent members of the Security Council. Even so, having the UN approve these resolutions greatly strengthened the legitimacy of efforts to expel Iraq from Kuwait and create and maintain the Coalition.

UN Security Council Resolutions on Iraq's Kuwaiti Invasion

Aug. 3	**Resolution 660:** Passed 14 to 0, with Yemen abstaining because it "did not have instructions." The resolution "condemn[ed] the Iraqi invasion of Kuwait"; demanded that Iraq "withdraw immediately and unconditionally" from Kuwait; and called on Iraq and Kuwait to begin "intensive negotiations for the resolution of their differences."
Aug. 6	**Resolution 661:** Passed 13 to 0, with Cuba and Yemen abstaining. Ordered a trade and financial embargo of Iraq and occupied Kuwait.
Aug. 9	**Resolution 662:** Passed 15 to 0. Declared Iraq's annexation of Kuwait null and void.
Aug. 18	**Resolution 664:** Passed 15 to 0. Demanded that Iraq free all detained foreigners.
Aug. 25	**Resolution 665:** Passed 13 to 0, with Cuba and Yemen abstaining. Empowered the United States and other naval powers to enforce the economic embargo against Iraq and Kuwait by stopping shipping bound there.
Sept. 13	**Resolution 666:** Passed 13 to 2, with Cuba and Yemen opposed. Allowed food and humanitarian aid to be sent to Iraq and Kuwait.
Sept. 16	**Resolution 667:** Passed 15 to 0. Condemned Iraq's aggressive acts against diplomatic missions in Kuwait.
Sept. 24	**Resolution 669:** Passed 15 to 0. Declared that only the Security Council's Sanctions Committee could permit food and other humanitarian assistance to be sent to Iraq and Kuwait.

Sept. 25	**Resolution 670:** Passed 14 to 1, with Cuba opposed. Expanded economic embargo to include air cargo.
Oct. 29	**Resolution 674:** Passed 13 to 0, with Cuba and Yemen abstaining. Held Iraq liable for all war damage and demanded release of hostages.
Nov. 28	**Resolution 677:** Passed 15 to 0. Condemned Iraq's attempts to drive Kuwaitis out of Kuwait and repopulate the country with Iraqis.
Nov. 29	**Resolution 678:** Passed 12 to 2, with Cuba and Yemen opposing and China abstaining. Gave Iraq until January 15 to comply with UN resolutions, after which "all necessary means" could be used to drive Iraq from Kuwait.

Several of these resolutions were notable not only because they strengthened international support for the anti-Iraq effort and provided additional legitimacy to the Coalition, but also because they departed from common UN practices. Resolution 661 was only the third UN resolution imposing economic sanctions against a state.[55] Resolution 665 was the first time the UN authorized the use of military force to compel compliance with economic sanctions. Resolution 678 was the first UN resolution authorizing states to use their own discretion to achieve a UN objective. Together, all the resolutions helped legitimize the Coalition's efforts to expel Iraq from Kuwait.

Second- and Third-Party Contacts

Although the United States was the primary architect of the Coalition, other states also used their good offices to help create and maintain the Coalition and move it toward its objectives. These second- and third-party contacts were important in adding legitimacy to the Coalition.

For example, Margaret Thatcher, in addition to strengthening U.S. resolve to oppose Iraq in the hours immediately after the Iraqi invasion of Kuwait, also talked to many European and British Commonwealth heads of state to convince them of the wisdom of opposing Saddam Hussein. Thatcher's calls, in conjunction with those of George Bush, brought considerable pressure to bear on European and British Commonwealth leaders, who may have been hesitant to join the Coalition.

On one occasion, Soviet Foreign Minister Eduard Shevardnadze also helped solidify the Coalition with third-party contact. On November 23, Shevardnadze flew to Urumji, China, to discuss the crisis with Chinese Foreign Minister Qian Qichen. The two foreign ministers "decisively demanded" that Iraq withdraw from Kuwait and obey UN resolutions on Kuwait. No public comment was made on military force, but there is little doubt that such discussions took place.[56] Six days after the meeting, the USSR supported and China abstained on Resolution 678.

Even Syrian President Assad played a role in second- and third-party contacts. In early October, after having met with U.S. Secretary of State James Baker, Assad flew to Teheran to meet with Iranian leaders. Before Assad's visit, Iran had called for a holy war against U.S. forces in the region. After Assad's visit, Iran called for a holy war against U.S. forces only if they remained in the Middle East for an extended time. The timing of the change in Iran's rhetoric may have been coincidental, but it is highly likely that Assad suggested such a change, possibly at Baker's request.[57]

In all likelihood, the Coalition would have been created and maintained its cohesion even in the absence of second- and third-party contacts. But the use of second- and third-party contacts enhanced the legitimacy of the Coalition's efforts against Iraq by strengthening the perception that such efforts were more than just U.S. policies.

CONCLUSION

In the final analysis, the Coalition that drove Iraq from Kuwait was created and maintained by a unique set of personalities, geopolitical realities, economic conditions, and domestic political situations. Despite its uniqueness, several concluding points must be stressed.

First, to a great extent, the Coalition was George Bush's personal creation. He created it and maintained it very much on his own, admitting to "enjoy[ing] trying to put the coalition together and keep it together."[58]

Second, the Coalition was created between and among leaders of states rather than between and among institutions of states. One reason for this was the perceived need for speed in early August 1990 to counter the possibility of continued Iraqi aggression. But one reason that the Coalition remained a leader-to-leader entity rather than evolving into an institution-to-institution entity was the role that personal diplomacy played in creating and maintaining the alliance.

Third, although U.S. forces by themselves could probably have deterred and defeated Iraq, thereby obviating the need for a Coalition, the existence of a broad, multifaceted Coalition helped legitimize first the U.S. military buildup in Saudi Arabia and then the use of armed force to expel Iraq from Kuwait. In essence, the existence of the Coalition permitted the U.S. government to argue that it was acting in concert with international public opinion and not unilaterally, thereby swaying public opinion in the United States and in the U.S. Congress to support a large military deployment and the use of military force.

Fourth, although the Coalition itself was diverse, the core of the Coalition was not. Twenty-five of the thirty-five Coalition members were Western alliance or Arab states. To a great extent, the rest of the world stayed on the sidelines.

Finally, the Coalition came together and stayed together not necessarily because of coincident or shared interests, but because of leadership perceptions of personal or national advantage for being in the Coalition or personal or national threat from Iraq. That the Bush administration could orchestrate these diverse perceptions to form a Coalition that was both diverse and successful was a truly impressive accomplishment.

NOTES

1. Table 1.1 includes as part of the Coalition's military forces two Soviet naval vessels that were operating in the Persian Gulf area during late 1990 and early 1991, even though these vessels were operating independently of the Coalition's command structure. Thus, Table 1.1 shows thirty-six states rather thirty-five.

2. For details of the main financial contributors to the war effort, see Table 1.3. Japan also deployed four mine countermeasures ships and one support vessel to the Persian Gulf after the conclusion of Operation Desert Storm.

3. *New York Times*, August 5, 1990.

4. Even with a large and diverse Coalition in place, it was not certain that the U.S. Congress would authorize President Bush to use U.S. armed forces to drive Iraq from Kuwait. In the House of Representatives, the vote was 250 to 183 in favor of the January 12, 1991 resolution supporting "the use of all necessary means" to end Iraq's occupation of Kuwait. In the Senate, the vote was much closer, 52 to 47. In the absence of a large and diverse Coalition, it is likely that three more senators may have opposed the resolution, thereby defeating it. See *New York Times*, January 11, 12, 13, 14, 1991.

5. For the text of the joint statement, see TASS, 1900 GMT, August 3, 1990, as reported in *Foreign Broadcast Information Service (Soviet Union)*, August 6, 1990, 10.

6. Harry G. Summers, Jr., points to this as the critical factor in the Persian Gulf War, arguing that "as long as the U.S.–Soviet alliance held, the end for Iraq was inevitable." See Harry G. Summers, Jr., *On Strategy II: A Critical Analysis of the Gulf War* (New York: Dell, 1992), 233. The analysis in this chapter takes a considerably different view of the importance of the de facto U.S.–Soviet alliance, arguing that it was a necessary but not sufficient condition to forming the anti-Iraq alliance, deploying external armed forces to the Middle East, and conducting the war against Iraq.

7. Robert Woodward, *The Commanders* (New York: Simon & Schuster, 1991), 223–24 [hereafter *Commanders*].

8. *New York Times*, August 3, 1990.

9. Woodward, *Commanders*, 224–29.

10. *New York Times*, August 6, 7, October 16, 1990; *Time*, January 7, 1991, 20; *Washington Post*, August 3, 6, 1990.

11. *Newsweek*, January 28, 1991, 58; *Time*, January 28, 1991, 31; *New York Times*, August 3, 1990; *Washington Post*, August 3, 1990.

12. Martin Walker, "Dateline Washington: Victory and Delusion," *Foreign Policy* (Summer 1991): 167.
13. Woodward, *Commanders*, 225, 237, 247–48.
14. *New York Times*, August 9, 1990; *Time*, January 7, 1991, 22.
15. Woodward, *Commanders*, 238.
16. Ibid., 240.
17. Ibid., 199–204, 240–44.
18. Ibid., 247–54.
19. Ibid., 259.
20. For additional details, see ibid., 267–73; *Time*, January 7, 1991, 22–23; *Newsweek*, January 28, 1991, 59.
21. *New York Times*, October 16, 1990.
22. *New York Times*, August 4, 5, 6, 1990. See also *Washington Post*, August 19, 1990. Jordan's Prime Minister Mudar Badran later implied that by mobilizing support for the anti-Iraqi resolution, Egypt had reneged on its agreement with Jordan to seek an Arab-only solution to the crisis. See Jordan television, as reported in *Foreign Broadcast Information Service (Middle East)*, August 6, 1990, 55.
23. See Table 1.3.
24. After additional phone calls from George Bush, Mubarak agreed to send Egyptian forces to Saudi Arabia. The first contingent of Egyptian troops landed in Saudi Arabia on August 11. See Joseph P. Englehardt, "Desert Shield and Desert Storm: A Chronology and Troop List for the 1990–1991 Persian Gulf Crisis," *SSI Special Report* (Carlisle, Pa.: Strategic Studies Institute, March 1991), 15.
25. Woodward, *Commanders*, 275–76.
26. For a fascinating Russian account of the meeting, see *Izvestiya*, August 17, 1990. See also *New York Times*, August 11, 12, 1990.
27. Saudi and Kuwaiti troops were already deployed.
28. *Washington Post*, August 5, 1990; Woodward, *Commanders*, 267.
29. Jean Edward Smith, *George Bush's War* (New York: Henry Holt, 1992), 124–25 [hereafter *Bush's War*]; Woodward, *Commanders*, 226.
30. For the complete text of the statement, see *Pravda*, September 10, 1990.
31. *New York Times*, November 20, 1990. See also TASS, 0006 GMT, November 20, 1990, as reported in *FBIS (Soviet Union)*, November 20, 1990, 12.
32. *Washington Post*, August 22, 1990.
33. *Time*, January 7, 1991, 22; *New York Times*, August 26, 1990.
34. Woodward, *Commanders*, 266.
35. One measure of the closeness between the United States and Israel and the importance that the United States placed on keeping Israel out of the conflict was the establishment of a special top-secret secure voice communication link between the Pentagon and the headquarters of the Israeli Defense Forces. For details, see ibid., 363.
36. See *New York Times*, on virtually a daily basis between February 9 to February 23, 1990, for details of the Soviet initiative. See also *Washington Post*, February 22, 1991, for a detailed assessment of the possible impact of the Soviet plan on the military campaign.
37. CNN News, August 5, 1990. See also *Washington Post*, August 4, 1990; Woodward, *Commanders*, 241, 255.
38. Woodward, *Commanders*, 251–52.

39. Ibid., 255, 260, 301; *Time,* January 7, 1991, 22; *Newsweek,* January 28, 1991, 59; *New York Times,* August 8, 1990.
40. He also had other objectives on these trips.
41. *New York Times,* August 31, 1990.
42. Woodward, *Commanders,* 333.
43. Author's conversation with Secretary Baker, January 28, 1994, in Washington, D.C.
44. Woodward, *Commanders,* 345.
45. *Washington Post,* December 30, 1990.
46. *Washington Post,* November 9, 1990.
47. *New York Times,* November 30, 1990; *Washington Post,* November 30, 1990. Bush's offer also had a downside beyond the United States. Prince Bandar and other Arab Coalition members were concerned that the United States offer might either be a weakening of the U.S. position or be interpreted in Baghdad as a weakening of the U.S. position. See Woodward, *Commanders,* 335–36; Smith, *Bush's War,* 218–20.
48. *New York Times,* November 30, 1990.
49. *Washington Post,* November 26, 1990.
50. *Washington Post,* September 1, 1990.
51. *Washington Post,* August 29, September 11, 1990; Smith, *Bush's War,* 127.
52. For the Iraqi government's statement on detainees, see *New York Times,* August 19, 1990. For France's decision to strengthen its naval presence in the Persian Gulf, see *New York Times,* August 20, 1990.
53. Smith, *Bush's War,* 157.
54. See *Washington Post,* October 4, 1990, for Saddam Hussein's statement that Iraq would not give up any Kuwaiti territory.
55. The first two times were against Rhodesia in 1967 and South Africa in 1977.
56. For Soviet coverage of the meeting, see TASS, 1209 GMT, November 23, 1990; Moscow Domestic Service, 1990 GMT, November 23, 1990; TASS, 1542 GMT, November 23, 1990, all as reported in *FBIS (Soviet Union),* November 26, 1990, 4–5.
57. Smith, *Bush's War,* 171.
58. *Washington Post,* September 11, 1990.

2

But Was It *Jihad?* Islam and the Ethics of the Persian Gulf War

Sohail H. Hashmi

INTRODUCTION

The Persian Gulf War was perhaps the most morally debated conflict in recent history. From August 2, 1990, until the present day, the war in its many dimensions has been the subject of just-war rhetoric and analysis by a truly diverse assortment of personalities and organizations. To date, at least half a dozen books and countless editorials and articles have been published on the ethics of the Gulf War.[1]

However, the public discourse on the justice or injustice of the war has largely neglected at least one-half of the discussion, for the conflict was the subject of intense moral evaluation and analysis within the Muslim world itself. Although the Gulf War offered an important opportunity for a truly cross-cultural dialogue on issues of war and peace in our international society, the opportunity went largely unrealized.[2] In the last week of January 1991, I watched CNN in Cairo as George Bush declared the conflict to be a "just war." A few hours later, on Egyptian state television, I listened as two senior religious officials explained how Islamic law (*shari'a*) fully sanctioned the war to liberate Kuwait. A few days earlier, I had heard several Jordanian officials compare Iraq's struggle against the Western "imperialists" and their Arab supporters to *jihad*. This was truly a cacophony of righteous rationalizations for war, appealing to different traditions, or different interpretations of the same tradition, all citing doctrine more alike than different, and yet—as is often the case with the West's encounter with Islam—talking completely past one another.

The exploitation of religion by authoritarian and often militantly secularist regimes during the Gulf War has led many students of Middle East politics to dismiss the appeals and justifications as nothing but crass propaganda. Even the religious appeals of the more sincerely motivated persons have been and indeed should be received with a degree of skepticism. As Michael Walzer has commented in his contribution to a volume entitled *But Was It Just?*, "Think of the perverse if exhilarating effect upon religion whenever the language of holiness is taken over by politicians."[3] The Muslim discourse on the ethics of the Gulf War certainly evinces its share of perversities. Nevertheless, as the crisis unfolded over the course of seven months, it also allowed ample opportunity for public and often vociferous debate on its ethical and legal dimensions. This Muslim discourse, when studied in the context of previous ethical and legal controversies centering on conflicts such as the Arab–Israeli wars, the Iran–Iraq War, the war in Afghanistan, and the ongoing conflict in Bosnia, emphasizes the continuing development of Muslim perspectives on the current role and future place of Islamic thought in international relations. This discourse also provides important answers to why so many Muslims all over the world opposed American policies in the war.

The ethical and legal debate was conducted on several different levels and with many objectives. First, at the individual level, a number of independent scholars in several countries published commentaries on the crisis in books, monographs, or interviews. These scholars came from both the ranks of the traditionally educated *'ulama* as well as the secularly, often Western, educated intellectuals. Second, a number of Islamist organizations and movements issued statements throughout the crisis. Often the purpose of such declarations was to strengthen their popular base by challenging state policies or pressuring the regime to adopt their own positions.[4] Third, at the state level were the *fatwas* (juristic opinions) issued by "establishment" *'ulama*, most notably in Egypt and Saudi Arabia. These statements were then used by the regimes as religious sanctions for their policies and as responses to the Islamist challenge. Fourth, at the international level were the declarations of several conferences convened to ascertain the opinion of the *umma*, the universal Muslim community, in support of either the Iraqi position or that of its opponents. These conferences were hardly independent of the states that sponsored them, namely Iraq and Saudi Arabia. They did not fail to issue communiqués fervently supporting their sponsors' positions. However, given the truly multinational nature of the conference's participants, including among them several highly respected scholars, the work of the conferences and the statements that were issued by them merit consideration.

This analysis of the Muslim discourse on the ethics of the war draws on the arguments advanced by individuals or groups at each of the aforementioned four levels. However, my primary focus will be on levels 3 and 4—that is, on the *fatwas* or formal juristic opinions rendered by *'ulama,* as well as the deliberations and declarations of the international conferences. To a large extent, these statements generated a dialectic, both shaping and reflecting the diverse moral positions on the conflict. They were thus at the center of the Muslim debate on the ethics of the war.

The principal ethical and legal issues raised by the war may be divided into the following roughly chronological categories:

1. The invasion of Kuwait by Iraq and Iraq's subsequent attempt to incorporate Kuwait
2. The introduction of American-led Western forces into the Persian Gulf region
3. The conduct of the war against Iraq by Coalition forces
4. The conduct of the Iraqi regime during its campaign against internal rebellion in the southern mainly Shi'ite regions and in the northern Kurdish regions.

ISLAM IN CONTEMPORARY INTERNATIONAL RELATIONS

Thirty years ago, Majid Khadduri, one of the leading scholars of Islamic international legal theory, wrote that "twentieth-century Islam found itself completely reconciled to the Western secular system [of international relations], a system which itself had undergone radical changes from its medieval Christian background."[5] Two dramatic developments have led to the reassessment of such views. The first is, of course, what has come to be popularly labeled the "Islamic resurgence." Contrary to scholarly expectations of the 1960s and 1970s, it has been Islamic movements which have emerged as well-organized, ideologically committed, and often mass-based challengers to the postcolonial, secular-nationalist regimes. The second development is the equally unexpected dissolution of the Soviet empire and the overnight disappearance of the Communist "threat." The new threat to Western values—and Western hegemony—in the international system has been identified by some journalists and academicians as "Islam."

However, both the Islamist challenge and the current fixation with the "Islamic threat" distort the extremely diffuse and divided state of Muslim approaches to politics. Far from being a monolithic or homogeneous political and social phenomenon, the "Islamic resurgence" is characterized by a number of contending approaches to and visions of political Islam. The Muslim discourse on the ethics of the Gulf War attests to the fact that the most underdeveloped aspect of contemporary Islamic political thought remains the field of international relations.

In practice, the Muslim world appears to have accommodated itself with an international system that reflects Western origins and dominance. Certainly, the Muslim states that emerged from the retreat of European colonialism did nothing to challenge the Third World pattern of seeking not an overthrow of the international system into which they were born, but instead full membership. All of the states, for example, sought and gained membership in the United Nations within two years of independence.

In 1969, representatives of twenty-four Muslim-majority states voted to create the Organization of the Islamic Conference (OIC), which today includes forty-nine member states. Its charter contains a statement of principles taken directly from the UN Charter, including the peaceful settlement of disputes and respect for state sovereignty—that is, territorial integrity and noninterference in the domestic affairs of states.

Yet conformity to the prevailing international system does not necessitate assimilation of all its norms, which ultimately are grounded in a specific cultural and religious context. Although many of the specific *legal* injunctions of the medieval Islamic theory of international law may be anachronistic in actual Muslim state practice, the general *ethical* framework from which the law was derived does influence the worldviews of both the state elites and their challengers. In other words, although the medieval theory is today clearly in disuse, its principles have by no means been repudiated by the majority of Muslim states. For example, the OIC voted in 1980 to establish an International Islamic Law Commission to "devise ways and means to put forward the Islamic point of view before the International Court of Justice and such other institutions of the United Nations when a question requiring the projection of Islamic views arises therein."[6]

Fourteen years after its founding, the commission has yet to meet, largely because the state elites that voted to create the commission realize that its findings may challenge not only the international system, but also their own positions within it. In the absence of any systematic and authoritative modern elaboration of an Islamic theory of international relations, the discourse consists largely of ad hoc applications of medieval law to contemporary events, including, of course, the Gulf War. Yet this process is in itself valuable in emphasizing the continuing relevance of Islamic theories of international relations in the minds of many Muslim scholars as well as politicians. Moreover, such discourse ultimately contributes to the evolution of modern Islamic approaches to international relations. Even without the formal deliberations and rulings of a body such as the proposed Islamic International Law Commission, the interpretation and revision of Islamic international law continues through these numerous informal means.

Two important aspects of the contemporary Islamic discourse are (1) political community, or the status of the sovereign, territorial state in relation to the Qur'anic ideal of the unified Muslim community, the *umma;* and (2) conflict and conflict resolution, or the definition of *jihad.* Since both of these issues figured prominently in discussions of the ethics of the Gulf War, we must consider each briefly.

Political Community

A few years after his migration to Medina in 622 C.E. (the Hijra), the Prophet Muhammad concluded a formal agreement that has come to be known as the Constitution of Medina. According to this document, all Muslims, including the immigrants who had accompanied the Prophet from Mecca and all those native to Medina, were to form a single community distinct from all others. This social and political organization was in keeping with the still ongoing Qur'anic revelation, which designated Muslims as one community (*umma wahida*) and enjoined them to retain their unity.[7]

The first Muslim community at Medina has served as a model of the virtuous polity for Muslim theoreticians for 1,400 years. The concept of the Muslim *umma* has been interpreted to mean not just shared values and culture, but, as in Medina, a single political community as well. Even as late as the twelfth century, when in reality the Muslim world had become fragmented into several distinct states, in theory the *umma* still meant a unitary Muslim state ruled by a single man, the *imam*, whose principal duty was to enforce Islamic law, the *shari'a*. Even theorists such as al-Ghazali (d. 1111) and Ibn Khaldun (d. 1406), who were among the first to attempt a reconciliation of Islamic theory with political realities by embracing the legitimacy of several Muslim states, could not entirely renounce the ethical ideal of a unified Muslim community.

The spread of Western imperialism in the Muslim world introduced further and more fundamental challenges to Islamic ideals. First, European powers redrew the political map of Muslim peoples according to their own interests. When they withdrew in the twentieth century, they left behind frontiers and states that had little historical or cultural relevance to the people who inhabited them. Second, European imperialism confronted Muslims with political ideologies and a nascent international legal framework, both of which were alien to them. To survive in this system, Muslims had to respond; but unlike the conditions under which medieval thought was developed, their responses were shaped by another, dominant civilization.

The most powerful idea that Europe disseminated to the rest of the world beginning in the second half of the nineteenth century was nationalism, the linkage of a single "nation" defined by ethnicity to a specific territory. The spread of nationalism among Muslim peoples is an extremely complex story. In the Arab Middle East, nationalism generally meant pan-Arabist schemes of unification of the Arab "nation" in revolt against the artificial states created by Europeans. Opposed to pan-Arabism from its inception was not a particular type of nationalism, such as Egyptian, Syrian, or Iraqi, but instead pan-Islamism. Pan-Islamism was essentially a revival of the *umma* paradigm, the idea that all Muslims everywhere constitute a single community apart from all others. Pan-Arabism was condemned by pan-Islamists as an obstacle to the realization of the Islamic ideal. Underlying much of their opposition was their awareness that one of the tenets of pan-Arabism was secularism. This secularism was sometimes explicitly formulated by pan-Arabists as the need to exclude Islam from the political arena. But as the challenge from pan-Islamists mounted, many pan-Arabists attempted to reconcile the two ideologies by emphasizing the centrality of Islam to Arab identity. Unity of the Arabs, they argued, was a logical and necessary first step to unity of all Muslims.

Pan-Arabism enjoyed its heyday in the 1950s and 1960s. Elucidated by ideologues such as Nasser and the Ba'athists, it came to be seen as firmly, even militantly, secular in its thrust, relegating Islam to the personal and cultural spheres. This brand of pan-Arabism met its demise, by general agreement, with the shattering Arab defeat to Israel in 1967. However, it would be premature to write its postmortem, since it has reemerged in the decades since in its more religiously oriented form. The pan-Arabists of the 1980s and 1990s have resurrected the old argument that an "Islamically sensitive" Arab unity is the precursor to Islamic unity. Although most Arab religious opposition organizations remain wary of old secularists in new Islamic guise, they themselves have become increasingly fragmented along national lines. Thus, unlike pan-Islamism in the early decades of this century, there is no coherent ideological response to the fusion of Islam and pan-Arabism today. This is the environment in which a leader like Saddam Hussein, despite a lifetime commitment to the militantly secularist Ba'athist ideology, can still lay claim among many Muslims to being a champion of the Islamic cause. Although the reality of the Muslim world is that it is divided into nearly fifty sovereign states, the sense that this arrangement is of a foreign and not an Islamic inspiration still underlies much of the political discourse.

Conflict and Conflict Resolution

Like other religious and moral systems, Islam attempted to limit human conflict by prescribing a certain set of criteria for legitimate wars. Within Islamic theory, the only legitimate war was *jihad,* the struggle to propagate the word of God to all people, through peaceful means if possible, through violent means if necessary. Since Muslims theoretically formed one community living under the laws of God, *jihad,* properly speaking, was not applicable within the Islamic realm according to the majoritarian Sunni view. Conflicts among Muslims were not wars, but faction, or civil strife, conveyed by the Arabic word *fitna,* meaning literally a "trial" or "test."

But Was It *Jihad*?

The ethical and legal approach to conflicts among Muslims has been shaped by a single Qur'anic verse dealing with the subject: "If two parties from among the believers fall into dispute, then make peace between them. But if one party transgresses beyond bounds against the other, then fight all of you together against the transgressor until it complies with the laws of God. But if it complies, then make peace between them with justice and be fair; for God loves those who are fair" (49:9).

This verse provided the basis in medieval law for the *ahkam al-bughat,* or the rules for dealing with rebellion within the Islamic community. The verse presumes the existence of a Muslim community, if not a supreme authority, that has the right to intervene in a dispute to resolve it before the beginning of hostilities. If one of the parties resorts to unacceptable means to resolve the dispute (presumably, if it begins hostilities), it becomes the duty of the collective Muslim community to fight the belligerent until it desists. It is important to note here that the verse maintains neutrality with regard to the merits of the causes. It is not the justice or injustice of a particular claim that provides the grounds for fighting, but the employment of illegitimate means by one of the parties. When the offending party desists, it becomes incumbent on the Muslim community to desist and to resolve the dispute by peaceful means. In other words, the goal of fighting under *ahkam al-bughat* is to rehabilitate, not to annihilate, the rebels.

Given the preferred outcome of intra-Muslim disputes, medieval jurists formulated a number of conditions governing the conduct of war against rebels. Among the most important of these was that captured rebels were to be treated as prisoners of war, not as murderers or traitors, and thus could not be killed. Moreover, in the event of a rout in battle, they were to be allowed unimpeded flight as long as they were not regrouping for another battle. Most important for the purposes of this discussion, rebels were to be fought without the assistance of non-Muslim forces, even more so if military command was in their hands.[8]

Verse 49:9 and numerous interpretations of it became the focus of the Muslim ethical discourse throughout the Gulf crisis. When the crisis began, *'ulama* who spoke in opposition to the Iraqi invasion consistently cited it and the medieval *ahkam al-bughat* as justification for the deployment of Coalition forces. In doing so, they hoped to take advantage of the strong bias in Islamic thought against *bughat,* or any undermining of legitimate political order. As the crisis mounted, however, the same verse was cited by supporters of Iraq in their condemnation of the Coalition. No better example is available of what I have earlier termed the ad hoc application of medieval Islamic international law to contemporary events. The resulting contradictions and confusions were to characterize the Islamic debate throughout the conflict.

RESPONSES TO DESERT SHIELD

When Iraqi tanks rolled across the Iraqi–Kuwaiti frontier on August 2, 1990, they availed themselves of the modern expressway linking Baghdad to Kuwait City, which had been financed by Kuwait's rulers during the Iran–Iraq War as an expression of brotherly affection for the people of Iraq. The Kuwaiti frontier was completely undefended, despite months of mounting tensions between the two countries. According to some postwar analysts, Saddam Hussein had given numerous indications of his intentions regarding Kuwait. In February and again in May 1990, he had devoted two major addresses before Arab summits to the topic of pan-Arab unity. The second speech was particularly noteworthy in its attempt to link pan-Arabism with Islam. It concluded by citing a Qur'anic verse which foreshadows the conflict Saddam Hussein may have anticipated at this point: "A great army is gathering against you."[9] Finally, in the weeks right before the invasion, Baghdad had waged a steady press campaign against Kuwait, alleging that Kuwait was deliberately undermining Iraq's postwar recovery by driving down international oil prices through overproduction. Yet when the invasion did occur, it astonished everyone, most of all the Arab leaders directly connected to the dispute.

Some of these leaders had hoped that the Iraq–Kuwait dispute would be resolved at the OIC Council of Foreign Ministers meeting in Cairo. When news of the Iraqi invasion reached the conference, the OIC ministers voted 37 to 5 to call on Iraq to withdraw immediately and unconditionally from Kuwait.[10] This vote is significant in that it is the first indication of the division among Muslim states, which would last through the conflict.

In Baghdad, the Revolutionary Command Council began releasing statements justifying the Iraqi invasion of Kuwait. The initial rationale was that Iraqi forces had been invited to intervene by the Free Kuwaiti Interim Government. This explanation gave way quickly to the claim that by its actions Iraq was merely reclaiming one of its ancient provinces, which had been severed from it by British imperialists. The "merger" declarations are again laden with religious rhetoric. The pan-Arab struggle—meaning physical unity in the Iraq–Kuwait context—is characterized as *jihad*. Those who oppose this definition of pan-Arabism, including specifically the emir of Kuwait, are compared to Qarun, a Qur'anic figure who symbolizes greed and pride. He exults in his riches instead of spending them on good causes. In the end, he and his wealth are swallowed by an earthquake.[11] By invoking the Qur'an's consistent theme of economic and social justice among Muslims, Saddam Hussein was tapping two powerful emotions: first, the resentment felt by many Muslims of the vast wealth that has flowed to the oil-rich states; second, the widespread view that the Gulf Arab leaders live a decadent lifestyle.

In the first few days after the invasion, the prevailing mood in the Muslim countries and particularly among the most active fundamentalist groups was generally anti-Iraq and consonant with the tenor of the OIC resolution. Although few groups rushed to the verbal support of the ousted al-Sabah family, Saddam Hussein was also no favorite of theirs due to his brutal campaign against Islamic opposition movements within Iraq and his eight-year war against Iran. However, this anti-Iraq consensus began to shift quickly following George Bush's declaration on August 8 of American military intervention, ostensibly to secure the Saudi border against Iraqi aggression.

The injection of American-led Western forces into the Gulf dispute had an obviously profound impact on both the policies as well as the discourse in the crisis. The presence of Western troops in the Arabian peninsula provided immediate grist for the Iraqi propaganda mill. Saddam Hussein exploited it by linking Iraqi compliance with Security Council resolutions calling for Iraq's withdrawal from Kuwait with Israeli compliance with earlier UN resolutions demanding Israel's withdrawal from the occupied Arab territories. The logic of the linkage was, of course, patently absurd, but given the strong American military action, the Iraqi regime was able successfully to link issues of Arab nationalism with Islam. The Western powers were once again enforcing their double standard in international politics: They would not enforce international law when Muslim issues, such as the Israeli occupation of Jerusalem, were involved, but they were all too ready to curb a powerful Arab state that challenged their own regional interests. Thus, when Saddam Hussein called on August 10 for *jihad* against "aggressive invaders" and their "collaborators," he found support among the organized Islamic movements as well as the masses in many Muslim countries.[12]

Hussein's appeal was not due to a sudden reevaluation of his Islamic "credentials," which remained suspect in the eyes of most Islamist groups. It stemmed rather from his ability to articulate the deep-rooted frustration with the perceived injustices of the current international system shared by many Muslims. While other Muslim leaders blustered, Saddam Hussein acted.

Saddam Hussein's "Call to Arabs and Muslims to Save the Two Sacred Shrines" received a religious imprimatur on the same day that it was broadcast. The General Secretariat of the People's Islamic Conference, an organization created in 1982 to resolve the Iran–Iraq War, issued a statement declaring the Iraqi cause to be a defensive war against external aggression. This type of *jihad* was a moral obligation on all Muslims, men and women, according to their "capabilities and situation." The statement also pointedly challenges the Saudi invitation to foreign troops. The presence of foreign forces in the Arabian peninsula, it declares, violates two prohibitions in Islamic law: (1) allowing non-Muslims to enter areas near the two sacred sanctuaries in Mecca and Medina; and (2) allying with non-Muslims to fight other Muslims.[13]

In response to the Iraqi calls for *jihad,* the religious establishments of Egypt and Saudi Arabia were mobilized to refute the arguments. On August 10, the office of the Shaykh al-Azhar, Jad al-Haqq 'Ali Jad al-Haqq, released that institution's first statement on the Gulf crisis. Al-Azhar has long been considered the religious mouthpiece of the Egyptian government, which frequently turns to it to legitimize controversial policy decisions, such as Anwar Sadat's peace treaty with Israel. Thus, not surprisingly, al-Azhar's statement condemns Saddam Hussein's action and calls on him to turn away from aggression in compliance with the requests of Egyptian President Hosni Mubarak. The entire document is restrained in its tone and does not present any significant assessment of the legal and ethical issues raised by the Iraqi invasion; rather, it portrays its own call for an end to the Iraqi occupation of Kuwait as being a moral obligation to guide a Muslim away from wrongdoing, in this case oppression (*zulm*). The statement is entirely focused on Saddam Hussein and depicts the crisis as being the result of his own actions without the complicity of either the Ba'athist regime or the Iraqi people.[14] This approach would, in fact, be maintained by virtually all the anti-Iraq Arab coalition until the beginning of Desert Storm.

One day after Shaykh al-Azhar's statement was published in the Egyptian press, another document reviewing the Gulf crisis was issued by the Rabitat al-'Alam al-Islami (Muslim World League) based in Mecca and largely controlled by the Saudi regime. This statement portrays itself as a refutation of the charges made by Saddam Hussein in his "Call to Arabs and Muslims." Mecca and Medina, it declares, are not under foreign occupation, but are being "tended by secure hands who cherish the religion and the sanctities of all Muslims." The statement ends by appealing to the Iraqi president to "fear God and spare the property and blood of Muslims" by withdrawing from Kuwait according to the OIC resolution. By complying with the OIC requests, the statement avers, Saddam Hussein would be complying with Qur'anic principles, encapsulated in verse 49:9, the basis for *ahkam al-bughat.*[15]

According to this verse, the party to be fought collectively is the one that has resorted to unacceptable means to achieve its ends. This was certainly the reason for the Rabita document's focus on this particular verse, and the reason why this verse would continually be cited in subsequent statements against Iraq. Saddam Hussein was the *baghi,* the rebel, because he had employed unacceptable means in resolving his dispute with the Kuwaitis. His principal transgression was not that his army had violated the sovereignty of an independent state (this legal argument was used primarily in "secular" fora, such as the Arab League and the UN); rather, it was that he had fomented civil strife and outright war among Muslims. By designating Saddam Hussein as the *baghi,* the *'ulama* were hoping to capitalize on the strong presumption against civil strife that underlay the medieval *ahkam al-bughat.*

However, the anti-Iraq *'ulama's* attempts to focus the debate on the Iraqi aggression proved largely unsuccessful. By this time, the focus of the debate had shifted decisively away from the Iraqi invasion of Kuwait to the American intervention in the dispute. In the four and a half months separating the Iraqi occupation of Kuwait and the launching of the allied air campaign, the anti-Iraq Coalition was largely on the defensive, steadily justifying the presence of non-Muslim forces in the Arabian peninsula. The issue grew in importance in direct proportion to the increase of Western forces in the Persian Gulf.

In mid-August, the Saudi government released a statement issued by a conference of senior *'ulama* which declared the necessity of availing all possible means to defend the Muslim *umma* and invested Muslim leaders with the obligation of undertaking all measures to ensure the elimination of the threat against Muslim lives and property.[16] One prominent member of this conference, Shaykh 'Abd al-'Aziz ibn Baz, later published a detailed justification for seeking non-Muslim assistance in the conflict. The Prophet Muhammad had received the assistance of non-Muslims during some of his military campaigns. Seeking such assistance, argues Ibn Baz, is obligatory (*wajib*) for a Muslim ruler when necessary (*darura*) for the safety and security of Muslims.[17]

In addition, al-Azhar's bureau of legal interpretation (Dar al-Ifta') released a juristic opinion (*fatwa*) in September which declared that the Gulf crisis was an affliction on both the Muslim community (*umma*) and on the entire world. Seeking the assistance of non-Muslims was legitimate under the circumstances, especially because foreign forces had come for a specified mission, which was to end the Iraqi occupation of a Muslim state.[18]

Finally, on September 10 through 12, the Muslim World League convened in Mecca a full-scale conference, attended by hundreds of religious scholars and activists from several countries, to present the "Islamic perspective" on the Gulf crisis. In its communiqués, the conference declared that Iraq's invasion of Kuwait violated clear Islamic principles concerning the inviolability of life, property, and honor among Muslims as well as the sanctity of agreements and treaties between governments. Iraq's alleged reasons for its invasion, including redistribution of wealth, were characterized as "socialist satanism" and "thievery." In the end, the conference endorsed the presence of foreign troops on Saudi soil due to the necessity of securing Saudi frontiers from the Iraqi threat. However, the endorsement was less than unequivocal, since the conference also suggested that the OIC create an Islamic military force for collective security among Muslim states. An Islamic force would "free the region of the use of any non-Islamic force."[19]

The idea of an "Islamic army" put forth by the League conference highlights some of the contradictions and dilemmas confronted by the pro-Coalition *'ulama* in justifying Operation Desert Storm. By repeatedly citing verse 49:9 and the *ahkam al-bughat,* they themselves had opened the door for strong condemnation of the anti-Iraq Coalition. As critics pointed out, the Qur'anic verse commands Muslims to resolve disputes among themselves. There is no mention of involving outside parties. Indeed, the Qur'an does contain several verses forbidding Muslims from taking non-Muslims as *awliya',* meaning "allies" or "protectors." Supporters of Iraq frequently quoted verse 60:1: "O you who believe! Take not My enemies and yours as friends (or protectors)." In context, the verse's injunction relates specifically to the pagan Arabs who had persecuted the Prophet Muhammad and the earliest Muslim community. But quoted out of context, the verse could easily be used in condemning a Coalition that included former European colonialists, the United States, and Israel. Even when the Prophet had accepted the assistance of non-Muslims, the pro-Iraqi *'ulama* pointed out, he had never used such help to fight against Muslims. This policy had been so consistently maintained by his four immediate successors, the "rightly guided caliphs," that it became incorporated by wide juristic consensus as a point of Islamic law.

As the January 15, 1991 deadline for Iraqi withdrawal approached, both the anti- and the pro-Iraqi forces launched a final campaign to buttress Muslim support for their positions. This round began with the announcement in Baghdad of another meeting of the People's Islamic Conference. The conference got underway on January 6, with a stream of Iraqi Ba'athist officials working assiduously to portray Saddam Hussein as a *mujahid* (one who wages *jihad*) and a latter-day Salah al-Din (Saladin). Apparently, the irony of this comparison was lost on the speakers, since Saladin was Kurdish, not Arab. At the climax of the conference, Saddam Hussein himself presented an address suffused with religious imagery: "We are fighting for the sake of honor in this world. Prior to that, we were fighting for the principles of the God of the heavens and earth. ... Our preparation is of a level that will defeat the aggressive armies because the slogan of *Allahu akbar* [God is most great] is the lofty banner our fighters are guided by and believe in."[20] Indeed, the words *Allahu akbar* had appeared overnight on the Iraqi flag.

The Baghdad conference concluded officially on January 11 with the declaration that the conflict was not one of governments but of Islamic peoples against infidels. Because Iraq was battling in defense of the honor and lives of Muslims, *jihad* was an individual moral duty for all Muslim men and women *(fard 'ayn)*. The conference urged volunteers from all Muslim countries to join Iraqis in the field of battle.[21]

While the Baghdad conference was in full swing, a rival anti-Iraqi wing of the same organization, the People's Islamic Conference, was continuously issuing its own statements from Saudi Arabia in what ended up becoming the battle of the Baghdad versus the Mecca conferences. As pro-Iraqi members of the conference's executive committee were opening the Baghdad conference, other members declared it illegal because most of them had not been consulted or had not agreed to it.[22]

On the day that the Baghdad conference issued its call for *jihad* should Iraq be attacked, the Mecca conference issued its own declaration entitled the "Declaration of Mecca."[23] This statement is a systematic treatment of the principal issues raised by attacks against the anti-Iraq Coalition. It begins by attempting to appropriate the legitimacy of religious interpretation: "The *'ulama* of Islam are required to explain the facts and give a wise opinion to the *umma* on every occasion, especially when sedition occurs and confusion is rife." In this situation, it is a "sin" to remain silent when Islam is being portrayed "as a religion that appeases the oppressors and approves tyranny—whereas repelling injustice on earth is one of the great objectives of Islam." The statement continues by explicitly attacking the motives of the Baghdad conference and declaring the illegitimacy of its declarations because the Iraqi regime "uses Islam only as a tool." What follows is a list of the Ba'athist regime's past crimes against Islam (including repression of Kurds, Shi'ite activists, and senior *'ulama* who opposed the regime), as well as their present crimes, which include the invasion and destruction of a Muslim country and the diversion of attention away from legitimate Islamic causes, including specifically the Palestinian *intifada*. No Muslim, the declaration continues, should lend any support to the Iraqi regime because "this appeasement tempts the regime to persist in its inflexible stance. This stance is the wide gateway to the hell of war."

What follows next is a brief elaboration of the main themes the anti-Iraq Coalition had been propounding in the preceding three months. First, the declaration attempts once more to separate the Iraqi people from the Iraqi regime, explicitly calling on them to save their homeland from the devastation of war by rising against Saddam Hussein. Second, it addresses the Iraqi army and, on the authority of a tradition of the Prophet, declares that Iraqi troops who persist in supporting an unjust cause will not be considered martyrs deserving paradise, according to the Qur'anic conception, but rather criminals deserving eternal punishment in hell. Third, it attempts to diminish Saddam Hussein's appeal among many Muslim groups due to his belligerent anti-Israeli stance by declaring that the Palestinian issue remains "Islam's greatest cause."

All of these points were part of a new approach to the Iraqi leader. He was no longer an errant Muslim in need of friendly counsel. Now, according to many *'ulama*, he was simply the head of a secular, atheistic Ba'athist regime that had to be fought by all available means.[24]

Finally, the statement addresses the issue central to anti-Coalition sentiments in the Muslim countries: the presence of Western forces in this Coalition. Criticism of the decision to include non-Muslim forces in opposition to Iraq is dismissed as "propaganda trickery." The Iraqi regime, the declaration reads, is the direct cause for the arrival of the foreign forces due to its initial aggression and its threatening the security of Saudi Arabia and all other Gulf states. "It is the right of the victims of aggression and those threatened by it to pursue the means for repulsing the aggression."

The ultimate result of the Mecca conference was to sanction *jihad* to repulse the Iraqi occupation of Kuwait because the struggle against sedition (*fitna*) and oppression (*zulm*) is obligatory for Muslims. The theoretical basis had been laid for the launching of Desert Storm.

RESPONSES TO DESERT STORM

The beginning of the air campaign on January 17, 1991 exacerbated all the controversies of the past months. Naturally, *jus in bello* rather than *jus ad bellum* concerns now dominated the discussion. With regard to the ethics of Desert Storm, the anti-Iraq Coalition was remarkably incoherent. Iraq's response to the air campaign violated a number of Islamic provisions on proper conduct in war: for example, discrimination between military and civilian targets when it launched Scud missile attacks against civilian centers in Saudi Arabia and Israel; and protection of the natural environment when it leaked millions of barrels of oil into the Persian Gulf or when retreating troops set fire to Kuwaiti oil wells. Yet the pro-Coalition *'ulama* did not address in any systematic way these specific *jus in bello* issues. When religious figures did speak on the conduct of the war, it was generally to issue sweeping declarations that Saddam Hussein was entirely responsible for the calamity of war being experienced by the Iraqi people.

The silence of the pro-Coalition *'ulama* was due apparently to the fact that the Muslim Coalition partners were unprepared for the scope of the massive allied air bombardment of Iraqi targets. General unease with the conduct of the war is evident from numerous attempts by several Coalition governments, as well as a number of independent Muslim organizations, to convene an emergency meeting of the OIC foreign ministers in order to achieve an immediate cease-fire. Popular sentiment against the allied air campaign intensified when both the Saudi and the Egyptian governments blocked such moves. Thus, the Islamic discourse remained focused—as it had throughout the crisis—on the issue of Western involvement in the conflict. The pro-Coalition *'ulama* remained on the defensive throughout Desert Storm because of the widespread outrage in the Muslim world at the prosecution of the war. One month into Desert Storm, at a conference in Riyadh convened specifically to clarify the laws of *jihad,* Shaykh Ibn Baz was still justifying on Islamic grounds the presence of Western troops in the Coalition.[25]

Several American commentators on the Gulf War have written on the alleged absurdity of prewar Western concerns about popular Muslim opposition to war against Iraq. Charles Krauthammer, for example, has gone so far as to suggest that the lesson from the actual Muslim response to the war is that the Arab "street is largely an echo of the palace."[26]

Such assessments of the Muslim response fail to appreciate the widespread concerns and unease—even among those who had most vocally condemned the Iraqi invasion and occupation of Kuwait—with the way the war was fought. For example, in an interview published in the Moroccan newspaper *Al-'Alam* on February 3, 1991, a senior Moroccan religious scholar, Shaykh 'Abd al-'Aziz ibn Siddiq, declared that although Iraq had been the precipitator of the crisis, the *baghi*, the rules of warfare in the *shari'a* do not permit the prosecution of the war to suppress the sedition in the way the allied campaign was progressing. The allied strategy did not discriminate well enough, charged Ibn Siddiq, between combatants and noncombatants, and no Muslim could countenance the mass killing of children, women, and the old to achieve the suppression of sedition. Similar statements were issued by religious figures in several countries, including those in the Coalition.

The Allied campaign against Iraq officially ended on February 28, 1991. What followed immediately after was a two-month-long civil war for the overthrow of the Ba'athist regime and, indeed, the dismemberment of the state of Iraq itself. Saddam Hussein's internal war to suppress the Kurdish and Shi'ite rebellions raised profound ethical issues in Islamic theory, including the right of resistance to an oppressive regime versus the value of political order and the right of humanitarian intervention by outside parties versus state sovereignty. The Muslim discourse on these issues belies their importance, for there was virtually none. All of the official religious establishments formerly justifying the war now fell remarkably silent on events transpiring within Iraq itself. This silence was perfectly in keeping with state policies which favored the maintenance of a united Iraq—even one governed by a *baghi*—rather than the emergence of separate political entities. The only noteworthy exception to this policy was Iran, whose government not only issued appeals for united Muslim action against the Ba'athists, but actively supported both the Shi'ite and Kurdish resistance to the Iraqi army.[27]

In short, the Muslim discourse on Desert Storm constitutes a missed opportunity for a systematic and comprehensive review of Islamic approaches to just means in war. Such a review would have addressed not only the issue of who may intervene in Muslim disputes, but also the definition of "noncombatant immunity," "collateral damage," "proportionality of means," and "reciprocity" in Islamic thinking today. Finally, such a review would have addressed a largely neglected area: the legitimacy of weapons of mass destruction—weapons that several Muslim countries have tried to acquire and ones that Saddam Hussein has repeatedly threatened to use—according to Islamic moral evaluation.

CONCLUSION

Wars rarely end the way those who fight them intend. One Qur'anic verse frequently cited during the Gulf War admonishes as follows: "Fear sedition and tumult (*fitna*), which afflicts more than only those who are oppressors among you."[28] The Gulf conflict's ramifications certainly go well beyond the Iraqi invasion and annexation of Kuwait.

Based on the ethical and legal discourse considered in this chapter, it is possible, I believe, to draw some general conclusions on the war's impact on evolving Islamic conceptions of world order. First, with regard to conflict and conflict resolution, the war highlighted the trend in recent decades for Muslim theorists to define *jihad* in terms of defensive war, thus attempting consciously or unconsciously to achieve a convergence of *jihad* with just-war concepts as elucidated in the West. During the Gulf War, both sides appealed to the idea of *jihad* to lend legitimacy to their policies. Both sides consistently maintained that they were fighting defensive struggles to repulse aggression: Iraq's invasion of Kuwait for the Coalition or the Western "intervention" in the dispute for supporters of Iraq. There was little religious support for the violent means Iraq had used to resolve its dispute with Kuwait.

The support that Saddam Hussein did garner came from his linkage of the invasion to broader "Muslim concerns," such as the Palestinian conflict, the redistribution of wealth among Arab states, and pan-Arab unity. Many Islamist groups have used similar rhetoric for decades to justify their violent methods within various Arab states. Since the entrenched "corrupt" and "un-Islamic" regimes ruling many Muslim states will not cede power peacefully, such groups charge, they must be overthrown by violent means. When Saddam Hussein declared that the invasion and annexation of Kuwait was an Arab *jihad,* he understood and manipulated an idea that has broad popular appeal: The modern *jihad* is for internal reform and strengthening of the Muslim *umma*.

Second, the war emphasized the continuing ambivalence within the Muslim world toward the legitimacy of the contemporary international state system. The foremost issue here remains the status of the sovereign territorial state in Islamic ethical and legal thought. It is instructive that the most common rationale for repelling the Iraqi aggression given by pro-Coalition *'ulama* was not based on the inviolability of territorial frontiers, but on the sedition and strife within the Muslim community that the Iraqi invasion precipitated. When directly asked if the war was being fought to liberate Kuwait, Shaykh Ibn Baz responded, "No, it is because of [Iraq's] oppression, rejection of religion, and aggression against neighboring Muslims during its subjugation of Kuwait."[29]

The widespread opposition to the Western military intervention on behalf of the Gulf states is also derived, I believe, from this general unease with the contemporary international state system. The Gulf War increased the disillusionment and cynicism that many Muslims feel toward the relevance of international law and ethics. The Western powers, and particularly the United States, were seen as exploiting the United Nations and international law to achieve their own particular interests. After the war, the Western powers have continued to apply a double standard based on their own national interests: Sanctions against Iraq are strictly maintained, but sanctions against Serbs in the former Yugoslavia are only sporadically enforced.

Thus, although the Gulf War may have dealt yet another blow to pan-Arabism, it has strengthened the call of pan-Islamism. Throughout the crisis, the OIC was the object of vociferous attacks from numerous sources for its inability to mount a purely Islamic response to the Iraqi invasion. Even the pro-Coalition *'ulama* were forced to accept the Western military support as a necessity and not the Islamic ideal. The ideal, even for supporters of the Coalition, would have been a Muslim collective security force.

The calls for a collective Muslim response foundered, of course, on the actual structure of the OIC, an organization of nearly fifty independent and often mutually hostile states. The struggle to transform the OIC from a collection of sovereign states into an instrument of the Islamic *umma* predates the Gulf War, but it has assumed greater impetus in the war's aftermath. This issue will be only one of several that characterize Islamic international thought and practice well into the next century.

NOTES

The author is grateful to the SSRC MacArthur Foundation Fellowship in International Peace and Security for its financial support during research for this chapter.

1. See the review essay by Stanley Hoffmann, "Bush Abroad," *New York Review of Books*, November 5, 1992, 54–59, which lists and surveys several works on the ethics of the Gulf War.

2. One noteworthy exception is the conference conducted by the United States Institute of Peace. The proceedings have been published by the Institute in David Smock, ed., *Religious Perspectives on War* (Washington, D.C.: United States Institute of Peace, 1992). The discussion of Muslim perspectives is, however, extremely brief and superficial.

3. Michael Walzer, "Justice and Injustice in the Gulf War," in Jean Bethke Elshtain et al., eds., *But Was It Just? Reflections on the Morality of the Persian Gulf War* (New York: Doubleday, 1992), 2.

4. A review of the Islamist responses to the Gulf War in seven countries may be found in James Piscatori, ed., *Islamic Fundamentalisms and the Gulf War* (Chicago: American Academy of Arts and Sciences, 1991).

5. Majid Khadduri, "The Islamic Theory of International Relations and Its Contemporary Relevance," in J. Harris Proctor, ed., *Islam and International Relations* (New York: Praeger, 1965), 35.

6. Abdallah al-Ahsan, *OIC: The Organization of the Islamic Conference* (Herndon, Va.: International Institute of Islamic Thought, 1988), 36.

7. "Verily, this Community of yours is a single Community, and I am your Lord and Cherisher: therefore serve Me" (Qur'an 21:92). "And hold fast, all together, by the rope which God [stretches out for you], and be not divided among yourselves; and remember with gratitude God's favor on you; for you were enemies and He joined your hearts in love, so that by His grace, you became brethren; and you were on the brink of the pit of fire, and He saved you from it. Thus does God make his signs clear to you: that you may be guided" (Qur'an 3:103).

8. See the detailed review by Khaled Abou El-Fadl, "*Ahkam al-Bughat*: Irregular Warfare and the Law of Rebellion in Islam," in James T. Johnson and John Kelsay, eds., *Cross, Crescent, and Sword* (Westport, Conn.: Greenwood Press, 1990), 149–78.

9. Ofra Bengio, ed., *Saddam Speaks on the Gulf Crisis: A Collection of Documents* (Tel Aviv: Tel Aviv University Press, 1992), 98 [hereafter *Saddam Speaks*]. The Qur'anic verse reads, "Men said to them: 'A great army is gathering against you': and frightened them: but it [only] increased their faith. They said: 'For us God sufficeth, and He is the best disposer of affairs'" (3:173). Saddam Hussein cited this verse again at the conclusion of his call for *jihad* on August 10, 1990.

10. The five members voting against the OIC resolution were Jordan, Mauritania, Palestine, Sudan, and Yemen.

11. Bengio, *Saddam Speaks*, 119–24. The Qur'anic verses referring to Qarun are 28:66–72.

12. Foreign Broadcast Information Service–Near East and South Asia (FBIS–NES)-90-156, 46.

13. FBIS–NES-90-157, 31.

14. *Al-Ahram*, August 10, 1990, 1.

15. *Rabita*, September 1990, 14–15.

16. FBIS–NES-90-157, 26.

17. *Rabita*, September 1990, 13.

18. *Al-Ahram*, September 12, 1990, 8.

19. *Rabita*, October 1990, 13–27.

20. FBIS–NES-91-009, 3–4.

21. *Al-Thawra* (Baghdad), January 13, 1991, 2, 9.

22. FBIS–NES-91-008, 3.

23. *Rabita*, February 1991, 6–10. Excerpts of the declaration in English translation are found in FBIS–NES-91-009, 4–7.

24. See the statements of Shaykh Muhammad al-Sha'rawi in *Rabita*, January 1991, 8–11, and of Shaykh Ibn Baz in *Rabita*, March 1991, 10–12.

25. *Rabita*, March 1991, 8–14.

26. Charles Krauthammer, "On Getting It Wrong," *Time*, April 15, 1991, 70.

27. For more detailed discussion of the Muslim response to the Kurdish and Shi'ite crises within the context of humanitarian intervention, see Sohail Hashmi, "Is There an Islamic Ethic of Humanitarian Intervention?" *Ethics and International Affairs* 7 (1993): 55–73.

28. Qur'an 8:25.

29. *Rabita*, March 1991, 14.

Part II
BRINGING THE EAGLE TO THE GULF DESERT: AIRLIFT, SUPPLIES, AND LOGISTICS

In his book *The Art of War,* published in 1838, Baron Antoine Henri De Jomini rhetorically queried, "Is logistics simply a science of detail? Or, on the contrary, is it a general science, forming one of the most essential parts of the art of war? Or, is it but a term consecrated by long use, intended to designate collectively the different branches of staff duty . . . ?" In answering his own questions he concluded, "the term *logistics* [is] . . . nothing more or less than the science of applying all possible military knowledge."[1]

This having been said by one of the "gods" of military science, one might suppose that military leaders, scholars, and experts might know a great deal about things like logistics, or even about important support functions like airlift and sealift. You might suppose in today's military parlors that these same leaders would know what United States Transportation Command (USTRANSCOM) is and what its role was in the Persian Gulf War. Sadly, few experts, let alone people, are familiar with anything more than general aspects of what airlift, sealift, or logistics are all about. This same ignorance exists with regard to the role these vital functions performed in the Persian Gulf War. To this end, this part of the book provides two chapters that cover all the aforementioned topics.

1. Lieutenant Colonel David C. Rutenberg and Jane S. Allen, *The Logistics of Waging War: American Logistics, 1774–1985, Emphasizing the Development of Airpower* (Gunter AFB, Ala.: Air Force Logistics Management Center, 1987), iv.

The more popular books and news items recounting the Allied experience in the Gulf War spend little, if any, time covering these "less interesting" topics. Nonetheless, they were major components in the Allied victory; especially during the buildup phase of Desert Shield. However, as John W. Leland (in "Air Mobility in Operations Desert Shield and Desert Storm: An Assessment") and William Suit (in "Sustaining the War Machine: U.S. Air Force Logistics Support during the Gulf War") both note, the vital role of these functions was critical to Allied victory and did not end when the war began. Intratheater supply movements and field-level repair operations remained critical throughout Desert Storm and after the war ended.

These two chapters detail the significant part all these support functions played in getting the troops, supplies, and weapons systems to the Gulf. As these chapters indicate, if an army marches on its stomach, then the outcome of the Gulf War was inevitable since the Allied forces were the best supplied in history and the Iraqis one of the worst.

—William Head

3

Air Mobility in Operations Desert Shield and Desert Storm: An Assessment

John W. Leland

The first military airlift command (MAC) aircraft to arrive on the Arabian peninsula, a C-141 from Charleston Air Force Base (AFB), South Carolina, landed at Riyadh Air Base (AB), Saudi Arabia, on 8 August with an advance team from the U.S. Central Command Air Forces (CENTAF).[1] Only airlift combined the speed and flexibility needed to deploy rapidly tens of thousands of U.S. troops to a distant theater. An equally massive sealift, in concert with thousands of airlift missions, transported the vast quantities of material needed to resupply the forces deployed to the Persian Gulf area of responsibility (AOR). Airlift remained the principal means of transporting troops and for deploying time-sensitive materiel. Along with the airlifters, tanker aircraft made up the other component of the air mobility equation. During the conflict, American refueling aircraft also supported the war effort.[2]

Desert Shield soon became the most massive airlift in the history of air power. It was the first large strategic deployment of combat forces by air. By its sixth week, Desert Shield has surpassed the Berlin Airlift (1948–1949) in total ton-miles flown.[3] Air Force Chief of Staff General Merrill A. McPeak later described MAC's contribution to Desert Shield "as the equivalent of a Berlin Airlift every six weeks."[4] The statistics tell the story. During the Berlin Airlift, U.S. aircraft moved 1.78 million tons an average distance of 300 miles, but the MAC airlift system had moved nearly 550,000 short tons of cargo between the United States and Europe to the

Persian Gulf by the time most of the deployed forces had returned to their home bases by late April 1991. Whereas the average distance from a European operating base to Berlin was 300 miles, it was about 7,500 miles from the U.S. East Coast to the Persian Gulf region.[5] A comparison of Desert Shield and Desert Storm with the Berlin Airlift follows.[6]

Comparison: Desert Shield and Desert Storm MAC Airlift with U.S. Participation in the Berlin Airlift[7]

	Operation Desert Shield/Storm* (Strategic Airlift)	Berlin Airlift
Duration	9 Months	15 Months
Distance	6,330 Miles	300 Miles
(Average from onload) Average Ton-Mile Daily	13.6 Million	1.2 Million
Missions	19,780	189,960
Short Tons	548,000	1.78 Million
Passengers	590,956	62,750

*7 Aug 90–19 Apr 91

In assessing the Desert Shield airlift, the magnitude of the operation and the long distance from the continental United States to the Persian Gulf region must always be kept in mind. Desert Shield reaffirmed the often-made statement that airlift is a total system, dependent on the smooth working of many integral components. These include, but are not limited to, the availability of aircrews, suitable operating bases, and the ability of aircraft to be maintained in a timely fashion. The various elements of the airlift system must operate smoothly to produce maximum efficiency. This assessment will focus on the planning and management of the Desert Shield and Desert Storm airlift. It will discuss the contributions of the Civil Reserve Air Fleet (CRAF),[8] the total force policy, C-130 operations, and air refueling. Also examined is the extent to which the Gulf War might serve as a model for future operations.

General Hansford T. Johnson, who served as both Commander in Chief, U.S. Transportation Command (CINCUSTRANSCOM), and Commander in Chief, Military Airlift Command (CINCMAC), believed that one of Desert Shield's major lessons had already been learned from Operation Just Cause, the 1989 U.S. military operation in Panama. Just Cause, he said, marked a turning point in U.S. military doctrine. It demonstrated that "once our nation decides to intervene, we intervene very quickly ... with overwhelming force."[9] So it was with Desert Shield.

Lessons applicable to air mobility arose daily, even hourly. Commanders, midlevel managers, and technicians fine-tuned the airlift system to deal with new requirements, unanticipated difficulties, and ever-changing circumstances. The need to move tens of thousands of troops quickly gave MAC no time to build an airlift system from scratch. Rather, the airlift's success resulted in large measure from MAC having perfected a seamless airlift system over five decades. In 1990, this system was mutually dependent on strategic airlift, intratheater airlift, the commercial airlines, and the integration of the active duty, Air Force Reserve (AFRES), and Air National Guard (ANG) forces.[10]

General Johnson was committed to identifying and correcting problems quickly.[11] MAC's assessment of the airlift began during Desert Shield's second week, when General Johnson directed Headquarters (HQ) MAC's Command Analysis Group (CAG)[12] to form a "lessons learned" working group composed of representatives from across the MAC staff. When the group issued its report in late 1990, it proposed solutions to 120 identified lessons. The lessons ranged from issues of logistics, manpower, and disaster preparedness to an examination of how effectively HQ MAC was organized for war. The CAG conducted dozens of studies during the conflict. It often confirmed by quantitative and qualitative analysis the instinctive answers to questions proposed by airlift managers assigned to HQ MAC's Crisis Action Team (CAT).[13]

The pattern of operations begun in Desert Shield's first week continued until the redeployment airlift was largely completed in April 1991. Ninety percent of the strategic airlift missions were staged through four European bases: Torrejon AB, Spain (31 percent); Rhein–Main AB, Germany (27 percent); Zaragoza AB, Spain (18 percent); and Ramstein AB, Germany (14 percent). Other European bases used by MAC were RAF Upper Heyford, United Kingdom; Rota AB, Spain; Lajes AB, Azores; and Sigonella AB, Italy. This relatively small number of en route bases made the aggregate airlift system more vulnerable to variables such as weather and ramp congestion.[14]

Desert Shield validated the importance of having an airlift system in place that could expand as escalating requirements dictated. The intense August airlift would have been even more demanding without MAC having an established en route system at Torrejon, Rhein–Main, Ramstein, and Zaragoza. The cadres of trained MAC people, already present at these bases, were quickly augmented with temporary duty personnel to support the surge of missions that stopped en route to the Arabian peninsula.[15] Time was a valuable commodity in August 1990, when an Iraqi invasion of Saudi Arabia seemed likely. It was appropriate, then, that in the aftermath of the war, General Johnson emphasized to Secretary of Defense Richard B. Cheney the importance of the United States retaining both a Central European and an Iberian peninsula base. He asked that the USTRANSCOM be consulted on any base closure issues "affecting the global strategic mobility mission."[16]

Unlike Operation Just Cause in Panama, no approved transportation plan existed for Desert Shield. Initially, Persian Gulf deployment requirements were based on a United States Central Command (USCENTCOM) operation plan for Southwest Asia that was still being coordinated among the organizations that supported USCENTCOM. Members of the CAT reviewed all of the operations plans existing for Southwest Asia. None fit the circumstances because a scenario involving an Iraqi invasion of Kuwait had never been used.[17]

General Johnson described the mood of airlift customers in August 1990 as one in which "everybody wanted to rush off to the war."[18] Delays and inherent difficulties arose because too many users of airlift wanted to move troops and cargo forward as quickly as possible. No Time-Phased Force Deployment Data (TPFDD)[19] existed for the Desert Shield scenario. Without an approved transportation plan, unit deployments were simply based on gross estimates of requirements. The need for Desert Shield to begin at maximum speed and volume became more difficult without an approved transportation plan. If, for example, a Time-Phased Force Deployment Data List (TPFDDL) reported that a given unit was ready for airlift on day 5 with 500 tons of cargo and 500 troops, MAC scheduled whatever combination of C-5s, C-141s, or contract commercial aircraft was needed to satisfy the requirement. The CAT quickly discovered that the airlift requirements being submitted through the TPFDDLs by dozens of Army, Air Force (USAF), Navy, and Marine Corps (USMC) organizations were unreliable indicators of a unit's true airlift needs.[20] Onload locations were often wrongly stated, and the terms *outsize* and *oversize* cargo were frequently applied incorrectly.[21] These circumstances caused the following types of inefficiencies: Too much airlift was scheduled, not enough airlift was tasked, or the wrong type of airlift was planned.

The problem of unreliable TPFDDLs was fixed early. A Requirements Validation Cell was created within MAC's CAT and staffed around the clock, usually with six to nine validators. Cell members telephoned every unit requesting airlift to confirm the departure dates and quantities of cargo and passengers reported in the TPFDDLs. This, too, did not always go as planned because it sometimes took several calls to find someone who could state with certainty a unit's true airlift requirements. Unreliable TPFDDLs remained a major problem throughout the operation. The telephone cell never disbanded. Even in the late stages of the redeployment, MAC still called the units to confirm the accuracy of the requirements stated in the TPFDDLs.[22]

Changing requirements and priorities were no less troublesome than unreliable TPFDDLs. "More than anything else," said MAC's senior CAT director, "changing requirements were our greatest difficulty" in August

1990. The Joint Operation Planning and Execution System (JOPES), the services' automated deployment system, created the sequence for each unit to deploy. The JOPES, however, could not cope with the magnitude of rapidly changing requirements. One day the USCENTCOM changed its airlift priorities seven times between the 1st Fighter Wing at Langley AFB, Virginia, and the 82nd Airborne Division, Pope AFB, North Carolina. Aircraft already on their way to one of these bases had to divert to other locations.[23] During the first three days of September, the 101st Division Air Mobile, Fort Campbell, Kentucky canceled twenty-eight C-5 and twenty-five C-141 missions.[24] During the surge period of August and early September, the airlift system was often able to generate aircraft more readily than the supported units could mobilize personnel and cargo. MAC responded by sending aircraft to the major onload locations at one-hour intervals rather than at half-hour intervals, as was done during the deployment's first weeks.[25]

The frequent changing of airlift requirements, especially in the first days of a major operation, is likely to occur again. Even with more accurate TPFDDLs, supported commanders will always be redefining their transportation requirements as circumstances dictate. Major General Vernon J. Kondra, who became MAC Director of Operations on 23 August 1990, made the point: As requirements change, "it becomes a dynamic, evolving, changing thing. You'd better understand it's going to happen, no matter how hard you try. . . . It absolutely will not go away."[26]

By the end of August, the MAC system had completed nearly 1,700 strategic airlift missions to the Gulf region.[27] General Kondra, at this time, found the greatest difficulties to be rooted in there not being a total airlift system firmly in place. The absence of a total system stemmed in part from the USCENTCOM not assigning MAC a base on the Arabian peninsula from which aircrews could rest and fresh crews stage to fly the inbound C-5s and C-141s back to one of the European bases.[28]

The absence of a stage base complicated aircrew management. For safety reasons, aircrews were normally not to exceed 125 flying hours in thirty days and 330 hours in ninety days. To support the lengthy Desert Shield missions, General Johnson increased these maximums to 150 hours and 400 hours, respectively.[29] He also increased the maximum crew day from sixteen hours to twenty hours.[30] Given the delays in loading aircraft, C-5 and C-141 missions from the United States to Europe were lasting up to seventeen hours. Similarly, many of the round-trip missions between Europe and the Persian Gulf that should have lasted less than twenty hours sometimes stretched to thirty or more hours because of unloading and refueling delays.[31] Some pilots accrued flying time so rapidly that they exceeded the monthly flying-hour ceilings and were grounded.[32]

The absence of a stage base prevented aircrews from completing their cycle of mandatory crew rest in the AOR. This circumstance required augmenting the basic C-5 and C-141 crews departing Europe for Southwest Asia with an extra pilot (three pilots instead of two) so that the same aircrew could return the aircraft to a European base. The pilot augmentees helped the primary crewmembers with their flying duties or rested themselves when deploying between the United States and Europe and on the missions to and from the Persian Gulf region. Yet even when not at the controls of a strategic airlifter, the pilot augmentees still accumulated flying time that counted toward their thirty- and ninety-day flying-hour maximums.[33]

In September 1990, to help slow the rapid accumulation of flying time, HQ MAC implemented a system of pilot pools at the four major European bases. Approximately 200 C-5 and C-141 pilots were apportioned among the four bases on three-week temporary duty assignments. The pilot pools enabled a significant number of pilots to remain in Europe for an extended period and conserved flying time by reducing the need for pilot augmentees to shuttle between the United States and Europe so frequently.[34]

Jeddah New Airbase, Saudi Arabia—with its plentiful supplies of fuel and considerable ramp space—was MAC's first choice for an in-theater stage base. Had Jeddah New become MAC's stage base, refueling time in the AOR would have been reduced greatly. On 20 September 1990, US-CENTCOM offered MAC Cairo West AB, Egypt, as an in-theater stage facility. Cairo West, however, could not support extensive refueling operations and would still have required the cargo transports to refuel at their offload points in Saudi Arabia. The offer also carried the proviso that the airlifters had to depart Cairo West within twenty-four hours after the outbreak of hostilities to make room for other USAF planes. By this time, the pilot pools were working so well that MAC declined the offer.[35] Having a stage base in a distant theater became one of Desert Shield's most important lessons for air mobility. A Rand Corporation study later reported that the absence of an in-theater stage base had reduced the strategic airlift capability by 20 percent during Desert Shield and Desert Storm.[36]

During the deployment of the defensive force that was completed by about 20 September, MAC averaged 100 to 105 onloads daily from approximately thirty-five U.S. locations. Although there were delays loading in the United States, an even more serious bottleneck existed in the theater, in large part because airlift customers insisted that a disproportionately large number of their missions land in Dhahran, Saudi Arabia. General Kondra used this analogy to describe the difficulties: "We had a 4-foot opening trying to push airlift through that 7,000-mile-long hose and come out a 4-inch nozzle at the other end. It didn't work very well. You've got to have the offload bases to handle what you're pushing through the flow."[37]

Subsequent analysis of Operation Desert Storm revealed the need for patience by both the customer and the airlift provider. Pressures to move passengers and cargo too quickly in the operation's first days wasted airlift when C-5s and C-141s were sent to aerial ports of embarkation only to find that the cargoes were not ready to load. Pushing the maximum number of aircraft through the en route system had been done instinctively at first, because neither MAC nor its customers would accept anything less than an intense, all-out effort. General Kondra later stated that the haste to demonstrate a maximum effort had "clogged the system and worked it to death for no appreciable gain."[38]

Desert Shield confirmed that airflow planning was an art, not a science. The three factors of changing priorities, en route system variables, and delays in unloading and servicing aircraft in the AOR required great scheduling flexibility. Techniques developed during years of peacetime exercises soon became established procedures. By late August, airflow managers in the CATs at HQ MAC, 21st Air Force, and 322nd Airlift Division, Ramstein AB, Germany began an unofficial system of assigning each aircraft a slot time—or time window—during which an aircraft was scheduled to arrive at one of the airfields in Saudi Arabia. Slot times, assigned in fifteen-minute increments, enabled airflow managers to know consistently about how many aircraft were at each of the offload locations. In late August and September, slot times were assigned two days in advance. When the system became more refined in October 1990, slot times were assigned up to four days prior to an aircraft's scheduled arrival. Slot times remained in use throughout the Gulf War.[39]

By Desert Shield's third month, some airlift customers were reporting unacceptable delays in MAC's delivery of critical spare parts to the Arabian peninsula. To ensure customer satisfaction, on 31 October MAC initiated Operation Desert Express, which provided for the next-day delivery of "show-stopper" spare parts to Dhahran and Riyadh. These highest-priority spare parts were transported to the Arabian peninsula on a single C-141 mission that departed Charleston AFB, South Carolina, daily at 1200 local time. Logisticians had only to have their high-priority materials at Charleston by 1030 to ensure next-day delivery. Army, USMC, Navy, and USAF customers were each allocated a percentage of the cargo space. Airlift managers adjusted the service allocations as USCENTCOM's requirements dictated.[40] Desert Express resulted in part from a lesson MAC had learned before: If an airlift customer perceives a problem, then a problem exists. As General Kondra put it, "When you provide a service, you have to be 100% right every time, because people only remember the bad service. They don't remember the good."[41]

When the deployment of an offensive force began in late November 1990, a large portion of the American forces and equipment sent to Saudi Arabia came from Germany. This created the requirement for an overnight delivery of critical spare parts from Europe as well as from the United States. MAC responded by initiating European Desert Express in December

1990. In this operation, a dedicated C-141 operated daily from Rhein-Main AB to Dhahran.[42] When the stateside Desert Express operation began experiencing some cargo backlogs in early 1991, a second dedicated daily flight from Charleston to the Arabian peninsula commenced on 13 February 1991.[43]

Desert Express, however, carried a price. Since airflow planners assigned no slot times to other airlifters within an hour of the dedicated C-141s' arrivals at Dhahran and Riyadh, there was some reduced flow in the total airlift system. Planners estimated that this caused the MAC system to lose the equivalent of four C-141 offloads daily.[44] Nevertheless, by the time the redeployment began in early March 1991, the aggregate Desert Express missions had airlifted more than 2,700 short tons of cargo.[45]

The strategic airlift missions to the AOR averaged approximately 100 per day in August and September[46] and fifty missions daily in October and November.[47] The signal for a more intense airlift tempo occurred on 8 November, when President Bush ordered an additional 250,000 troops to the Persian Gulf region, thereby raising the size of the deployed American force to about 430,000 men and women. The reason for this second deployment, the president said, was to create "an offensive military option" if Iraqi forces failed to withdraw from Kuwait by the 15 January 1991 deadline the United Nations had imposed. Many of the Phase II troops came from the U.S. Army's VII Corps, Stuttgart, Germany. Although most of VII Corps's equipment was transported by sea, nearly all its troops were deployed by air. Also sent to Saudi Arabia in Phase II was the 3rd Armored Division, Frankfurt, Germany, and several Marine units from the continental United States.[48]

MAC managed its Phase II airlift drawing on the lessons it had learned since early August. The strategic airlift missions were now scheduled based on the ability to offload and refuel aircraft in the AOR. "How many aircraft can we put through daily to Dhahran, King Fahd, Jubail, and the other Saudi bases?" was the critical question asked.[49] "When we really started becoming efficient was when we worked the requirements backwards," General Kondra explained.[50]

If MAC now recognized the importance of scheduling missions based on the ability to offload, too many airlift customers had not learned the importance of sending their passengers and cargo to locations other than Dhahran, where 65 percent of the August missions had landed. Dhahran was the best airfield in Saudi Arabia, but there were other bases available to airlift nearly as good. As the deployment progressed, Army and USMC customers continued to schedule most of their passengers and cargoes for Dhahran in order to marry their inbound troops with equipment that was arriving by sealift at the nearby Ad Damman and Al Jubayl port facilities. By late September 1990, King Khalid Military City and King Fahd International Airport—the latter only a short distance from Dhahran—had been opened to airlift. Yet not until December 1990 did airlift customers validate more than 50 percent of their monthly cargoes for locations other than Dhahran.[51]

The airlift's second phase began slower than MAC either desired or expected. Although MAC was ready to accelerate the airlift when President Bush ordered the second major deployment, the Phase II airlift did not get fully underway until the first week of December. Airlift planners attributed the delay partially to some European Command organizations being in the mindset of receiving forces rather than of deploying themselves.[52]

Cargo to resupply the deployed forces continued backing up at Dover AFB, Delaware, and Tinker AFB, Oklahoma, the two major aerial ports in the continental United States. Partly at MAC's urging, USCENTCOM established several sustainment cargo diversion teams composed of representatives from all the services. The teams went to Dover, Tinker, and the Defense Logistics Agency at Mechanicsburg, Pennsylvania. Here they identified nonpriority cargo and arranged for its movement over land to an appropriate seaport for movement by sealift. To illustrate the dimension of the problem, one team diverted more than 1,200 tons of rations for sealift which, if transported by air, would have required the equivalent of sixty C-141 missions.[53]

Throughout the Gulf War, MAC relied heavily on the civil airline industry to help satisfy its enormous airlift requirements.[54] On 7 August 1990, the day that President Bush issued the Desert Shield deployment order, two World Airways DC-10 passenger aircraft departed from Pope AFB, North Carolina, for Dhahran with more than 500 troops from the 82nd Airborne Division at neighboring Fort Bragg. Volunteer commercial airliners had completed about thirty missions to the Arabian peninsula[55] when the requirement for airlift became so great that General Johnson activated the CRAF's Stage I on 17 August 1990.[56] His action marked the first time in the CRAF's thirty-nine-year history that any of its stages had ever been activated.[57] Although the CRAF Stage I activation put a total of thirty-eight aircraft (seventeen passenger and twenty-one cargo aircraft) at MAC's disposal, it actually added only ten airplanes above those the civil air carriers had already volunteered. The important point, however, is that twelve of the thirty-eight aircraft were the wide-bodied Boeing 747s that MAC needed to transport troops.[58]

Since the CRAF had never been activated before Operation Desert Shield, some problems naturally occurred. A troublesome issue became securing Title XIII insurance, which guarantees an airline government-sponsored war risk protection not available from commercial insurance companies. The Federal Aviation Administration (FAA) grants indemnity insurance to the CRAF, and the Department of Defense (DOD) pays for any aircraft lost. The airlines reported that too much time had been spent in Desert Shield's first days obtaining Title XIII insurance on a mission-by-mission basis. If an aircraft had to be rescheduled, the paperwork began anew. Three weeks after the first CRAF mission arrived on the Arabian peninsula, the FAA authorized blanket approval on a weekly basis for all the commercial flights that were supporting Desert Shield. Nonetheless, the absence of streamlined procedures for obtaining indemnity insurance during the critical month of August had resulted in duplicated effort, delayed missions, and too often an inefficient use of airlift.[59]

The civil air carriers played no less an important role in the Phase II deployment than they had during the Phase I airlift. On 17 January 1991, the day the air war began, the lingering backlog of cargo at Dover AFB was the major reason for activating CRAF's Stage II. Given the urgency of moving more cargo, MAC told the Stage II carriers that only long-range, international (LRI) cargo aircraft need respond, even though the passenger aircraft called up in Stage II later participated in the redeployment airlift. The Stage II activation brought the total number of aircraft activated in both stages to seventy-six LRI passenger and forty LRI cargo aircraft.[60]

Meanwhile, in the continental United States and Europe, civil airline crews learned from the media of Iraq's Scud missile attacks on Israel and Saudi Arabia and that the missiles might be armed with chemical warheads. Some airlines refused to send missions to the airfields that were within Scud range because their crews did not know how to use chemical warfare protective gear.[61] Airlift managers had planned to distribute chemical warfare equipment to the CRAF aircrews after they landed in the AOR and simply had not anticipated the airlines' concerns.[62]

MAC resolved the problem by sending teams to the airlines' en route stops at Frankfurt, Rome, Brussels, and other locations. Here the CRAF crews were given chemical warfare gear and shown how to use it. The teams also gave the CRAF aircrews intelligence briefings.[63] To address further the concerns of the airline crews, MAC ceased scheduling commercial missions into the AOR between 1600Z and 2100Z, the period when Scud launches were most likely to occur.[64] General Johnson later said that the CRAF pilots' concerns should have been anticipated and dealt with sooner.[65]

From August 1990 through May 1991, the civil air carriers completed more than 5,000 missions. Since the CRAF had never been activated before August 1990, the lingering question had always been, "How well will the CRAF operate if called upon to support wartime requirements?" Clearly, the CRAF's most important lesson was a positive one. Overall, the CRAF had worked well, even though some broad questions, such as improving the system of indemnity insurance, remained. So it was that General Johnson described the CRAF carriers as "tremendous heroes." "I couldn't be more pleased with the system," he said.[66]

The first major implementation of the total force policy also occurred during the Gulf War and confirmed the critical role of the Air Reserve

Component (ARC) to the air mobility mission. In the autumn of 1990, the active strategic airlift force was authorized for seventy-six C-5s and 234 C-141s.[67] Another twenty-eight C-5As and eight C-141s belonged to the AFRES. The ANG had eleven C-5As and eight C-141s authorized.[68] On Desert Shield's first day, General Johnson directed that all of the ARC's C-5s and C-141s participate in the airlift. He also asked aircrews from the Guard and Reserve to volunteer. Many Guard and Reserve crewmembers did so, but not enough of them volunteered to operate the ARC aircraft for an extended period of time.[69]

In 1990, about half of the C-141 crews and 60 percent of the C-5 crews belonged to the ARC. The CAG projected that 44 percent of the C-141 crew force would reach the 150 flying-hour ceiling in the airlift's first thirty days.[70] This prompted MAC on 25 August[71] to activate three C-5 and two C-141 Reserve squadrons, which equated to about 19 percent of the ARC's strategic airlift aircrew capability. Nonetheless, the rapid rate at which crewmembers were accumulating flying hours continued. Some crewmembers, especially C-5 pilots, were exceeding the flying-hour limits, but another week passed before MAC decided to activate the ARC's remaining C-5 aircrews. Neither did it activate any additional C-141 squadrons until 9 September 1990.[72] Ultimately, the aircrews of all seven C-5 squadrons and eleven of the fifteen C-141 squadrons were activated. General Johnson later said he should have asked for a selected ARC activation sooner.[73]

In MAC, more than 7,600 nonmedical personnel were selectively called up before combat operations began in mid-January 1991.[74] When President Bush ordered a partial mobilization of Reservists in all the services on 18 January 1991, 22,000 ARC men and women—60 percent of the USAF total—belonged to MAC.[75] Commencing with the first selective call-ups in late August 1990, MAC deployed active duty officers and airmen from its East Coast bases at McGuire AFB (New Jersey), Charleston, and Dover to the European en route locations to support transit operations there. Personnel from the East Coast bases were replaced stateside by activated Guard members and Reservists. Temporary accommodations had to be found for the ARC men and women who backfilled at the three East Coast bases for the ones sent overseas. Military billeting and off-base accommodations at or near the East Coast bases were taxed to the limits. Many ARC personnel had to be billeted far away from their temporary duty (TDY) bases. Clearly, it would have been better to have kept most of the active duty force at home station and moved the ARC personnel forward.[76]

Air transportation during the Persian Gulf War consisted of much more than thousands of strategic airlift missions. MAC C-130s made up the second component of the total airlift system. By the end of January 1991, approximately 144 MAC C-130s were fulfilling USCENTCOM's requirements for in-theater airlift. These aircraft were assigned to six wings at bases in Oman, the United Arab Emirates, and Saudi Arabia.

Although the beddown of fighter squadrons had been USCENTCOM's top priority in August 1990, theater airlift was also critical to the war effort. By the end of the month, sixty-four C-130s were operating in the AOR. Brigadier General Fredric N. Buckingham, the first Commander of Airlift Forces (COMALF), managed MAC's C-130s in the AOR on behalf of the Central Air Forces' commander, Lieutenant General Charles A. Horner. General Buckingham and his staff were among the first U.S. forces to arrive on the Arabian peninsula. Their responsibilities included setting up the Airlift Control Center, creating a C-130 infrastructure, and establishing the 1610th Airlift Division, Provisional, to which the C-130 airlift wings were soon made subordinate. In mid-October, General Buckingham was succeeded by Brigadier General Edwin E. Tenoso, who served as the COMALF until mid-May 1991.

Determining how many C-130s were needed to support General Schwarzkopf proved a challenge for General Tenoso and suggested an issue that might crop up again. Theoretically, MAC's entire C-130 inventory could have been deployed, but the COMALF wanted only enough C-130s to meet USCENTCOM's wartime requirements. During the force buildup from August 1990 to mid-January 1991, General Tenoso kept asking the Army to estimate its airlift requirements once hostilities commenced. Its spokesmen responded that the Army's wartime airlift requirement would be minimal, given its plans to rely principally on ground transportation. General Tenoso, however, believed that once the war started, U.S. ground forces would want all the airlift they could get. "Airlift will be like free candy," he quipped. "Everybody will want some." The nearly 14,000 C-130 sorties flown from 17 January through the end of February 1991 proved him right.[77]

The COMALF kept pressing Army and USMC planners to define their airlift requirements for activities such as troop transport, food distribution, and aeromedical evacuation. Based on these discussions and the recommendations of his own staff, General Tenoso proposed 144 C-130s as the number of tactical airlifters needed to support USCENTCOM's wartime theater airlift requirements. USCENTCOM eventually agreed.[78]

That no C-130 aircraft or crews were lost in the AOR confirmed the quality of C-130 flight training. Nevertheless, the Persian Gulf War demonstrated the need for better C-130 integration training in anticipation of future conflicts. General Tenoso urged that C-130 aircrews fly more training missions, not just with other airlifters but also with fighters, Airborne Warning and Control System aircraft (E-3s), and other airborne command, control, and communications systems, as they had done during the Persian Gulf War.[79]

Desert Storm also demonstrated the need to add high-altitude airdrop training to C-130s' peacetime training curriculum. In January 1991, airlift planners had considered airdropping supplies to Allied forces from high altitude, given the absence of terrain masking in the desert and the likelihood that the threat at high altitude would be less than from small arms fire at low altitude. The few C-130 crewmembers so trained were mostly Guardsmen and Reservists who had gained their proficiency in high-altitude airdrop in Vietnam. Although no high-altitude airdrops were made during the Gulf War, General Tenoso urged that C-130 crewmembers be given this training in preparation for the next contingency.[80]

With the C-130s under USCENTCOM's command and control, the supply system in the AOR required the C-130 wings to obtain spare parts through CENTAF logistical channels. Delays stemming from CENTAF's unfamiliarity with airlift often resulted in the provisional wings circumventing the established supply system and requesting spare parts directly from their home units. The importance of setting up an efficient resupply system quickly when mobility forces "chop"[81] to another command in wartime was demonstrated during Desert Shield and Desert Storm. "If we had to come over . . . and fight a war in the first two or three weeks, our planes' mission capability could very well have been down . . . just because our supply system was nonfunctional," General Tenoso cautioned. Yet overall, General Tenoso could rightly state that "by every measure, we supported our users in an outstanding fashion."[82]

From 18 to 28 January 1991, C-130s airlifted elements of the XVIII Airborne Corps from King Fahd International Airport to Rafha Airfield, in northern Saudi Arabia, near the Iraqi border. This intense airlift supported General Schwarzkopf's flanking maneuver, which he called the "Hail Mary Pass."[83] C-130s flew the mission corridors at ten-minute intervals in radio silence. During the airlift to Rafha, C-130 sortie rates increased from 200 per day to more than 300 daily and peaked at more than 350 sorties during one twenty-four-hour period. Nearly 14,000 troops and more than 9,300 short tons of cargo were transported in this fast-paced demonstration of air mobility.[84] For all of Operations Desert Shield and Desert Storm, the C-130s flew almost 13,900 missions and 47,600 sorties and logged 76,000 flying hours to transport more than 242,000 passengers and 174,000 tons of cargo.[85]

MAC shouldered the burden for airlift but did not carry the entire load. Tankers from the Strategic Air Command (SAC) played a small, but significant, role by transporting 74 percent of SAC's passengers and 56 percent of its own cargo.[86] SAC action officers sometimes referred to the tanker airlift as a "Little MAC" operation. Tankers moved a total of 14,208 passengers and 4,817 short tons of cargo. Operating in a purely cargo-transport role, the KC-10 transported more than 25,100 tons of cargo and moved 4,185 passengers during the Persian Gulf War.[87] Before the deployment, USAF planning guidance stated that twenty-three of SAC's fifty-seven KC-10s (40 percent) would be available for strategic airlift in a major regional contingency. The twenty-three KC-10s would have provided an additional 2.54 million ton-miles per day. As it happened, an average of only seven KC-10s operated in a dedicated cargo role from mid-August 1990 to the outbreak of hostilities. Not until the war began were twenty KC-10s released and committed exclusively to airlift. A greater use of the KC-10 as an airlifter is predicted in future contingencies.[88]

Of course, air refueling of U.S. and United Nations Coalition aircraft was the primary mission of tanker aircraft during Desert Shield and Desert Storm. SAC sent 256 KC-135s and forty-six KC-10s to the AOR,[89] and they performed an impressive number of missions. For all of Desert Shield and Desert Storm, USAF tankers flew more than 34,000 sorties. KC-135s and KC-10s made over 85,000 air refuelings and offloaded more than 1.2 billion pounds of fuel. Tankers refueled both American and Allied aircraft using the boom/receptacle and probe/drogue configurations.[90]

The Gulf War tanker assessment confirmed much that SAC had been doing correctly in its management of the USAF's air refueling mission. SAC tankers deployed to twenty-one bases in twenty-one overseas nations during Desert Shield and Desert Storm. Nearly 100 tankers operating from nine countries maintained the Atlantic and Pacific air refueling bridges, which moved more than 1,000 bomber and fighter aircraft to the Persian Gulf Theater. As with airlift, ARC volunteers furnished timely and much needed tanker expertise during the deployment's first days. Nearly 5,200 ANG and AFRES men and women were activated to support tanker operations, confirming the critical wartime role of these forces for air refueling as well as for airlift.[91]

A comparatively small number of strategic airlift missions were air refueled. Early in the deployment, some missions were air refueled in the AOR because of refueling limitations on the ground in Saudi Arabia. General Johnson pointed out that the long distance from the continental United States to Saudi Arabia negated the advantages of air refueling on most missions. The en route bases in Europe were roughly equidistant from the continental United States and the Persian Gulf. Each airlift leg from the continental United States to Europe and from Europe to the Arabian peninsula was about 3,500 nautical miles. Allowable cabin loads were based on these 3,500-mile legs. Little would have been gained from air refueling C-5s and C-141s unless it were done at both ends of the mission. It was more practical to launch from the East Coast of the United States to a base in Spain or Germany, change crews there, and send the mission on to its final destination.[92]

As Operation Restore Hope in Somalia later demonstrated,[93] air refueling could sustain airlift over these long distances, but only if staging bases were closer to the main area of operations. Cairo West, Egypt, and first Jeddah New and then Taif ABs in Saudi Arabia were the stage bases for the airlift to Somalia. Even if there had been stage bases on the Arabian peninsula for air-refueled C-5s and C-141s during the Gulf War, aircrew changes would have been required at the heavily congested bases. Staging through Europe during Desert Shield had given MAC increased flexibility in managing the crew force since, on most missions, crewmembers did not have to be qualified for air refueling.[94]

Insufficient airspace to support all of the Allies' air refueling requirements became the most limiting factor for tanker operations once the war began. Limited airspace was a problem not just over Saudi Arabia but also in the refueling areas along the Turkish/Iraqi border and over the Mediterranean Sea. To make maximum use of the airspace available for air refueling, SAC employed a combination of air refueling tracks and anchors, in which tankers remained in orbit to perform short-notice air refuelings. During the most intense periods of flying activity, airspace congestion prevented using additional tankers. Airspace congestion for the tankers was compounded by the language barriers between the tanker crews and many of the air traffic controllers who were coordinating air traffic in the Persian Gulf region.[95]

To some senior military leaders, the Gulf War revealed weaknesses in the organization of the USAF. Referring specifically to air mobility assets, General Johnson had no doubt that a single manager controlling the majority of airlift and tanker forces would improve future mobility operations. "We found in DESERT SHIELD/DESERT STORM that we didn't coordinate very well on bedding down big airplanes," he said. Having most USAF tankers and airlifters assigned to a single command will enable the manager to "better use . . . limited assets to project forces, to give true Global Reach."[96]

The war, in fact, proved a catalyst for the reorganization of the USAF. A new major command structure soon provided an organizational framework in keeping with the Secretary of the Air Force's landmark policy document, *The Air Force & U.S. National Security: Global Reach—Global Power,* published in June 1990. Activation of the Air Mobility Command (AMC) and concurrent inactivation of the MAC and SAC on 1 June 1992 brought into a single organization most of the Air Force's tanker and airlift assets. Air Force planners believed that Global Reach could be accomplished more effectively by integrating the airlift and tanker forces. To further this objective, in early 1992, a new Tanker Airlift Control Center, located at HQ MAC, began serving as the single planner, scheduler, and executor for all airlift and tanker missions worldwide.

Frequently asked during the Desert Shield and Desert Storm assessment was the question, "Can the Gulf War be seen as a model for future conflicts?" Certain aspects of the conflict set it apart from past contingencies and suggest that a similar set of circumstances is unlikely in the near future. For one thing, Saddam Hussein's hesitation to invade Saudi Arabia gave time to build an international Coalition to oppose Iraq's aggression by diplomatic and military means. It enabled forces to train for war in an unfamiliar desert environment and to assemble by airlift and sealift the vast stockpiles of munitions, spare parts, and supplies needed for a campaign against a formidable adversary.[97] The 7,500-mile distance to the Persian Gulf from the U.S. East Coast made Desert Shield a worst-case scenario. On the other hand, American forces benefited from an excellent infrastructure on the Arabian peninsula and plentiful supplies of fuel in Saudi Arabia and at the en route bases. And Allied air superiority negated the threat of Iraqi interceptors to the transport aircraft.[98]

In another sense, AMC's leaders viewed Desert Shield and Desert Storm as a model for future military contingencies. Instead of a superpower confrontation, the Persian Gulf War had been a massive, well-orchestrated, multinational response to a regional conflict that threatened the economic stability of many nations. In the future, the AMC will likely be called on to move forces over thousands of miles with a minimum of advance warning. The theaters of operation will probably be places that have little or no infrastructure, unlike the Arabian peninsula, where American forces benefited from modern airfields, roads, and seaports.[99]

In sum, Persian Gulf operations corroborated the truth of the often-made statement that airlifters and air refuelers perform their wartime missions in peacetime. When the United States goes to war, the only thing that changes significantly for airlifters and air refuelers is the intensity of the effort. The success of air mobility in the Persian Gulf War was many years in the making. For MAC, the experience garnered in Vietnam, Grenada, Panama, and elsewhere contributed immeasurably to the successes of 1990–1991. This, of course, was by design, for it was by flying hundreds of humanitarian, exercise, and other missions every year for five decades that MAC and its predecessor commands had trained for war. So, too, had the tanker force prepared for the Persian Gulf War by performing tens of thousands of air refueling missions in peacetime and during the Southeast Asia War. As C-5s, C-141s, C-130s, KC-135s, KC-10s, and contracted commercial aircraft streamed toward the Arabian peninsula in August 1990, airlifters and air refuelers drew on these many years of experience. They emerged from the war with new knowledge, which had been garnered from the first major military operation of the post–Cold War era.

NOTES

1. Hist (S/Decl OADR), MAC, 1990, p. 160, info used (U).
2. Address, Gen H. T. Johnson, CINCUSTRANSCOM/CINCMAC, to Capital Chapter Airlift Association, Andrews AFB, Maryland, 28 Mar 91 [hereafter Andrews Address].
3. Address, Gen H. T. Johnson, CINCUSTRANSCOM/CINCMAC, to National Research Council, Atlanta, Georgia, 11 Jun 91 [hereafter Atlanta Address].
4. Andrews Address.

5. Rprt, MAC/XOCCR, "MAIRS DESERT SHIELD Histories," Aug–Sep 90 [hereafter MAIRS Rprt].

6. Any comparison of the Berlin Airlift with the Persian Gulf War requires qualification, because the Berlin Airlift was also a remarkable accomplishment. During the fifteen-month Berlin Airlift, American C-47s and C-54s transported a daily average of 3,853 tons to Berlin. This was roughly 44 percent more cargo than the 2,149 tons MAC airlifted daily to the Arabian peninsula. Just three German airfields had supported the 1948–1949 operation, but MAC organic transports and commercially contracted aircraft eventually were landing at a dozen airfields in the AOR. The relatively small C-47s and C-54s were manually loaded and unloaded. This made the Berlin Airlift a much more labor-intensive operation. See Rpt, MAC/XPY, "DESERT SHIELD/STORM Analysis," Apr 91; R. D. Launius and C. F. Cross II, MAC History Office, *MAC and the Legacy of the Berlin Airlift,* Apr 89, pp. 58–60 [hereafter *MAC Legacy*].

7. Atlanta Address; Launius and Cross, *MAC Legacy*; Brfg Slide, AMC Command Presentations, "Comparison: DESERT SHIELD/DESERT STORM with the Berlin Airlift," 1991; MAIRS Rprts, Sep–Nov 90.

8. The CRAF was the program by which participating airlines committed varying numbers of aircraft to support wartime airlift in exchange for a proportionate share of DOD peacetime airlift contracts. Some airlines not participating in the CRAF volunteered aircraft to support Operation Desert Shield.

9. Intvw, J. K. Matthews, USTRANSCOM Historian, and J. H. Smith, MAC Command Historian, with Gen H. T. Johnson, CINCUSTRANSCOM/CINCMAC, Dec 92, p. 4 [hereafter Johnson Intvw].

10. Address, Gen H. T. Johnson, CINCUSTRANSCOM/CINCMAC, to Little Rock Community Council, Little Rock, Arkansas, 21 Jul 91 [hereafter Little Rock Address].

11. Andrews Address.

12. A directorate assigned to the Deputy Chief of Staff for Plans and Programs.

13. Rprt, MAC CAG, "DESERT SHIELD Working Group: Report of Lessons Learned," n.d.; Maj Gen V. J. Kondra, MAC DCS Operations, "Notes for Operation DESERT SHIELD/STORM," 7 Apr 92, edited by Clayton Snedeker, 21 AF Historian [hereafter Kondra Notes]; Intvw, J. W. Leland, MAC Office of History, with Col D. J. Bottjer, MAC Senior CAT Director during DESERT SHIELD/STORM, 9 Sep 92, p. 9 [hereafter Bottjer Intvw].

14. Hist, USTRANSCOM/HO, "DESERT SHIELD/DESERT STORM: 7 Aug 90–10 Mar 91," Vol I, 18 May 92, p. 31 [hereafter TRANSCOM Hist].

15. Intvw, J. W. Leland, with Maj Gen V. J. Kondra, MAC Deputy Chief of Staff for Operations, 14 May 91, p. 3 [hereafter Kondra Intvw].

16. Excerpt from Statement, CINCUSTRANSCOM to Senate Committee on Armed Services, "Airlift," 10 Mar 92, p. 7, in TRANSCOM Hist, Vol. I, p. 31.

17. Bottjer Intvw, p. 5.

18. Ibid., p. 9.

19. Drawn from a database known as a Time-Phased Force Deployment Data (or TPFDD), a TPFDD List (or TPFDDL) specifies the loading sequence for each unit deployment and matches it with specific allocations of air or sea transportation resources.

20. Point Paper, MAC/XOOXA, "Soft Requirements," 10 Jul 91.

21. *Oversized* describes an item of cargo that exceeds the usable volume of a standard 463L airlift pallet (104 inches × 84 inches × 8 feet), the standard pallet carried by USAF military cargo transports. *Outsized* is the term which describes a size of cargo that exceeds the capabilities of a C-141 and requires air movement by a C-5.

22. Bottjer Intvw, p. 9.
23. Ibid., p. 6
24. Kondra Notes, p. 27.
25. Rprt, by MAC CAT, "Flow Cell Logs," Aug–Sep 90 [hereafter Flow Cell Logs].
26. Kondra Notes, p. 150.
27. Hist (S/Decl OADR), MAC, 1990, p. 250, info used (U).
28. Kondra Intvw, p. 1; Kondra Notes, p. 8.
29. Johnson Intvw, p. 18.
30. Hist (S/Decl OADR), MAC, 1990, p. 171, info used (U).
31. Bottjer Intvw, p. 6.
32. Hist (S/Decl OADR), MAC, 1990, p. 172, info used (U).
33. Ibid.
34. Ibid., p. 174; Kondra Notes, p. 30.
35. Kondra Notes, p. 34.
36. USAFE Force Structure Brfg to AMC Vice Commander, 10 Feb 93, Historian's Notes.
37. Kondra Intvw, p. 1.
38. Ibid., pp. 149–50.
39. Flow Cell Logs, Sep–Nov 90.
40. Hist (S/Decl OADR), MAC, 1990, pp. 214–18, info used (U).
41. Kondra Notes, p. 25.
42. Msg, CDRAMC/AMCSM to CDRARCENT FWD/G-4 and CDRARCENT SUPCOM PROV/AMC-SWA, "DESERT EXPRESS—Saudi Arabia/Europe," 191115Z Dec 90.
43. Msg, MAC CAT to USTRANSCOM CAT, "Double DESERT EXPRESS Mission Concept," 090310Z Feb 91.
44. Flow Cell Logs, Nov 90–May 91.
45. Appendix 14, "DESERT EXPRESS/EUROPEAN DESERT EXPRESS," as of 10 Mar 91, in TRANSCOM Hist, Vol I, p. 136.
46. D. F. Bond, "DESERT SHIELD Airlift Slackens," *Aviation Week & Space Technology,* (8 Oct 90), p. 76.
47. Rpts, MAC/XOCCR, "MAIRS DESERT SHIELD History," Oct and Nov 90.
48. M. R. Gordon, "Bush Sends New Units to Gulf to Provide Offensive Option," *New York Times,* 9 Nov 90, p. 1.
49. Kondra Notes, p. 51.
50. Kondra Intvw, p. 2.
51. Kondra Notes, pp. 11, 69.
52. Ibid., pp. 57, 62–63.
53. Rpt, GAO to the Chairman, Senate Committee on Armed Services, "DESERT SHIELD/STORM: AMC's Achievements and Lessons for the Future," Jan 93, p. 24.

Air Mobility

54. CRAF Stage III, with 506 aircraft committed, could only be activated by the President or Congress in response to a national defense emergency.
55. MAIRS Rprt, Aug 90.
56. Kondra Notes, p. 10.
57. Memo for Record, Gen Johnson, CINCMAC, "CRAF Stage I Activation," 17 Aug 90.
58. A 747, for example, could transport almost twice as many passengers as the smaller Douglas DC-8.
59. Rprt (S/NF/Rel UK Only), Rand Corporation (Project Air Force DESERT SHIELD Assessment Team), "Project Air Force Assessment of Operation DESERT SHIELD: The Buildup of Combat Power—Technical Applications," Vol II, Jan 92, pp. 79–80, info used (U).
60. TRANSCOM Hist, Vol I, p. 10.
61. Johnson Intvw, p. 24.
62. Kondra Notes, p. 10.
63. Msg, MAC CAT to 1610 ALDP/COMALF, "CRAF Chemical Warfare Defense (CWD) Operations Guidance," 111400Z Feb 91; Msg, MAC CAT to USCENTAF Rear, "Request for Assistance Expanding CWD Equipment Issue," 140744Z Feb 91.
64. Kondra Notes, p. 114.
65. Johnson Intvw, p. 24.
66. Ibid.
67. Rprt (FOUO), MAC/QS, "Command Data Book," Oct 90, p. 13, info used (U).
68. Mgt Inf Summary, by MAC/XPPD, "MAC Air Reserve Components," 15 Nov 90.
69. Johnson Intvw, p. 18.
70. Kondra Notes, p. 6.
71. *Reserves* in this context includes both AFRES and ANG personnel.
72. Rpt, GAO to the Chairman, Senate Committee on Armed Services, "DESERT SHIELD/STORM: Air Mobility Command's Achievements and Lessons for the Future," Jan 91, p. 38.
73. Johnson Intvw, pp. 18–19.
74. Hist (S/Decl OADR), MAC, 1990, pp. 184–88, info used (U).
75. Msg, SECAF to ALMAJCOM-SOA/CC, "Execution—Presidential Declaration of Partial Mobilization," 222245Z Jan 91.
76. Kondra Intvw, p. 11.
77. Intvw, Dr Gary Leiser, 22 AF Historian, with Brig Gen Edwin E. Tenoso, Commander, Airlift Forces (COMALF) in Saudi Arabia during Operation DESERT SHIELD/STORM, 28 May 91, p. 12 [hereafter Tenoso Intvw].
78. Ibid., pp. 12–13.
79. Ibid., p. 19.
80. Ibid., p. 20.
81. Change of Operational Control (CHOP): the date, time, and/or point at which the responsibility for operational control of a force passes from one operational control authority to another.
82. Tenoso Intvw, p. 22; Rprt, Tenoso, 1610 ALD(P)/CC to Johnson, CINCUSTRANSCOM/CINCMAC, n.s., 6 May 91.

83. Point Paper, AMC/HO, "Overview of the DESERT SHIELD/DESERT STORM Airlift," 6 Aug 92; Little Rock Address.

84. Point Paper, by AMC/HO, "C-130 Support of the 'Hail Mary Pass' Flanking Maneuver During Operation DESERT STORM," 10 Nov 92.

85. MAC News Service, "C-130s in Operation DESERT SHIELD/DESERT STORM," Apr 91.

86. Rprt (S/Decl OADR), SAC/XP, "DESERT SHIELD/DESERT STORM Tanker Assessment," 23 Sep 91, pp. 2–12, info used (U).

87. Ibid., pp. 9–10, info used (U).

88. TRANSCOM Hist, Vol I, p. 31.

89. Rprt, USAF/PA, "USAF White Paper—Air Force Performance in DESERT STORM," Apr 91, p. 9.

90. Rprt (S/Decl OADR), SAC/XP, "DESERT SHIELD/DESERT STORM Tanker Assessment," 23 Sep 91, pp. iv, 1–9, info used (U).

91. Ibid., p. iv, info used (U).

92. Johnson Intvw, pp. 31–32; Brfg, AMC TACC/DOO, "0800 RESTORE HOPE Update," 12 Dec 92.

93. This was the peacetime deployment of 25,000 U.S. troops to Somalia to ensure the distribution of food to several million starving Somalis in December 1992.

94. Hist (S/RD), SAC, 1990, p. 334, info used (U).

95. Rpt (S/Decl OADR), SAC/XP, "DESERT SHIELD/DESERT STORM Tanker Assessment," 23 Sep 91, pp. iv, 8–12, info used (U).

96. Johnson Intvw, p. 63; Hist (S/FRD), SAC, 1991, pp. 22–25, info used (U).

97. Atlanta Address.

98. Address, Gen H. T. Johnson, CINCUSTRANSCOM/CINCMAC, to National Aviation Club, Washington DC, 28 Mar 91.

99. Ltr, USTRANSCOM/TCPA, to Johnson, USTRANSCOM/CC, "DOD DESERT SHIELD/STORM Film Questions," 6 Aug 91.

4

Sustaining the War Machine: U.S. Air Force Logistics Support during the Gulf War
William Suit

What accounted for the apparent ease with which the U.S.-led, UN-sanctioned Coalition dismantled the world's fourth largest military force? The basic answer is that the United States and its Allies built a military machine capable of defeating the Warsaw Pact and, despite Saddam Hussein's belief to the contrary, proved willing to use it to protect their vital interests. The Coalition force of 800,000 troops fielded better-trained and more motivated personnel, utilized superior weapons and support systems, employed these assets more creatively, and was supplied and maintained by a logistics network that dwarfed that of Iraq. The Coalition enjoyed an enormous advantage in airpower, eventually employing over 1,800 combat aircraft from nine countries.[1]

Common sense dictated that a Coalition including the premier Western military powers—the United States, the United Kingdom, and France—in alliance with the major Arab powers—Egypt, Syria, and Saudi Arabia—could defeat Iraq if war erupted. However, had the Iraqi army continued its blitzkrieg through Kuwait on into Saudi Arabia, the war to drive the Iraqis back into their own country would have unfolded differently, for the Coalition would have had to begin the war without the logistics base assembled, unhindered, during the Gulf War. General Colin Powell, Chair, Joint Chiefs of Staff (JCS), later noted, "It would have taken us a lot longer, and it would have been a much more difficult proposition, to have to kick the Iraqi army out of Saudi Arabia as well as Kuwait."[2]

Fortunately, the worst case did not occur. Iraq chose not to invade Saudi Arabia, whether intimidated by the initial American show of force in support of the desert kingdom, or satisfied to pause and digest Kuwait; only Saddam Hussein knows. Either way, the choice proved fortuitous to the Coalition that formed to confront Iraq, for it gave the U.S.-led forces time to assemble the military machine that liberated Kuwait.

The United States Air Force (USAF) and U.S. Central Command (CENT-COM) had prepared for a Middle East war, but desert warfare had never been the leading focus of USAF preparations. Nevertheless, USAF personnel and equipment adapted very well to the vast expanses and harsh environment. Non-NATO nations substantially contributed to the war effort, but NATO/Cold War–oriented ground, sea, and air forces comprised the bulk of the Coalition combat units. From the late 1940s until the late 1980s, the Air Force had trained and equipped its personnel primarily to fight a standing start war against the numerically superior Warsaw Pact. Outnumbered, NATO armed forces planned to repel a Warsaw Pact attack by employing innovative battle tactics—the AirLand Battle—and by fielding technologically superior weapons and more highly skilled personnel.[3]

Fortunately, during Desert Storm the Coalition confronted a far less fearsome foe—dangerous, but not the Warsaw Pact. Iraq fielded a huge army equipped with thousands of main battle tanks, armored personnel carriers, long-range artillery pieces, and chemically and conventionally armed tactical and medium-range ballistic missiles. The 600-combat-aircraft Iraqi Air Force had obtained most of its equipment (much of it modern and chemical warfare capable) and training from the Soviet Union and France. One of the most formidable Arab air forces (certainly the largest), it was still inferior in numbers, technology, and training to the air forces assembled against it. The Coalition rapidly established air superiority without suffering a single confirmed air-to-air combat loss. The enemy's ground forces and extensive air defenses posed a more serious challenge, but again the air-to-ground war devastated Iraq's war machine at a cost of only thirty-four Coalition aircraft lost; tragic, but in proportion to the number of combat sorties flown, this was an astonishingly small number.[4]

The Air Force's logistic operations successes during Desert Shield and Desert Storm were the result of long-term planning and preparation. Over the years, Air Force logisticians and planners expended great effort and expense to make the USAF a mobile force. This mobility proved invaluable. As Winston Churchill once observed, "Strange as it may seem, the Air Force, except in the air, is the least mobile of all services," because "[a] squadron can reach its destination in a few hours, but its establishment, depots, fuel, spare parts, and workshops take many weeks, and even months, to develop."[5]

Comprising the largest element of Coalition airpower, the USAF contributed one-half of the aircraft. Supporting so large a force challenged the

USAF's logistics community. But with the Air Force geared for a standing start war with the Warsaw Pact and fleshed out by the defense buildup begun in 1979, the Air Force Logistics Command (AFLC) made what its Commander, General Charles C. McDonald, described as "an almost transparent transition to wartime operations."[6]

Lieutenant General William G. Pagonis, Commander of U.S. Army Central Support Command, directed the overall logistics support effort in the CENTCOM area of responsibility (AOR). His greatest task involved coordinating the massive U.S. airlift and sealift operations and piecing together a logistics infrastructure that met the needs of U.S. forces and, wherever possible, complemented the logistics needs of other Coalition members. As AFLC Commander, General McDonald stood at the center of USAF logistics effort, a task that involved working closely with logisticians from the other Air Force commands, numerous contractors, CENTCOM, the Defense Logistics Agency (DLA), U.S. Transportation Command (TRANSCOM), U.S. Army logisticians, U.S. Navy logisticians, and Coalition members dependent on AFLC for logistics assistance through the International Logistics Center (ILC).[7]

For several reasons, the Air Force was able to rush substantial combat forces and logistics support to the AOR more quickly than the other services. Foremost, the Air Force's heavy fighting machines, aircraft, flew to the AOR. Equally as important, the Air Force was organized and trained to airlift necessary support equipment and personnel concurrent with the movement of combat aircraft. Thus, when the JCS ordered USAF combat, strategic airlift, tactical airlift, and support units to the AOR, USAF logisticians stood ready to provide instant support. The key was having the necessary munitions, spares, and equipment available in air transportable configurations ready for shipment aboard cargo aircraft with deploying squadrons.

War Readiness Spares Kits (WRSK) contained the necessary spare parts to keep a squadron flying for approximately thirty days. Standard Air Munitions Packages (STAMP) contained a varying quantity of one type of munition, chaff, or flare. Standard Tank, Rack, Adapter, and Pylon Packages (STRAPP) contained these and associated items for specifically configured aircraft of a particular squadron. All of these were kept ready for immediate loading aboard C-141 Starlifter transports or equivalent cargo aircraft that would fly to the squadron's theater airfield. Because of this logistics preparation and continuous training, every deployed squadron could move into a bare base and begin combat operations almost immediately. This is precisely what happened when the first F-15 squadrons flew to Saudi Arabia. Each squadron deployed with the equivalent of twenty C-141 cargo loads of materiel and 500 personnel. Building the logistics base to sustain the forces eventually employed during Desert Storm required much more.

Beginning with the first hectic week of Operation Desert Shield, massive amounts of support materiel poured into the AOR as the Air Force tackled the task of creating the air base and supply system required to house and maintain hundreds of aircraft and thousands of personnel. Accordingly, the Air Force began to rely more heavily on the transportation network established by U.S. Transportation Command (TRANSCOM) and CENTCOM for the intertheater and intratheater movement of such bulky supplies as fuel, munitions, and vehicles.[8]

The movement of so large a force, so far, and so fast loomed as an unprecedented logistics feat. TRANSCOM directed the overall airlift and sealift effort, while Military Airlift Command (MAC) and Military Sealift Command (MSC) executed the movement of personnel and materiel. Due to the urgency of the earliest deployments, the MAC heavy airlifters—C-5As, C-5Bs, and C-141s—rushed the troops and equipment into the AOR that provided the initial thin defensive screen. The massive airlift continued unabated through the war. On 18 August 1990, forty-one Civil Reserve Air Fleet (CRAF) aircraft and crews joined the effort, and on 17 January 1991 the secretary of defense activated an additional 146 CRAF aircraft and SAC pressed some of its KC-10s into airlift service. By the end of March 1991, the combined MAC and CRAF air fleet had flown over 17,000 strategic airlift missions in support of the war.[9]

The first USAF aircraft to fly into Saudi Arabia found state-of-the-art facilities, such as those at King Khalid Military City and Dhahran, at their disposal. The Saudis possessed numerous modern bases with extensive ramp space and infrastructure, which they merely turned over to arriving American and British forces. As the buildup continued, Coalition air forces set up operations at military and commercial airfields in all of the Gulf Cooperation Council (GCC) countries.[10] By the time the war began, USAF aircraft engaged in the conflict also operated out of Diego Garcia, the United Kingdom, Spain, and Turkey. In addition to the considerable existing runway and ramp space made available to Coalition air forces, the Saudi Arabian cities Jubail and Dhahran provided massive port facilities. With modern air and sea terminals available immediately, MAC and MSC moved hundreds of thousands of troops and billions of pounds of supplies and equipment into the AOR with unprecedented dispatch.[11]

However, a means of rapid spares delivery to the AOR did not exist until MAC established Desert Express in mid-October 1990. Desert Express provided a daily, regularly scheduled C-141 flight between Charleston AFB, South Carolina, and Dhahran, Saudi Arabia. Each armed service received an allotted daily tonnage. The cargo service worked extremely well, enabling technicians to receive "show stopper" items within seventy-two hours after placing a requisition. A second daily flight was added for service between Charleston AFB and King Khalid Military City in February 1991, and MAC began a third daily flight between Europe and the AOR (European Express) the same month.[12]

The host nations (Saudi Arabia in particular) provided more than just dock space and runways. The Saudis also supplied food, water, fuel, housing, and transportation equipment, utilizing every available resource in support of the Coalition forces. When faced with an initial shortage of land transport, the Saudi government pressed into service the fleet of yellow buses kept on hand for the annual Moslem pilgrimage to Mecca. Saudi trucking companies provided tractor trailers and drivers to move materiel from aerial and sea ports to Coalition operational bases. Saudi oil refineries poured out aviation fuel at such a rate that the country actually resorted to importing some petroleum products for domestic use. Building contractors and vendors supplied building material and labor for expansion of existing facilities and construction of new facilities. Local caterers fed the troops, and local cleaning services washed their uniforms. Grateful for the Coalition's support, the Saudi government eventually paid for all services rendered. Coalition forces gathered in other GCC nations received similar support, though on a smaller scale. As shown, the importance of host nation support (HNS) cannot be overstated.[13]

Prepositioned assets represented the second major source of materiel support available in the AOR. Large quantities of war supplies and equipment lay dispersed in warehouses and ships throughout the region. USAF-dedicated assets were kept in storage at five land-based sites and aboard three ships. USAF items prepositioned ashore in the AOR included hard-wall shelters, temper tents, aircraft hangers, power generation and distribution equipment, water purification and distribution equipment, kitchens, vehicles, air flight support equipment (barriers and lighting), and munitions. The afloat prepositioned ships contained aircraft ammunition, general-purpose bombs, cluster bomb units, rockets, chaff and flares, and miscellaneous asset hardware. The USAF also maintained fuel and petroleum, oil, and lubricant (POL) tankers in the area. Prepositioned materiel proved to be a wise investment, for having the supplies and equipment in theater saved an equivalent of 1,800 airlift missions and provided supplies and infrastructure materiel for twenty-one of the principal airfields. The other armed services also kept assets prepositioned in the area. Notably, the five Diego Garcia–based U.S. Marine, Maritime Prepositioned Squadron 2 ships that reached Jubail on 15 August 1990 carried M-60A1 tanks, support vehicles, and supplies that equipped the 7th Marine Expeditionary Brigade, the first heavy land-based U.S. firepower to reach the imperiled kingdom.[14]

Although the Air Force remained prepared for war at all times, the rapid and massive deployment quickly exposed materiel shortfalls. Several of these shortages involved preparing the aircrews for the harsh heat of the Arabian Desert. For example, in the first few months, almost all U.S. troops deployed with uniforms designed for the temperate climates of Europe or

North America. To meet the need for hundreds of thousands of desert camouflage uniforms, the DLA immediately pressed its uniform factory at the Defense Personnel Support Center, Philadelphia, into overtime production and placed emergency orders with several contractors. In addition to the need for regular uniforms, the possibility of Iraqi chemical warfare attacks created an urgent requirement for chemical protective suits, not only for Americans, but also for the Saudis. Again, within weeks, the DLA managed to locate new contractors to augment the production of the few vendors who had ongoing contracts. However, working on an aircraft in the desert heat while wearing a chemical suit stretched the endurance of any human. To provide relief from the heat, the San Antonio Air Logistics Center (one of five AFLC-operated depots) rushed the production of the Multi-Man Intermittent Cooling System, a portable air conditioning unit that allowed ten persons wearing special vests to plug hoses into the unit and receive forced chilled air into the vests. In a commendable show of productive capacity, the manufacturer began delivering the units for use in the field by October 1990. Adding to the supplies required for desert deployment, the DLA provided countless tubes of lip balm, bottles of sunscreen lotion, pairs of sunglasses, and cans of foot powder.[15]

One hundred and forty-four CENTAF-controlled USAF C-130s performed the bulk of tactical intratheater airlift, and by late March they had flown over 45,000 sorties distributing 158,800 tons of cargo and 184,000 passengers. Hundreds of Coalition helicopters (mostly U.S. Army) and a limited number of non-USAF fixed-wing aircraft also provided tactical airlift. In addition, CENTAF utilized 100 contractor-operated tractor trailers for linehaul operations, dubbed the "Blue Ball Express," complementing the much larger U.S. Army linehaul effort. The CENTAF effort alone delivered 31,000 short tons of munitions, general cargo, and vehicles during Desert Shield. Understandably, the day before hostilities commenced, the foreign national tractor trailer drivers walked off the job. The Air Force quickly replaced them with 200 USAF drivers for combat linehaul delivery. During the war, these blue suit truck drivers delivered 14,400 tons of cargo. After hostilities ceased, foreign nationals resumed driving responsibilities.[16]

Although strategic airlift proved crucial for rapid deployment, the large-scale movement of heavy and bulky materiel such as armor, vehicles, munitions, and fuel required sealift. As of early February 1991, the United States alone utilized a total of 269 ships in support of the war. Just as MAC called on the CRAF, MSC pressed into service seventy-one Ready Reserve Force ships and chartered an additional 108 dry cargo ships and forty tankers. The U.S. Marine prepositioned ships from Diego Garcia reached Saudi Arabia first, and eventually all twenty-five U.S. military prepositioned ships (including USAF petroleum, oil, and lubricant and munitions ships) deployed worldwide sailed to the AOR.[17]

Providing logistics support to the fighting units in the AOR involved hundreds of thousands of persons, both military (active duty, reserve, and National Guard) and civilian (civil service and contractor). Primarily a procurement, depot maintenance, and depot modification command, the AFLC deployed a relatively small number of personnel to Southwest Asia. In total, the AFLC deployed 1,702 personnel worldwide in support of Desert Shield and Desert Storm. The flying units themselves provided the vast bulk of deployed maintenance personnel. In addition to the military and DOD civilian personnel deployed, thousands of contractor personnel served in the AOR as technical representatives and in base support roles.[18]

Combat Logistics Support Squadron (CLSS) Aircraft Battle Damage Repair (ABDR) teams and CLSS Rapid Area Distribution Support (RADS) teams constituted the bulk of AFLC personnel deployed to the AOR. The command deployed 621 CLSS personnel (549 active duty and 72 reserve) divided among forty-two ABDR teams (thirty-nine active duty teams and three reserve teams). Demonstrating their great value, the teams performed battle damage repair on thirty aircraft and completed combat maintenance and depot-level repair on combat, transport, tanker, and CRAF aircraft. At the peak of the buildup, a total of 136 CLSS personnel deployed with RADS Supply and Reconstitution/Augmentation Teams (SATs) and Packaging Reconstitution/Augmentation Teams (PATs) to bolster existing supply and packaging operations. In addition, the SATs and PATs established complete operations, such as a Base Supply Store and Transportation Management operations.[19]

The bulk of the assets prepositioned in the AOR, as well as those procured for use in Southwest Asia but held in storage in the continental United States (CONUS), comprised bare base assets. Though owned by operational commands, the AFLC procured the systems and assisted in assembling them when deployed. The Air Force developed three types of bare base systems. Tactical Air Command (TAC) owned Harvest Bare, a collection of prefabricated hardwall shelters that, when fully assembled, provided support for five squadrons. CENTAF utilized only portions of this system during the war. A second system, Harvest Eagle, included sets of tents designed for housekeeping support, each of which could support 1,100 personnel. United States Air Forces Europe (USAFE), Pacific Air Forces (PACAF), and TAC each owned four sets, but CENTAF utilized only two sets. The most comprehensive system, Harvest Falcon, included shelters, tents, kitchens, water systems, electrical systems, and air conditioning systems to support 55,000 personnel and 750 aircraft. Air Force logisticians designed Harvest Falcon specifically for use in Southwest Asia. The entire system deployed in segmented units—fourteen host and twenty-three tenant packages. When Operation Desert Shield commenced, 30 percent of the system's equipment was prepositioned in the AOR, 52 percent was in storage at CONUS locations, and 18 percent was still in the procurement pipeline. In addition to the aforementioned bare base assets, the

Air Force also deployed fifteen Air Transportable Hospitals, each a fifty-bed unit.[20]

Air Force Base Engineering Emergency Forces (Prime BEEF) teams (usually deployed in fifty-member teams) assembled the prepackaged assets and Rapid Engineer Deployable, Heavy Operations Squadrons Engineer (RED HORSE) teams constructed runways, drilled wells, and built revetments. Readiness in Base Services (Prime RIBS) teams (generally nine to twenty-five members) followed to provide kitchen, billeting, laundry, and mortuary services. Drawing on these assets, units deployed to established or bare base airstrips and, where necessary, rapidly erected air-conditioned tents, mess halls, showers, latrines, water and electrical systems, air traffic flow control units, and aircraft shelters. In addition, the teams also extended runways, ramps, and aprons. AFLC contributed 115 civil engineers from Hill AFB, who deployed to Saudi Arabia with the 388th Tactical Fighter Wing (TFW) to assist with the beddown of the wing at a bare base site.[21]

CENTAF required a great number of vehicles to handle cargo, fuel aircraft, pick up and deliver materiel, construct base housing, and perform a host of other tasks. The original operational deployment plan for Southwest Asia called for 6,244 vehicles of all types, including tow tractors, 40-ton (40K) loaders, P19 fire trucks, High Mobility Multi-Wheel Vehicles (HMMVs), general-purpose vehicles, special-purpose loaders, and fuel trucks to support fourteen sites. However, after the mid-November buildup, the number of vehicles required jumped to 9,326 to support twenty-five sites. When Desert Shield began, the Air Force had 3,418 vehicles prepositioned in the AOR, both ashore and aboard afloat prepositioned ships. The USAF stored an additional 824 vehicles at Seymour Johnson AFB, North Carolina. To meet the shortfall between requirements and immediately available assets, the Air Force leased vehicles from Saudi contractors, and AFLC command levied (emergency requisitioned from USAF Major Commands [MAJCOMs]) 2,000 vehicles, drawing primarily on War Reserve Materiel (WRM) stocks stored in Europe.[22]

In addition to the large numbers of vehicles, CENTAF required hundreds of common support equipment (CSE) items necessary to service and maintain aircraft. This equipment included munitions loaders and trailers, rapid-assemble munitions systems, maintenance stands, floodlight carts, aircraft jacks and towbars, air conditioners, liquid nitrogen carts, and liquid oxygen carts. Despite heavy use in a harsh environment, the CSE maintained an average 94 percent mission capable (MC) rate. Aircraft maintenance crews also required high-technology Automatic Test Equipment (ATE) to maintain the sophisticated aircraft and subsystems. CENTAF, USAFE, and SAC utilized thirty-six complete ATE sets, and USAFE deployed an additional partial set to Incirlik AFB, Turkey. The test sets proved to be equally rugged, operating at an average 95 percent MC rate. As with the aircraft and vehicles, keeping the CSE and ATE functioning at these high rates required skilled technicians and a reliable flow of spares.[23]

Providing fuel for the aircraft involved in Desert Shield and Desert Storm proved to be an enormous task. With the Coalition forces virtually sitting atop the world's largest petroleum reserve, purchasing fuel did not present a problem. Once Saudi Arabia adjusted production at its refineries to meet military needs, the oil-rich kingdom merely gave the Coalition what gasoline, diesel fuel, and aviation fuel each member required. During the buildup and the war, Coalition forces consumed over 890 million gallons of jet fuel. However, even the extensive Saudi infrastructure did not have the capacity to get this volume of fuel from the refineries into the aircraft. To augment the transportation, storage, and servicing needs of the USAF (and in many cases CENTCOM, CRAF, and Coalition aircraft), CENTAF established an extensive fuels transportation and servicing network. At the peak of Desert Storm operations, CENTAF employed 2,061 supply and fuels personnel. To store and issue fuel, the Air Force deployed 100 R-14 pumping modules, 200 R-9 refueling trucks, and 700 50,000-gallon fuel bladders. In addition, fuels personnel also utilized numerous other specialized equipment types, such as liquid oxygen and liquid nitrogen storage and dispensing tanks and equipment.[24]

CENTAF prepositioned munitions, primarily general-purpose types, at three AOR sites and aboard three munitions ships. Each squadron deployed with air-transportable STAMP, which provided immediate, though limited (4,009 short tons deployed), munitions stocks. During the early months of Operation Desert Shield, munitions activities centered on distributing the prepositioned stocks to the combat aircraft units and improving the munitions storage facilities at these operational sites. However, as the tempo and volume of munitions shipment arrivals and distribution activity increased, the lack of a central munitions depot began to hinder munitions activities. CENTAF therefore constituted the 4401st Munitions Maintenance Squadron in October 1990 and established a provisional munitions depot at Al Kharj, Saudi Arabia. Given the cushion of time and the elimination of the Soviet threat, the Air Force was free to draw on CONUS, PACAF, and USAFE stocks of preferred munitions (both guided and unguided). In total, the Air Force shipped 556,900 short tons of munitions to the AOR via 358 surface ship movements and 693 aircraft missions. Upon arrival in the AOR, USAF munitions were shipped to Al Kharj and redistributed to operating locations by tactical airlift C-130s (32,000 short tons) or by truck (49,000 short tons). USAF aircraft eventually expended 150 million pounds of ordnance. USAF units did not cancel a single mission for lack of munitions, and no aircraft sortied without a full munitions load. SAC B-52Gs came close to running short of 500-pound bombs, but MAC and SAC (utilizing KC-10s) emergency airlifted 132 C-141–equivalent loads of 500-pound bombs to the B-52G forward operating bases, which allowed SAC to sustain planned sortie rates.[25]

As noted earlier, the aircraft that deployed to AOR bases brought along their own WRSK and STRAP to provide an immediate thirty-day combat support capability. Few units, however, actually maintained completely stocked WRSK. Having to act rapidly, many units cannibalized nondeployed aircraft to fill out WRSK. The cannibalized items were then replaced from AFLC stocks. Within a week of the first deployment, the Air Force began planning for spares support beyond the thirty-day in-theater supply. CENTAF logisticians decided to keep the WRSK intact and use them as tools for spares inventory control. The logisticians chose to follow this course because the Air Force did not deploy the Tactical Shelter Systems (which included full-up supply computers), but each unit did deploy with their Combat Supply System (CSS) computers, which were designed to maintain the accountability and inventory accuracy of the WRSK. Moreover, the Air Force did not have sufficient personnel or operational supply support infrastructure available to warehouse sustainment stocks. Fortunately, the CSS computers gave each unit an inventory control system, and the WRSK shipping containers served adequately as storage containers. Initially, deployed units received stock replenishment and Mission Incapable Parts (MICAP) support from their home station (where WRSK accountability remained), which requisitioned the spare from the applicable source of supply and then forwarded it to the AOR. As time passed, various units altered this WRSK replenishment procedure; some home base Stock Control clerks cut spares shipping time by arranging for spares to be shipped directly from the source of supply to the AOR, while others transferred kit responsibility to the combat supply system established in the AOR. To further enhance spares and maintenance support, deployed units received Follow On Spares Kits (FOSK) and High Priority Mission Support Kits (HPMSK). Air Force logisticians made up HPMSKs specifically for the U.K.-based F-111 squadrons because their only planned combat mission was to fight in place from their U.K. air bases, thus negating the need for air-mobile WRSKs. FOSKs added to the WRSKs the shop replaceable units (SRUs) and economic order quantity (EOQ) items necessary to support intermediate-level maintenance.[26]

Having each unit resupplied through their home station proved too slow and cumbersome for an extended deployment. CENTAF therefore established and began operating the CENTAF Supply Support Activity (CSSA) in October 1990. Composed of approximately 100 men and women from various Air Force and DLA organizations, the CSSA normalized in-theater supply accounts by channeling requirements from the twenty-one individual AOR supply accounts to a single location at Langley AFB, Virginia. Acting as a clearinghouse, the CSSA received requisitions transmitted via secure military satellite link from Thumrait, Oman, to Fort Dietrick,

Maryland, where the message traffic was forwarded over a dedicated commercial line to Langley AFB. The CSSA then forwarded the supply requisition to the appropriate air logistics center or DLA supply center. During the course of the operation, the CSSA processed between 45,000 and 60,000 transactions a day. The turnaround time for AFLC-supported items hovered around one week for high-priority items and two to three days for "show stoppers."[27]

Keeping track of the items in the logistics pipeline vexed early supply efforts, with personnel in the field often reordering the same item when specific information regarding delivery could not be obtained from AFLC. Not sure if the original item was lost in the pipeline, the AOR technician would order another as a precaution. The problem was that once the item left the hands of the AFLC shipper, AFLC lost visibility of the item until the consignee sent notification that the item had arrived. Both MAC and MSC tracked items from the time they took possession until the item was offloaded from their ship or aircraft. Because the AFLC, MAC, and MSC tracking systems were not linked, finding a particular item in the logistics pipeline proved very difficult and time consuming. Computer specialists at HQ AFLC solved this problem by developing the Air Force Logistics Information File (AFLIF), a computerized information system that tapped into MAC and MSC databases, allowing AFLC to track the movement of every item shipped from the time it left an AFLC facility until the item reached the AOR. With this en route visibility, AFLC could even divert shipments when a high-priority requisition had been received for an item already shipped.[28]

As noted earlier, Iraq possessed both chemical and biological warfare capabilities and had previously used chemical weapons against Iran and rebellious Iraqi Kurds. Fortunately, Saddam Hussein refrained from using these weapons against Coalition forces. However, preparing for the worst case, Coalition troops deployed with chemical protective gear and decontamination equipment, which afforded some degree of protection. Unfortunately, the Coalition forces could not shield aircraft and support equipment from chemical or biological contamination, thus presenting a serious problem—the Air Force did not have the equipment or procedures in place to handle contaminated reparables. In the course of a chemical or biological weapon attack, ventilated reparable equipment would have been subject to contamination. Of particular concern, electronic circuit board conformal wiring coatings could absorb these agents. Once exposed, neither AFLC nor any other DOD organization possessed the means to detect, monitor, or decontaminate the reparables. Additionally, neither the field technicians, AFLC depot technicians, nor contractors were equipped to perform repairs on contaminated SRUs, Line Replaceable Units (LRUs), or other expensive reparables. Furthermore, AFLC, TAC, and MAC had not established marking, packaging, or shipping procedures for contaminated equipment. As a result, to ensure the safety of all those who might come in contact with a contaminated reparable, from the technician and packagers in the field to the repair technician in a depot shop, the Air Force would have had no choice but to keep all potentially contaminated reparables in the AOR until a safe method of detection, packaging, shipping, decontamination, and decontamination verification had been devised.[29]

Establishing intermediate level maintenance (ILM) capability in the AOR proved to be a key to the achievement of the high sortie rates sustained by USAF aircraft. The tactical air units deployed with a mix of aviation packages (which included maintenance, avionics ILM for F-15s, electronic countermeasures [ECM] test stations, and low altitude navigation target infrared rader for night [LANTIRN] test stations), ILM packages, WRSK, and FOSK. Thirty days after initial deployment, CENTAF deployed the ILM packages to provide sustained jet engine intermediate maintenance, avionics intermediate maintenance, and heavy fabrication shop maintenance. To avoid shipping engines to the CONUS for repair, CENTAF arranged to ship spare engines to USAFE Jet Engine Intermediate Maintenance (JEIM) "Queen Bee" facilities, where 437 engines were eventually produced. USAFE fighter wings hosting JEIM "Queen Bee" facilities included 50th TFW, Hahn AFB, Germany; 36th TFW, Bitburg AFB, Germany; 48th TFW Lakenheath AFB, United Kingdom; 20th TFW, Upper Heyford, United Kingdom; 401st TFW, Torrejon AFB, Spain; 86th TFW, Ramstein AFB, Germany; and the 81st TFW, Bentwaters AFB, United Kingdom. MAC also manned Rhein–Main AFB as a regional repair center for LRU repair, T-56 engine repair, and C-130 Isochronal (ISO) inspection. Adding to the in-theater C-130 support capabilities, MAC established a propeller shop in the AOR. In addition, one Avionics Intermediate Station (AIS) deployed to each AOR air base, and CENTAF established a single Precision Measurement Equipment Laboratory (PMEL) at Riyadh to service the entire theater.[30]

Beginning with the first days of Desert Shield, activity at every AFLC Air Logistics Center, major modification and repair depots, increased. In the rush to get aircraft to the operational commands, AFLC accelerated the programmed depot maintenance (PDM) or depot modification of seventy aircraft, including five B-52s, eleven C-5s, forty-one C-141s (thirty-five organic and six contract), seven C-130s, and six F-111s. In addition to accelerating aircraft production, AFLC surged the production of over 90,000 commodity items, filling 70,000 Desert Storm requisitions.[31]

The immediate, massive airlift requirements of Operation Desert Shield quickly saturated MAC's and AFLC's airlift capacity. Therefore, over the course of Desert Shield and Desert Storm, AFLC added 488 missions to its logistics airlift (LOGAIR) operations. LOGAIR, a contractor-operated air cargo service, linked the Air Force's CONUS depot facilities and provided regularly scheduled flights to meet the materiel movement needs of AFLC and its customers, the other USAF commands. However, over one-half of the added flights supported U.S. Army units within the CONUS preparing for deployment to the AOR, which required these LOGAIR flights to divert to off-line Army airfields. The bulk of the Army cargo airlifted by LOGAIR consisted of DLA war readiness materiel.[32]

The nearly one-way flow of 463L pallets, straps, and nets into the AOR came close to creating a war-stopper situation. Under tremendous pressure to unload arriving aircraft as quickly as possible and then get them serviced and back into the air to make room on the crowded ramps and aprons for more inbound planes, ground crews found little time to remove cargo from the pallets or load available empty pallets onto outbound aircraft. In addition, ground crews could handle and stack cargo much more easily with the cargo firmly strapped to a pallet, particularly when the paved storage lots became full and the crews were forced to store cargo on sand. Additionally, once unloaded at an AOR air cargo port, thousands of pallets dispersed to forward operating bases, where, as happened in Southeast Asia a quarter century earlier, the 463L pallets ended up serving alternative uses, such as tent floors, trench reinforcements, or as revetment walls. As a result, the USAF expected to suffer a 35 percent net and pallet attrition rate over the entire deployment and redeployment. To forestall a critical shortage, the sole pallet manufacturer, AAR Brooks & Perkins, surged production of the 463L and nets seven days after Desert Shield began. Moreover, the Air Force rushed to use its entire war reserve materiel stockpile of 463Ls, the Air Staff and JCS organized a pallet and net recovery team, and Germany donated 2,096 pallets and 3,092 nets to MAC.[33]

Due in great part to excellent logistics support, the USAF's aircrews, ground crews, sophisticated aircraft, subsystems, and weapons performed admirably. Through six weeks of unrelenting combat operations, support personnel kept the complex machines' mission capable rates higher than normal peacetime rates. Mission capable rates for the primary combat aircraft involved are noted in Table 4.1.

From August 1990 until the cease-fire on 28 February 1991, the Air Force rushed to assemble a massive logistics support structure in the AOR and worked under equally pressing time constraints to fill the supply lines. Following the rapid victory, the flow of supplies slowed dramatically, and the Air Force's logisticians began the arduous task of returning the fighting units and equipment to their home bases and disassembling and reconstituting the air-mobile and prepositioned assets. Based on wartime lessons learned, the Air Force began the time-consuming and expensive task of replenishing and reposturing materiel to support its forces should they again be called to war.

In conclusion, several observations regarding USAF logistics support can be made based on Desert Shield and Desert Storm experience. First, the war demonstrated that technological superiority made possible a swift, de-

Table 4.1
Aircraft Mission Capable Rates[34]

AIRCRAFT	# DEPLOYED	COMBAT SORTIES	MC RATE
F-4G	62	900*	87.5%
F-117	42	1,300*	85.8%
F-15C/D	120	5,900*	94%
F-15E	48	2,200*	95.9%
F-16	249	13,500*	95.2%
A-10	144	8,100*	95.7%
F-111F	84	4,000*	85%
EF-111	18	900*	87%
B-52G	74	1,600*	81%

Approximate numbers.

cisive air war victory at the cost of few Coalition casualties and minimal collateral damage. If the USAF hopes to maintain its decisive edge in the future, it must maintain a fielded force technologically superior to that of any potential enemy. Second, although conditions during Desert Shield and Desert Storm were ideal for providing logistics support to the deployed combat forces, it is unlikely such ideal conditions will be present in any future conflict. Therefore, the USAF must retain an industrial base, spares and supplies inventory, and airlift capability sufficient to support and sustain the combat forces from the first hours of a standing start war. Similarly, the USAF must continue to steamline maintenance through such initiatives as the move from three-level maintenance to two-level maintenance, which will ultimately reduce the number of personnel and amount of equipment that must deploy with a combat squadron.

NOTES

1. The growth and use of Iraqi military power are described in Stephen Pelletiere, Douglas V. Johnson II, and Leif R. Rosenberger, "Iraqi Power and U.S. Security in the Middle East," Carlisle Barracks, Pa., Strategic Studies Institute, U.S. Army War College, 1990; Ronald E. Berquist, *The Role of Air Power in the Iran–Iraq War* (Maxwell AFB, Ala.: Air University Press, 1988). Documents hereafter cited are available in the Air Force Materiel Command (AFMC) Office of History, Wright–Patterson AFB, Ohio.

2. Powell quote in "Powell says Iraqi Potential to Take Ports Worried U.S., Early Move Could Have Extended Gulf War," *Washington Post,* 16 Mar 1991.

3. For a description of CENTCOM contingency planning prior to the Gulf War, see Testimony of General Norman Schwarzkopf, Congress, Senate, Committee

on Armed Services, *Threat Assessment; Military Strategy and Operational Requirements,* 101st Cong, 2nd sess. 8 Feb 90, 590–637.

4. The late 1980s Soviet–American military balance is examined in *Soviet Military Power, Prospects for Change 1989* (U.S. DOD, 1989). NATO and Warsaw Pact forces and doctrine are specifically addressed on pp. 92–112. For an analysis of the Gulf War and the role of airpower, see George T. Raach et al., *Conduct of the Persian Gulf War,* Final Report to Congress, 3 vols. (U.S. DOD, Apr 92); Norman Friedman, *Desert Victory* (Annapolis: Naval Institute Press, 1991); Richard Hallion, *Storm over Iraq: Air Power and the Gulf War* (Washington: Smithsonian Institution Press, 1992); Eliot A. Cohen et al., *Gulf War Air Power Survey Summary Report* (Washington, D.C.: USGPO, 1993). Coalition fixed-wing aircraft losses from all causes totaled thirty-six: twenty USAF; thirteen U.S. Navy and Marine; and thirteen British, Saudi, Kuwaiti, and Italian. One cannot surmise that because the Coalition so easily routed the Iraqi armed forces, the Warsaw Pact likewise could have been overwhelmed. However, a full array of Warsaw Pact and NATO equipment was employed on both sides, and U.S. and Western European equipment clearly demonstrated a qualitative edge. For Russian reactions to the war, see Benjamin S. Lamberth, *DESERT STORM and Its Meaning, The View from Moscow* (Santa Monica: RAND, 1992).

5. Winston Churchill quoted in Charles M. Westenhoff, ed., *Military Air Power: The CADRE Digest of Air Power Opinions and Thoughts* (Maxwell AFB, Ala.: Air University Press, 1990), 42.

6. General Charles C. McDonald quoted in "AFLC Chief Sees War Tab Reaching $1.1 Billion," *Fairborn Daily Herald,* 23 Apr 1991.

7. For a broad examination of U.S. military logistics during the Gulf War, see GAO Report GAO/NSIAD-92-26, DESERT SHIELD/STORM Logistics: Observations by U.S. Military Personnel, Nov 91, microfiche repro.; Air Force Logistics Management Center (AFLMC) Final Report LX912097, Air DESERT SHIELD/ DESERT STORM Logistics Lessons Learned, AFLMC, Mar 92, microfiche repro.; Raach et al., *Conduct of the Persian Gulf War,* Appendix F, *Logistics Build-up and Sustainment,* microfiche repro.; William G. Pagonis and Jeffrey L. Cruikshank, *Moving Mountains: Lessons in Leadership and Logistics from the Gulf War* (Boston: Harvard Business School Press, 1992), 63–158.

8. White Paper, AFLC/XPOX, "Air Force Logistics Command Operations in DESERT STORM," Jul 90; Brfg, by HQ AFLC, "DESERT STORM/STORM Lessons Learned," 12–13 Jul 91 [hereafter "Lessons Learned"]; "Half Audie Murphy, Half Jack Welch," *Business Week,* 4 Mar 91, 42–43 [hereafter "Half Murphy, Half Welch]; "DESERT SHIELD/DESERT STORM Supply Lessons Learned," by AFLMC, Gunter AFB, Alabama, Mar 92. Aircraft that deployed during wartime relied on WRSK for initial spares support, whereas units that expected to fight in place, such as those located in Europe, relied on Base Level Self-Sufficiency Spares (BLSS) for initial wartime spares support. For a comparison of the these wartime spares management tools, see AFLMC Report LS902011, "Base Level Self-Sufficiency Spares Versus War Readiness Spares Kits Analysis," by AFLMC, May 91, microfiche repro.

9. Desert Shield Strategic Airlift is examined in William R. Tefteller, executive research project, Strategic Airlift Support for U.S. Forces Deployment to Operation Desert Shield, Industrial College of the Armed Forces, Apr 91, microfiche repro.

For pre–Gulf War and post–Gulf War analysis of CRAF, see Mary Chenoweth, Rand case study N-2838-AF, The Civil Reserve Air Fleet: An Example of the Use of Commercial Assets to Expand Military Capabilities during Contingencies, Jun 90, microfiche repro.; Brooks L. Bash, research report, "CRAF: The Persian Gulf War and Implications for the Future," Naval War College, 19 Jun 92; William H. Sessons and Thomas J. Maxson, research report, "Civil Reserve Air Fleet: Looking From DESERT STORM to the Future," Army War College, Apr 92.

10. The Gulf Cooperation Council was a collective security organization formed by Kuwait, Bahrain, the United Arab Emirates, Oman, Qatar, and Saudi Arabia in May 1981. For discussions of this organization, see "GCC: Safety in Numbers," *Jane's Defence Weekly* (31 Mar 90), 587–88, 590–91, 594–95, 597–602; W. Jack Dees, "Gulf Security and the Gulf Arab Contribution," Naval War College, 6 Jun 91, microfiche repro.

11. "U.S. Buildup Puts Strain on Saudis, Hosts Hand Over Air Bases, Box Lunches to Massing Americans," *Washington Post*, 27 Aug 90; David F. Bond, "Troop and Materiel Deployment Missions Central Elements in Desert Storm Success," *Aviation Week & Space Technology*, 22 Apr 91, 94–95; Mitchell and Payne, "Half Murphy, Half Welch," 42–43.

12. David A. Fulghum, "MAC 'Desert Express' Rushes Priority Supplies to Mideast," *Aviation Week & Space Technology* (3 Dec 90): 20–22; Brfg, "Lessons Learned"; Talking Paper, by AFLC/LGTX, "DESERT EXPRESS," 5 Jul 91; Joint Universal Lessons Learned System (JULLS) Rprt, No. 31838-44257 (00003), by HQ AFLC (Jerry Riffe), "Standardizing Express Transportation System Operations," 12 Mar 91.

13. David F. Bond, "Troops and Materiel Deployment Missions Central Elements in Desert Storm Success," *Aviation Week & Space Technology*, 22 Apr 91, 94–95; Michael Wines, "Saudis Plan to Supply U.S. with Fuel for Military Use," *New York Times*, 23 Aug 90; John J. Fialka, "U.S. Troops Replace Building Boom as Source of Profit for Saudi Business," *Wall Street Journal*, 27 Dec 90; *Final Report to Congress*, Appendix F, F12–17. Responsibility sharing is discussed in ibid., Appendix P, P1–9. In Katsuaki L. Terasawa and William R. Gates, "Burden Sharing in the Persian Gulf War: Lessons Learned and Implications for the Future," Naval Postgraduate School, Monterey, California, Aug 92, the authors argue that based on self-interest (control of their oil supplies and sovereignty), with the exception of Kuwait, the Gulf states may not have contributed as much to the war effort as their stake in the outcome justified, whereas Germany and Japan may have contributed more (money and materiel) than their stake in the outcome warranted.

14. Peter Grier, "Middle East: Laying the Groundwork," *Military Logistics Forum* (Sep 87): 19–25; James Kitfield, "Lifeline Across the Sea," *Government Executive* (Nov 90): 30, 32; Ray P. Linville, "Maritime Prepositioning: A Logistics Readiness and Sustainability Enhancement," *Air Force Journal of Logistics* (Winter 1984): 2–7; "Air Force Performance in DESERT STORM," Department of the Air Force White Paper, Apr 91, 9; Brfg, by AFLC Director of Operations and Contingency Plans to USAF Scientific Advisory Board Cross Matrix Panel, "AFLC—Partners in Warfighting," Wright–Patterson AFB, Ohio, 24 Apr 91.

15. Tom Shoop, "Supply Demands Exceed Korea and Vietnam," *Government Executive* (Nov 90): 35–38; Ross Day, "New Cooling System Battles Desert Broiler," *Kelly Observer* (30 Aug 90).

16. Sum Rprt, "Logistics Support for DESERT SHIELD and DESERT STORM," by HQ AFLC, 30 Mar 91, 10–15, appendixes [hereafter "Logistics Support"]; James Ott, "Desert Shield Deployment Tests CRAF's Viability," *Aviation Week & Space Technology* (10 Dec 90): 31–32; David F. Bond, "Troop and Materiel Deployment Missions Central Elements in Desert Storm Success," *Aviation Week & Space Technology* (22 Apr 91): 94–95; James C. Hyde, "MAC Flying Nonstop to Support Desert Storm," *Armed Forces Journal International* (Mar 91): 12–13.

17. For examinations of sealift operations, see Carl T. Broght and Sharon R. Hale, "Strategic Sealift for DESERT SHIELD Not a Blue Print for the Future," Naval War College, Jun 91, microfiche repro.; Robert B. Lambert, "Sealift In Operation DESERT SHIELD," U.S. Army War College, Mar 91, microfiche repro.; Ronald F. Rost et al., *Sealift in Operation DESERT SHIELD/DESERT STORM: 7 August 1990 to 17 February 1991* (Alexandria, Va.: Center for Naval Analysis, 1991), microfiche repro.; John P. Morse, research rprt, "The RRF in Operation Desert Storm: A First Look," Naval War College, May 91, microfiche repro.

18. Brfg, "Lessons Learned"; Ltr/Atch, AFLC/DPX to AFLC/XPO, "Inputs for the DESERT STORM White Paper," 21 May 91; Talking Paper, by AFLC/SGSP, "AFLC Medical Response for Operation DESERT STORM," 24 Apr 91; Ltr/Atch, AFLC/CK to AFLC/XPO, "Inputs for DESERT STORM White Paper," 23 May 91; William Flannery, "Supporters Outnumber Lead Players in Desert," *Washington Times*, 4 Feb 91; Denise Kalette, "Civilians among Unsung Heroes of War," *USA TODAY*, 6 Jun 91. Although AFLC and AFSC deployed relatively few personnel, these commands experienced many of the same deployment snags as TAC, MAC, and SAC. The AFLMC made a preliminary study of SAC Desert Shield and Desert Storm mobility data as part of a larger study. The results are presented in AFLMC Final Report LX912080, Analysis of DESERT SHIELD Deployment Data, AFLMC, Mar 92.

19. Talking Paper, by AFLC/LGMA, "Combat Logistics Support Squadron Maintenance," ca. 12 Jul 91; Talking Paper, "Combat Logistics Support Squadron (CLSS) Rapid Area Distribution Support (RADS)," by AFLC/LGTX, 19 Jun 91; Brfg, "Lessons Learned." The ABDR teams deployed with ABDR kits, which Desert Shield and Desert Storm experience showed needed to be reconfigured. See AAR, "AOR Assets (ABDR Kits)," by HQ AFLC/MATP, n.d.

20. Brfg, "Lessons Learned"; Talking Paper, by AFLC/XRCO, "DESERT SHIELD/DESERT STORM Bare Base Support."

21. Ronald B. Hartzer, "Engineering and Services in Operation DESERT SHIELD," *Air Power History* (Fall 1991): 20–27; Ltr/Atch, AFLC/CE to AFLC/XPO, "Inputs for the Desert Storm White Paper," 24 May 91; Phil Rhodes, "They Came. They Saw. They Built." *Airman* (Sep 91): 42–45; Lee Ewing, "Building an F-16 Team from Scratch," *Air Force Times* (24 Dec 90): 14–15, 22.

22. Talking Paper, by AFLC/XRCO, "Vehicles," 12 Jun 91; JULLS REPORT, No. 32039-17154 (00005), by AFLC (Jerry Riffe), "Accountability of Vehicles," 12 Mar 91. For a description of the various vehicle types and specialized equipment, see Christopher F. Foss and Terry J. Gander, eds., *Jane's Military Vehicles and Logistics* (Couldson, Surrey: Jane's Information Group, 1991), 422–23, 429–30, 550–51, 580–81, 594–96, 631–32.

23. Brfg, by AFLC/XRC, "Commodity Support for Operation DESERT SHIELD/STORM," 25 Apr 91.

24. Sum Rprt, "Logistics Support," 9. For a description of fuel distribution at the wing level, see Joseph M. Pinckney, "The War in the Gulf: Fuels Branch Makes a Difference," *Air Force Journal of Logistics* (Summer 1991): 28–32. Various refuelers and storage bladders are described in *Jane's Military Vehicles and Logistics,* 422–23, 429–30, 580–81. The USAF, U.S. Army, and Marines also used jet fuel in their diesel-burning ground vehicles, the latter two with some reservations. For an analysis of the use of Jet A-1 fuel in lieu of DF-2 fuel, see Belvoir Research, "Development & Engineering Center Report 2527, Performance of Fuels, Lubricants, and Associated Products Used During Operation DESERT SHIELD/STORM," Aug 92, microfiche repro.

25. Sum Rprt, "Logistics Support," 1–2; Briefing, Presented to USAF Scientific Advisory Board, by AFLC/LGW, "DESERT SHIELD/STORM AFLC Munitions Experience," 25 Apr 91; "DESERT SHIELD/DESERT STORM Munitions Lessons Learned," by AFLMC, Gunter AFB, Alabama, Apr 93. For more on USAF munitions, see David Fulghum, "USAF Nears Completion of 30 GBU-28s, Plans Advanced Penetrating Bomb," *Aviation Week & Space Technology,* 20 May 91, 22–23; "Harm Missiles Enhanced for Possible Gulf Mission," *Aviation Week & Space Technology,* 15 Oct 91, 79; Benjamin Weiser, "No Shortage of Bombs, Missiles Forseen for U.S.," *Washington Post,* 25 Jan 91; William Neikirk, "War Barely Dented U.S. Arsenal," *Chicago Tribune,* 15 Mar 91.

26. Sum Rprt, "Logistics Support," 5–6; Talking Paper, by AFLC/XRII, "Follow on Spares Kits," 19 Jun 91; Brfg, "Lessons Learned"; JULLS Rprt, No. 32857-54653 (00009), by HQ AFLC (Jerry Riffe), "War Readiness Spares Kit Deployment," 2 Apr 91; "AF Desperate to Get Spare Plane Parts," *Dayton Daily News,* 23 Nov 90; Gen Charles C. McDonald, Letter to the Editor, *Dayton Daily News,* 7 Dec 90. For an examination of C-130 WRSK use and resupply during Desert Shield and Desert Storm, see Kim L. Davey, "C-130 War Readiness Spares Kit (WRSK) Resupply during Contingency Operations—A DESERT SHIELD/STORM Analysis," master's thesis, Air Force Institute of Technology, Sep 91.

27. Sum Rprt, "Logistics Support," 6–7; Msg, AFNEWS Kelly AFB TX/11B to AIG 9333/PA/DP/CC et al., "Supply Line Victory" (Intrv with Maj Gen James W. Hopp, AF Director of Logistics Operations) R162200Z, Apr 91; Talking Paper, by AFLC/XRII, "CENTAF Supply Support Activity (CSSA)," 19 Jun 91. For an abbreviated examination of USAF supply activities based on postwar reports, see AFLMC Final Report LS912085, DESERT SHIELD/DESERT STORM Supply Lessons Learned, AFLMC, Mar 92.

28. Brfg, by AFLC/LGT, "Air Force Logistics Information File," 25 Apr 91; Talking Paper, by AFLC/LGTX, "Intransit Item Visibility for Cargo," 23 May 91.

29. Brfg, by AFLC/XRC, "Commodity Support for Operation DESERT SHIELD/STORM," 25 Apr 91; Talking Paper, by AFLC/SGBE, "Chemical Warfare Agent Detection and Decontamination of Reparables," 19 Jun 91; Test Rprts, (1) "Aircraft Decontamination Using Common Air Force Aircraft Ground Equipment–Forced Air Field Test," Joint Operational Test & Information Directorate, (2) "Effects of Extended Flight on Aircraft Contamination Using C-130 Military Transport Aircraft," Joint Operational Test & Information Directorate, U.S. Army Dugway Proving Ground, Jul 92.

30. Sum Rprt, "Logistics Support," 2–4, appendixes; AAR, by SA-ALC/LPE, "In-theater 'Queen Bee,' " n.d.

31. Talking Paper, by AFLC/LGSI, "Acceleration/Surge," 28 Jun 91; Brfg, by AFLC/XR, "Weapon System Performance," 25 Apr 91.
32. Talking Paper, by AFLC/LGTX, "AFLC Logistics Airlift (LOGAIR) Support," 19 Jun 91.
33. Talking Paper, by AFLC/XRCO, "463L Pallets and Nets," 28 Jun 91; JULLS Report, No. 32039-74029 (00006), by HQ AFLC (Jerry Riffe), "Strap Management, 12 Mar 91. 463L pallets were designed for use on USAF cargo aircraft. Constructed from balsa wood and aluminum, each pallet cost approximately $1,000. For more on 463Ls for noncargo movement purposes during the Vietnam War, see Ray L. Bowers, *The United States Air Force in Southeast Asia: Tactical Airlift* (Washington, D.C.: Office of Air Force History, 1983), 256.
34. White Paper, by HQ USAF, "Air Force Performance in DESERT STORM," Apr 91, 3–6; Sum Rprt, "Logistics Support," appendixes; Brfg, by AFLC/XR, "Weapon System Performance." For statistical analysis of B-52G, KC-135, KC-10, C-5, and C-130 Desert Shield and Desert Storm performance, see Richard Hallion, "Reaching Globally, Reaching Powerfully: The United States Air Force in the Gulf War," USAF White Paper, Sep 91; Brfg, by C-130 SPM, "C-130 WSPAR," 14 Mar 91.

Part III
THE AIR WAR: PLANNING AND COMBAT

In April 1991, shortly after the Allied victory in the Persian Gulf War, the Tufts University Institute for Foreign Policy Analysis hosted a U.S. Air Force symposium in Boston. For two days, senior USAF officials, along with civilian airpower enthusiasts, lauded the decisive victory which airpower, particularly the Air Force, had so recently delivered. The general theme of this symposium was that great technology, great airplanes, and great leadership, all brought together under the aegis of a great air campaign plan, had made a reality of the prophecies of Italian theorist Giulio Douhet and U.S. airpower enthusiasts from Billy Mitchell to Colonel John A. Warden III.

American airpower had performed well. In fact, airpower was arguably so dominant that it raised in the minds of many the idea that warfare had been fundamentally changed. Indeed, there were the usual claims that airpower, if it did not win the war all by itself, could have won it given a little more time and operational latitude. In addition, there were those who also held that the United States now enjoyed the kind of technological advantage over almost any potential foe that the machine gun had afforded nineteenth-century European colonial powers over native armies throughout the world.

However, in the minds of many historians like myself, what was missing was any real articulation of history; the study of which has been traditionally—and often conveniently—neglected by airpower enthusiasts. For instance, the air component of Desert Storm was not the world's first modern air campaign in which precision-guided munitions played a key role. Linebacker I, the airpower response to a fourteen-division North Vietnamese invasion of South Vietnam in 1972, holds that distinction. Indeed, many of the weapons used so effectively in Desert Storm were around in 1972 in earlier versions: The RF-4 Phantom, the F-4G Phantom II Wild Weasel anti–surface-to-air missile aircraft, the F-111, the B-52, as well as the Navy A-4, A-6, and the Navy and Air Force A-7 aircraft all served in the Vietnam War. Laser-guided bombs were first used in the late 1960s to destroy antiaircraft guns in Laos and to destroy bridges during Linebacker I, where they played a key role. Many of the support aircraft—planes such as the KC-135 tankers, C-5 and C-141 transports, and C-130 tactical transports—date from the Vietnam War and before. Furthermore, although more than twice the bomb tonnage fell on North Vietnam during the six months of Linebacker I than were dropped on Kuwait and Iraq during the thirty-nine-day air component of Desert Storm, the proportion between precision-guided munitions and standard aerial-delivered munitions (dumb bombs) was about the same. So was the outcome: Airpower was pivotal but not the decisive element in either operation.

Of course, there were fundamental differences between Linebacker I and the air campaign in the Gulf War. Linebacker I was a near-classic interdiction effort, and it succeeded in all of its primary objectives. The air component of Desert Storm, on the other hand, was more strategic in its thrust and focused on what was defined as Iraq's center of gravity. Under the guiding principles of John Warden's "air campaign concept," Iraq was depicted as a dynamic system amenable to a five-rings model. Saddam Hussein and the Iraqi military leadership lay at the center of the rings. The deployed Iraqi Army was, on the other hand, at the outer, fifth ring. The constructs of the parameters of this approach to warfare distinctly reflect the ideas posited by Douhet and other strategic bombing enthusiasts for the last three-quarters of a century. Because the enemy was depicted as a system, the governing paradigm was that if the nerve center was attacked, the ability of the leadership to communicate with its fielded military forces would be degraded to the point that they would be virtually irrelevant. Airpower could win the war without the use of ground forces.

As was the case in Vietnam, although the U.S. Air Force performance was good tactically, hitting targets and causing destruction did not deliver decisive victory. After thirty-nine days of bombing, Iraqi forces were still ensconced in Kuwait. Despite some 109,876 sorties flown by the Coalition (the U.S. Air Force flew about 65,000 sorties), neither Hussein nor Bush believed airpower had been employed decisively. Hussein certainly did not because Iraqi forces did not begin to leave Kuwait until the Coalition ground forces began their offensive. Bush did not believe in the purported decisiveness of airpower because he did, indeed, order the ground forces to attack to dislodge the Iraqis in fulfillment of the UN mandate.

The following chapters deal with that part of the air campaign which is most positive: its tactical and operational accomplishments. Daniel

T. Kuehl's chapter focuses more generally on many of these issues as well as how these operations were carried out. Colonel David A. Deptula was, indeed, one of the primary architects of the air campaign. He is also an accomplished operator with many hours of flying to his credit. He recounts the numerous tactical accomplishments of airpower. His chapter, and the others in this part, provides a wealth of insight into the operational aspects of the war.

Particular attention should be accorded to the chapter by Mark D. Mandeles. Perhaps the most profound change in the way wars are fought, and in the military technology that makes that change possible, is in the realm of information and communications. Innovations like the Global Positioning System and secure FAX systems, although not as spectacular as television footage of a single bomb going in the window of an enemy headquarters, were perhaps far more significant to the way in which the war was fought and to the final outcome.

The Revolution in Military Affairs (RMA), however, is not now the exclusive property of the United States. Much of the technology of the Gulf War is currently available to any nation willing to invest in it. Furthermore, it is not likely that a future Saddam Hussein will be as strategically inept. To build a paradigm for the future based on the perceived accomplishments of airpower in Operation Desert Storm and the flawed five-ring concept behind the strategic air campaign could prove disastrous.

As was the case in Vietnam, in the Gulf War the United States and its Allies had the technological advantage over the enemy. The much more sanguine outcome of the Gulf War notwithstanding, technology does not win wars. Wars are won by the side which develops a strategy appropriate to the war at hand. The side which can incorporate its technological advantages into a coherent strategy will have a distinct advantage. Indeed, it is my desire that these chapters and my introduction to them might be the focus and foundation of a truly fruitful and historical debate and discussion of the truths of both viewpoints. Only in this way can past experiences in war benefit the U.S. Air Force specifically, and the U.S. military in general.

—Earl H. Tilford, Jr.

5

Thunder and Storm: Strategic Air Operations in the Gulf War

Daniel T. Kuehl

The issue of strategic bombing remains perhaps the most controversial and uncertain of any surrounding the employment of airpower in the Gulf War. The importance of airpower per se in modern war is not at issue: Virtually any soldier, analyst, or political leader recognizes that in any conflict between modern technologically advanced states, military victory is highly unlikely without dominance in the air. The question centers instead on the contributions made by strategic airpower, defined as airpower brought to bear against a state's vital internal centers of gravity, rather than airpower devoted to support and cooperation with surface forces on the battlefield. This chapter will evaluate the effectiveness of strategic airpower in meeting the military and political objectives set by Coalition leaders. Before doing that, however, it will be useful to touch on some aspects of how strategic air operations in the Gulf War were planned and executed, which will in turn shed some light on the overall evaluation of those operations.

THE PLAN'S CONCEPTUAL ORIGINS

Even with the relatively sudden outbreak of the crisis in August 1990, some prewar planning had been done on how to employ airpower against Iraq. Just a month before the Iraqi invasion, U.S. Central Command (US-CENTCOM) planners conducted a command post exercise,[1] Internal Look 90, based on what was then only a hypothetical Iraqi attack on Kuwait and Saudi Arabia. The exercise target list for air operations resembled the later wartime target list in many ways, but there were critical differences, especially in the sequencing and focus of air attacks. Even the exercise target lists compiled by the joint CENTCOM planners and the USAF-only component (CENTAF) contained significant differences in focus, which hinted at some of the difficulties that would arise later during the war. Internal Look 90, and the regional defense plans on which it was based, concentrated on the ground defense of Saudi Arabia, not a slashing offensive into Iraq. Possibly the greatest conceptual difference between the Internal Look air scheme and the actual air campaign was the sequencing of attacks against what could be considered true strategic targets, such as enemy leadership and national command and control targets. What Internal Look 90 categorized as "long-range interdiction" operations came at the end of the scenario; in January 1991, these "strategic" attacks would instead open the war.[2]

That these attacks took place at all was the result of a resurgence within the USAF of the belief in conventional (nonnuclear) strategic airpower. Nowhere was this belief more powerful than in the Directorate of Plans at HQ USAF, where a relatively unknown colonel, John A. Warden, led a group of airpower advocates who had been thinking of how to best use airpower in just such a situation. Warden had developed a concept for explaining his theories of strategic conventional air operations. Sometimes and erroneously referred to as a "strategy" for strategic air attacks, his Five Strategic Rings (working inward, from lowest to highest priority, they were fielded military forces, population, infrastructure, key production, and leadership) were more accurately a "marketing tool" (Warden's words) and a framework within which to discuss airpower.[3]

The Iraqi conquest of Kuwait gave Warden's airpower planners an opportunity to put their theories into practice. The situation facing U.S. political and military leaders in the first week of August 1990 was critical; the one-sided outcome of the Gulf War can too easily blind one to the disparity of strength at the beginning of the crisis. General Norman Schwarzkopf, Commander in Chief USCENTCOM (usually CINCCENT or just "the CINC"), asked the USAF for help in planning possible offensive operations against Iraq should Saddam Hussein's forces cross into Saudi Arabia.[4] Using President Bush's four stated objectives—Iraqi withdrawal from Kuwait; restoration of the Kuwaiti government; security and stability of the region; protection of Americans abroad—as their only planning guidance, Warden's planners went to work, even as the first U.S. forces began deploying to the Gulf.

Starting early on August 9, they worked throughout the day and into the night drafting a conceptual air campaign plan. In pointed rejection of the incrementalism of the Vietnam War's Rolling Thunder air campaign, Warden called his plan Instant Thunder. Its intent went beyond ejecting

Iraqi forces from Kuwait, for that would merely recreate the status quo ante bellum and leave open the door for a repeat invasion at a later date. Instant Thunder was to be quick, violent, and focused on true Iraqi strategic centers of gravity—targets such as national-level leadership and command-control facilities, electric power, Iraq's capability to develop and possibly deliver weapons of mass destruction (nuclear, chemical, biological, and so-called NBC systems), and its military capability to reach beyond its borders with airpower or Scud missile attacks. The next day, General Schwarzkopf fervently endorsed this first effort and told them to keep working on the plan.[5]

A fair question is why the Air Staff was constructing an air campaign plan instead of CENTAF, which had the formal mission of doing precisely that. Part of the reason is that CENTAF at that moment was utterly focused on two activities, each of which vied to occupy 100 percent of its attention: getting forces to the theater (which included arranging for bases at which to land, fuel, munitions, etc.), and planning how to defend Saudi Arabia should the Iraqi forces poised just across the border continue their attack, which in early August was a real fear. Another less obvious reason is that CENTAF was simply not staffed with strategic airpower advocates. The core of CENTAF was the USAF's Ninth Air Force, an element of the Tactical Air Command. Over the years, the USAF had developed a philosophical schism over the use of conventional, nonnuclear airpower. One element, perhaps the largest, saw airpower's role as primarily that of supporting and cooperating with friendly ground forces. Another element, of which Warden and his fellow airpower thinkers were perhaps the leading exponents, saw a wider role for airpower in air operations that would at times parallel, and at times operate independently of, ground operations.[6] Given the extant conditions during early August, it is perhaps not surprising that the CENTAF staff focused on the Iraqi forces in the Kuwait Theater of Operations (KTO) while Checkmate looked deeper into Iraq.

General Schwarzkopf directed Colonel Warden to expand the Checkmate effort; representatives of the other Services were added, Strategic Air Command eagerly sent some planners, and work intensified as the Instant Thunder concept began to take on the appearance of an actual plan, with targets grouped into categories and priorities and target folders expanded with accumulated intelligence. A week later, Warden flew to Saudi Arabia with four of his Checkmate planners to brief Lieutenant General Charles A. "Chuck" Horner, the CENTAF commander, and turn the plan over to him. Horner's reception was cool to hostile; aside from the obvious criticism that the plan ignored the Iraqi forces already in Kuwait, Horner's Vietnam-era sensitivity to interference from Washington, D.C., made him question this plan born in the "ivory towers" of the Pentagon.[7] Warden returned to Washington, but he left both his briefing/plan and his four assistants in Riyadh.[8]

When Horner asked Brigadier General Buster Glosson to take over the task of planning an air campaign, Glosson reviewed the plan and saw some merit. Noting that it was "not a bad place to start," Glosson assembled a small group of air planners and charged them with the task of developing a strategic air campaign against Iraq. Using the Instant Thunder plan as a starting point and working in absolute secrecy, they began building an air campaign designed strategically to paralyze Iraq right from the opening strikes. The plan now belonged to CENTAF.[9]

Aside from the obvious space limitations that prevent telling the entire history of the air campaign planning that took place between General Glosson's initial review of the Instant Thunder plan and the start of the war, this story has been adequately told elsewhere.[10] By early September, Glosson had what he felt was an executable plan and the forces with which to carry it out, although the following months saw significant additions to both the forces and targets. Whereas Instant Thunder had eighty-four targets, for example, the final prehostilities Desert Storm plan had more than 300; in August, General Horner had less than seventy-five aircraft capable of delivering laser-guided bombs, whereas by mid-January this figure had nearly tripled. The final plan had five major objectives and twelve specific target sets, as follows:[11]

1. Isolate and incapacitate the Iraqi regime

    —Leadership and command centers
    —Electricity
    —Telecommunications and command, control, and communications (C3)

2. Gain and maintain air supremacy

    —Strategic integrated air defense system (IADS)
    —Iraqi Air Forces and selected airfields

3. Destroy capacity for NBC warfare

    —Known NBC research, development, production, and storage

4. Eliminate Iraq's offensive military capability

    —Military production and storage
    —Scud missiles, launchers, production, and storage
    —Oil refining and distribution (not production)
    —Naval ports and facilities

5. Cause the collapse of the Iraqi Army in Kuwait

    —Rail lines, bridges, roads, and lines of communications
    —Republican Guard

Strategic Air Operations

It is easy to assume from the phrase "air campaign plan" that the air war unfolded in accordance with a single detailed plan, but such was not the case. Instead, extremely detailed plans existed only for the first two days of operations (the third had been roughed out but was still fragmentary), along with a general concept for how later operations against any given set of targets would evolve and a planning framework that placed air operations within four distinct phases: a strategic air campaign of approximately a week; an intense two-day effort to suppress enemy air defenses in the KTO; a week-long effort against the Republican Guard; and a longer effort against other Iraqi forces in the KTO. In the initial Instant Thunder concept, these phases were sequential, but the final Desert Storm plan telescoped them so that they were executed simultaneously.[12]

This was due both to the overwhelming amount of airpower available to air planners and the subtle redirection of emphasis by theater (as opposed to air) planners from the air campaign as the primary effort against Iraq to a necessary prelude to a ground offensive against Iraqi forces. The actual Desert Storm campaign plan in fact combined the air planners' third and fourth phases into a "Battlefield Preparation" phase and made a ground campaign the fourth and final planned phase of operations. The maturation of the air campaign plan during the months preceding the war was accomplished by Glosson's "Black Hole" planners, who for most of the period worked in isolation from the rest of the CENTAF staff. Although this was necessary to ensure tight security over the offensive planning effort, it had the unfortunate effect of creating "we and they" attitudes that split the staff, led to hard feelings, and in some ways hampered the efficient flow of intelligence and targeting data. The fact remains, however, that Glosson's planners did a superb job of transforming a brilliant concept into a devastating plan. How it unfolded, and what it accomplished, are the next two parts of the story.

EXECUTION

The air attack that the Coalition unleashed the night of January 17 (times and dates reflect those in theater; it was still January 16 in the United States) was unprecedented for its tactical sophistication and strategic vision. There is neither space nor need to describe here in detail the first night's attacks nor to tabulate in detail the war in the air: This has been done elsewhere. Instead, it may be useful to provide a statistical overview of the strategic aspects of the air campaign. The daily conduct of the air war was governed by the lengthy and detailed Air Tasking Order (ATO), which provided the information on targets, routes, radio call signs, etc., all of which the aircrews needed to carry out their missions. Before the ATO was prepared, however, General Glosson's strategic air planners, led by Lieutenant Colonel Dave Deptula, prepared a Master Attack Plan (MAP) that listed the targets for that day's operations and matched assets (aircraft) against them. The MAP was the key planning tool of the war because it reflected the planners' strategic priorities and decisions on what targets needed to be struck to meet the military and political objectives. The targets in the MAP target list (referred to as the Master Target List, or MTL) reflected the following categories and was designed to meet the five wartime objectives[13]:

A	Airfields and associated facilities (i.e., aircraft shelters)
C	Chemical weapons (R&D, bunkers, etc.)
C3	Command, control, and communications
E	Electricity
L	Leadership
N	Nuclear (R&D, production, etc.)
O	Oil
RR	Railroads, bridges, and lines of communications
RG	Republican Guard
SAD	Strategic air defenses
SCUD	(Missiles, launchers, transporters, production facilities)
SAM	Surface-to-air missiles
MS	Military support (industries, depots, warehouses, etc.)

Planners had another category of sorts, a line for "Other" strikes, into which virtually all operations against Iraqi ground forces in Kuwait were lumped.

The Air Force's postwar Gulf War Air Power Survey (GWAPS) prepared a detailed compendium of statistics that included tabulations of daily strikes arranged by MTL categories and by the categorization used by intelligence officers.[14] The following discussion is based on the MTL tabulation, since it most closely reflected the thinking of the air planners. Using the argument that their highest priorities were to achieve air dominance quickly by paralyzing the Iraqi integrated air defense system (IADS) and then strike those targets that supported the Iraqi ability to threaten the region and exercise strategic direction of its society and forces, six target categories appear to have been the core of the strategic air campaign: strategic air defenses (SAD), nuclear and chemical facilities (N and C), and the electric, leadership, and command and control systems (E, L, and C3). This methodology indicates that the strategic air campaign reached its crescendo in the war's first twenty-four hours, when 32 percent of the 1,223 strikes carried out by Coalition aircraft struck targets in those six categories.[15] The need to negate quickly Iraq's strategic air defenses was apparent in the weight of effort directed against those targets, fully one-quarter of the total during the war (159 of 626). Over the course of the war's first five days,

Strategic Air Operations 117

25 percent of the strikes would hit those six categories. Since by war's end that had fallen to only 7 percent of the total strikes, it can be seen how much emphasis planners put on those categories early in the war; on only four other days would the percentage of strikes against those target categories rise to double figures.[16]

What does this apparently dry tale of statistics tell? For starters, it is apparent that the strategic aspect of the air war was, in strictly numerical terms, a relatively minor part of the war. More than 70 percent of the strikes carried out during the war (31,578 of the 41,309 tabulated against the MTL target categories) were against "Other" targets, which in most cases translates into Iraqi ground forces in Kuwait. Only two other categories received more than a thousand strikes: the combined Military/Support category, and Airfields, which was the focus of the "shelter busting" effort that destroyed a significant portion of the Iraqi Air Force in its hardened aircraft bunkers. The Military/Support category alone absorbed nearly twice as much effort as the three key target categories of Electricity, Leadership, and C3, which were the core of the effort to paralyze Iraq's strategic leadership. A third feature of the strategic air campaign, one that literally leaps out of the tabulation of strikes by aircraft, is the utterly disproportionate role played by one aircraft, the F-117 "stealth fighter." The world's premier "strategic" bomber, the B-52, carried out just 111 strikes against these six key target categories, only one-eighth the contribution of the F-117. The effort to destroy the most vital nodes of the Iraqi strategic leadership, the L and C3 categories, rode the back of the F-117, which carried out fully 45 percent of this effort. This performance helped to break the decades-old paradigm that had translated *strategic* into *nuclear* and relegated all other elements of offensive airpower into a battlefield role. It was a vindication of sorts for what Warden and others had been saying about the strategic potential of conventional airpower.[17]

One further element of the strategic air effort worth mentioning in this brief discussion is how quickly worldwide media and telecommunications systems can transform an incident into "An Incident." On the night of February 13, F-117s carried out thirty-two strikes against Iraqi leadership targets. One of those was the Al Firdos bunker, one of ten such facilities in Baghdad that planners believed had been activated to provide C3 to the Iraqi leadership. Unknown to Coalition planners, large numbers of Iraqi civilians had been using this bunker as an air raid shelter, and hundreds were killed when the bunker was destroyed. Iraqi authorities escorted newsmen through the ruins even while fires were being extinguished and bodies were being brought out, and Cable News Network (CNN) cameras beamed the grisly images to the world via satellite.[18]

Perhaps in other wars, with less immediacy of news coverage, this tragedy would have been recognized for what it was: an unfortunate but historically typical accident of war. The impact on planners, however, was immediate. In the two weeks preceding the attack, over two dozen targets had been struck in Baghdad; but in the two weeks following, the target list shrank to five. General Glosson had to brief General Schwarzkopf on all Baghdad targets planned for attack, and the media interest in the incident was "intense," as Schwarzkopf noted in his autobiography.[19] The combination of gripping real-time visual imagery on television, coupled with a public conditioned by film of bombs routinely going down ventilator shafts and striking exactly where aimed, time after time, had established airpower's omnipotence. The public had come to expect perfection in an activity—war—which can never be perfect. This perception—and the media and telecommunications capabilities that helped create it—has the potential to affect significantly the future use of U.S. military force.

ASSESSMENT

As soon as the cease-fire went into effect, analysts and advocates began collecting data on the strategic air campaign and issuing verdicts on its effectiveness or lack thereof. At first these efforts were supported by rather skimpy bracing, because the data were both scattered and being collected. The first attempt to take an analytical and somewhat detached view of the strategic air campaign was the Department of Defenses's own official study, the *Conduct of the Persian Gulf War,* often known as the Title V report. Despite being produced by a joint team of officers from all the Services that was inevitably subject to some Service position marking and parochialism,[20] the Title V report was remarkably objective. It briefly outlined the air operations during each week of the war and discussed some of the major events and themes. It then examined strategic air operations by assessing the major goals and accomplishments in each of the target categories cited earlier.

At about the same time that the Title V effort was starting, the USAF was beginning its own assessment of airpower in the Gulf War. Secretary of the Air Force Donald Rice commissioned the aforementioned independent GWAPS, patterned after the World War II–era United States Strategic Bombing Survey (USSBS—known among airpower historians as the "us bus"). GWAPS was headed by Eliot Cohen, a civilian academic with no ties to the USAF, and his staff included about a dozen USAF officers and about fifty civilians, many of whom had previous military experience.[21] Although its charter was to examine all elements of airpower in the Gulf War, support as well as combat, a key focus was the strategic air campaign.

Title V opened its discussion of the strategic air campaign's results by observing that although no two conflicts are exactly alike, the opportunities for strategic air operations present in this conflict would likely be present in future ones, for "all modern industrial and military powers share certain universal vulnerabilities . . . [such as] computer dependent C3 systems; net-

Strategic Air Operations

worked air defense systems ... and easily located sources of energy." It then noted that the quick attainment of the initial air objective, seizing control of the air, enabled the air planners to bring the full weight of the available airpower to bear continuously against the full range of targets throughout Iraq and the KTO.[22]

GWAPS opened its discussion of "What Did the Air Campaign Accomplish?" by weighing the effects and effectiveness of air operations against the objectives established by the Coalition. It noted that any attempt to evaluate the effectiveness of air operations had to take into account not only direct effects, such as destroying hardened aircraft shelters, but also indirect effects, like forcing the Iraqis to disperse their aircraft, and even more distant second-order consequences, such as the political and legal implications of the Iraqis parking their aircraft next to historical and cultural sites.[23]

The Title V report opened its examination of strategic attacks against the twelve key target categories by discussing what some considered to be the three systems most vital to the leadership center of gravity: the leadership, electric, and telecommunications/C3 categories. Title V noted that the attacks against those targets had forced Iraq's senior leadership to operate on the move and caused them to use less secure, and more easily intercepted and exploited, communications systems. Saddam Hussein's ability to exercise rigid and rapid command of his forces "deteriorated rapidly." Approximately 60 percent of military landline communications, for example, passed through the civil telephone system, which was severely degraded when F-117s destroyed key telecommunications sites in Baghdad early in the war. Attacks against Hussein's secure communications links to his fielded forces significantly reduced these systems, although their repairability and redundancy meant that air planners frequently had to reattack some of these facilities.[24]

GWAPS also examined these target categories, although it included electricity with oil in what seemed to be a discussion of energy-related targets. Attacks against leadership and C3 employed primarily precision-guided munitions (PGMs) because many of these attacks were carried out by the F-117s and the targets were located in the heavily urbanized areas. Planners had hoped these strikes would disrupt the Hussein regime and degrade its strategic connectivity to a sufficient degree that Saddam Hussein would be unable to control Iraq and his forces. GWAPS noted that these ambitious goals had not been reached: At the war's end, Saddam Hussein was still firmly in control of his regime, and the Iraqi forces in the KTO, although overwhelmed by the Coalition ground offensive, still possessed sufficient C3 to issue a withdrawal order and attempt to redeploy some of the most valuable Republican Guard units. Nonetheless, GWAPS noted, the Iraqis must have suffered "some, if not *considerable* [italics in original], disruption and dislocation." The difficulty was with the evidence, or rather the paucity of it: Not enough conclusive evidence was available to say with any certainty whether the effort failed or came within inches of succeeding.[25]

The attacks on the Iraqi electric network were at once one of the most notably successful and hotly debated elements of the air campaign. The Iraqi electric grid rapidly went down, in part because of direct destruction of key nodes and in part because of the cascading effects of system failure. Additionally, some plants were voluntarily shut down by the Iraqis themselves, to prevent their destruction. At issue is not how quickly the Iraqi electric grid failed (eleven plants were hit in the first two days), but what effect this had on Iraq's key centers of gravity and the conditions that came afterward, for the loss of electric power also meant the loss of the modern elements of the Iraqi water and sanitation systems. Although virtually everyone agrees that cutting the power to an air defense headquarters or weapons production facility is clearly a useful and legal objective, many of these same facilities had backup power systems, and there is no way to determine which or how many of these facilities failed to function because of the interruption of or loss of electric power. Although these targets were valid and appropriate under the existing laws of war, many have questioned whether the Iraqi civil populace paid too high a price for these attacks after the war in the form of reduced sanitation, outbreaks of disease, and increased infant mortality.[26]

In the absence of more complete data from Iraqi sources, however (which may well not be forthcoming for years, if ever), it remains impossible to assess confidently the direct results of these attacks. Some view this as proof that the attacks on Iraqi electricity were a strategic failure, and others take the position that common sense dictates that any nation that loses 85 percent of its electric supply must be in serious long-term trouble. The question cannot currently be solved by empirical means but is an active subject of study.[27]

Two important targeting categories that suffered less heavily than planners had hoped were the Iraqi nuclear, biological, and chemical (NBC) target sets, and Iraq's Scud missile production and launch capability. Iraq's known nuclear research facilities were targeted and, in most cases, heavily damaged, but postwar investigations by UN teams sent into Iraq found that the Iraqi nuclear program was much larger than had been suspected during the war.[28]

Whereas the target list in mid-January contained only three targets related to nuclear research and production, the postwar UN inspectors saw more than twenty sites related to Iraq's nuclear effort. The Iraqis also used the five months leading up to the war to good advantage, dispersing much of the equipment outside of facilities likely to be targeted. Attacks against Iraq's chemical warfare (CW) production capabilities fared better, although it again became evident after the war that our prewar knowledge of the size and scope of the Iraqi programs was greatly understated. Title V assessed that 75 percent of the Iraqi CW production capability had been destroyed. A tougher task, however, was destroying those agents that had already been produced and were in storage. Despite a significant effort against these facilities, GWAPS noted that postwar UN inspectors discovered some 150,000 chemical munitions. Attacks against facilities related to Iraq's biological warfare (BW) efforts were more successful, with all known BW research and production facilities destroyed.[29]

If any one target set proved to be frustrating, it was the Iraqi Scud missile program. The targeting plan was threefold: Strike the fixed launch sites, to prevent their immediate use; strike the long-term research and production facilities, to negate any future Iraqi threat; and suppress the Iraqis' mobile launchers, which could take missiles out into the desert and fire them at Israel and the Gulf states to the south. The campaign to destroy the Scud production effort was inconclusive, and the Title V Report noted that the UN inspectors determined that the Iraqis had removed key equipment and components before the war started.[30]

GWAPS went even further and stated that no evidence was available that proved that the entire counter-Scud effort had killed even one mobile launcher. The Iraqi Scud reaffirmed Clausewitz's maxim about war being an enterprise between two thinking and reacting opponents, for the Iraqis used mobility, concealment, and camouflage to continue Scud operations throughout the war.[31] This is not to say, however, that the anti-Scud campaign did not bear some fruit. Launch rates for Scuds declined sharply after the first week of the war (4.7 per day during the first week), and they declined again after the second week. Although the last two weeks saw the rates climb again, the overall rates for weeks 2 through 6 still totalled only 1.5 per day. Additionally, the Iraqi practice of salvoing multiple missiles in mass launches, a tactic much in evidence during the Iran–Iraq War of 1980–1988, was apparently affected by the counter-Scud effort, for the time span between Scud launches increased until the fifth week of the war.[32]

As these excerpts from the Title V report and GWAPS show, both were evenhanded and analytical examinations of airpower in the Gulf War. What neither they nor other studies of the war have done, however, is to move beyond the relatively narrow perspective of individual target categories to attempt a broader, overall view of strategic airpower in the Gulf War. In this sense, they were typical of much American thought concerning strategic airpower in that they were essentially reductionist in nature, using successively more powerful lenses to view elements of the enemy nation and system in greater detail but losing in the process a more holistic, all-encompassing view of the state. One analyst of the war, William Arkin of the Greenpeace organization, stated that "the air war was clean on a strategic level, but irrelevant to the defeat of the Iraqi army,"[33] a view that has been echoed by other observers without considering whether the war had other military and political objectives, which it plainly did. An equally important objective was to reduce Iraq's long-term threat to its neighbors and to the entire region. The Iraqi Army occupying Kuwait at the outset of hostilities in January 1991 was primarily an understrength conscript force that posed no significant threat to anyone except the unfortunate citizens of Kuwait. To weaken sufficiently Iraq's potential threat required attacks on several elements of Iraqi power. Its strategic offensive military forces had to be reduced; its program to acquire weapons of mass destruction had to be halted; and its internal stability needed to be shaken.

The strategic air campaign was the only way to strike directly at all three of these factors. The Iraqi Air Force was essentially destroyed, which not only negated it as a threat but also left Iraq open to attack from other quarters. The Scud force, while not destroyed immediately during the course of the war, was destroyed after the war during the UN inspections that were conducted while Iraq was prostrate and under the constant threat of renewed air attack. The Republican Guard was not destroyed as hoped, and although it had been hurt (both by the air campaign and the ground offensive that brilliantly exploited the results of air attacks on the Iraqi ground forces), it remained the most potent combat force Saddam Hussein had left.[34] The Iraqi NBC program was derailed, partly during the air campaign (as described earlier) and more completely as a result of the UN inspections. It is worth remembering that these inspections took place long after the victorious American ground forces had left Saudi Arabia; if Saddam Hussein proved too intransigent and intractable for the UN to tolerate, it was not another ground campaign that would punish him but rather a renewal of the strategic air attacks against which he had no defense. Although this was an unforeseen and somewhat fortuitous result, it was important nonetheless and points out the potential for airpower to control a political situation on the ground merely through an implied threat.

Finally, and perhaps most important, what were the overall conditions in Iraq and what were the problems facing Saddam Hussein after the war? This discussion is related to a broader question: What is the primary objective for strategic air attack? Is it to generate results that are directly traceable to the battlefield, or is it something of less immediate but longer-lasting significance? Science offers us the term *entropy*, meaning the degree of disorder in a system, which may serve as a useful analogy for airpower. The modern state is a complex "system of systems" whose complexity offers vulnerabilities, strengths, and opportunities for strategic airpower to introduce entropy into its functioning. Analysis that looks only at the parts of the system without considering its overall state of function runs the danger of describing the forest by discussing the individual trees. It is obvious from what happened immediately after the end of the Gulf War that the Iraqi "system" was in shaky condition: Two of the country's three major ethnic groups, the Kurds in the north and the Shias in the south, were in open revolt; Iraqi citizens were openly critical of the regime to the world's media on the streets of Baghdad; the infrastructure of daily life (communications, water, electricity, etc.) were in shambles; and programs that Iraq had poured its national treasure and hopes into (especially its nuclear program) were either in pieces or unusable.[35]

What brought Iraq to this condition? It certainly was not the defeat of the Iraqi Army in Kuwait. Iraq's losses during the grinding eight-year war with Iran were far worse, and because of Saddam Hussein's control of the internal Iraqi media, the average Iraqi knew little of events in Kuwait. What they did see, especially from the perspective of the larger cities, was the constant evidence of Coalition omnipotence in the air and the inability of Saddam Hussein to prevent the daily passage of Coalition airpower through Iraqi skies.

It is impossible to point to the results obtained in any single targeting category as being responsible for the increasing dislocation of the Iraqi system, and equally impossible to ascribe all of the dislocation in the Iraqi system to the impact of strategic air operations. The embargo certainly played a part, as did the Iraqi defeat on the battlefield. But the central factor in the weakening of the Iraqi regime was the cumulative impact of the entropy generated in the Iraqi society and regime by the strategic air campaign. In six weeks, the rather modest effort devoted to attacking Iraq's strategic core eliminated key nodes in the infrastructure that supported Iraq's position as a major regional power (with larger aspirations), generated conditions of open revolt that could (with modest Coalition help) have fragmented Iraq and toppled the regime, and forced that regime, after it survived these threats, to acquiesce in humiliating inspections by UN inspectors. The message for the future is that any modern military-industrial state has precisely the same systemic vulnerabilities that Iraq possessed: vulnerable energy supplies, vulnerable C3 nodes and networks, leadership vulnerable to disruption and dislocation, and a nation open to American airpower. Strategic airpower is a fact, and it worked in the Gulf War.

NOTES

1. Called such because it did not involve the actual operations of forces or equipment. It was in the nature of a wargame that forced planners to develop plans and options in response to a hypothetical scenario.

2. Thomas A. Keaney and Eliot A. Cohen, *Gulf War Air Power Survey Summary Report* (Washington, D.C.: USGPO, 1993), 29–31 [hereafter *GWAPS Summary Report*]. The eleven volumes of the GWAPS study, ten of which are available in unclassified versions, are without question the most thorough, balanced, and exhaustive source of information on airpower in the Gulf War. The GWAPS effort, of which this author was a member, favorably compares with the legendary United States Strategic Bombing Survey, although the two efforts were not identical and

had different objectives. For the best account of the USSBS effort, see David MacIsaac, *Strategic Bombing in World War II: The Story of the United States Strategic Bombing Survey* (New York: Garland, 1976).

3. ECL, "From Obscurity to Omnipotence: Theory Influences the Air War," *Army,* March 1991, 16; Richard P. Hallion, *Storm over Iraq: Air Power and the Gulf War* (Washington, D.C.: Smithsonian Institution Press, 1992), 116–117 [hereafter *Storm over Iraq*]. Hallion's book, although perhaps a bit too uncritical of airpower's performance in the war, does probably the best job of any one book of explaining the technological basis for airpower's dominant role in the war. For more on Warden's theories on airpower, see his book *The Air Campaign: Planning for Combat* (Washington, D.C.: NDU Press, 1988), and his article "Employing Air Power in the Twenty-first Century," in Richard H. Schultz, Jr., and Robert L. Pfaltzgraff, Jr., eds., *The Future of Air Power in the Aftermath of the Gulf War* (Maxwell AFB, Ala.: Air University Press, 1992), 57–87.

4. James A. Winnefeld, Preston Niblack, and Dana J. Johnson, *A League of Airmen: U.S. Air Power in the Gulf War* (Santa Monica: RAND, 1994), 56 [hereafter *A League of Airmen*]. This is a well-balanced, one-volume account of airpower in the war; many of its major conclusions track closely with GWAPS.

5. *Conduct of the Persian Gulf War* (Washington, D.C.: USGPO, 1993), 91–92 [hereafter called *Title V*]; Keaney and Cohen, *GWAPS Summary Report,* 36. *Title V* was in many ways a remarkable effort, and one that is surprisingly balanced and objective given its nature as an "official" history. The team that produced it, of which this author was a member, overcame most (but not all) of the prejudices and parochialism which inhabit the Pentagon and the Service staffs that reside therein.

6. Hallion, *Storm over Iraq,* 115–18.

7. Keaney and Cohen, *GWAPS Summary Report,* 37; Rick Atkinson, *Crusade: The Untold Story of the Persian Gulf War* (New York: Houghton Mifflin, 1993), 60–63 [hereafter *Crusade*]. Atkinson's book is a fascinating account of the war, virtually impossible to put down; and its account of airpower, at least those incidents of which this author has personal knowledge, ring true.

8. By far the most influential of these was Lieutenant Colonel Dave Deptula, who became General Glosson's chief strategic planner in the Special Planning Group, better known as the "Black Hole." Deptula not only had Glosson's and Horner's confidence, but he was in constant contact with Warden and the "Checkmate" planners in the Pentagon. In a real sense, Deptula was the key link between "Checkmate" and the "Black Hole" before and during the war and thus played the indispensable role in keeping the plan true to its strategic conceptual origins.

9. Winnefeld et al., *League of Airmen,* 68.

10. See, for example, virtually any of the sources already cited: *Title V,* Hallion, *Storm over Iraq;* Atkinson, *Crusade;* Winnefield et al., *League of Airmen;* and Keaney and Cohen, *GWAPS Summary Report,* especially its separate volume on planning the air campaign.

11. *Title V,* 95.

12. Keaney and Cohen, *GWAPS Summary Report,* 50.

13. *GWAPS Statistical Compendium,* "Introduction to Table 185, Strike Counts by Master Target List Categories," 516.

14. It is important here to delineate what is meant by *strike.* A strike is defined

Strategic Air Operations 125

as the delivery of a weapon or weapons by one aircraft against a specific, individual target. A strike is not a sortie, which has always meant the flight of an aircraft from takeoff to landing, but which does not mean the delivery of weapons against a target. F-15Cs on a fighter sweep, for example, flew sorties but not strikes. Since the intent of the statistical tables on which this section of the narrative is based was to portray accurately the use of airpower against ground targets, and since the employment of precision-guided munitions (PGMs) quantitatively and qualitatively caused a significant change in the nature of aerial warfare, GWAPS used the strike as a statistically useful gauge. Thus, one F-16 dropping its (unguided) bombs on an artillery position totals one strike; one F-117 dropping its two PGMs on a bridge and a headquarters bunker tallies two strikes; and an F-111F dropping its four PGMs on a bridge, aircraft bunker, oil pumping station, and communications site would be credited with four strikes.

15. *GWAPS Statistical Compendium,* Table 186, "Daily Strikes by Master Target List Categories," 518–19.

16. Ibid., Table 186, "Daily Strikes by MTL Categories."

17. Ibid., Table 185, "Strikes by MTL Categories." Obviously, there are virtually endless ways to sort and analyze these data. That, in fact, was one of GWAPS' express objectives: to create as complete and exhaustive a database as possible for the use of future analysts and researchers.

18. Atkinson, *Crusade,* 275–77, 285–88. After the war William Arkin, a member of the Greenpeace organization, visited the Al Firdos and other similar bunkers and noted (and photographed) areas that were identified in English and Arabic as "EMP Hardened," which means that whatever equipment or facilities were behind those doors had been hardened to withstand the electromagnetic pulse (EMP) effects that normally result from nuclear detonations. Arkin did not offer any explanations for why a civilian air raid shelter needed to be EMP hardened, but he noted accurately that a communications switching site or command and control node would benefit from such hardening. Data contained in a briefing presented to GWAPS, October 31, 1991.

19. Title V, 615–16; Keaney and Cohen, *GWAPS Summary Report,* 68–69; Atkinson, *Crusade,* 290–96; H. Norman Schwarzkopf, with Peter Petre, *It Doesn't Take a Hero* (New York: Bantam, 1992), 435.

20. For example, intense debate among team members occurred over the use of the term *air campaign,* with some non-USAF members of the team seeing this as an attempt by the Air Force to stress the independent aspects of airpower in the war, and Air Force members pointing out that the term only reflected common usage during the war, by news commentators and senior military political figures alike. The term stayed, but not until negotiations at the general officer level were settled.

21. Keaney and Cohen, *GWAPS Summary Report,* ix.

22. Title V, 148.

23. Keaney and Cohen, *GWAPS Summary Report,* 55–56; Title V, 98.

24. Title V, 150–52.

25. Keaney and Cohen, *GWAPS Summary Report,* 69–71.

26. See the Middle East Watch's report, *Needless Deaths in the Gulf War* (Washington, D.C.: Middle East Watch, 1991) or the report of a health team from Harvard, Harvard Study Team: *Harvard Study Team Report: Public Health in Iraq*

After the Gulf War, published in May 1991. This view ignores the fact that it was the UN-mandated embargo that prevented, and still prevents, the rapid shipment to Iraq of replacement gear for damaged electric facilities and, especially, the wilfull intransigence of the Iraqi regime and its own decisions on the allocation of resources inside Iraq that have prolonged the UN-imposed embargo.

27. A 1993 graduate of Air University's School of Advanced Airpower Studies, Major Tom Griffith, authored a study ("Attacking Electrical Power") that assessed such attacks as having little utility. My view (contained in a pending piece for the *Journal of Strategic Studies,* "Airpower vs. Electricity: Electric Power as a Target for Strategic Air Operations") takes a more positive view. RAND has done a study of electric targeting, and a group of students in the 1994 class at Air University's Air Command and Staff College (where Colonel John Warden serves as Commandant) studied the issue and wrote their conclusions in a group student thesis.

28. *Title V,* 154.

29. *Title V,* 154–55; Keaney and Cohen, *GWAPS Summary Report,* 78–82.

30. *Title V,* 156.

31. It was ironic that planners focused on the Scud's "military insignificance" and neglected the political impact that was almost certain to result from the use of Scuds against Israel. Although planners had foreseen how technically and tactically difficult it would be to track and attack mobile Scud launchers, it does not appear that any significant planning had been done before the war concerning this possibility. When the war came and the Coalition was faced with a crisis in Israel, planners had to cobble together an anti-Scud effort that did, in the event, experience great difficulty locating and tracking Scuds.

32. Keaney and Cohen, *GWAPS Summary Report,* 83–90.

33. Winnefeld et al., *League of Airmen,* 279; pages 276–80 contain an interesting compilation of published views on the air campaign, ranging the entire spectrum from "it won the war" to "it was ineffective."

34. At the war's end, the Republican Guard had suffered approximately 50 percent losses in its key equipment, tanks, artillery, and other armored fighting vehicles, which could be replaced from other stocks in Iraq. See Keaney and Cohen, *GWAPS Summary Report,* 105–7.

35. Many of the reports documenting these conditions came from journalists who visited Iraq after the war. For some of the reports, see Milton Viorst, "Report from Baghdad," *New Yorker,* June 24, 1991, 55–73; Michael Massing, "Can Saddam Survive?" *New York Review of Books,* August 15, 1991, 59–68; Caryle Murphy, "Intermission in Iraq: Fear, Loathing, and $48 Beer . . . ," *Washington Post,* September 8, 1991, C3, and, in the same issue by Yasmine Bahrani, " . . . and Sorrow in the Mail"; and Ray Wilkinson, "Nothing Left to Lose," *Newsweek,* July 22, 1991, 29.

6

Parallel Warfare: What Is It? Where Did It Come From? Why Is It Important?
David A. Deptula

In the early morning hours of January 17, 1991, Major Greg Biscone was leading the first of two B-52s against Wadi Al Kirr airfield—a recently completed forward operating fighter base in central Iraq. His targets were the taxiways between the runway and the base's hardened aircraft shelters. The crewmembers never thought they would go on this mission. They thought Saddam would pull out before it came to war. The co-pilot felt they were all going to die if they did go—a senior general on a visit to their base told them a third of their crews might never return. However, the initial apprehension of entering combat disappeared after they started engines, and they were more concerned with getting the mission off on time, and bombs on target, than they were with anything else. "Don't screw up," Biscone recalls thinking as he and his crew with the callsign of "Ghost" took off from Diego Garcia, over 2,000 miles from their target.

Skimming over the desert at nearly 500 miles per hour at 300 feet, they approached their target. It was a moonless night and blacker than the inside of a tar pit. There was so little light that the night vision goggles did not work, nor did the low-light TV system—by definition it needed some light, and there was none. The ingress was uneventful until Iraqi early warning radars lit up their electronic warning receiver. In the face of the black, moonless night and rocky desert with no horizon, prudence warned against going any lower. In the face of potential antiaircraft artillery (AAA) fire and a serious surface-to-air missiles (SAMs) threat, however, prudence lost.

They descended to 200 feet, counting on the radar altimeter and terrain avoidance systems to keep them from hitting the ground.

The lumbering bomber, flying almost within a wingspan of the ground, made it to the target area, successfully avoiding both the threats and the ground. As they approached their bomb drop point, they climbed to the appropriate altitude for release. With light from the airfield helping their night vision devices, they could see people unloading trucks at the airfield. The crew could see the people turn to look up in their direction. The bomb bay doors made a loud noise as they opened, sounding as if they were "ripping the air." To Biscone it seemed like an eternity before the bomb release light came on in the cockpit, and he was afraid the sound of the doors opening would warn the antiaircraft artillery gunners of their presence before bomb release. It did, but the bombers' multiaxis attack beat them—by the time the guns began firing, the gunners could only fire at the receding noise of the egressing B-52s.[1]

Less than an hour earlier, stealthy F-117s had struck the heart of the enemy—Baghdad—in the opening minutes of the war. Tomahawk Land Attack (Cruise) Missiles (TLAMs) followed, striking critical electric systems and government centers. F-15Es, part of an initial covert entry scheme into Iraq, attacked known Scud launch facilities that were a threat to Israel. While Biscone and his flight were departing the target area in central Iraq, similar attacks to his were occurring at four other forward operating fighter bases spread across Iraq. At the same time, thirteen F-117s flew against twenty-two separate targets, including command leadership bunkers north of Baghdad, communications exchanges in Baghdad, interceptor operations centers in Kuwait, satellite downlink facilities, and other command and communications nodes around the country. Out west near H-3 airfield, a force package of thirty aircraft took away the Iraqis' ability to air deliver a chemical attack. On the opposite side of the country, just north of Basrah, thirty-eight fighters attacked Shaibah airfield. Meanwhile, forty-four aircraft stripped away the medium-altitude SAM defenses in the area west of Baghdad near Al Taqqadum airfield, the Haybannya oil storage area, and three chemical weapon precursor facilities to prepare for the following days' daylight attacks.

Before the crews of Ghost cell landed back at Diego Garcia, Republican Guard headquarters in the Basrah area, as well as regular Iraqi ground forces near the Saudi border, came under attack. All the suspected biological weapons storage facilities were targeted, and critical oil supply and storage facilities were hit. The northernmost reaches of Iraq came under attack as conventional air-launched cruise missiles (CALCMs) fired from B-52s flying from the United States hit electric facilities at Al Mawsil. Before the end of the first twenty-four–hour period of the war, bombs hit enemy bridges, military support and production factories, and naval facilities as well. The pair of thirty-year-old bombers led by Major Biscone were only two of over 1,300 "offensive" sorties flown in the first twenty-four–hour period of the Gulf War.[2] It was not the quantity of sorties flown, however, that led to the success of this first night of air attacks (which were a precursor to the entire Gulf War air campaign), it was how they were used.

PARALLEL WARFARE: WHAT IS IT?

The first night of the Gulf War air campaign was the opening act of a drama of immense significance in the evolution of warfare. Prudence dictates that promise of change and revolution in the conduct of war should be viewed with a healthy dose of skepticism. However, the air campaign in the Gulf was more than a promise, it was a reality. One hundred fifty-two discrete targets made up the master attack plan for the opening twenty-four–hour period of the Gulf air war.[3] This number excludes regular Iraqi Army forces and surface-to-air missile sites, which were also targets over that period. The Gulf War began with more targets in one *day's* attack plan than the total number of targets hit by the entire Eighth Air Force during the years 1942 and 1943 combined.[4] A review of summary reports from World War I, World War II, the Korean War, the Vietnam War, and the Arab–Israeli wars of 1967 and 1973 indicates that the first day of the Gulf War saw the largest number of air attacks on separate targets in the shortest period of time in the history of warfare.

What allowed planning against such a large number of targets in so short a time? What was different about the concept of the air campaign in the Gulf War from previous air campaigns? What does this mean for the sizing, shaping, and use of military forces in the future? This chapter explores these key questions to understand better the transformation of warfare seen in the Gulf War and how those changes anticipate future warfare. Our nation and our military leaders can only gain from exploring the potential these changes present and developing a military ready and able to meet the challenges of the future.

The Gulf War Coalition accomplished its stated military objectives quickly and with relatively few losses of life on both sides. In that regard, the Gulf War put a mark on the wall—an indelible mark—in terms of casualty tolerance, a fact confirmed when the unfortunate deaths of eighteen American soldiers led to the termination of U.S. operations in Somalia in 1993. Little tolerance for casualties has been a consistent factor in the early 1990s debate over how the United States should address conflict in the Balkans; it will continue to have a significant—perhaps even decisive—impact on the future use of force. The quick conduct of the Gulf War, achieving unprecedented military effectiveness with relatively few casualties, is clearly an important lesson for future success.

In short form, the lesson is a strategy that emphasized our strengths and avoided Saddam's. More specifically, we capitalized on a new construct of warfare to paralyze Saddam's control of his forces, and then we went on to neutralize the enemy's capacity to fight, undermine its will to fight, reduce its military production base, and create the conditions to control its capacity to construct weapons of mass destruction. This construct of warfare allowed us to avoid dashing headlong on the ground into Iraq's vast defensive armies, which would have given Saddam the potential to cause high numbers of Coalition casualties.

The construct of warfare employed during the Gulf War air campaign has become known as *parallel warfare*.[5] The term comes from basic electrical circuit design. Anyone experiencing the frustration of Christmas lights on a series circuit versus a parallel circuit will recognize the analogy. In the series circuit depicted at the top of Figure 6.1, when the switch closes, electrons flow from the battery to light the five light bulbs illustrated. However, electricity must pass through each light before the next is lit in a sequential flow. In the parallel circuit at the bottom of Figure 6.1, when the switch closes, electricity reaches all the lights virtually at the same time, exhibiting simultaneous flow. Applying the same concept to the application of force in war yields the terms *serial* (sequential) and *parallel* (simultaneous) warfare (see Figure 6.2)—a simplistic analogy perhaps, but accurate.

In air campaigns before the Gulf War, force was primarily applied in a sequential fashion to "roll back" enemy defenses before attacking targets of the highest value. Area and point defenses had to be eliminated *before* war planners could get to what they really wanted to attack. The upper portion of Figure 6.2, "Series Warfare—Sequential Attack," depicts a generic example. First, the early warning sites are put out of action to mask ingress of friendly strike packages. Next, operations centers controlling enemy defensive fighters, antiaircraft artillery, and surface-to-air missile systems are targeted to force defensive systems into autonomous operation, which destroys the integrated enemy defense systems. Enemy defensive force elements are targeted, and finally the target of value, in this case leadership, can be hit. The huge effort required to suppress enemy air defenses and the time required to accomplish these tasks in sequence limit the feasibility of attacking several high-value targets simultaneously.

Targets of highest value are generally those most protected by an adversary. It makes perfect sense to reduce enemy defenses before attacking these high-value targets, for two principal reasons. First, reducing enemy defenses increases the probability of reaching the target with sufficient force to attack it successfully. Second, reducing enemy defenses makes it easier to attack key targets without sustaining prohibitive losses. The Eighth Air Force's mission to Schweinfurt, Germany, on October 14, 1943—sustaining 20 percent bomber losses—is a familiar and dramatic example of what happens when enemy defenses are fully functional and effective. High losses encountered in attempting to strike German targets before suppressing

Figure 6.1
Basic Electric Circuits

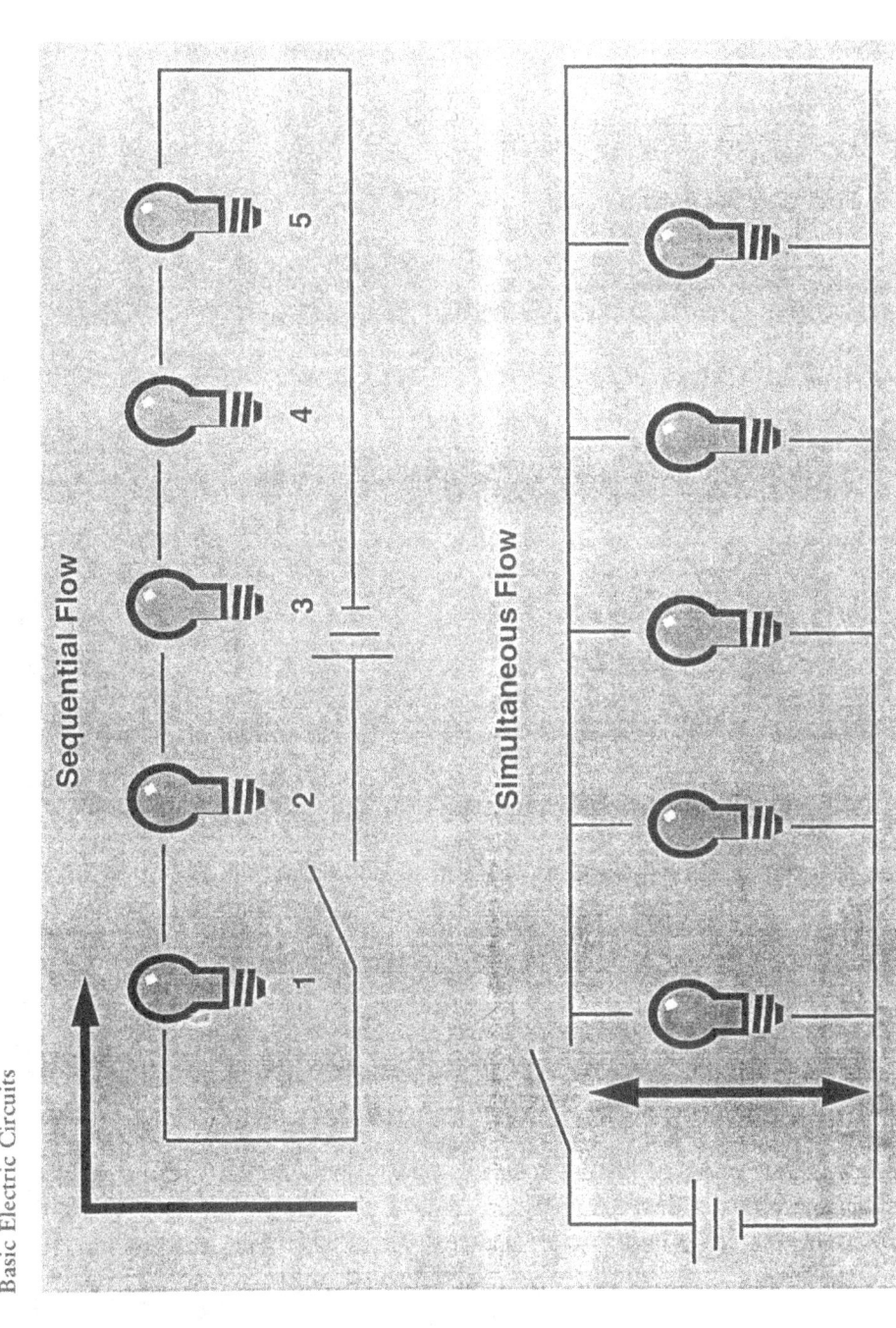

Figure 6.2
Series versus Parallel Warfare

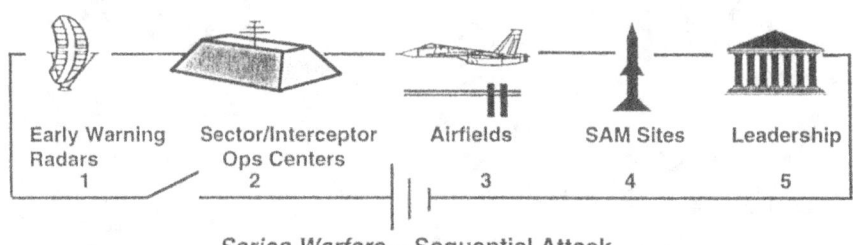

Series Warfare —Sequential Attack

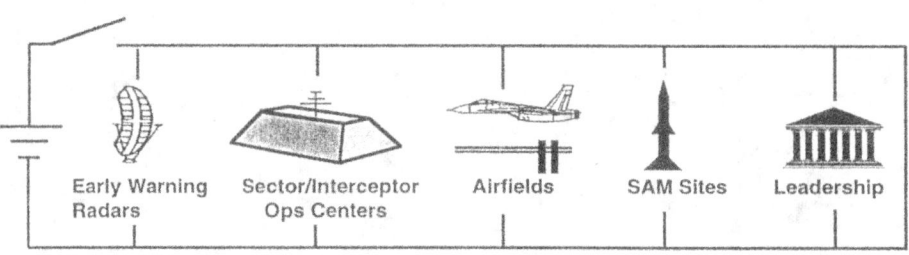

Parallel Warfare—Simultaneous Attack (Weighted Against Air Defense)

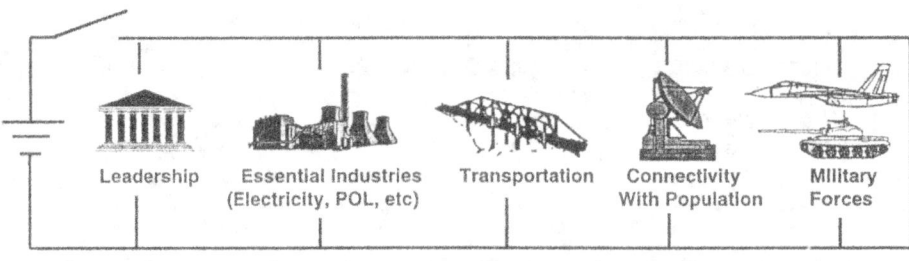

Parallel Warfare—Simultaneous Attack Against All Vital Enemy Systems

Luftwaffe fighter defenses made it imperative for the Allies to undertake a concerted effort to achieve control of the air. This was a necessary step to reduce friendly losses and a requirement before daylight "precision" bombing began to achieve substantial impact against the German war machine.

The middle section of Figure 6.2 depicts simultaneous attack against the same set of targets, as in the previous case. Possessing the ability to hit all the elements of an air defense system simultaneously is desirable in terms of facilitating attacks on high-value targets, but this situation still leads to a somewhat sequential application of force. The majority of targets are defenses en route to, and in the area of, the target of value. This kind of simultaneous attack can be accomplished with large force packages of non-stealthy aircraft in discrete areas of a theater or on a one-time raid against a limited target set. However, the large force packages to suppress enemy air defenses tend to limit the total number of areas struck in this manner. To hit an entire theater set of high-value targets requires many attacks in a similar fashion.

A capacity for simultaneous attack on the entire array of high-value targets with little or no need to suppress enemy air defenses opens the door to monumental changes in the conduct of war—enables surprise at the tactical level, a larger span of influence, fewer casualties, paralyzing effects, and shorter time to impose effective control over the enemy. The lower portion of Figure 6.2 depicts simultaneous attack against a wider array of high-value targets than in the previous case. Leadership facilities, key essentials such as refined oil and electricity, transportation nets, connectivity between the leadership and the population, and fielded military forces all come under attack at the same time.[6] The capacity to have a controlling effect on the enemy's ability to act as it desires is clearly much higher in this case than in the previous examples.

More high-value target coverage in a short time is not the only benefit of parallel attack. When combined with a strategy to render adversaries ineffective in controlling their state or organization, essential industries, transportation infrastructure, population, or forces, the ramifications of parallel attack extend well beyond the arithmetic advantage of hitting more high-value targets in a shorter time.

The successful prosecution of parallel war requires much more than compressing the timing of sequential attacks into one simultaneous attack. Parallel war requires exploiting three dimensions: time, space, and levels of war. In the opening hours of the Gulf War, all three dimensions were capitalized on. In terms of time, within the opening hour and a half, over fifty separate targets were on the master attack plan. Within the first twenty-four hours, over 150 separate targets were designated for attack.[7] In terms of space, the entire breadth and depth of Iraq was subject to attack. No system deemed critical escaped targeting because of distance from the origin of a strike. In terms of levels of war, Saddam's national leadership facilities (strategic level), Iraqi air defense and Army operation centers (operational level), and Iraqi-deployed fighting units—air, land, and sea—(tactical level) all came under attack simultaneously.

Simultaneous application of force (time) across each level of war without inhibition of geographical location (space) describes the physical conduct of parallel warfare. However, the crucial principle defining parallel warfare is how time and space are exploited in strategic terms of how force is applied and for what purpose or policy at each level of war.

For hundreds of years, the only way to get to an enemy's center(s) of gravity was through destruction of the enemy's defending forces. One legacy of centuries of surface warfare is the common view that the intrinsic purpose of military force is the destruction of an enemy's military force. Adding to the weight of this legacy is the almost religious military following of Clausewitz's monumental work, *On War*. Unsurpassed in its contribution to the theory of war, *On War* is susceptible to misinterpretation for a variety of reasons—among others, its philosophical mode of expression and the fact that is was unfinished (a draft) when its author passed away. Regardless, many who read *On War* are prone to misinterpret it as reducing warfare to the physical destruction of opposing forces in "decisive" battles.[8]

Ultimately, the purpose of war is to compel an adversary to do what you want it to do. Use of force to *control* rather than *destroy* an enemy's ability to act lends a different perspective to what might be the most effective use of force. Terms that describe how application of force against elements of a system can achieve control include *render ineffective, negate, disable, prevent, neutralize, limit, reduce, stop,* and so forth. Force used to control a system rather than destroy it may lead to the same operationally relevant result as destruction, but with much less use of force. Control allows the use of conserved force not used for destruction to expand the number of additional systems exposed to control through force application. For example, shutting down the power grid that provides electricity to the air defense system around Baghdad requires much less force to *negate* the air defense system than destroying each element of that air defense system. At some point, effective control of enough of the adversary's enabling operational-level systems will paralyze the enemy's ability to function at the strategic level. At that stage, the enemy has no choice but to acquiesce to the will of the controlling force.

The object of parallel war is to achieve effective control over the set of systems relied on by an adversary for power and influence—leadership, population of the adversary state or organization, essential industries to survive and exert influence, transportation and distribution, and military forces.[9] Action to induce specific effects rather than destruction of the systems making up each of these centers of gravity is the foundation of parallel war. The crux of parallel war is not its physical elements, but rather its conceptual ones.

PARALLEL WARFARE: WHERE DID IT COME FROM?

Parallel warfare is thus the simultaneous application of force (in time, space, and at each level of war) against key systems to effect paralysis on the subject state or organization's ability to function. The object of parallel warfare is effective control of the enemy's strategic activity.

Simultaneous attack in any type of warfare has always been a desirable element contributing to success in war. Historically, it has been used to achieve surprise in an opening move of a longer-lasting sequential series of campaigns or in campaigns and operations of short duration. Japanese attacks against Pearl Harbor and the Philippines within a matter of hours are an example of the former, whereas the Arab–Israeli War of 1967 and the raid on Libya in 1986 are examples of the latter.

There are three primary reasons why simultaneous attacks never evolved to the degree of parallel war demonstrated in the Gulf War: the requirement for mass to compensate for a lack of precise weapons delivery; the high resource requirements to suppress the ever-increasing effectiveness of enemy air defenses; and the absence of a concept of operations focusing principally on effects rather than destruction to achieve control over an opponent. Combined, the first two imperatives precluded sustaining continuous attacks against the entire array of an enemy's vital target systems. Because the means to overcome these elements were not technologically mature before the mid-1980s, they could not join with the third, and most critical, element necessary to make parallel war a reality—a concept of operations at the operational level of war aiming to achieve the effect of control over entire enemy systems rather than ultimate destruction of enemy forces.

The idea of targeting large systems to achieve debilitating effects is not new. It was a central tenet of the strategic air offensives against Germany and Japan during World War II, and it had been theorized many years before. Early in the twentieth century, theories were put forth about the vulnerability of modern nation-states to air attack of their highly centralized, interdependent political and economic structures. Lord Montague in 1909 spoke of crippling an entire nation through air attacks on "nerve centers" like London. The targeting of "government buildings, the Houses of Parliament, the central railway stations, the central telephone and telegraph offices, and the stock exchange" are all attacks against the nation's central nervous system that would produce a "massive and fatal paralysis."[10] Similar theories were advanced by Italy's Douhet, America's Mitchell, Britain's Tedder, and others. Their ideas were summarized well in an early statement of the United States Army Air Corps: "Disruption or paralysis of [vital] systems undermines both the enemy's *capability* and *will* to fight. Proper selection of vital targets in the industrial/economic/social structure of a modern industrial nation, and their subsequent destruction by air attack, can lead to fatal weakening of an industrial enemy nation."[11]

Early work on identifying critical targets vulnerable to air attack was conducted by the Air Corps Tactical School (ACTS), the forerunner of the current Air University. Searching to formulate doctrine for an air offense against modern industrialized states, students there began a systematic evaluation of industrial, economic, and social development complexes in the United States. Air Corps Tactical School findings led to a "subtle but very significant variation from the doctrines of Douhet and Mitchell. The latter advocated destruction of factories and industrial centers and population centers. The school favored destruction or paralysis of national *organic systems* on which many factories and numerous people depended."[12]

The findings went on to identify electric power systems, transportation systems, railroads, fuel, food distribution, steel manufacturing, and other manufacturing industries vital to the operation of the economic and industrial well-being of the state. Parallel war takes these ideas one step further, aiming not just to impede the *means* of the enemy to conduct war or the *will* of the people to continue war, but the *ability* of the entire spectrum of a society at each level to have control of its vital functions.

Precision—An Enabling Factor in Parallel War

The difficulty in extracting the maximum potential from earlier theories of strategic attack was a shortcoming in execution. Even when control of the air was wrested from the Luftwaffe in the spring of 1944 and Allied aircraft were free to roam the Axis skies at will, the level of "precision" bombing still required a thousand aircraft to succeed against one target. Only a very small percentage of bombs dropped usually hit their targets. Over the entire Second World War, only about 20 percent of the bombs aimed at targets designated for precision attack fell within 1,000 feet of their aim point.[13] The large number of aircraft needed to achieve success made simultaneous attack against a multitude of targets technically impossible. Generally, target sets were attacked in sequence, even after control of the air was secured, because large numbers of aircraft had to be massed repeatedly to debilitate just one target set.

The World War II campaigns against the German ball-bearing and aircraft production industries took seven months—in part set back by the lack of air superiority over Germany. Even with air superiority, however, the requirement for mass to overcome the relative lack of precise delivery led to a transportation campaign taking five months and an oil campaign taking six months. These relatively long periods of time focusing against one target set at a time gave the enemy time to recover in other target systems, making it even more difficult to paralyze more than one target system at a time. "To knock out a single industry with the weapons available in 1943 and early 1944 was a formidable enterprise demanding continuous attacks to effect complete results."[14]

In World War II, air commanders were "compelled to substitute sheer tonnage for precision."[15] However, World War II also witnessed the first effective combat use of precision-guided munitions (PGMs). The first such Allied guided bomb, the Azon bomb (VB-1), was employed in combat with excellent results against bridges in Burma during late 1944 and 1945.[16] The challenge of dropping bridges during the Korean and Vietnam Wars spurred the further development of PGMs. Vietnam saw the first large-scale use of laser-guided bombs (LGBs), with over 4,000 being dropped between April 1972 and January 1973.[17]

By the time of the Gulf War PGMs overcame the necessity to mass aircraft before achieving successful attack against a target. During the Gulf War over 9,000 LGBs were used out of a total of approximately 220,000 bombs.[18] This seemingly small portion of the total number of weapons dropped understates the consequence of their effect. In some cases, *a single* aircraft and *one* PGM during the Gulf War achieved the same result as a 1,000-plane raid with over 9,000 bombs in World War II—and without the associated collateral damage.[19] The enormous leverage of the effectiveness of PGMs in successfully striking a target offset the need for mass attacks to achieve a high probability of success.

Stealth—Technological Leverage

As aerial weapons delivery accuracy improved after World War II, so did air defenses. By the early 1970s, radar detection and radar-guided surface guns and missiles were highly lethal against air attack. Experience in the Vietnam War and the 1973 Arab–Israeli War indicated that highly defended targets would yield to successful attack only with large force packages of aircraft. Designed to get strike aircraft into and out of a target area, each force package contained—besides the bomb-dropping aircraft—aircraft to suppress enemy early warning and surface-to-air missile acquisition radars, to destroy or jam enemy defensive missile systems, and to defend against enemy aircraft attacks. A typical force package during the Linebacker I campaign in Vietnam consisted of sixty-two combat aircraft (not including air refueling support) to get sixteen fighter-bombers in and out of the target area.[20]

Even though weapons delivery had become more precise by the early 1970s, the high number of support, force protection, and defense suppression aircraft to protect strike aircraft successfully reduced those available to attack and hence reduced the number of potential targets coming under attack at any one time.

Avoiding radar detection until it is too late to react effectively can drastically reduce the effectiveness of any air defense system. It was this stimulus that led to research in techniques to reduce radar cross section—a measure of the ability of a radar to "see" a signal return from a radar-reflective target. These "stealth" techniques saw early application on reconnaissance aircraft and drones in the late 1950s and 1960s. In the mid-1970s, aircraft designers were asked to study stealth fighter configurations; and by late 1978, development of the Lockheed F-117 began. The aircraft first flew in June 1981 and became operational in October 1983. The last of fifty-nine F-117s built was delivered in July 1990.[21] The next month, some of them were deployed to Saudi Arabia to prepare for the most effective use of combat aircraft to date.

The combination of stealth and precision radically reduces the number of aircraft, supporting personnel, and infrastructure required to strike effectively a large number of targets. The significance of the stealth and precision combination was first captured in October 1990 in a relationship calculated from the version of the air campaign master attack plan existing then: *"The planning effectiveness of the F-117 (stealth) is illustrated by the fact that it accounts for only 5% of the combat aircraft (30/580) yet it strikes 44% of the first 24 hour targets"* (emphasis in original).[22] During the entire war, the F-117 stealth aircraft flew less than 2 percent of the total combat sorties while attacking 43 percent of the targets on the master target list.[23]

A comparison of the first nonstealth aircraft attack in the Basrah area with a wave of F-117 strikes in the same time frame illustrates the enormous leverage of the stealth/precision combination. The nonstealth force package consisted of thirty-eight aircraft and three drones attacking one target with three aim points. The force package consisted of four A-6s and four Saudi Tornadoes dropping bombs on the target. Four F-4Gs provided suppression for a particular type of SAM, five EA-6Bs provided jamming of Iraqi early warning and acquisition radars, seventeen F/A-18 fighters were carrying radar-homing missiles to suppress SAMs, and four other F/A-18s provided air-to-air protection—thirty-eight aircraft, with only eight dropping bombs on three aimpoints. At the same time, twenty stealth aircraft (F-117s) were targeted against thirty-seven aimpoints in other areas with the same and even higher threat intensity,[24] an over 1,200 percent *increase* in target coverage using 47 percent *fewer* aircraft.

Effects versus Destruction

Open a targeting manual, and you find mere words about targeting to achieve effects, but pages and chapters written about damage expectancy, probability of damage, and weaponeering to achieve levels of destruction. This focus on destruction is a result of the two traditional strategies of armed conflict: annihilation and attrition. Annihilation relies on overwhelming force or mass to defeat the enemy through outright destruction. Attrition relies on exchanging blows to exhaust an enemy gradually before it exhausts you.[25]

Another concept of warfare is based on control—the idea that an enemy organization's ability to operate as desired is ultimately more important than destruction of the forces it relies on to protect its operations or exert influence. To render the enemy force useless is just as effective as eliminating the enemy force itself in terms of securing favorable conflict termination. Furthermore, controlling an adversary can be accomplished quicker, and with far fewer casualties. In words attributed to Sun Tzu, "Those skilled in war subdue the enemy's army without battle. They capture his cities without assaulting them and overthrow his state without protracted operations."[26]

Rather than *the* operative means to inhibit enemy activity, destruction should be viewed as one of a variety of means acting as a catalyst to achieve control over enemy activity. In this approach, destruction is used to achieve effects on each of the systems the enemy organization relies on to conduct operations or exert influence—not to the destroy the systems, but to prevent them from being used as the adversary wants. Effective control over adversary systems facilitates achieving the political objectives, making the use of force necessary.

Generally, conventional planners and intelligence personnel tend to think about targeting in terms of "the required number of sorties to achieve the desired damage against each target."[27] The bread and butter of a targets officer involve "determining the quantity of a specific weapon required to achieve a specified level of damage to a given target."[28] An evaluation of the effectiveness of the air campaign during the Gulf War demonstrates the propensity to focus on individual target damage rather than the effects of those attacks on the system under attack.

On February 15, 1991, the Iraq target planning cell received a report on the progress of the air campaign in accomplishing its target set objectives. For the electric target set, the analysis concluded that the objective was not met because all the targets in the primary and secondary electric set were not destroyed or damaged to a specific percentage.[29] In actuality, the electric system was not operating in Baghdad, and the power grid in the rest of the country was not much better off. The effect desired in attacking this system was not destruction of each of the electric sites, but to stop temporarily the production of electricity in certain areas of Iraq. In this case, the planning cell had previously learned the operating status of the Iraqi electric grid from a separate intelligence source and had already reduced strikes against electric sites to maintenance levels.[30] The determinant of whether to plan a strike on an individual site was whether the electric system was operating in the area of interest, not the level of damage or lack thereof to an individual site.

During the war, some power plant managers shut down their electric plants to avoid targeting. To the air campaign planners, that was great news because against those sites we achieved our desired effect without exposing a Coalition member or noncombatant Iraqi to danger and without expending any ordnance, and this freed air resources for another task—Sun Tzu's dictum fulfilled.

Although the virtues of planning to achieve systemic effects were discussed early in the conceptual phase of the air campaign planning effort, the initial attack planning was done on the basis of traditional destruction-based methodology. For example, early in the process,[31] intelligence identified two major sector operations centers (SOCs) providing command and control of Iraqi air defenses—one in Baghdad, and one at Tallil air base in southern Iraq. Each was hardened to protect two underground command and control bunkers. Weapons experts and target planners determined it would take eight F-117s with a mix of GBU-27 and GBU-10 2,000-pound bombs to destroy the bunkers at each SOC. At that time, since only sixteen F-117s were available for planning, destroying the two SOCs meant using all the available F-117s.

However, once intensive planning for the offensive air campaign began in theater on August 21, 1990, it became evident that the combination of precision and stealth provided by the F-117 would enable attack of the wide array of high-value targets in the heavily defended Baghdad area. The attack flow planner began thinking of ways to reduce the high F-117 requirement to destroy the two critical SOCs.[32] At that time, effects became more significant than destruction in constructing the targeting plan. An event on August 30, 1990 emphasized the importance of effects rather than destruction. On that date, the director of the special planning group, accompanied by his attack planner, went to Manama, Bahrain to brief the CENTCOM naval component commander on the air plan. During the trip, they read an intelligence analysis of the Iraqi air defense network and became aware of not just two SOCs in Iraq, but four. Associated with each of these SOCs were three to five interceptor operations centers (IOCs), and associated with the IOCs were a number of radar reporting posts. Although the sectors operated independent from each other, each sector's IOCs were interconnected and could pick up the entire sector load.

The known targets in the strategic air defense system expanded almost tenfold with the additional information. This significantly increased the challenge in attaining the operational objective to "render Iraq defenseless and minimize threat to allied forces."[33] For the initial attack plan, the effect desired was to shut down the air defense command and control system in certain areas, enabling nonstealth aircraft to approach their targets without resistance. However, there were not enough stealthy F-117s to destroy each of the newly discovered nodes of the air defense system.

The solution lay in effects-based rather than destruction-based targeting. A 2,000-pound bomb could go off in the other end of the building the planners were working in, and although the planning group would survive, it would abandon the facility to seek shelter. The point is that the SOCs and IOCs did not require destruction. Targeting only had to render them ineffective, unable to conduct operations through the period of the ensuing attacks by nonstealthy aircraft.

By September 6, 1990, the attack plan that originally had eight F-117s targeted on one SOC was rewritten, putting no more than two F-117 loads on any particular SOC.[34] This greatly multiplied the number of stealth/ precision strikes for use against other targets—IOCs, biological and chemical weapons storage facilities, and other critical targets.

In the August 16, 1990 attack flow plan, sixteen F-117s were targeted on two SOCs—an 8-to-1 aircraft-to-target ratio. The opening twenty-four hours of the air war found 42 F-117 sorties flying 76 target attacks:[35] almost a 1 to 2 aircraft-to-target ratio. Compared to the original plan, just over 2 ½ the stealth strike sorties were attacking 38 times the target base.[36]

The process of planning for effects is complex. Planners in conjunction with intelligence must determine which effects on each enemy system can best contribute to the fulfillment of the military and political objectives of the theater campaign. This depends on the specific situation, political and military objectives, centers of gravity, target systems, and weapon system capabilities. Since an air campaign plan is highly dependent on the weapon systems available for its execution, an effective plan must extract maximum impact from available weapon systems—not in terms of absolute destruction of a list of targets, but in terms of effects desired on target systems.

Concept of Operations

Strategy is the orchestration of means to accomplish ends. The process of selecting air assets (i.e., planes and missiles) (means) and assigning them against target systems to achieve specific effects (ends) is the air strategy for an air campaign. It is generally explained in a concept of operations (CONOPS). A concept of operations is usually written as a series of paragraphs describing friendly force intentions and the sequence of operations to accomplish the command's objectives. Of concern here is not so much the process or format of a CONOPS, but rather the philosophy underlying the development of air strategy.

The focus of the command and control organization developed for planning and execution of air-to-surface attack in the Vietnam War, the Tactical Air Control System (TACS), was on allocating sorties to individual targets in support of ground operations. To a large extent, ground commanders selected the targets and set priorities for the majority of operations processed by the central element of the TACS, the Tactical Air Control Center (TACC).[37] Effectiveness in air-to-surface operations was measured in terms of responsiveness and efficiency in destroying individual tactical-level targets. Battle damage assessment focus was on destruction of individual targets of the kind seen earlier in the electric target example. The function and organization of the TACS led many to confuse the efficiency of hitting individual targets with the effectiveness of achieving campaign objectives.[38]

Between the Vietnam War and the Gulf War, the TACS was established in doctrine as the air command and control system for conventional war.[39] Improvements to the TACS focused on improving responsiveness through joint training with the Army, enhancing sortie production rates, and incorporating modern systems, such as the computer assisted force management system (CAFMS), to process large air tasking orders (ATOs) quickly. Emphasis was on improving process—little effort or time was spent on developing air strategy or providing tools for the planning of air strategy. The "marriage" between Tactical Air Command (TAC) and the Army's Training and Doctrine Command (TRADOC) in the 1980s elevated the Army's doctrine of AirLand Battle as TAC's air strategy in regional conflicts.[40] Basic Air Force instructional documents on target planning had a complete chapter on AirLand Battle targeting, but no mention of principles or guidelines for conventional strategic attack.[41] The Air Force's largest and most influential conventional air command, TAC, entered the 1990s with its vision of conventional war confined to supporting the Army—only one element of its versatile potential.[42]

Absent any place in the established planning process for conventional theater air warfare beyond support of land forces on the battlefield, it should come as no surprise that the principal focus of most Central Command Air Force (CENTAF) TACC planners and intelligence personnel arriving in Riyadh in the late summer of 1990 was on tactical operations. With dedication and a sincere commitment to applying airpower in the best way they knew how, TACC personnel were the product of their past. The previous twenty-five years and established procedures for the design of an air tasking order led them to a conventional force planning focus—based on a mechanistic application of sorties against a list of individual targets in a sequential fashion. The process was often referred to as "servicing a target list."

The offensive air campaign employed against Iraq in early 1991 came together between August 1990 and January 1991. On August 8, 1990, CINC-CENTCOM asked the vice chief of staff of the Air Force to put together an air option for potential use against the Iraqis. The effort resulted in Instant Thunder—an initial concept of operations, a draft operations plan (OPLAN), and an initial cut of a first twenty-four–hour attack plan. Embracing the concept on August 17, the CINC directed the key planners to deliver the concept to his Joint Forces Air Component Commander (JFACC), who was also acting as CINC-forward in Riyadh. Although not comfortable with the completeness of Instant Thunder and feeling it lacked attention to defensive response to further Iraqi aggression, the JFACC did ask some of the Washington-based planners to remain in theater to form a nucleus of an offensive planning organization. It was known simply as the

Parallel Warfare

special planning group, and later as the "Black Hole" because of its highly classified status, which required special access clearance.

The architects of the air campaign did not limit themselves to the "servicing a target list" approach. The design of the air campaign grew out of a mindset questioning how to impose force against enemy systems so every effort would contribute directly to the military and political objectives of the Coalition. Planning began with a critical examination of potential strategic centers of gravity and their constituent operational systems, and it led to identifying the set of individual targets making up each system. Assessment of whether to continue or stop attack against a particular system's target set was dependent on achieving the effects desired on the system. Individual targets only became important if the system was still operating. If the effects desired were achieved, it did not matter that individual targets may not have been hit. Returning to the electrical example, it did not matter to the Black Hole planners, as it did to the intelligence analyst, that several individual targets in the electric target set remained undamaged—the electric *system* was shut down.

Figure 6.3 illustrates the subtle, but significant, difference between the destruction-based and effects-based approaches to war fighting. The upper half of Figure 6.3 shows two methods of the series targeting approach—a single prioritized list, and multiple target set lists prioritized in sequence. The serial approach is to target those elements of an adversary's defenses that restrict access to targets of critical value. For example, early warning radars, air defense systems, command and control nodes, and airfields are hit before production, government, and leadership facilities. This series methodology can be applied against an adversary's entire target base, or against a group of individual targets. This is not unlike the approach taken in World War II. However, attacking one target system at a time allows the others to continue operation or recover if previously attacked.

The parallel attack scheme is shown in the lower half of Figure 6.3. The theoretical application of force in a parallel attack strategy involves the application of force against all targets in each target system at one time. With correct identification of target systems and appropriate targets critical to each system, if each target is hit the effects desired within each system will occur. The simultaneous application of force in such a manner would enable friendly control over the adversary systems. In reality, however, the number of aimpoints to conduct such a campaign will generally exceed the conventional resources available to hit all of them simultaneously. The difference between the total number of aimpoints and the number of assets required to hit each will influence campaign duration.

If all the target set aimpoints cannot be hit in one attack, then those with the most significant impact in each set should be hit first. Counter air operations, for all the reasons as in the past, become a primary consideration if the attack force is not fully stealthy. Targeting is weighted to paralyze

Figure 6.3
Air Campaign Attack Schemes (Series versus Parallel)

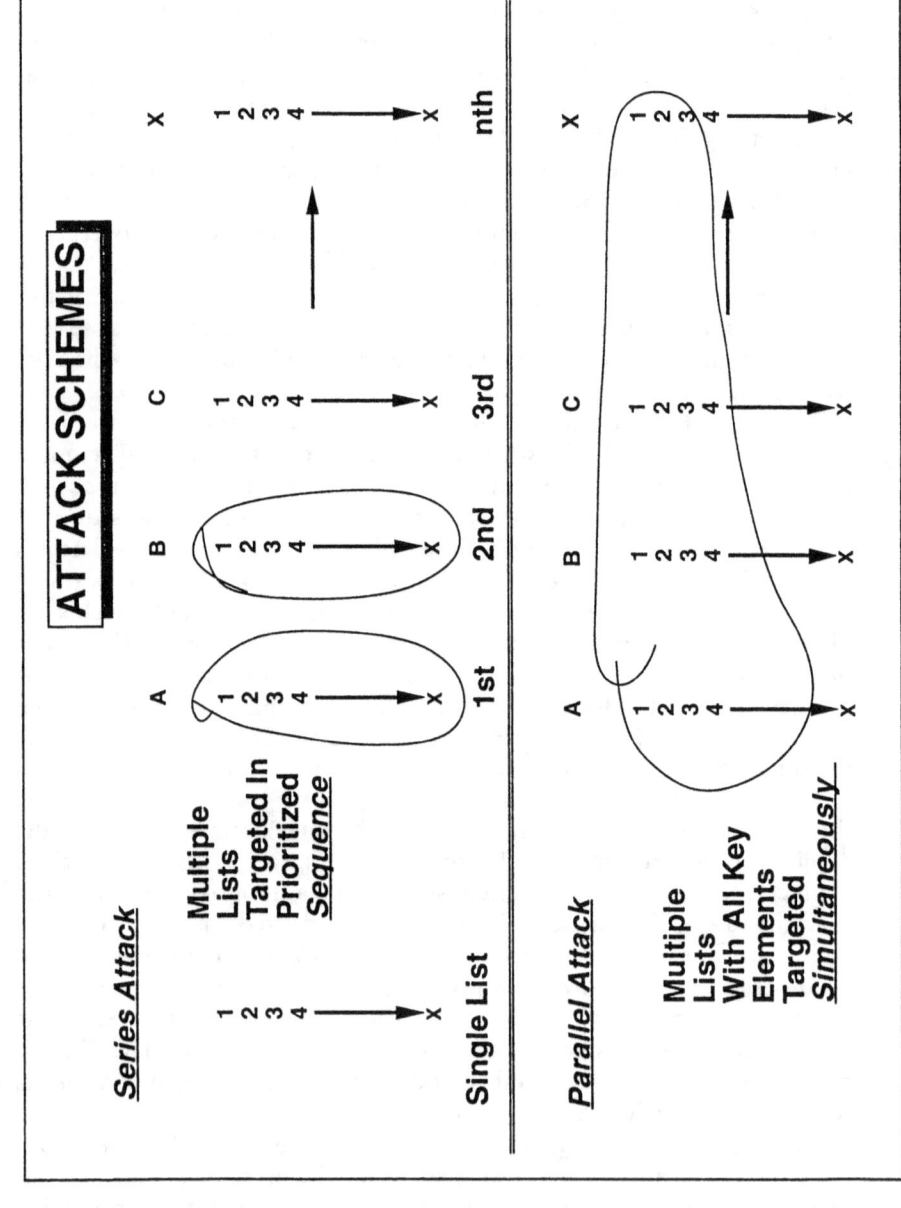

the air defense areas in which nonstealthy assets would operate. This is the reason for the skewing depicted in the lower half of Figure 6.3 toward the target sets A, B, C, etc., notionally representing air defense, airfield, and the command and control target sets. The weight of strikes against other target systems can increase with the attainment of air superiority, and air attacks continue until the desired effect for each objective is obtained.

What Figure 6.3 does not show, and what must be understood about the "theoretical" application of force is (1) that intelligence about an enemy, strategic centers of gravity, the constituent operational systems, and the set of individual targets making up each system is never complete; and (2) an enemy will attempt to negate the effects of the actions taken against it while trying to respond effectively. War is dynamic. No theory completely captures all its operative elements for every situation. As a consequence, parallel war may involve more than one set of force application, even if the resources are available to attack all the known elements of all the identified systems that might affect the enemy. Any enemy may react to attack in ways not anticipated or may have elements unknown to the friendlies, or the friendlies may not possess the capacity to counter an enemy move quickly and effectively—any or all of these contingencies may change the calculus of the original parallel attack formula, requiring additional application of force and lengthening the time to achieve desired effects.

Mobile Scuds, bad weather, untimely battle damage assessment (BDA), incomplete intelligence, and a variety of other frictions extended the duration of the Gulf War air campaign.[43] An attraction of parallel war is its potential to reduce the time duration of conflict relative to previous wars. However, until we can have certain knowledge of all the elements affecting the conduct of war in each situation—highly unlikely—the application of force to achieve war-winning effects will take a finite, but unknowable, amount of time. Duration of parallel war is determined by how well its dynamic elements are understood and how effectively the functioning systems of an adversary can be paralyzed.

In 1990, the confluence of three elements allowed the planning of an air strategy based on simultaneous attack against the entire array of target sets in a sustained air campaign. The elements were stealth, precision, and an operational plan that focused on effects rather than destruction. Stealth obviates the need for large numbers of suppression and force protection assets to strike a heavily defended individual target—air superiority is inherent in the nature of stealth itself. Precision reduces the number of assets required to achieve a specific effect against an individual target. A focus on systemic effects rather than individual target destruction leverages assets for strikes against other targets.

Thus, parallel warfare came from the combination of mature airpower technologies with a strategy based on achieving systemic effects rather than individual target destruction.

PARALLEL WARFARE: WHY IS IT IMPORTANT?

Parallel warfare is the manifestation of the revolution in military affairs occurring in the 1990s. More than a means to apply new weapons resulting from technological innovation, parallel warfare calls for a basic realignment in war planning. In this sense, it meets the definition for some of a military revolution.[44] For others, the revolution is yet to occur.[45] Semantics aside, the character of warfare is changing and the degree of that change is considerable—analogous to the difference in worldviews between Ptolemy and Copernicus. The implications of parallel warfare are many, but the most significant are three of high order: First, parallel war can replace attrition and annihilation as the most effective means to compel an adversary to cease undesirable behavior. Second, parallel war provides effective use of current weapon systems while transitioning to those emerging from advances in technology. Third, to best exploit the potential of parallel war, the military must institute organizational changes.

Parallel War Can Replace Attrition and Annihilation

War colleges teach two principal forms of warfare: attrition and annihilation. The Gulf War demonstrated another: paralysis through the application of parallel war. The strategies of annihilation and attrition rely on the mechanistic application of aircraft, tanks, warships, or other forms of force input against individual targets. The aggregation of individual target destruction is the ultimate method of success and measure of progress in these schemes of war. In parallel war, the determinant of success is output, or effective control of systems that the enemy relies on to exert influence. Changing the way we think about the application of force may produce more effective use of force.

The combination of stealth and precision redefines the concept of mass. Mass, in the sense of an agglomeration of a large number of forces, is no longer required to achieve a devastating effect on a system of forces, infrastructure, government, or industry. One well-placed modern PGM can do the work of thousands of dumb munitions from the past. No longer do large numbers of surface forces require movement, positioning, and extensive preparation before achieving dominant effects over an enemy. In the first twenty-four hours of the Gulf War, the enormous leverage of stealth, precision, and effects-based planning allowed targeting forty-two stealth aircraft sorties armed with PGMs (along with three EF-111 sorties) against more targets than the complete air and missile force launched from the entire complement of six aircraft carriers and nine TLAM launching ships in the theater.[46]

Surface forces will always be force elements of the military, but not always for the purpose of massing to overwhelm an enemy before imposing control. It requires more aircraft to transport a light infantry division than to move the total number of PGMs delivered during the entire Gulf War.[47] What moves into a theater should be determined by what can most effectively influence an adversary, not a rote response reflecting how war was fought in the past. Furthermore, the massed forces—air, ground, sea—present a lucrative target now much more vulnerable to enemy attack particularly as weapons of mass destruction proliferate among potential hostile states. Mass, which in the past was a valued principle of war, in some situations now becomes a vulnerability.

Since the ability to impose effects is independent of the massing of forces, the *projection* of force becomes much more important than the *deployment* of force. The objective of presence of force in a region or the massing of force is ultimately influence. The operative element in achieving influence is the threat or actual use of force to achieve a particular effect. If the same effect can be imposed without the presence or large-scale massing of forces, then deployment of forces can be replaced by the projection of forces that can achieve the same effect. A recipient of a PGM does not know or care if the weapon came from near or far or from what kind of platform or from what kind of base. For military, political, and economic reasons, the capability to project force to achieve influence has immense advantages compared to deploying force for the same purpose.

The evolving security environment requires greater responsiveness—the ability to act in hours rather than weeks or months; long range—the ability to span the globe without forward basing; effective punch—the ability to deliver weapons with precision to achieve desired effects; and high leverage—the ability to reduce personnel, support, and overall dollar cost. Paul Nitze, a former secretary of the Navy and eminent authority on defense, notes that: "we cannot depend on getting conventional ground forces into a hot spot quickly enough to deter further aggression, or should deterrence fail, to prevent an early fait accompli by an invader. Long-range bombers . . . can provide firepower with speed and reach, and demonstrate seriousness of intent in a way that missiles or carrier battle groups cannot."[48] Focusing on influence, the end of strategy, rather than presence, the traditional means to achieve it, enables us to consider different and perhaps more effective ways to accomplish the same goal with fewer resources.

Systems-based intelligence analysis is critical to the application of parallel war. Without adequate information about what an adversary relies on to exert influence and conduct operations, parallel war cannot be effective. This potential vulnerability can be reduced by exploiting advances in space-based systems, communications technology, and rapid information transfer by reducing the need for forward-based organizational elements. Intelligence during the Gulf War is a good example of the rudimentary use of these capabilities. Much of the intelligence used in planning and execution of the Gulf War air campaign came from outside the theater.

Redefining the concept of mass, relying on force projection rather than force deployment, and aiming to control adversary systems rather than using attrition and annihilation to destroy them require changes in the current approach to force management. The changes required may include more reliance on out-of-theater command, control, communications, computer, and intelligence (C4I) organizations; distributive intelligence architecture; and "off-board" systems that can provide information direct to the user of that information. These structural changes can reduce reaction time for effective use of intelligence, reduce the requirement for forward basing, and enable effective force application without having to deploy large command and support elements. Each of these changes moves vulnerable control nodes away from the enemy. Changing the manner in which we think about the application of force requires changing the way we structure to employ it.

Parallel War Exploits Today's Weapons with Promises for the Future

We are in a transition phase of the ongoing revolution in military affairs. Parallel war clearly departs from the traditional strategies of attrition and annihilation, but we fight with the tools available today and will do so for the duration of their service life. We must carefully manage the transition to the new instruments of war to assure that their development is not predicated on the theories of the past and to adapt current systems to this more lucrative strategy. It will be a difficult transition. The tendency to retain orthodox concepts and doctrine is strong when the means on which those concepts and doctrine were built still make up the preponderance of weapons. Although military doctrine is invaluable in establishing a basis for application of force, it must not be allowed to constrain application of force in ways that might prove effective, but different from traditional modes. Parallel war provides a useful construct on how to conduct war that can bridge the gap between the weapons of today and the weapons of the future. It allows useful application of current weapon systems as we acquire a new generation of tools to exploit the concept.

During the major drawdown of forces at the end of the twentieth century, it is imperative that new weapon systems and those retained from force cuts meet the demands of the evolving security environment. However, "the widely held assumption about post Cold War force levels has been that we can make do with less of the same: the same weapons and technology [of the past], but in radically reduced numbers."[49]

The results of the 1993 DOD "Bottom Up Review" tend to confirm this observation, which is no surprise since the weapons systems for the near term exist today. The apparent significance of the new elements that enabled the military success in the Gulf—the impact of revolutionary technologies such as stealth along with the mature state of precision and new concepts for the employment of those systems—may be diminishing as the footprints of the Gulf War recede in the sands of time, covered by the inertia of past war-fighting paradigms.[50] Current weapons were built for strategies of the past. We must guard against reverting to the better-known past, allowing inertia to distort strategies of the future, or allowing a previous "monopoly" of a mission area to inhibit more effective application of new technologies or operational concepts.

The air campaign in the Gulf used bombs and missiles on aimpoints of individual targets to achieve a specific effect within the parent system. The air campaign gave us a view of the leverage that stealth, precision, rapid and secure information transfer, ready access to accurate positional information, and other cutting-edge technological systems can provide. However, although the aircraft/PGM match of the early 1990s was orders of magnitude beyond the systems used during World War II, it is crude compared to the ideal means for the conduct of parallel war. We must continue to explore follow-on systems that will provide even higher leveraged effects. As technological innovation accelerates, "nonlethal" weapons will become the operative means to conduct parallel war. Some were used during the Gulf War with resounding success.

The ability to achieve effects directly against systems without attacking their individual components would allow a more preferable application of the concept of parallel war than we are capable of today. Indeed, the ultimate theoretical application of parallel war would involve no destructive weapons at all—effects are its objects, not destruction. Nonlethal weapons, information warfare, and space-based systems have the potential to approach that theoretical goal and are the next step in the evolution of tools for the conduct of parallel war.

The Military Must Recognize the Requirement for Organizational Change in Battlespace Management to Best Exploit the Potential of Parallel War

The end of the Cold War and the dramatic reduction in military forces of the United States have accelerated the need for effects-based military strategy. We can no longer afford duplicative systems but, more pertinently, we may no longer have the option of overwhelming force or an abundance of weapon systems to conduct war in the future. Today, the permanence of the philosophies of attrition and annihilation tends to inhibit the development of organizations and acceptance of doctrine that apply to parallel war.

The Coalition was fortunate to have an overwhelming number of air forces in the Gulf War. When elements of one force component chose to ignore the joint air planning process, the Joint Forces Air Component Commander (JFACC), in the interest of avoiding doctrinal strife, could afford to rely on forces directly under his command to accomplish theater objectives.[51] In the future, the luxury of each Service component force doing its own thing may not be an option. Decisions on the use of force must be made on the basis of how they can have the most effect in accomplishing the joint force commander's theater objectives.

Although nonlethal weapons and information warfare will allow us to capitalize further on the concept of targeting for effects while continuing to limit casualties, only new organizations and doctrine aiming to exploit the parallel war strategy can fulfill the full potential of this concept. Nonlethal weapons and information warfare should enhance the ability of all our forces to conduct operations to achieve desired effects. In this respect, recent attempts to develop and write joint military doctrine are helpful when their focus is on weapon system capabilities and effects-based planning rather than employment environment or presumptions of attrition and annihilation. The Gulf War was a joint endeavor, and that is important to keep in mind. We must make sure, however, that the true meaning of *jointness* is understood. It is not the equal use of each Service in every war, but rather the use of the most effective force for a given situation. To paraphrase President George Bush, jointness is the use of the right force at the right place at the right time and, one could add, for the right purpose.[52]

An example of capability-based weapons allocation was the incorporation of the Tomahawk Land Attack (Cruise) Missiles (TLAMs) as part of the Gulf War air campaign. The Navy's original TLAM target list had many targets suitable for both aircraft and TLAM strike. The strategic air campaign planners' capability-based perspective, and the JFACC's unified targeting of both aircraft and TLAMs, made it possible to avoid duplication and maintain focus on the air plan objectives by using the two types of systems synergistically. TLAMs were used to keep pressure on Baghdad during the day and to take out soft targets, while the F-117s with GBU-27s were employed at night against hard targets requiring penetration. Each system's capabilities were exploited not to achieve service co-participation, but because their capabilities enhanced attainment of the air campaign objectives. Optimum parallel war is dependent on a functional organization encompassing not just the air component, but the entire theater campaign (i.e., a joint force land component commander, a joint force naval component commander, as well as a joint force air component commander).

Parallel warfare changes the basic character of war. It has the potential to reduce deployment, forward basing, fighting, casualties, time, and forces previously required to win in war.

CONCLUSION

In the Gulf War of 1991, airpower—from all the Services—proved its potential as a definitive military instrument. Airpower did not act in isolation, however. It worked in conjunction with magnificent support from surface forces. Sea forces conducted a maritime interdiction campaign before and during the application of airpower. Ground forces first helped to protect Saudi Arabia and subsequently reoccupied Kuwait after the air campaign had so incapacitated the enemy that Coalition ground forces could move with minimal casualties. Retired Marine Corps General Bernard Trainer and Michael Gordon conclude in their 1995 book, *The Generals' War,* "It was also the first war in history in which airpower, not ground forces, played the dominant role."[53]

Although the tenets of parallel war could be applied in every medium of warfare, the characteristics of airpower[54]—speed, range, flexibility, precision, and lethality—fit seamlessly with this strategic construct. Airpower has the potential to achieve effects at every level of war directly and quickly. As a result, it will remain the dominant means for conducting parallel war for the immediate future. However, more important than the characteristics of airpower is the strategic perspective associated with its most effective use—a perspective that views the theater or globe, as well as the aerospace medium, as an indivisible whole in which weapons are selected based on their ability to influence.

Parallel war has the potential to reduce force requirements, casualties, duration of conflict, forward basing, and deployment of forces previously required to win in war. Parallel war changes the basic character of war. The Desert Storm air campaign gave us a glimpse of its potential. The change in warfare is only just beginning. Airpower systems will evolve beyond manned aircraft, but the philosophy behind the use of those systems will remain. It is an evolution of the philosophy born with the airplane—the antithesis of attrition and annihilation warfare—and it is the philosophy of control over an adversary's strategic activity by direct influence and effect on the adversary's ability to act. It is strategic vision, rather than flying skills, that will add value to the ongoing transformation of war. In reality, the parallel approach is a springboard for better linking military, economic, and political elements to conduct national security strategy in-depth.

Some in the Russian military, studying closely the conduct of the Gulf War, recognize the potential of new military technologies and strategies for the orchestration of war. Identifying Desert Storm as one of the "rare 'turning points' " in military affairs fixing the evolution of warfare at the "juncture of two epochs in military art," they see the end of multimillion-man armies and the emergence of "aerospace war" as the determinant of military actions. Acknowledging that strategic objectives can be achieved through direct use of "aerospace strikes," they have gone so far as to postulate that "victory can be achieved without the seizure and occupation of territory by ground forces."[55]

Whether such proclamations are accurate or not is not relevant. What is relevant, however, is the potential danger that exists if our own military institutions become blind to the possibility of change in the nature of war.[56] Seeing new technologies only as a means to modernize a preferred way to conduct war, rather than a means to exploit change in the nature of war, may prove disastrous. Potential antagonists recognize the significance in the "revolution in military affairs" now underway—it would behoove us to do the same.

The title of a front page article in the July 15, 1994 *Wall Street Journal* reads, "How Wars Are Fought Will Change Radically." The way war *is* fought *has* changed radically—a revolution in the planning of war *has* occurred. Paralysis through parallel warfare was the basis for air campaign planning in the Gulf War. The challenge for a military steeped in the traditions, paradigms, and strategies of the past is recognizing the change, embracing it, and capitalizing on it before someone else does. Machiavelli said, "There is nothing more difficult to carry out, nor more doubtful of success, nor more dangerous to handle, than to initiate a new order of things." He might also have added that there is nothing more worthwhile.

NOTES

1. Major Greg Biscone, Langley AFB, Virginia, transcript of interview with author, October, 11, 1993, and Colonel Terry A. Burke, Commander, 4300 Provisional Bombardment Wing, narrative from the recommendation for the Distinguished Flying Cross to the crews of Ghost cell.

2. Eliot A. Cohen et al., *Gulf War Air Power Survey*, Vol. 5, *A Statistical Compendium and Chronology* (Washington, D.C.: USGPO, 1993), 253 [hereafter GWAPS].

3. Plan (S), "Master Attack Plan, 10 Jan 1991 with Changes 1, 2, 3," printed January 16, 1991 at 2121h Riyadh time. The master attack plan was a new planning document designed by the author specifically to facilitate planning the Gulf War air campaign. A script providing direction for the construction of the air tasking order (ATO), it specified targets, the timing of attacks, the aircraft force packages for each attack, and, in some cases, the specific weapons for the strike aircraft. Information extracted is unclassified.

4. Roger A. Freeman, *Mighty Eighth War Diary* (London: Jane's Publishing Co., 1981), 9–161. Between August 17, 1942—the Eighth AF first heavy bomber raid—and December 31, 1943, the Eighth AF flew 171 attacks. Subtracting leaflet missions and accounting for multiple targets hit on one mission, attacks were flown against 124 distinct targets. This number includes all Eighth AF missions flown in the European theater of operations, not just those flown against Germany.

5. The term was coined by members of the Air Force Directorate of Warfighting Concepts Development (AF/XOXW). It first came into common use immediately after the Gulf War.

6. The five systems mentioned here were ones used to model Iraq in the early design of the Gulf War air campaign. See John A. Warden III, "Employing Air Power in the Twenty-first Century," in Richard H. Shulty, Jr., and Robert L. Pfalt-

zgraff, Jr., eds., *The Future of Air Power in the Aftermath of the Gulf War* (Maxwell AFB, Ala.: Air University Press, 1992), 64–82.

7. Plan (S), "Master Attack Plan, 10 Jan 1991." Information extracted is unclassified.

8. "It was an easy step for Clausewitz's less profound disciples to confuse the means [of war] with the end, and to reach the conclusion that in war every other consideration should be subordinated to the aim of fighting a decisive battle." B. H. Liddell Hart, *Strategy* (New York: Meridian, 1991), 319. Although Liddell Hart is generally attributed by scholars as being unfair in his interpretation of Clausewitz, this quote captures today what many modern officers take away from *On War*.

9. For further elaboration of these particular systems and their use as a strategic model for an adversary, see John A. Warden III, "The Enemy as a System," *Airpower Journal* (Spring 1995), 41–50.

10. Lee B. Kennett, *A History of Strategic Bombing* (New York: Charles Scribner's Sons, 1982), 43; Lee B. Kennett, *The First Air War, 1914–1918* (New York: The Free Press, 1991), 44.

11. Haywood S. Hansell, *The Strategic Air War against Germany and Japan* (Washington, D.C.: USGPO, 1986), 10.

12. Ibid., 12.

13. *The United States Strategic Bombing Survey, Summary Report (European War) 1945*, reprinted in *The United States Strategic Bombing Surveys (European War) (Pacific War)* (Maxwell AFB, Ala.: Air University Press, 1987), 13.

14. Ibid., 18.

15. Richard G. Davis, *Carl A. Spaatz and the Air War in Europe* (Washington, D.C.: Center for Air Force History, 1983), 283.

16. Wesley Frank Craven and James L. Cate, eds., *The Army Air Forces in World War II*, Vol. 6, *Men and Planes* (Chicago: University of Chicago Press, 1955; new imprint, Washington, D.C.: Office of Air Force History, 1983), 259.

17. Thomas A. Keaney and Eliot A. Cohen, *Gulf War Air Power Survey, Summary Report* (Washington, D.C.: USGPO, 1993), 226 [hereafter *GWAPS, Summary*].

18. Ibid.

19. To have a 90 percent probability of one bomb hitting a 60' × 100' target (size of a small bunker) would take 9,070 bombs with B-17 accuracy (3300' CEP) compared with the accuracy of one bomb (10' CEP) dropped from aircraft equipped to drop LGBs (F-117, F-111, F-15E, A-6, RAF Tornados, and Buccaneers). Briefing chart, AF/XOXW, Fall 1990.

20. Karl J. Eschmann, *Linebacker, The Untold Story of the Air Raids over North Vietnam* (New York: Ivy Books, 1989), 32.

21. Richard P. Hallion, *Storm over Iraq, Airpower and the Gulf War* (Washington, D.C.: Smithsonian Institution Press, 1992), 293–94.

22. Memo (S), Secretary of the Air Force Staff Group (SAF/OSX), Memo for Secretary Rice, October 9, 1990, 90, 4. Information extracted is unclassified.

23. "F-117 Target Analysis," April 19, 1991, by author. Of 688 targets on the MTL (corrected for duplication), 298 were attacked by F-117s. Data from (S) "Master Target List," March 1, 1991, Central Command Air Force (CENTAF) Iraq Target Planning Cell and 37th Tactical Fighter Wing Mission Electronic Database, March 1991. The F-117 flew 1,299 of 74,091 combat sorties (1.75 percent)

between January 16, 1991 and February 28, 1991. The definition of combat sorties used here includes only Coalition fighter or bomber aircraft, not tankers, airlift, or other types of support. Data from (S) GWAPS, 334–35. Information extracted is unclassified.

24. Plan (S), "Master Attack Plan, 10 Jan 1991." Information extracted is unclassified.

25. Practitioners of annihilation strategy were Alexander, Caesar, and Napoleon. Examples of attrition warfare are Washington's strategy during the Revolutionary War, Grant's campaign in Virginia, and German General Von Falkenhayn's strategy of exhaustion in the trenches of World War I. For more on this subject, see Gordon A. Craig, "Delbruck: The Military Historian," in *Makers of Modern Strategy, from Machiavelli to the Nuclear Age*, ed. Peter Paret (Princeton: Princeton University Press, 1986), 341–45.

26. Sun Tzu, *The Art of War*, trans. by Samuel B. Griffith (New York: Oxford University Press, 1971), 79.

27. "The TACC Targeting Process," in *Target Intelligence Standard Operating Procedures*, used by targeters of the CENTAF Intelligence organization in 1990–1991.

28. Air Force Pamphlet (AFP) 200-17, *An Introduction to Air Force Targeting*, June 23 1989, 21.

29. Paper (S), CCJ-2-T Fact Paper, "Subject: Electric Power Facilities Analysis D + 29," February 15, 1991. Information extracted is unclassified.

30. In the absence of theater-based intelligence concerning effects of attack on target *systems* in addition to the outcome of attacks on individual targets, planners obtained this information daily by secure FAX directly from a variety of agencies in Washington, D.C. These strategic assessments were valuable in determining when, and how much, to change focus in constructing the daily master attack plans.

31. August 7, 1990 to August 17, 1990—the development period of an air option for the use of force in the Gulf crisis. The title of the briefing for the Commander in Chief, U.S. Central Command (CINCCENTCOM), on August 17, 1990 describing this air option was "Iraqi Air Campaign, Instant Thunder." The several-hundred–page operations plan accompanying the presentation was entitled "Proposed Iraq Air Campaign, Operation Instant Thunder, STRATEGIC AIR CAMPAIGN against Iraq to Accomplish NCA Objectives."

32. The "attack flow plan" was the precursor to the "master attack plan," which was given that title on August 27, 1990 to deconflict it from the various iterations of earlier "attack flow plans."

33. In constructing the master attack plan, each target set was viewed as a system with a specific operational-level objective associated with it. Achieving the operational objective of each target set contributed to rendering a higher-order parent strategic level center of gravity ineffective. Fielded military forces were the parent strategic level center of gravity of which the strategic air defense system was an operational element. The operational objectives for each target set were specified on the master target list sent to the CINC, CJCS, and SECDEF in early January 1991.

34. Plan (S), "Master Attack Plan, 6 Sep 1990." Information extracted is unclassified.

35. "Target attacks" are the number of lines associated with an aircraft or force

package attacking a target in one of the twelve JFACC target categories on the first twenty-four hour master attack plan.

36. "Campaign Flow, Update as of 16 Aug [1990] 2000L," *Instant Thunder* briefing chart 21; Plan (S), "Master Attack Plan, 10 Jan 1991." Information extracted is unclassified.

37. "Once the TACC has received the LCC (land component commander) . . . nominations and . . . prioritized target list from the BCE (battlefield control element), the TACC plans the . . . sorties and support packages to meet the LCC request. Additionally, it matches air assets against the target list to provide the forces required to achieve the requested effect on *each target*" (emphasis added). From the *Joint Operational Interface of the Ground Attack Control Capability Study* (Langley AFB, Va.: 1986), explaining how ground attack control is envisioned to fit into the twenty-first–century TACS, in Thomas H. Buchanan, *The Tactical Air Control System: Its Evolution and Its Need for Battle Managers*, Research Report No. AU-ARI-87-1 (Maxwell AFB, Ala.: Air University Press, 1987).

38. For an insightful study and analysis of the USAF command and control system for the conduct of conventional war, see J. Taylor Sink, *Rethinking the Air Operations Center, Air Force Command and Control in Conventional War*, School of Advanced Airpower Studies Thesis (Maxwell AFB, Ala.: Air University Press, June 1993).

39. TACM 2-1, *Aerospace Operational Doctrine: Tactical Air Operations*, April 15, 1978.

40. "On April 21, 1983, General Charles A. Gabriel, CSAF, and General E. C. Meyer, CSA, signed a memorandum of understanding on 'Joint USA/USAF Efforts for Enhancement of Joint Employment of the AirLand Battle Doctrine.' The two services agreed to engage in joint training and exercises 'based on the AirLand battle doctrine as promulgated in Army FM 100-5, Operations, 20 August 1982.'" Richard G. Davis, *The 31 Initiatives* (Washington, D.C.: Office of Air Force History, 1987), 35.

41. Air Force Pamphlet (AFP) 200-18, *Target Intelligence Handbook, Targeting Principles*, October 1, 1990.

42. "Tactical aviators have two primary jobs—to provide air defense for the North American continent and support the Army in achieving its battlefield objectives." General Robert D. Russ, USAF (Commander of TAC), "Open Letter to the Field," *AirLand Bulletin 81-1* (Langley AFB, Va.: TAC-TRADOC ALFA, March 31, 1988), 7.

43. In the JFACC's "Theater Air Campaign" progress briefing to Secretary of Defense Richard Cheney and Chairman of the JCS, General Colin Powell, in Riyadh on February 9, 1991, one of the charts depicts that by the day before the briefing, February 8, 1991, twenty-three days into the air campaign, only eleven were "effective flying days."

44. Dan Goure, "Is There a Military-Technical Revolution in America's Future?" *The Washington Quarterly* 16 (Autumn 1993): 179.

45. The closing sentence of the GWAPS summary report states, "The ingredients for a transformation of war may well have become visible in the Gulf War, but if a revolution is to occur someone will have to make it." See Keaney and Cohen, *GWAPS, Summary* (Washington, D.C.: USGPO, 1993), 251.

46. Plan (S), "Master Attack Plan, 10 Jan 1991." Information extracted is unclassified.

47. It takes 618 C-141 and eighteen C-5 loads to move a light infantry division. To move the entire number of PGMs used in the Gulf War requires only 450 C-141 loads. *Military Traffic Management Command, Transportation Engineering Agency Deployment Planning Guide, Appendix C—Strategic Movement Requirements,* August 19, 1991.

48. Paul H. Nitze, "To B-2 or Not to B-2?" *Washington Post,* July 17, 1994, C4.

49. Ibid.

50. "It is a given that air power theory is enjoying a renaissance that is completely unrealistic in light of the reality of the Gulf War or of capabilities achievable in any reasonable timeframe." Attributed to Army Chief of Staff Gordon Sullivan in "Sullivan to Raise the Stakes on Roles & Missions," *Inside the Army* 6, no. 31 (August 1, 1994): 12. Russian military leadership takes the opposite view. General-Major I. N. Vorob'yev views the Gulf War as "one of those rare 'turning points' in military affairs" prompting "a radical re-examination of the structure of armed forces and the roles of particular branches," and he calls "for a 'new military thinking' on the part of 'our generals and officers' who are still locked into the 'inertial thinking' of the World War II generation." Mary C. FitzGerald, *The Impact of the Military-Technical Revolution on Russian Military Affairs,* Vol. I (Washington, D.C.: Hudson Institute, August 20, 1993), 5–6 [hereafter *Impact of Technical Revolution on Russian Military*].

51. Royal N. Moore, Jr., "Marine Air: There When Needed," *U.S. Naval Institute Proceedings* (November 1991): 63–70. "This way I didn't have to play around with the [joint air planning] process while I was waiting to hit a target. I kind of gamed the ATO process." "The Navy's trouble was that they tried to do it very honestly and write just what they were going to fly." Others in the USMC who dealt with the JFACC planners on a daily basis had a different perspective: "To those that had day to day dealings with the Air Force it became readily obvious that the JFACC's primary concern was to coordinate the efforts of theater aviation, deconflict airspace, and increase efficiency of the air campaign." Colonel J. W. Robben, Marine Liaison, CENTAF, USMC, *Operation Desert Shield/DESERT STORM After Action Report,* March 18, 1991, Enclosure 2, 16, in P. Mason Carpenter, *Joint Operations in the Gulf War: An Allison Analysis,* School of Advanced Airpower Studies Thesis (Maxwell AFB, Ala.: Air University Press, June 1994), 51.

52. President George Bush, "Address to the Air University," Maxwell AFB, Alabama, April 13, 1991.

53. Bernard Trainer and Michael Gordon, *The Generals' War: The Inside Story of the Conflict in the Gulf* (Boston: Little Brown Inc., 1995).

54. Note that I use the term *airpower,* not *aircraft*—in fact, *aerospace power* would be even more accurate.

55. FitzGerald, *Impact of Technical Revolution on Russian Military,* i–6.

56. See, for example, Brigadier General Robert J. Scales, Jr. et al., *Certain Victory: The United States Army in the Gulf War* (Washington, D.C.: Office of the Chief of Staff, U.S. Army, 1993), 388. "Desert Storm confirmed that the nature of war has not changed ... the strategic core of joint warfare is ultimately decisive land combat."

7

Command and Control in the Gulf War: A Military Revolution in Airpower?
Mark D. Mandeles

The Romans said, "if you would have peace, you must be prepared for war." And while we pray for peace, we can never forget that organization, no less than a bayonet or an aircraft carrier, is a weapon of war. We owe it to our soldiers, our airmen, and our marines to ensure that this weapon is lean enough, flexible enough, and tough enough to help them win if, God forbid, that ever becomes necessary.[1]

INTRODUCTION

Military revolutions occur, not as the result of deployment of a single weapon or technology,[2] but when a set of technologies and associated operational concepts transform the nature and character of warfare *and* the relevant personnel and military organizations are able to deploy and exploit the set of technologies.[3] In such revolutions, new tactical, operational, and strategic problems and solutions emerge, link, and re-form with varying degrees of resolution. The success of the U.S. air forces in the war against Iraq—the technical capabilities and performance of weapon platforms and munitions employed during the conflict (such as the F-117A aircraft and precision-guided munitions)—led some defense analysts to argue that the U.S. military was beginning to undergo a military revolution.[4] However, command and control in the Gulf War was hampered by extensive uncertainty, imperfect information, equipment shortfalls, and the incompatibility of multigenerational equipment. These factors kept the U.S. command and control and weapons operational capability from reaching the ideal performance of a "reconnaissance-strike complex"—a military organization integrating capabilities from microelectronics, telecommunications, sensors, automated decision support systems, and long-range precision munitions.[5] Military organization for command and control of the Gulf air war limited the effective employment of personnel and new weapons systems. One aspect of command and control of U.S. air forces during Operation Desert Storm will be used to illustrate this point: uncertainty in the relationship between centralized planning, command, and control conducted by the Tactical Air Control Center (TACC) in Riyadh and decentralized execution of the Air Tasking Order (ATO) by the wings. Identifying organizational deficiencies does not detract from the heroism and astounding wartime performance of American and Allied military personnel at all levels. The spectacular summer victory of the Iraqis, climaxed by the fall of Kuwait, hit the Emir of Kuwait, the House of Saud, and the United States "like a cold douche."[6] In response, the remarkable U.S.-led international Coalition employed airpower to crush the world's fourth largest conventional army, thereby avoiding a long and bloody land war. The Air Force led the way in deploying forces to deter[7] an Iraqi invasion of Saudi Arabia, and in preparing and supplying the forces that defeated the Iraqi military. Between January 17 and February 28, 1991, approximately 120,000 U.S. and Allied air sorties were flown. This figure translates into a daily average of 2,780 sorties, with a peak of about 3,300 sorties on February 24. Within the total number of sorties, approximately 1,600 strike sorties were flown daily, for a total of 68,960.[8]

In comparison to past air campaigns, these numbers are very large. Air operations were executed twenty-four hours a day. No other air force had ever conducted a campaign at this tempo. The size and pace of the campaign exceeded the expectations of even the most optimistic U.S. Air Force leaders and outstripped the capacity of systems and equipment to plan and communicate effectively in the rapidly changing battlefield.

In addition to generating and executing a large number of sorties each day, the air campaign against Iraq was the first to

1. Make enemy command, control, and communication nodes a priority target;
2. Use airpower to damage significantly and demoralize a land army;
3. Direct air attacks on a twenty-four–hour basis; and
4. Apply standoff, wide area, airborne radar systems—such as E-3A AWACS, E-2C Hawkeye, TR-1 ASARS, and E-8A JSTARS, aided by EC-130E ABCCC—to (a) air surveillance, air traffic control, and air superiority fighter intercept; (b) precision, high-resolution standoff radar imagery of ground targets; and (c) wide area standoff surveillance of moving ground targets with selected spot imagery and real-time broadcast of ground situation to multiple ground stations.[9]

Military Revolution in Airpower 159

Moving, modifying, manning, and managing a large military (or civilian) organization is a difficult assignment under even the most benign conditions, and the conditions under which the Air Force was operating were far from favorable. The Kuwait Theater of operations covered more than 1 million square miles, an area more than twice the size of the World War II European Theater and fifteen times the size of the Korean Theater of Operations. In Saudi Arabia, the air, naval, and ground forces of many different nations assembled to overcome cultural, language, and organizational differences; harsh environmental conditions; and political constraints. In the end, despite these many obstacles, the Coalition succeeded in achieving its primary objective of ejecting Iraqi troops from Kuwait with low Coalition casualties.

It is these impressive and significant airpower achievements (supplying, moving, watching, and fighting) that tempt many to hail the advent of a military revolution. But not all of the ingredients necessary for a military revolution were present. A close examination of how the command and control system performed shows that significant organizational changes are needed, without which the Air Force will not be able to exploit new technologies and evolving concepts of operation.

UNCERTAINTY: THE TRANSITION FROM STATIC TO DYNAMIC PLANNING

The following case study, adapted from the *Command and Control* volume of the *Gulf War Air Power Survey*, examines how F-16s from the 363 Tactical Fighter Wing (TFW) and F-111s from the 48 TFW were coordinated with support aircraft to attack targets in the Baghdad area.[10] Figure 7.1 is a map showing key target areas.

The case study illustrates three important issues relevant to the realization of a military revolution: (1) Planners faced many obstacles in reliably assessing damage, and imperfect information about recently accomplished missions degraded the planners' perception of the progress of the campaign. (2) The organizational complexity of scheduling many different aircraft placed great analytical, computational, communication, and negotiating demands on planners. (3) There were persistent problems in communication between the planners and the wings, partially because of the complexity and size of the ATO, but also because of the many changes planners made to the ATO after it had been sent to the wings.

The planning and execution of two separate aircraft packages on January 21, 1991, or Dday plus 4 (D + 4) of the air campaign, illustrates senior leaders' beliefs about controlling the air campaign and the difficulty of dynamic planning. Figure 7.2 provides a simple outline of the planning process. At least five versions of the Master Attack Plan (MAP)[11] for the D + 4 ATO were produced (containing these two packages) by January

Figure 7.1
Map of Assigned Targets

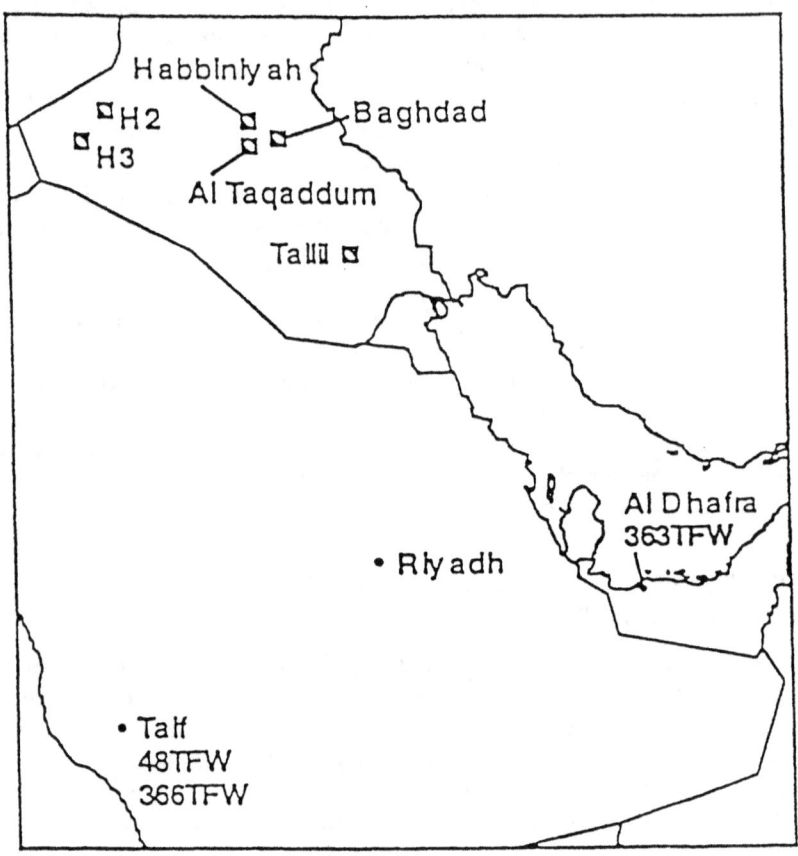

20 at 8:02 P.M. The first package was composed of F-16s from the 363 TFW at Al Dhafra, and the second package was made up of F-111s from the 48 TFW at Taif. The initial MAP development for this tasking began on January 19 around 8:00 A.M. The relevant ATO organized attacks from January 20 at 11:20 P.M. to January 22 at 5:01 A.M.[12]

In the initial rough draft of the MAP for January 21 (written on January 19), a forty-aircraft F-16 package from the 363 TFW was assigned targets in the Baghdad area with a time on target (TOT) at 1:00 to 1:30 P.M., and an eight-aircraft F-111 attack package from the 48 TFW was assigned targets in the Tallil area with a TOT at 2:30 to 2:45 A.M. Both packages were supported by suppression of enemy air defenses (SEAD) forces, EF-111s and F-4Gs.[13] The second version of this MAP (prepared on January 19, 9:00 P.M.), was nearly identical to the first pencil draft.[14]

Figure 7.2
The Planning Cycle

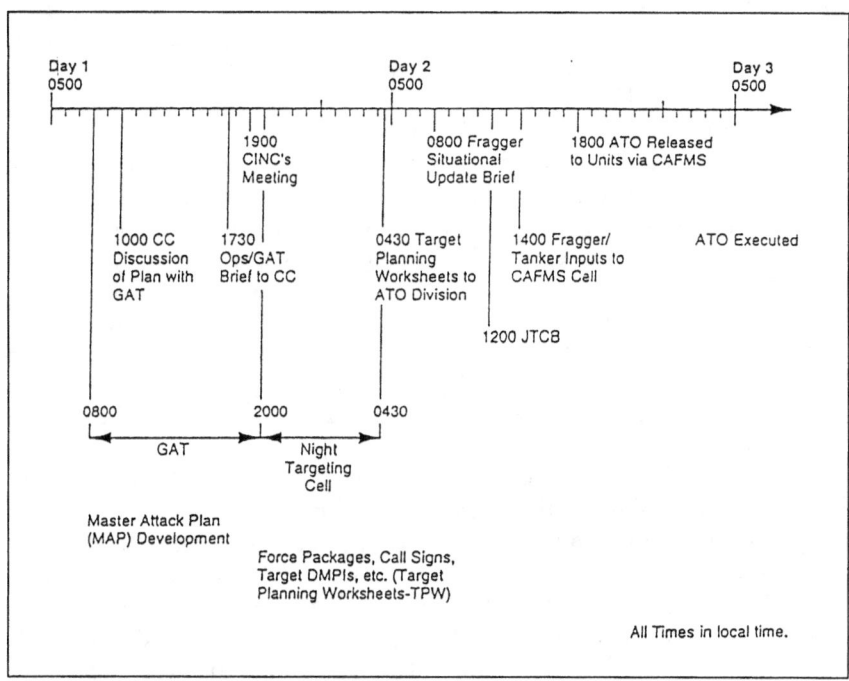

Legend:

ATO: Air Tasking Order

CAFMS: Computer Assisted Force Management System

CC: Component Commander (Lieutenant General Charles A. Horner, the Joint Force Air Component Commander)

CINC: Commander in Chief (General H. Norman Schwarzkopf)

DMPI: Desired Mean Point of Impact

GAT: Guidance, Apportionment, and Targeting Cell

JTCB: Joint Target Coordination Board

Ops: Operations

Comparison of the Target Planning Worksheets (TPWs) that were prepared to translate the draft MAPs into the ATO reveals conflicting instructions. The F-16 aircraft from the 363 TFW were called package A. The TPW listed package A's TOT against Baghdad area targets as 1:15 to 1:30 P.M., approximately the same TOT listed in the draft MAP. However, the number of F-16s in the package was reduced from forty to twenty-four. The TPWs supported package A with F-4G aircraft from the 35 TFW and EF-111 aircraft from the 366 TFW.[15]

The F-111 aircraft from the 48 TFW were called package D. In both drafts of the MAP (the initial pencil copy and the 9:00 P.M. version) and the corresponding TPWs, the F-111s were assigned targets in the Tallil area, with the TOT block between 2:30 A.M. and 2:45 A.M. The TPWs assigned the same F-4G and EF-111 mission numbers to support both the F-16s (package A) and F-111s (package D).[16] However, the aircraft assignments changed. During Desert Storm, it was common for the same flight of F-4Gs and EF-111s to support different attack packages. In this type of situation, the different package targets generally were near each other, and the TOTs were synchronized. In the case of the D + 4 ATO, however, the targets—Tallil and Baghdad—were approximately 200 miles apart, and the TOTs (1:00 to 1:30 P.M. for package A and 2:30 A.M. for package D) were eleven hours apart. Consequently, the same SEAD support could not have been used to support both attack packages.

The D + 4 ATO instructions for package A (the 363 TFW's F-16s) were identical to the tasking in the corresponding TPWs. Although minor errors crept into the ATO with respect to some of the support missions (e.g., the TPW listed F-15C missions for escort and sweep, whereas none were listed in the ATO), the essential information remained the same.[17] However, part of the ATO tasking for package D (the 48 TFW's F-111s) did not match the MAPs or the TPWs. For example, the information for the sweep/escort support did not match the TPW. More important, the target in the ATO was changed to the H2 airfield (see Figure 7.1).[18] No record of the reason for this change, or the change itself, was found.

The ATO transmitted on January 20 at 6:55 P.M.[19] was based on the MAP completed on January 19 at 9:00 P.M. and the TPWs based on that MAP. In this ATO, as in the TPWs, the SEAD support assignments for package A (the F-16s) and package D (the F-111s) were in conflict; the SEAD could not support packages separated by widely different times and locations. The origin of this conflict between instructions contained in the MAP and ATO may be found in the procedures for completing and publishing the ATO. In particular, Guidance, Apportionment, and Targeting (GAT) planners often reexamined and revised the MAP even after it had been converted into TPWs and the ATO.

Another MAP was printed at 2:27 P.M. (the operator entered January 20, 2:00 P.M. into the computer file). The job for package A printed in this MAP was identical to the earlier MAPs. The MAP still listed forty F-16s in the package instead of the twenty-four tasked in the TPWs and the ATO. However, changes to the package were written in pencil on the printed MAP. The F-16 package was lined out, the TOT was changed to between 4:00 and 4:30 A.M., and the target was changed to the H2 and H3 airfields (see Figure 7.1). The tasking for package D (the F-111s) remained essentially unchanged.[20]

The next MAP, and the first one approved (and signed) by Brigadier General Buster C. Glosson,* was printed at 6:48 P.M. This MAP assigned package A against the H2 and H3 airfield complexes with a change in TOT, as the penciled changes to the previous MAP indicated (forty F-16s were still listed). Package D still was assigned targets in the Tallil area. Pencil changes on this MAP indicate that package D was "retargeted to H2," which matched the published ATO tasking.[21]

A final MAP, printed at 8:02 P.M. and signed by Brigadier General Glosson and Lieutenant Colonel David A. Deptula (the chief GAT planner), was identical to the previous 6:48 P.M. version. Package A remained assigned against the H2 and H3 airfields. Package D continued to be assigned to attack targets in the Tallil area, despite the tasking in the published ATO and the penciled change on the previous (6:48 P.M.) MAP.[22] Then, at one point in the planning process, someone assigned both packages A and D to attack the area of the H2 and H3 airfields. The change in package A's target area and TOT was not entered into the ATO, and it is not clear whether the change was passed via telephone to the 363 TFW. Moreover, no version of the MAP showed a reduction from forty to twenty-four in the number of F-16s assigned to strike the target. The ATO's target change, assigning package D (the F-111s) to attack the H2 airfield, was not specified in the corresponding MAPs. The ATO also did not include synchronized SEAD support. The suppression aircraft, as specified in the tasking order, still could not support both packages.

The TACC *Change Log* for the January 21 ATO included three notes that might relate to package A. The first note concerned a minor confusion about the responsibility for sweep and escort. The second note adjusted air refueling control times for package A's F-16 that could have supported the changes to the F-16s' target and TOT found in the later versions of the MAP. The third note is confusing. The TACC change log identified the F-16 aircraft in package A by individual mission number and assigned them to strike the "C-7 Chem Prod Fac/Al Taqaddum Afld" (see Figure 7.1).[23] This target does not match any of those assigned in previous MAPs or the published ATO.

What finally happened? All twenty-four 363 TFW F-16s in package A successfully launched and attacked targets. However, the F-16s attacked neither the initial Baghdad area targets nor the H2 and H3 airfield targets identified later in the MAP. Mission Reports (MISREPs) obtained from the 363 TFW indicate that the unit attacked the Habbaniyah Possible Chemical Warfare Production Facility Number 2 and the Al Taqaddum airfield—

*Brigadier General Buster C. Glosson combined staff and line responsibilities as director of the Campaign Plans Division and command of the 14th Air Division (Provisional), through which he had operational control of all tactical fighter units in the theater.

targets approximately 30 miles west of the initial Baghdad area targets. These targets agreed with the revision found in the TACC *Change Log*. All the TOTs for these attacks were in the original TOT block (1:00 to 1:30 P.M.) specified in the first MAP and corresponding ATO.[24] The GAT planners (who worked in the Royal Saudi Air Force building in Riyadh) entered some of these results into their tracking system. Eight F-16s were shown to have struck the Habbaniyah Chemical Warfare facility (see Figure 7.1). Whether these were the eight F-16s from the 363 TFW is not known. The sixteen F-16s that attacked the Al Taqaddum airfield were not noted in the log.[25]

The 48 TFW's MISREPs tell another story. The ATO assigned the F-111s of the package to targets in the H2 airfield area. Of the eight F-111s assigned these targets, only two aircraft released weapons on target. Upon AWACS direction, four aircraft aborted the mission due to lack of tanker support. Two others aborted because of computer or inertial navigation system problems.[26] According to Computer Assisted Force Management System (CAFMS) data, the F-4G mission support package was aborted.[27] It is not known whether other F-4Gs provided support. The EF-111 support from the 366 TFW flew as scheduled in the ATO. It is not known where the aircraft flew.[28] GAT planners did not know what happened either. The GAT's records show that no F-111 aircraft hit the H2 targets assigned to the F-111s in package D for that day. However, forty F-16s attacked that target.[29]

One explanation for this level of confusion on D + 4 is that the GAT planners were beginning to learn how to engage in "dynamic" planning, or planning while attacking, an activity far more difficult than planning in the absence of combat. Brigadier General Glosson also was concerned that diplomatic efforts would lead to a premature end of the air campaign.[30] This concern led him to urge GAT planners to strike all important Iraqi strategic targets as quickly as possible, introducing a constant source of instability. It may be argued that the frequency and tempo of changes ordered by GAT officers early in the air campaign induced a cycle of changes and instability that affected the entire campaign. Since the planning and execution of the ATO cycle involved overlapping activities, the ATO planning process was unable to reach a steady state. Systemic errors were introduced into the planning process by the frequency and tempo of changes to the ATO.[31] In addition, the tenuous nature of the interactions between the GAT planners and the wings, multiplied over one day's (approximately 1,600) strike sorties and then multiplied by the duration of the air campaign, provided a rich source of uncertainty and imperfect knowledge. Clearly, although the Coalition was winning from the start of combat, the size, difficulty, and tempo of the planning effort—as the GAT planners constructed daily plans for more than 2,000 sorties—vitiated the ability of senior leaders and planners to know *specifically* how the air campaign was proceeding. They had a poor understanding of how little they knew about the effect of attacks on such critical Iraqi target systems as the Iraqi nuclear weapons program.[32]

A MILITARY REVOLUTION REALIZED?

This case suggests that a military revolution cannot be achieved solely by improvements in technical weapon system performance (e.g., replacing the F-117A with the F-22). A military revolution based on intelligence, surveillance, targeting sensors, stealth platforms, and long-range precision munitions ultimately depends on an organizational design capable of supplying appropriate and timely information to decision makers and operators. To be effective, the organizational design requires prior analysis of the kinds of decisions made by operating officials, the data needed to make those decisions, and an understanding of how to use the data. Simple "fixes" to improve the quality of information or to secure new types of information are not enough. These fixes must be implemented with reference to the way the entire organizational system operates and must cope with work and communication flows, errors, and damage. For it is the organizational system that will determine whether information is overlooked or incorporated effectively into the decision process and whether the system can operate if its vulnerable elements are attacked.[33]

The events of January 20–21 air campaign illustrate in microcosm important and compelling issues about command and control. First, building and executing an ATO for a static environment (where the planners had months to prepare a detailed plan for the initial attacks) was very different from preparing a plan while fighting and evaluating incoming results (where imperfect information and uncertainty were the rule and not the exception). Anticipating this difference, General Horner would not permit his planners to prepare a detailed attack blueprint beyond the first two days. Yet the Air Force has shown minimal recognition of the need to examine the efficiency–effectiveness trade-offs and vulnerabilities of TACC organization to operate in such an uncertain combat environment.[34] In June 1992, the Defense Science Board described the present organizational structure as one that produced

[1] the lack of readiness which characterized our posture on August 1, 1990, [2] the lack of interoperability of the force deployed, [3] the failure to anticipate the kind of weapons and sensor interactions which became so obviously necessary during Desert Shield, [and] [4] the failure to realistically exercise this contingency scenario and learn from it when it was recognized as the most probable use of military forces. It is the same structure that has consistently [5] failed to address the identification problem in a comprehensive way, [6] failed to create and practice concepts for BDA for the weapons and sensors which were clearly evident, and [7] failed to

anticipate the roles that space sensors, communications, and navigation systems would be required to play in this, the most likely, application of U.S. forces. . . . [T]he basic institutional processes have not changed.[35]

Second, during Desert Shield, the Coalition created a large communication system that transformed the character of military command and control by dispersing decision making and multiplying the number of possible informal communications channels. The presence, for example, of the Secure Telephone Unit-III (also known as the STU-III) made inevitable all sorts of exchanges (unknown and unauthorized by senior leaders) between U.S. defense and intelligence agencies based primarily in North America and theater-based planners and operators. The communications technology diffused both the information needed to run the air campaign and the awareness of the campaign's progress, thereby undermining the concept of central direction of the air effort.[36] In reaction, some analysts now call for direct control of weapons by a centralized group of planners and targeteers (in or out of theater) to minimize the sensor-to-shooter time intervals.

Third, to control large numbers of air sorties during the Gulf War, the Air Force built a complicated organizational architecture. This organization combined sensor technology, satellite communications, and compartmented information with many people in numerous agencies having myriad occupational specialities and perspectives and sometimes conflicting organizational responsibilities. The structure had so many linkages and pathways that naming them—let alone tracing all the connections—may be impossible. The ability of humans to calculate and compute options declines with increasing complexity of problems. As human-organization-machine systems become more integrated, complex, and interdependent, the probability of organizational impairment or failure increases. The availability of secure communications within the theater and between the theater and intelligence and analytic agencies in the United States allowed officers to compensate for the organizational failures of the formal TACC by creating ad hoc solutions. But at some point, the organization of people, agencies, and weapons systems may become so complicated that the kind of ad hoc solutions and fixes that typified Gulf War command and control may not suffice.

Fourth, during the Gulf War there was a difference between what senior leaders and planners believed they could manage and the reality of the war. At each level of CENTAF, key officers believed they were managing the chaos of war. However, when the activities of the many significant participants are pieced together, the problem is that neither planners nor Lieutenant General Horner—the JFACC—knew the details of what was happening in the air campaign or how well the campaign was progressing. For example, Lieutenant General Horner believed he "had real-time control of the air. The only thing I didn't have real-time control of was the F-117s because when they go Stealth, they go silent, but they were generally in Baghdad anyway."[37] Yet this case study and other evidence show that bomb damage assessment was often inadequate or nonexistent, and communications between the GAT and the wings were often confusing. As a result, Horner's quotations are revealing for what they show he knew (or did not know) about the conduct of the war effort at the unit level. Horner may have had real-time control of aircraft at times. But those times were short. Furthermore, the control of operations exercised by the GAT planners was constrained by their lack of adequate BDA and by their conflicts with CENTAF intelligence officers.[38]

In one respect, the sheer numbers of aircraft available may have been decisive in avoiding critical command and control failures that could have resulted in Coalition casualties and losses. When a key GAT planner complained that some air assets were not being used to their greatest effect (e.g., Marine AV-8Bs), Brigadier General Buster C. Glosson responded that there was no need to cause an internal squabble among the Services over doctrine. The Coalition had so many aircraft in theater that it could do whatever its leaders wanted done, and he could afford to let the Marine Corps do what it wanted to do.[39]

Since the beginning of organized warfare, the central problem of command and control has been an intellectual one of organizing—and then gaining access to—information, knowledge, and understanding. Despite improvements in the administration of command and control, the problem of organizing information, knowledge, and understanding has not been solved. The great complexity of modern fighting forces only exacerbates organizational shortcomings. Over time, military and nonmilitary technologies, and the size of the forces involved, have altered and modified the equipment and tactics of command and control. The lethality, mobility, and velocity of contemporary military forces create great opportunities for commanders but also place great demands on the command and control system—the people, equipment, and organizations. Advances in weapons and military support technology are outracing the ability of available command and control organizations to employ and control them.[40]

The F-16/F-111 case study illustrates the difficulties encountered in controlling an air campaign and in documenting what was accomplished. Most of the aircraft deployed to the Gulf did not carry on-board videotape equipment capable of recording munition impact. But even when aircraft had such a capability (the F-15E, F-117A, and F-111F), planners often did not know the results of attacks, either because the information arrived late or because it simply did not exist. In the absence of the cold, hard facts, planners had to assume that attacks were carried out as planned and were effective.

The argument that the Gulf War produced a military revolution assumes that planners understood the appropriate enemy target systems[41] and had appropriate information about the effect and effectiveness of just-completed attacks. However, due to the absence of such information, knowledge, and understanding, the Desert Storm air campaign resembled more a simple target list servicing than a campaign won by the analytical and intellectual feats of planners using airpower to shape the battlefield.

In large measure, victory was due to ample resources in numbers of aircraft, munitions, and fuel and the skills of pilots, aircrews, and support personnel. The encounter with Iraq provides a subtext similar to that advanced by Leo Tolstoy's novel describing the Franco–Russian War, *War and Peace*. Neither victory nor defeat were the result of rationally managed physical or political encounters: The specific commands of Napoleon and his Russian counterpart, Marshal Mikhail I. Kutuzov, simply not did matter.

CONCLUSION: NEW DIRECTIONS FOR AIR FORCE ORGANIZATION

Prospects for an emerging military revolution depend on organizations which can exploit new weapons and communications technologies. What is needed is a rigorous evaluation of real and experimental results concerning the organization of command and control. The effort must examine critical, long-held assumptions about the organization and control of airpower. It is tempting to call for more technology and centralized, tighter control to address the weaknesses illustrated by this case. But the centralized planning and control of airpower provides obvious targets for attack and tends only to exacerbate the negative consequences of uncertainty and imperfect information, not to control them. If present trends continue, the United States may be able to apply theater-based airpower against only weak, small opponents incapable of attacking the vulnerabilities inherent in tightly coupled, complex, and complicated human-machine-organization systems. Peer opponents may resist effectively massed U.S. airpower of the sort used against Iraq. Accordingly, the Air Force should prepare for formidable enemies and explicitly evaluate organizational models appropriating features from a "loosely coupled" system.

Loose coupling avoids overburdening a central planning and control organization that—no matter how well supported by computers—cannot be supported. Furthermore, because loosely coupled organizations are more creative, adaptive, and open to innovation in response to rapidly changing conditions, unexpected problems are easier to handle.[42] Limitations of space here preclude discussion of the trade-offs between tightly and loosely coupled organizations and the utility of each type to coordinate large air campaigns. It should be noted, however, that in the Gulf War, real-time and near–real-time control of forces was exercised by AWACS, JSTARS, and ABCCC from forward areas (rather than from headquarters) in the air–ground portion of the air campaign. These aircraft and their on-board controllers changed the air combat organization in the direction of more loose coupling.[43] It remains to be seen whether the Air Force will develop the organizational structures and procedures to address and resolve the difficult coordination problems (and exploit the communications technology) associated with such loose coupling.

The structure of an organization does not merely describe authority relationships or communication patterns. Rather, it predicts the nature of the problems the organization encounters and the solution to those problems. As senior congressional analyst John M. Collins put it, "Wartime arrangements should be established during peacetime. At the very least, peacetime and wartime setups should correlate closely."[44] We should hope that as the task environment changes—as has occurred due to advances in stealth, precision guidance for munitions, and communications and sensor technologies—so too will the organizational structure. This relationship often is called adaptation or organizational learning. However, there is no guarantee that such adaptation will take place. When the organization's menu of responses—its standard operating procedures—does not change, the organization cuts itself off from the empirical information it needs to accomplish its tasks. We need look no farther than the performance of Saddam Hussein's military to see the consequences of self-delusion and the absence of self-criticism. It takes time and thought to solve organizational communication and coordination problems and to design effective command and control organizations. The rapidity of technological change makes the design task difficult. As General George C. Marshall once noted, "It is utterly impossible to improvise military organizations, and it requires more than a year to build them."[45]

NOTES

I have had outstanding help from knowledgeable, kind, and gracious colleagues in identifying and excising errors of all types from this chapter. These colleagues include Thomas C. Hone, Laura L. Mandeles, Jacob Neufeld, and Sanford S. Terry. Of course, I am responsible for the errors they were unsuccessful in persuading me to remove. I also thank the wonderful staff of the John Marshall branch of the Fairfax County (Virginia) Public Library for securing countless books through interlibrary loan.

1. Excerpt from the opening statement by Representative William Nichols (D-Ala.), House Armed Services Committee, "Hearings on the Reorganization of the Department of Defense," February 19, 1986.

2. However, one new technology may trigger qualitatively higher performance of a set of technologies and capabilities. Such was the case with the use and diffusion of the stirrup during medieval times. The Battle of Hastings, for example, matched the military methods of the seventh century (Harold's Anglo-Saxons) against those of the eleventh century (William's Normans). Harold fought without

cavalry, and the English could do nothing except stand and take punishment from a mobile striking power. Lynne White, Jr., *Medieval Technology and Social Change* (London: Oxford University Press, 1972), 72.

3. See, for example, John W. Bodnar, "The Military Technical Revolution: From Hardware to Information," *Naval War College Review* 46, no. 3 (Summer 1993): 7–21.

4. William J. Perry, "Desert Storm and Deterrence," *Foreign Affairs* 70 (Fall 1991): 66; Ashton B. Carter, William J. Perry, and John D. Steinbruner, *A New Concept of Cooperative Security, Brookings Occasional Papers* (Washington, D.C.: The Brookings Institute, 1992), 3, 29–30; Richard P. Hallion, *Storm over Iraq: Air Power and the Gulf War* (Washington, D.C.: Smithsonian Institution Press, 1992). See also Dan Gouré, "Is There a Military-Technical Revolution in America's Future?" *The Washington Quarterly* 16, no. 4 (Autumn 1993): 179.

5. Thomas C. Hone, Mark D. Mandeles, and Sanford S. Terry, *Gulf War Air Power Survey* 1, Pt. 2, *Command and Control* (Washington, D.C.: USGPO, 1993) [hereafter *GWAPS C&C*].

6. With apologies to James Lea Cate and E. Kathleen Williams, who wrote, "The spectacular spring victories of the Nazis, climaxed by the fall of France, hit the United States like a cold douche." Cate and Williams, "The Air Corps Prepares for War, 1939–1941," in Wesley Frank Craven and James Lea Cate, eds., *The Army Air Forces in World War II, Volume I, Plans and Early Operations January 1939 to August 1942* (Washington, D.C.: USGPO, 1983), 127.

7. Obviously, without access to the objectives and decision calculus employed by senior Iraqi decision makers, we do not really know whether the deployment of U.S. forces deterred an Iraqi invasion of Saudi Arabia, or whether Saddam Hussein intended to invade Saudi Arabia.

8. The GWAPS staff defined a strike as the delivery of a weapon or weapons against a specific target. This definition entails no evaluation of the effectiveness of that strike. A strike sortie is defined in terms of the following mission categories: air interdiction, close air support, defensive counterair, and offensive counterair. See Lewis D. Hill, Doris Cook, and Aron Pinker, *GWAPS* 5, Pt. 1, *A Statistical Compendium*, 403–5.

9. Defense Science Board (DSB), *Lessons Learned During Operations Desert Shield & Desert Storm* (U) (Washington, D.C.: DOD, May 1992), 60, 62 [hereafter *Lessons Learned*].

10. For background on the ATO planning cycle and Master Attack Plan, see Hone et al., *GWAPS C&C*, 8–24.

11. The MAP was a command and control innovation developed by Lieutenant Colonel David A. Deptula, the chief planner in the GAT. The purpose of the MAP was to focus planning efforts on simultaneous and relentless attack on Iraqi targets, relationships among targets to be attacked, and operational-level effects. Target Planning Worksheets (TPWs), an existing planning tool, were used to transfer information from the MAP to the ATO. The MAP was an essential tool for the planners to facilitate the planning process and to centralize authority in the hands of the planners. See Hone et al., *GWAPS C&C*, chaps. 6 and 7.

12. The records cited in this case study are housed at the Air Force Historical Research Agency, Maxwell Air Force Base, Alabama. The designation of records

reflects the style employed by GWAPS staff. GWAPS, CSS Safe 6, DESERT SHIELD 20 January 1991, Air Tasking Orders (ATO).

13. GWAPS, Black Hole (BH) Box 1, Folder 9, Master Attack Plan, D + 4, 21 Jan 91, 5th 24 Hours.
14. Ibid.
15. Target Planning Worksheets, ATO D + 4, 21 Jan 91, HQ 9AF, Shaw AFB, N.C., Lieutenant Colonel Jefferey Feinstein.
16. Ibid.
17. GWAPS, CSS Safe 6, DESERT SHIELD 20 January 1991, ATO.
18. Ibid.
19. Ibid.
20. GWAPS, BH Box 1, Folder 9, Master Attack Plan, D + 4, 21 January 1991, 5th 24 Hours.
21. Ibid.
22. Ibid.
23. GWAPS, TACC ATO Changes, New Acquisitions Number 370.
24. 363 TFW Mission Reports, 211700Z, 211730Z, 211730Z Jan 91, GWAPS Missions Data Base.
25. Target Attacks By Day By Aircraft H-Hour-Day +32, GWAPS, Box 2, Folder 56.
26. 48 TFW Mission Reports, 210415Z, 210640Z, 210850Z, and 211327Z Jan 91, GWAPS Mission Data Base.
27. GWAPS Mission Data Base.
28. Ibid.
29. Target Attacks By Day By Aircraft H-Hour-Day +32, GWAPS, Box 2, Folder 56.
30. Although Soviet Secretary General Mikhail Gorbachev offered political support to the Coalition, there were concerns that the Soviets simultaneously were pursuing another agenda. Five days after the start of the air campaign, Soviet officials were still attempting to broker a peace agreement. These Soviet efforts continued. On January 29, 1991, a joint statement by Secretary of State James Baker, III and Soviet Foreign Minister Alexander Bessmertnykh asserted that a cease-fire was possible. On February 11, Soviet envoy Yevgeny Primakov arrived in Baghdad to discuss a possible cease-fire with President Saddam Hussein. Andrew Rosenthal, "Bush Demands Iraq Start Pullout Today Despite Its Assent to 3-Week Soviet Plan," *New York Times*, January 23, 1991, 1; Bill Nichols and Johanna Neuman, "U.S. Soviet Cease-fire Plan Offered," *Washington Times*, January 30, 1991, 1; Rick Atkinson, "Bush: No Immediate Plan to Start Ground War, U.S. Will Rely 'For a While' on Air Power Against Iraqis," *Washington Post*, February 12, 1991, 1.
31. This situation is similar to that described by W. Edwards Deming, "On Some Statistical Aids toward Economic Production," *Interfaces* 5 (August 1975): 1–15.
32. See Barry D. Watts and Thomas A. Keaney, *GWAPS* 2, Pt. 2, *Effects and Effectiveness*.
33. Mark D. Mandeles, "Between a Rock and a Hard Place: Implications for the U.S. of Third World Nuclear Weapon and Ballistic Missile Proliferation," *Security Studies* 1, no. 2 (Winter 1991): 251.
34. Paul Bracken argues that there is not enough "fresh thinking . . . that starts with a clean sheet of paper and examines the revolutionary impact of technology

on U.S. strategy and force structure." "The Military After Next," *The Washington Quarterly* 16, no. 4 (Autumn 1993): 157. This view is compatible with the argument advanced by Earl H. Tilford, Jr., that the Air Force has long had great difficulty distinguishing myth from history. See *Crosswinds: The Air Force's Setup in Vietnam* (College Station, Tex.: Texas A&M University Press, 1993). Barry D. Watts echoed this view: "The U.S. Air Force [has a] tendency to prefer uncritical advocacy of air power's capabilities and past achievements." See "Book Review," *Air Power History* 40, no. 4 (Winter 1993): 56.

35. DSB, *Lessons Learned* (U), June 1992, 61–62.

36. General H. Norman Schwarzkopf's memoirs detail the daily exchanges and limitations imposed by top national security officials in Washington, D.C. H. Norman Schwarzkopf with Peter Petre, *It Doesn't Take a Hero* (New York: Bantam Books, 1992). See also Hone et al., *GWAPS C&C*, especially chaps. 4, 6, 7, and 8; Teresa R. Clark, Richard A. Gunkel, Lawrence L. Lausten, Barbara A. Phillips, and Mitchell P. Slate, *GWAPS*, 4, Pt. 2, *Space Operations;* Thomas A. Keaney and Eliot A. Cohen, *GWAPS Summary Report*, chap. 8.

37. Interview, Barry Barlow, Richard G. Davis, and Perry Jamieson with Lieutenant General Charles A. Horner, Commander, Ninth AF, March 4, 1992.

38. See Hone et al., *GWAPS C&C*, chaps. 6–8, especially pp. 182–85, 255–62.

39. Interview Office of Air Force History, with Lieutenant Colonel David A. Deptula, SAF/OSX, November 29, 1991.

40. Martin van Creveld, *Technology and War: From 2000 B.C. to the Present* (New York: The Free Press, 1989); Mark D. Mandeles, "Understanding Command and Control in Complex Military Organizations" (Alexandria, Va.: The J. de Bloch Group, 1993).

41. The difference between particular targets and target systems and the causal relationship between war objectives and target systems are discussed in Watts and Keaney, *Effects and Effectiveness*.

42. See Martin Landau, "On Multiorganizational Systems in Public Administration," *Public Administration Research and Theory* 1, no. 1 (January 1991): 5–18. An extended discussion and comparison of loosely coupled organization with tight hierarchies as applied to command and control is provided in Mandeles, "Understanding Command and Control in Complex Military Organizations."

43. Hone et al., *GWAPS C&C*, chap. 9.

44. John M. Collins, "High Command Arrangements Early in the Persian Gulf Crisis," CRS Report for Congress, 90-453 RCO, September 21, 1990.

45. George C. Marshall, *Selected Speeches and Statements of General of the Army George C. Marshall* (Washington, D.C.: The Infantry Journal, 1945), 221.

Part IV

THE GROUND WAR: THE ARMY AND THE MARINES

Most of us are familiar with General Schwarzkopf's much ballyhooed "end run" around the Iraqis' right flank and television news pictures of long lines of surrendering Iraqi troops. Many of us recall the almost humorous sound bite on CNN news of one English-speaking, American-educated Iraqi "drafted" soldier wearing a Chicago Bears tee-shirt under his fatigues, surrendering to news cameramen, and asking "What took you so long? I haven't had any real food for weeks!" So many books, including the general's own autobiography, have explained in detail how the Allied ground forces won a smashing conventional military victory over such an apparently formidable foe misled by Saddam Hussein.

At the time, some wild news reports claimed that as many as 300,000 Iraqis died in the war. There were macabre stories of U.S. bulldozers burying hundreds, even thousands, of enemy soldiers alive. More recently, responsible reports from both the military and civilian sources suggest that the actual Iraqi battle deaths range anywhere from 15,000 to 25,000. As we now know, few were elite Republican Guard forces, and most were poorly trained and often unwilling recruits. Much of the armor and vehicle traffic destroyed in the spectacular battles in the north were in fact already abandoned. Indeed, these more recent facts came into focus with the reemergence of Saddam Hussein's forces near the Kuwaiti border in early October 1994.

The following two chapters seek to explain more fully the role of the Army, Marine Corps, and Allied forces in the Persian Gulf War.

Larry E. Cable, in his chapter "Playing in the Sandbox: Doctrine, Combat, and Outcome on the Ground," examines in great detail the actual factors involved in the evolution of the combat plans that were used to execute the Allied campaign against the Iraqis. He looks at the personal relationships between the senior, and not so senior, commanders of all the Services and Allied nations involved in the ground war. He relates the difficulties in maintaining a cohesive alliance and the single-mindedness of the single commander—H. Norman Schwarzkopf. Unlike other articles and books of the past, Cable is not always complimentary of the general's tactics, planning, execution, or his often difficult personality. Using little-used and recently declassified primary data; interviews with many well-known and lesser known, yet important, participants; and his own personal knowledge of the planning phase, he weaves a tale of a much less perfect ground war than that portrayed by other writings, the popular CNN videotape, and General Schwarzkopf's autobiography, *It Doesn't Take a Hero*.

Among other things, John T. Quinn and Jack Shulimson, in "U.S. Marine Operations in the Persian Gulf War, 1990–1991," examine the reason the Marines, traditional shock and attack forces, were primarily used as decoys. They discuss frankly the relationship between Marine leaders and officers with General Schwarzkopf and his staff. They finally suggest that despite the seemingly secondary role the U.S. Marine Corps played, it was nonetheless significant and critical to the outcome.

In the end, both of these chapters, although written from decidedly different points of view (like most of the chapters in this book), raise important new questions about events that, as it turns out, were not well understood by most American scholars or citizens in the months and years that followed the Persian Gulf War. These studies will take us to the next stage of critical historical analysis of the ground portion of the Gulf War and help us grasp the real results and lessons from that conflict.

—William Head

8

Playing in the Sandbox: Doctrine, Combat, and Outcome on the Ground

Larry E. Cable

March 1991 was a great month for Americans, who shared the pervasive perception that the good guys had won decisively and completely in a very American war. It had been a moral crusade against a satanic adversary in which the forces of righteousness had, at little cost to themselves, crushed the minions of evil and sent them streaming along "Hell's Highway" back to the foul pit from which they had emerged six months earlier. As a bonus, the soul-sapping specter of Vietnam had finally been laid to rest along with the toxic dreams of Saddam Hussein.

It had been a good war, even a perfect one: The enemy had been easy to hate, combining an act of seemingly unprovoked aggression and a rhetorical style completely alien to the American mind; the response of the United States had been the formation of a Coalition under UN authority, which underscored the apparent highmindedness and altruism of the collective sacrifice. Finally, traditional American strengths had been articulated and employed. After the long, frustrating failures experienced with limited war in support of policy in both Vietnam and Korea, the crusading zeal of Americans expressed in an act of collective security under the direction of an American military rich in technology and management skills had brought the type of victory which we had so long associated with our military history.

There were some points of dissent in the wake of Iraqi armistice, but these were of little import, at least initially. Some carped that the victory was not as complete as it should have been given that Saddam Hussein was still in power. Institutional egos within the Department of Defense plumped, pumped, and postured, for victory is a fungible commodity and the real conquest was yet to come, as the Services maneuvered to escape the next megaton round of defense cutbacks. Partisans of the Air Force emphasized the decisive nature of the air war, arguing that with some prolongation the persistent dream of truly decisive strategic airpower would have been achieved. Unsurprisingly, the perspective of the Army was different, underscoring the spectacular speed of the ground war and the minuscule casualties received during the process of destroying a large portion of the Iraqi Army. The Navy pointedly noted the importance of its platforms to the air and ground wars alike, while the Marines ignored the force that waited afloat as part of an effort to deceive the Iraqis and congratulated themselves on having accomplished the difficult mission of liberating Kuwait City.

The clash of egos, both individual and institutional in nature, combines with the general visceral sense of well-being in the wake of the collapse of the Soviet Union and the evident victory in the "Persian Excursion" to limit detached and reasonably dispassionate examination of the war as a whole as well as its penultimate phase: the ground campaign. When this synergy is taken in conjunction with the reality that it will be another fifteen or more years before the larger portion of the currently classified materials dealing with the formulation and execution of policy during Desert Shield and Desert Storm will be available to historians, it must be concluded that any assessments made at this close proximity to the war must be tentative. A further reality must be acknowledged: Historians, having been denied their best tools, must rely more on the nonattributable sources so long a staple of journalism. The citations, notes, and similar scholarly paraphernalia with which histories are normally equipped will be absent for now, replaced by the processes of educated inference and discrete paraphrase so long the primary methodology of the intelligence analyst.

In Iraq and Kuwait, the United States finally was able to fight the war for which it had so long prepared: armored, mechanized, and potentially nuclear combat. That the war was not fought against the enemy or on the physical terrain for which U.S. and other forces had prepared for nearly a half century was in large measure irrelevant. Indeed, the absence of villages and towns scattered across Germany in an inconveniently dense array allowed a far more effective employment of the doctrine for high-mobility, high-firepower war. The removal of the villages, the absence of a credible nuclear capacity on the part of the Iraqis, the collapse of the Soviet Union (and with it any possibility of outside military or diplomatic support for Iraq), and the lengthy period provided the United States for diplomatic and logistic preparations assured a Coalition victory. There was nothing magical nor surprising about the quick battlefield success of the United States and its allies between February 24 and 27, 1991. It was the war for which long, extensive, and expensive preparations had been made, against an opponent vastly inferior in all respects to the original Soviet adversary.

The basis of U.S. Army doctrine over the past 150 years has been the Napoleonic experience as interpreted by Karl von Clausewitz and Antoine Jomini. A review of the various editions of Field Manual (FM) 100-5 *Operations* between the 1930s and 1970s shows a persistent focus on decisive combat leading to the destruction of the enemy's combat power and thus its political will to continue the war.[1] A common thread that linked all the editions between the end of World War II and the late 1970s was an emphasis on firepower as the determinate of victory. However, although the priority continued to rest on the destruction of enemy forces through superior firepower, from 1954 to 1962 the importance of mobility was increasingly emphasized until the two were on a par. The continued elevation of mobility was a necessary response to the demands of the nuclear battlefield posited for the NATO–Warsaw Pact version of Armageddon. As the destructive power of nuclear munitions had become greater and more greatly appreciated, mobility (or, in the terminology of the U.S. Army's principles of war, maneuver) became, at least implicitly, the first among equals. Given that U.S. and Allied forces were disposing ever greater firepower in widely scattered and highly mobile formations, the problems of command, control, and communications became all the more central to combat effectiveness. By 1962, command, control, and communications (C3) reached a level of importance equal to the other two doctrinal pillars. Shoot, move, talk had become the three-word slogan which summarized all ground combat and combat support activities.

The doctrinal construct erected for use in Europe was less than splendid when applied inappropriately in South Vietnam. Arguably, incorrect doctrine was a major, perhaps the major, contributor to the American defeat in Southeast Asia. It may be argued with equal or greater justification that the conceptualization of ground combat forces as a subordinate force multiplier to airpower, which conditioned U.S. field force operations from the summer of 1965 on, was both more responsible for the ultimate U.S. failure and made inevitable by the nature of U.S. Army doctrine.[2] Other than the realization by some that doctrinal failures played some role in the Vietnam outcome, the military, certainly the Army, behaved as though the unsavory and unsatisfactory little affair in the bush of Southeast Asia had never occurred.

Although there were no direct or immediate lessons learned from Vietnam obvious in the evolution of Army doctrine during the hollow years of the 1970s, it became evident by the end of that lamentable decade that the Army's doctrine makers had been neither asleep nor demoralized by the twin kicks of defeat and budget cuts. A new, or at least seemingly new, concept emerged: Air-Land (later AirLand) battle.

In several essential aspects, such as the continued emphasis on shooting, moving, and talking, the new AirLand idea constituted the refurbishment of old wine in old bottles by replacing stodgy labels with those of a more modern look. This was appropriate because the doctrine was still biased toward the European environment and the numerically superior Warsaw Pact adversary.[3] In other ways, the AirLand battle concept as formulated in 1982 and modified in 1986 represented a sophisticated understanding of the changed nature of the battlefield as a result of rapid evolution in war-fighting technologies. In particular, the accent placed on the depth of the battlefield with the corollaries stressing initiative, synchronization, rapidity of maneuver, and high operational tempo coupled with the capacity to sustain rapid, intense operations over time demonstrate an accurate appreciation not only of the realities governing the nightmare scenario of the "crimson tide" pouring through the Fulda Gap in eastern Iraq, but also the historical experience with ground combat, which had demonstrated repeatedly that rapid movement coupled with sustained high-tempo combat destroyed the structural integrity and effectiveness of the defender's C3 as well as, on occasion, the political will of the defender's command structure.[4]

Since no military doctrine is conceived in some Army ivory tower by theorists divorced from the institutional realities, it is not surprising that the AirLand concept, like a predecessor twenty years earlier, the Penatomic division,* is at least implicitly predicated on the need to show, regardless of changes in weapons or delivery systems, that ground combat will not only remain a necessity, but the centrality of successful war fighting and war winning. The underlying thrust, not only of the AirLand concept as it emerged in the years of scarce resources and fierce competition over roles and missions, but also of the doctrine as published in the 1980s as the Reagan administration defense expenditures accelerated with seeming exponential vigor, was that ground combat will never again be a force multiplier for airpower. The older relation of air operations supporting ground combat would be restored and maintained. The AirLand doctrine would place the Army in a better position regarding the institutional rivalries for budget, which have occurred constantly behind the facade of "jointness."

The new doctrine was adopted during a period of sustained budgetary abundance, which saw much new equipment enter the Army's inventory. In addition, the relative attractiveness of the military as compared to civilian employment opportunities during the majority of the Reagan years assured that the volunteer-based Army would recruit and retain people of high ability as compared with earlier periods in its history. The combination of new, far more sophisticated equipment and capable personnel po-

*This is a five-unit division (as opposed to a three-unit division), made up of smaller units in the fifties and sixties designed to survive independently in a nuclear environment.

tentiated the effectiveness of the AirLand concept, which, the Army candidly noted, depended in large measure on human factors.[5] By the time Kuwait became a primetime news dateline, the U.S. Army had a fine package for major regional conflicts, particularly since the nuclear dimension had been attenuated to the point of nonexistence with the collapse of the Soviet Union. Never before had the Army had the combination of a well-developed doctrine, so much excellent, new equipment, and so many competent, well-trained, and well-led troops. Further, it had engaged in two confidence-building operations in Grenada and Panama, which had beneficial effects both within and without the Army.

Because the exhibition season concluded with the arrest of Manuel Noriega, it was a bad time for an aggressor to challenge U.S. interests. It is, fortunately, beyond the scope of this chapter to consider the policies of the Reagan and Bush administrations toward Iraq and the messages which might or might not have been advertently or inadvertently sent to Baghdad. More important, it is not necessary to attempt the deconstruction of Saddam Hussein's reasoning or actual and ostensible goals in the August 2, 1990 invasion of Kuwait. All that is necessary to allow the development of an appreciation of the ground campaign is an understanding of the goals, definition of victory, and theory of victory developed by the United States and the nature, character, quality, strategy, and operational attributes of the Iraqi forces and command structure.

In essence, the United States' view of the Iraqi invasion of Kuwait and the formulation of a response to that event was identical to the American perspective on the North Korean invasion of South Korea in June 1950. In 1950 and in 1990, the global political order was in a state of flux, with the result that the United States not only had to formulate an appropriate global policy, but either discover or exploit a relevant opportunity to implement the policy through seizing the leadership role. In 1950, the overarching need was the firm establishment of a containment policy under American leadership within a collective security context. In 1990, the death of the Communist threat took containment with it to a common grave, with the result that the United States, as the only global power, was in the throes of redefining its role, caught between competing internal political imperatives of reemerging disengagement (exemplified by the "end of history" motif among intellectuals and the "peace dividend" theme among political leaders and public opinion molders, who were convinced that the United States had ignored its internal problems too long during the consuming struggle of the bipolar confrontation) and the pervasive sense of self-imposed moral obligation to promote peace, stability, human rights, and related virtues. The Iraqi invasion provided a perfect opportunity for the United States to settle this internal political struggle on the side of continued global engagement.

Given the similarity between the Korean and Kuwaiti contexts, it is not facetious to suggest that the U.S. policy response in 1990 was identical to that which had been formulated forty years earlier, a limited war in support of policy carried out through the United Nations as an action of collective security. In both cases, the execution of policy was facilitated by the absence of the Soviet Union, in 1950 through the miscalculation of Stalin's pique and in 1990 through internal economic crisis and political turmoil signaling impending collapse. Although the intelligence available to the Bush administration regarding internal Soviet dynamics is unknown and the several policy shifts undertaken by the Gorbachev regime were undoubtedly somewhat unnerving, the willingness of the administration to continue with preparations for Desert Storm during the final Soviet mediation efforts indicates a high likelihood that the administration correctly appreciated the new reality that the Soviet Union was in a terminal stage and would be both unwilling and unable to oppose the U.S.-led Coalition.

One of the most impressive feats of the Bush administration was its ability to concoct the frosting of moral crusade to cover the cake of limited war. The American public had never understood nor accepted the idea of limited war, let alone the reality, as demonstrated in Vietnam and, to a much greater degree, Korea. If the public and its all-too-representative body, the Congress, were to support a war, even a short one, it would be necessary to sell the war as a moral crusade against an unmitigated evil. President Bush and key subordinates were able to do this with great effect.

In accomplishing the necessary political task of selling an American military commitment to Kuwait and Saudi Arabia, the administration was able to capitalize on three factors: the capacity to define substantial, ostensible goals requiring the use of force in terms which comported well with defining American public values; the nature and past actions of the Iraqi government; and the background public recognition regarding the cruciality of Persian Gulf oil to both global and domestic economic stability. As a result, fundamental goals such as the definition of U.S. leadership in the post–Cold War world and the restoration of regional stability to the Persian Gulf states by reconstructing the balance of power in the area could be masked by explicit and implicit political goals of greater palatability to the American public.

The explicit aims of Bush administration policy were the restoration of the status quo ante bellum through the ejection of the Iraqi occupation forces; the punishment of Iraqi aggression through the removal of that nation's offensive capabilities, both actual and potential; and, at least implicitly, the removal of Saddam Hussein from power. These goals were rendered agreeable to the majority of Americans by two considerations: the memories of previous oil embargoes and the perceived nature of the Iraqi regime.

There is no doubt that the past and contemporary practices of the Iraqi government had been unacceptable to American norms. Once Iraq had lost the mantle of protection which it had enjoyed during the Iran–Iraq War, it was easy and effective to capitalize on all the previously downplayed actions of Saddam Hussein, such as the use of chemical weapons on Kurdish targets, as well as to view with palpable fear the Iraqi efforts to produce weapons of mass destruction. It was not without both reason and effect that Saddam Hussein was repeatedly compared invidiously with Adolf Hitler. Although there was no substantial justification for the assertion that Saddam Hussein had acted in ways that were qualitatively different from the actions of former American clients, such as the Shah of Iran or members of the U.S.-led Coalition (such as Syria's Assad), Saddam Hussein and his regime were portrayed as such.

During the lengthy preparations for offensive war which lasted from August 1990 to January 1991, the Bush administration was able to exploit effectively for diplomatic and political purposes the delay which has been imposed by the logistics challenge of providing a sufficiently large, well-enough supplied, and fully acclimatized force to accomplish the two explicit goals. Not only was the administration able to provide every appearance of having given peace a chance, it was able to utilize the inept diplomatic efforts of the Iraqis against them. Never before had military necessity been so well employed for building a coalition or assuring overwhelming support among the American people.[6]

The administration was less successful in defining victory than it was either in identifying ostensible and fundamental goals or in employing them in the development of international and domestic consensus. Although it was easy to define victory with respect to the explicit goals of restoring the status quo ante and reducing Iraq's offensive potential as well as the implicit goal of removing Saddam Hussein from power, it was not so easy to define victory in the context of the two underlying goals of redefining the role of the United States in an emerging global political order or of assuring regional stability through the restoration of a regional balance of power. As a consequence, although the definition of victory regarding important components of the overall American design was accomplished easily, a coherent and comprehensive definition was not. This lack made the development of a relevant theory of victory all the more complex and assured that the complete accomplishment of American aims was generally all the less certain.

During the months of waiting before any offensive operations would be possible, the major task of the administration and its chief military advisers after the construction of a Coalition abroad and a consensus at home was the development of a theory of victory which was both relevant to the realities on the ground in the area of operations and coherent with both the goals and the definitions of victory. At root there were two options available to the administration, which can be cast accurately in the terminology of the Cold War: containment and rollback. Under the containment option, the United States and its Coalition partners would draw and defend a line in the sand enclosing and isolating Iraq economically, diplomatically, and militarily. This, coupled with appropriate psychological and covert or clandestine operations, would not only place destructive pressure on the Iraqi armed forces and government, it would allow the exploitation of the deep fault lines which ran through Iraqi society. Favoring the containment option were considerations such as the low probability of risk and attendant American casualties. Working against the containment option was an old enemy: time. As the forty years of containment against the Soviet Union had shown, time must be expended in truly un-American quantities for it to work. Expenditure of time would be particularly dangerous given the strange bedfellow coloration of the Coalition, the uncertainty as to whether or not the Gorbachev regime could or would continue its course toward further political and economic reform and thus its diplomatic malleability, and the necessity of maintaining domestic political support by an American public which had just been relieved of the multigeneration burden of the Cold War. The rollback option would require active offensive operation by both air and ground forces, with a real risk of significant and perhaps politically debilitating American casualties, but it would have the advantage of providing a very high probability of victory within an acceptable period of time. In all probability, the time consideration more than any other factor pushed the administration rapidly to selecting the rollback option and, with it, a theory of victory dependent on offensive military operations. Although it would be hard to debate the premise on which the option was selected, the relevance of the theory of victory to the definitions of victory and to the fundamental political goals is open to discussion.

When the rollback option was selected, it became obvious that the United States would have to deploy a sizable combat force, both air and ground, ultimately numbering more than 530,000 troops, as well as the enormous logistics structure necessary to support it. It was also obvious that high-grade intelligence relevant to military planning would have to be developed concerning the defensive capacities of the Iraqi Army and Air Force. Further, it would be necessary to develop a plan which would allow for the effective meshing of Coalition forces, which varied widely in language, doctrine, equipment, training, and competence. Finally, it would be imperative that suitable training, liaison, and C3 be undertaken to allow effective implementation of the plan.

The AirLand battle concept places an appropriately high priority on systematic intelligence operations focusing on intelligence preparation of the battlefield.[7] In the intelligence preparation of the battlefield, as in the development of the plan for offensive operations, a critical element is the enemy.

Consider the dispositions, equipment, doctrine, capabilities and probable intentions of the enemy. Because of the strength of established defenses, commanders should aggressively seek gaps or weaknesses in the enemy's defenses. Enemy defensive preparations should be studied, obstructed and frustrated. Commanders plan to penetrate enemy security areas, overcome obstacles, avoid the strengths of established defenses and destroy the coherence of the defense. This requires active intelligence collection oriented on critical units and areas. Enemy reserves in particular must be identified and located as accurately as possible. Enemy air capabilities and air defenses are also vital aspects of the intelligence estimate since they effect [sic] friendly freedom of maneuver.[8]

In addition to the enemy, a prime focus of both intelligence preparations and planning activity is the terrain and weather affecting the presumed area of offensive operations. Of particular importance is identification and exploitation of terrain and weather conditions which would facilitate rapid movement to the enemy's rear.

The clear purpose of intelligence is to provide U.S. and friendly force planners with a clear, accurate, and timely picture of the enemy's strengths and weaknesses as well as the physical environment influencing military operations so enemy strengths might be either neutralized or avoided while enemy weaknesses are exploited. The AirLand concept as implemented by 1986 made explicit a notion which at best had been implied in previous doctrinal concepts: The strengths of U.S. forces should be matched against the weaknesses of the enemy.

It has been argued that the U.S. intelligence community, in particular the Central Intelligence Agency, failed to provide effective warning of the Iraqi invasion of Kuwait while the entire intelligence structure, civilian and military, failed to assess accurately the size and competence of the Iraqi forces in Kuwait at the time Desert Storm commenced.[9] Absent the relevant documents, it is impossible to conclude the degree to which this suggestion is tenable. Certainly there is evidence suggesting that the number of Iraqi troops in the Kuwaiti theater of operations was less than half that believed to be in place by U.S. intelligence analysts. Overestimating enemy strength as a basis for planning an offensive is certainly preferable to underestimating because it will help assure success rather than guarantee failure.

There are even stronger indications that the intelligence estimates regarding the number of Iraqi Scud missiles and launchers were wildly inaccurate perhaps by an order of magnitude. Although this may well have been the case, its importance should not be exaggerated, because the Scuds could have no military effect and their political consequences could be contained, particularly by a quick and decisive Coalition military victory. The importance of the Scud contretemps lies not in the relevance of this specific estimate to the proper application of offensive doctrine, but rather in the inferences which it allows regarding the utility of American overhead imaging systems and the capacity or utilization of U.S. and other special operations forces in reconnaissance missions. Again, there can be no definitive answers until and unless the relevant documents are declassified, but the underestimation of the Scuds, like the overestimation of the competence and number of Iraqi troops in southern Iraq and Kuwait, hints at a failure to utilize special operations forces properly in one of their most important roles: strategic, or long-range, reconnaissance.

While the press and public focused on the presumed size of the Iraqi forces as well as the potential usage of chemical and biological weapons by the Iraqis and the horrifying losses suffered by the Iraqis during the long and awesomely bloody stalemate of the Iran–Iraq War, the proliferating intelligence shops deluging the Arabian peninsula in pursuit of their parent institutions' imperatives shook together far more completely, effectively, and rapidly than had been the case during the Vietnam War. The Iraqi forces demonstrated a number of serious weaknesses which lent themselves to ready exploitation by firepower-heavy, high-mobility forces, such as those deployed by the United States, Great Britain, and France.

Some of the obvious and readily exploitable Iraqi deficiencies had been evidenced in the Iran–Iraq War.[10] The Iraqi command philosophy and communication system, reflecting the centralized, autocratic nature of the government, was rigid, hierarchical, and unable to accommodate fluid battlefield situations. Exacerbating this was Saddam Hussein's one genuine echo of Adolf Hitler: a need to intervene directly in operational and tactical matters, usually to the disadvantage of the Iraqi military. Bluntly, Saddam Hussein had already demonstrated the propensity to fill the role so ably created by Hitler: a de facto, unintentional secret weapon operating on behalf of his opponents. The Iraqi logistics system, showing its British origins and Soviet guidance alike, was of the "push" variety in which remote headquarters managed the allocation of supplies as well as the transport and distribution system down to the corps level. Because battlefield realities generally showed an unpleasant disinclination to match the programmatic dictates of a general headquarters, the Iraqi logistics tail could be perturbed much to the disadvantage of the dog it sought to wag. The Coalition capacity to interrupt the flow of soldiers and supplies was potentiated by the deficiencies of the road and rail net, which linked the major logistics depots near Basra with the Kuwaiti theater of operations. There were only three roads running from Basra to the corps headquarters in or near Kuwait. Further, since the corps headquarters averaged 150 kilometers from the forward troops, the opportunities for Coalition interdiction efforts were legion. Perhaps the most fatal and easily exploitable weakness of the Iraqi Army was its fundamental doctrine, which emphasized positional warfare with heavy static defenses providing a base of support for methodical and slow-moving offensives. In this, the Iraqis resembled the French in the

1930s building the world's largest trench, the Maginot Line, to mount slow, deliberate offensives controlled by a rigid command and communication system. The net effect of these weaknesses—particularly the last, the philosophical base of their doctrine—was to assure that every U.S. strength was almost automatically aligned against an Iraqi debility.

Almost as though to ensure that even the most inept intelligence system coupled with the most resolutely indifferent planners could not miss the sign mounted on the Iraqi rear which read, "Kick here," the Iraqi defense planners engaged in an exercise of mirror imaging in the positioning of their forces and fortifications. It became evident from the disposition of the Iraqi forces as well as the placement of the series of defensive works collectively dubbed the "Saddam Line" that the Baghdad command did not believe that an attack could proceed through the interior desert terrain of northern Saudi Arabia and southern Iraq. After all, the Iraqis must have reasoned, the ground is bad, the roads nonexistent, the lines of supply overly lengthy, and therefore the Coalition forces would not think of using the interior route. Again, the Iraqi high command resembled the French on the eve of World War II, who saw no need to fortify or even screen the Ardennes on the basis of belief that the terrain was too difficult to be used by invading Germans.

Believing that Kuwait City and Basra represented the centers of gravity and that the only likely axis of Coalition attack would be directly north from Saudi Arabia into Kuwait, the Iraqis concentrated their relatively low-mobility infantry divisions within Kuwait and into the former neutral zone, placing nineteen infantry, one mechanized infantry, and two armored divisions south of a line drawn west from Kuwait City. An additional two infantry, two mechanized, and four armored divisions were located on or south of a line drawn west from Bubiyan. Further west, in the desert interior near the villages of Busayyah and As Salman, the Iraqis stationed two understrength infantry divisions in what they must have presumed to have been a screening role. The relatively high-quality mobile forces of the Republican Guard, including two armored, one mechanized, and one special forces division reinforced by three regular army armored divisions, were based along the Iraq–Kuwait border near Safwan, in a mass maneuver role. Finally, a lone infantry division consumed supplies and wasted oxygen near Jallibah and Tallil on the Euphrates River. The disposition of the defending forces would have been adequate to the task provided that the following Iraqi assumptions were proven to be correct: Airpower was less important in a ground support role than as a "force in being" and thus was a wasting asset, the strategic defense was inherently more potent than the offensive because of its capacity to reduce progressively the attacker's political will, and the reinvention during the Iran–Iraq War of the tactical and operational art of the Western Front in 1916 remained true in 1991 and the only possible axis of advance was that through Kuwait.

Figure 8.1
Map Showing the Coalition Offensive

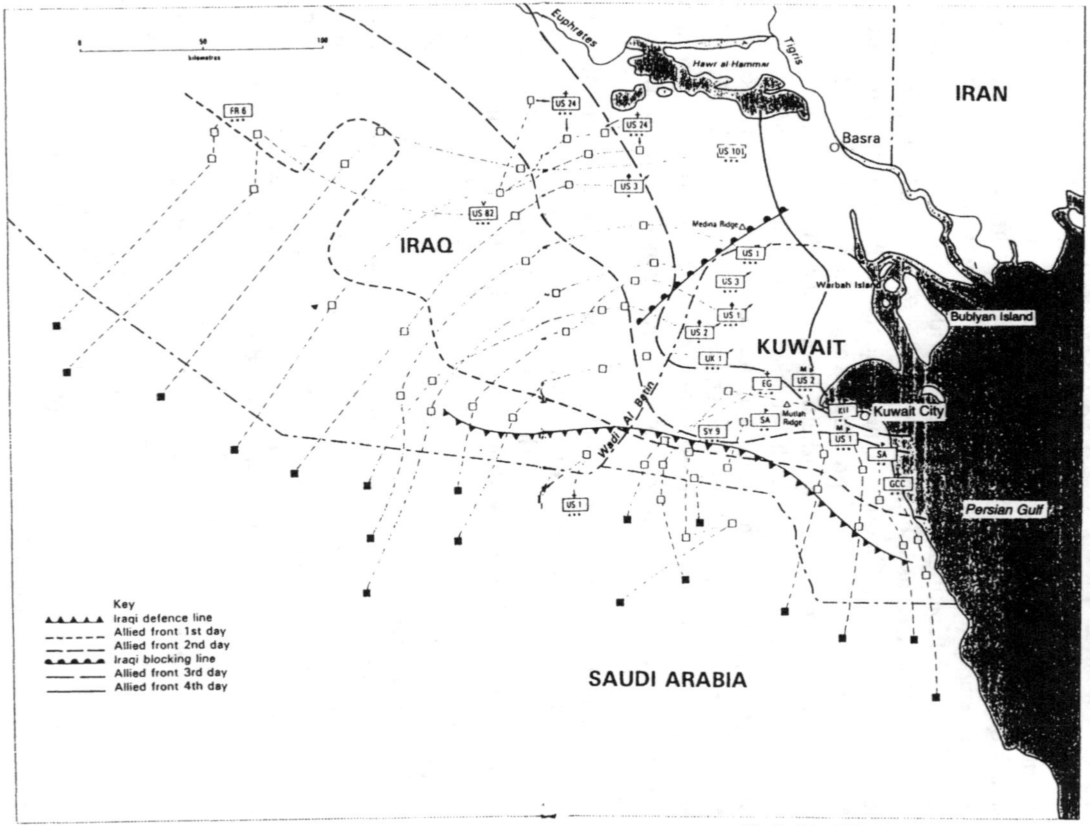

Although it may never be known how many permutations U.S. offensive planning underwent between October 1990 and the start of the air campaign on January 17, 1991, it would be instructive to speculate on whether or not the process mirrored that undertaken by the Germans preparing for war on the Western Front in 1939–1940. Is it possible that U.S. Central Command (USCENTCOM) planners under operational commander General Norman Schwarzkopf, like their German counterparts a half century earlier, made the mistake of playing to the calculations and assumptions of the defenders? In 1939, British, Belgian, and French strategy was predicated on the Germans attacking through the low countries with a mechanized version of the World War I Schleiffen Plan. Had the Germans executed this concept, which was the original design for war in the West, it is highly probable that victory would have proven elusive. In the 1939 event, the Germans were saved from this eventuality and the Allied defense was rendered irrelevant when the offensive blueprint was altered to provide for a sweeping armored drive through terrain presumed by the Allies to be impassable. It is difficult to conceive that USCENTCOM planners, in possession of moderately comprehensive and accurate intelligence regarding Iraqi dispositions, capabilities, and weaknesses, could have fallen into a similar error; however, given the expectation of Coalition air dominance and the capacity to destroy lines of supply and communication as well as both forward and follow-on forces, such an eventuality is not impossible.

General Schwarzkopf termed his final offensive concept "The Hail Mary Play," making reference to a desperate, last-second long pass which brings cliff-hanging victory in a football game. Not only is the term unacceptable hyperbola, it is completely inapposite. The Coalition offensive—as executed with a sweeping run around the Iraqi right flank, a fixing attack against the defender's main position, and a strong deception effort, in this case a threatened amphibious assault on the Kuwaiti coast—is precisely what was dictated by the AirLand concept:

> Envelopment is the basic form of maneuver in any doctrine which seeks to apply strength against weakness. Envelopment avoids the enemy's front, where his forces are most protected and his fires most easily concentrated. Instead, while fixing the defender's attention forward by supporting or diversionary attacks, the attacker maneuvers his main effort around or over the enemy's defenses to strike at his flanks and rear....
>
> Either variant can develop into an encirclement if the attacking force is able to sever the defender's lines of communication and prevent his reinforcement or escape.[11]

The doctrine that had governed U.S. Army operations for over a decade clearly emphasized the envelopment option over the frontal attack, which is charitably characterized as "the least economical form of maneuver, since it exposes the attacker to the concentrated fire of the defender while simultaneously limiting the effectiveness of the attacker's own fires."[12] Simply put, the first contingency developed for U.S. and Coalition forces, even before relatively detailed intelligence had been developed, should have been the one which was finally executed. Any other basis for planning would not only have violated sound doctrine without good reason, it would have thrown away every advantage the United States possessed in the search for quick, decisive, and low-bloodshed victory.

A second consideration reinforces the contention that the offensive plan as executed derives from the doctrinal emphasis on the "culminating point" of an attack, understood as the moment when the offensive force has expended its resources to such an extent that it ceases to have a militarily significant advantage over the defender and must halt before becoming weaker than the defender.[13] A frontal attack on prepared defenses, no matter how weakened these might be by air and artillery attack, would be more likely than a flanking alternative over rugged terrain (such as existed in the desert interior of Saudi Arabia and Iraq) to reach a culminating point without having achieved the desired end: the collapse of the Iraqi forces in Kuwait and coterminous Iraqi border areas. The only option which would have enjoyed a high probability of achieving victory, as variously defined by the several Bush administration political goals, was the one which finally was employed. Thus, it can be assumed that should USCENTCOM have proposed an offensive concept focusing on a frontal assault or on a too-limited flanking effort, it would have been disapproved by the Joint Chiefs of Staff, which, like its chairman, had demonstrated significant political acumen since the beginning of the Persian Gulf intervention.

A final argument in favor of the assertion that the characterization given the Coalition offensive by its operational commander was wrong is the purpose of attack as delineated by U.S. doctrine. The purpose of an attack, particularly a deliberate one, is the phase just prior to the culminating point: exploitation and pursuit. Only during this phase can the commander hope to gain a significant, decisive advantage over the defender, including "the relentless destruction or capture of fleeing enemy forces who have lost the capability to resist."[14] Exploitation and pursuit following an attack from an unexpected direction along an axis of advance which threatened the limited road and rail net supporting Basra and the forces southwest of that city would have been greatly facilitated by the Iraqi dispositions, assumptions, and weaknesses previously mentioned. The combination of an encircling force attacking from the interior, a direct pressure force moving up the coast road to and beyond Kuwait City, and the threat of amphibious operations anywhere along the Kuwaiti coast satisfied totally the requirements of U.S. doctrine.[15] Taken together, these three considerations lead ineluctably to the conclusion that if USCENTCOM offered any concept of operations other than the one finally executed, it would have constituted a major lapse. One can only await with interest the final declassification of the relevant materials so this matter might be resolved with finality.

The air campaign affected the details of the planned ground offensive in at least two important ways. First, it increased the flow of defectors from those Iraqi units stationed along the Saddam Line, with the result that a much clearer picture emerged regarding the combat capacity of the defensive forces. Many of the infantry units directly confronting Coalition forces along the Kuwait–Saudi Arabian border were understrength; contained large numbers of undertrained, even untrained, conscripts; were lacking a full complement of officers and noncommissioned officers; were short of supplies; and were desperately demoralized. This completed the picture of ineptitude and lack of a will to combat which the Iraqis had demonstrated during several border raids, most notably that at Khafji between January 30 and February 1, 1991. If it is true, as has been reported, that General Schwarzkopf said "he really began to think we are going to kick this guy's tail," and if he actually believed it, one can only wonder why it took the general so long to see reality.[16] Additionally, Coalition air dominance demonstrated that large Iraqi forces could not move at all by day and only rarely by night without a high risk of complete destruction. Linking the low quality of the defending forces with the inability of the Iraqis to move without fear of destruction at least as great as that suffered by the Germans in France in the days following the Normandy invasion, CENTCOM commanders became increasingly convinced that the direct axis advance along the coast road to Kuwait City would be accomplished without significant delay and with far fewer losses among the Saudi National Guard and Kuwaiti forces than originally feared. This would potentiate both the military and political effectiveness of the ground campaign. This potentiation was important because the air campaign had brought an Iraqi response which, although of no military value, had raised some potentially serious political and diplomatic problems.

The response was the barrage of Scud missiles. Although it was and remains impossible to fathom with precision Saddam Hussein's strategic vision either before or during and after the start of the air campaign, there are some indications that with the commencement of the aerial bombardment he lost some, if not all, faith in the ability of his military to defend successfully against the Coalition forces, and, as a result, again echoed Adolf Hitler in pinning his strategic hopes on the unlikely political makeup of the forces arrayed against him. The spine of the Coalition was provided by three Western forces—the United States, the United Kingdom, and France—conventionally seen by many in the Mideast as being not only colonial powers but the inheritors of the Christian Crusaders. If these could be split from the Moslem contingents; if the political ground within Egypt, Saudi Arabia, the United Arab Emirates, and, perhaps, Syria and Pakistan could be turned from a firm base to shifting sands, then the military Coalition would be fractured along its most vulnerable seam. The key to this would be the entrance of Israel into the war against Iraq. Should this almost universally hated perceived creation of the Christian West be provoked into a typically overly robust response to an attack, no matter how slight in initial effect, it was not unthinkable that the fellahin—the peasantry and urban proletariat of Egypt, Syria, and the Saudi Peninsula—would enthusiastically insist that their respective governments leave the war. A Scud missile, whose impact was far more psychological than physical—it was like a terrorist with a Radio Shack brain—an appropriate stimulus to elicit an overblown and counterproductive Israeli response. From the time the first Scuds fell on January 18, 1991 at Haifa and Tel Aviv carrying a cargo of fear (fear of chemical weapons with all that implies to the inheritors of the ghastly legacy of the Nazi camps, and fear of random, unpredictable death), the Israeli government was caught between the imperative to strike back with destructive, if not necessarily effective, fury and the diplomatic pressure for restraint imposed by the Bush administration, which quickly and accurately appreciated the potential of Israeli involvement. The pressure and inducements offered by the United States, coupled with the efforts of British and American ground special forces to locate and target Scud launchers, convinced the Israelis to forgo the risks and gratifications of reprisal. However, only an end to the war, an end which could be brought about quickly and certainly only by an overwhelmingly successful ground offensive, would finally end the perceived menace, and with it the Coalition-busting potential of the Scuds. As a secondary strategic gambit, also aimed at fracturing the Coalition by engendering a climate of pervasive fear through Scud attack, the Iraqis targeted the privileged urban elites of Saudi Arabia and the United Arab Emirates. Should this component of the Saudi and UAE population become sufficiently frightened, it had the potential to force the Arab governments to call off offensive operations. Again, only a speedy and undisputed victory over the Iraqi forces in the field could attenuate this potential political debacle with Israel. As the "Scud Hunt" demonstrated persuasively, airpower alone could not end the potential political debacle presented by elderly, technologically unsophisticated Soviet missiles to which a few, albeit important, wrinkles had been added by Iraqi technicians. Only the ground offensive could accomplish this, and then only if something approximating the annihilation of the Iraqi forces in the Kuwaiti theater of operations could be realized before the "culminating point" were reached.

On January 16, 1991, the day before the air campaign commenced, the Coalition forces were concentrated opposite the "Saddam Line" in positions which could be interpreted by the Iraqis as either defensive or offensive. From east to west between the eastern tip of the neutral zone and the coast, there were four corps areas: II Egyptian Corps, including the Syrian division; the U.S. VII Corps; the U.S. XVIII Corps, containing a Saudi contingent; and, next to the coast, the I Marine Expeditionary Force (MEF). Under the cover of the air attacks and supporting artillery barrages, the Coalition forces displaced to their final preattack positions. The U.S. XVIII Corps (82nd Airborne, 101st Air Assault, 24th Infantry [mechanized], and French 6th Light Armored) moved to the west of the neutral zone directly south of As Salman and As Samawah astride the main rail and road lines on the Euphrates River nearly 200 kilometers away. The U.S. VII Corps of five divisions (three armored, including the British 1st Armored, one armored cavalry, and one mechanized) moved into the neutral zone roughly 150 kilometers southwest of Jallibah and positioned perfectly to compel the withdrawal or force the destruction of the Iraqi Republican Guard. Immediately to the east of the neutral zone was the Joint Forces Command, North (JFC-N) with an offensive component of two Egyptian armored divisions and a composite task force of two mechanized brigades, one Saudi and the other Kuwaiti. The JFC-N faced one of the most imposing portions of the Saddam Line but would find that between the effectiveness of the air campaign, the ability of Egyptian artillerymen, and the demoralization of the Iraqis, the barriers, minefields, and bunkers were more of a photo opportunity than an obstacle. Immediately east of the JFC-N, barely more than 100 kilometers from Kuwait City, was the I MEF, which had been reinforced with an armored brigade for the assault. Finally, along the coast and moving straight up the coast highway was the Joint Forces Command, East (JFC-E) comprising two Saudi, one Omani, and two composite brigades. The first move would be made by the I MEF and JFC-E, moving first to draw Iraqi reserves forward to potentiate the enveloping blow to be delivered by the XVIII Airborne Corps and the VII Armored Corps, the latter the most potent concentration of armored firepower ever assembled in a single combat command.

The attack was the AirLand concept incarnate. It was an excellent doctrinal expression finally finding form in an operational plan to be executed by superbly equipped, well-trained, and well-led American, British, and French troops against a numerically and firepower-inferior defender, whose forward forces were already badly shattered and demoralized through a combination of effective air- and artillery-delivered fire, the ineptitude of the Iraqi chain of command, and, quite possibly, the strategic considerations of Saddam Hussein. Provided that USCENTCOM followed doctrinal guidance and decentralized command decisions; used timetables as control mechanisms, not rigid structures; and placed the emphasis on mobility, speed, and use of overwhelming fire when necessary; and provided that the U.S. logistics system could keep up with the enormous demands of the rapidly moving XVIII and VII Corps as well as the far from lethargic I MEF, the exploitation and pursuit phase of the offensive should be well developed long before the culminating point in the battle might be reached. A good idea, the AirLand battle concept, was on the verge of bringing good results, provided that the limits of soldiers, equipment, and materiel were not reached before the theory of victory achieved victory as defined, thus realizing the political goals established by the United States. Unfortunately, their limits were reached; so in the midst of putative success, the United States and thus the Coalition failed.

The reasons for this conclusion are not to be sought so much in the sands of Kuwait or Iraq or within the councils of CENTCOM as they are in the offices and conference rooms of the Pentagon and the White House, as well as in the collective mind of the American people. Unlike the war in Vietnam (in which the ultimate failure of the United States is to be found in the intellectual failure of American military doctrine, which was both irrelevant and counterproductive when applied against Viet Cong insurgent guerrillas), in the Persian Gulf War, the basic doctrine of the U.S. military in general and the Army in particular was completely relevant and effective; however, the national leadership failed to understand both the relationships between goals, definitions, and theories of victory and the absolute necessity of thinking beyond the first battle. In one particular, highly salient respect, General Schwarzkopf's characterization of his one great offensive as "The Hail Mary Play" was on target. Whether advertently or not, it was his only chance to throw for the winning touchdown, and the receiver tripped while crossing the goal line.

To understand what tripped the receiver with one foot over the line and one foot out of bounds as the clock counted down to the last second, it is necessary to revisit the various goals, the several definitions of victory, and the relevance of the AirLand battle–based offensive to these several, almost independent entities. Further, it will be necessary to consider the options available to the Bush administration as the 100-hour offensive was in progress, as well as the inducements and constraints which operated on it while selecting, if not the best, then what appeared at the time to be the least worst option. Finally, it will be appropriate to ask two questions: Was anybody thinking beyond the first battle, and what guidance might have been given USCENTCOM about the desired outcome of either the first or any succeeding battles?

Recall that the administration had stated two explicit goals and one partially explicit ostensible goal: the restoration of the status quo ante bellum through the forced removal of Iraqi forces from Kuwait; the destruction of Iraq's offensive capacity, including but not limited to its actual and potential weapons of mass destruction; and the removal of Saddam Hussein from power. This final goal, although not made as explicitly as the others, was clearly necessary if Iraq were to be denied an offensive capability over time. The ostensible goals were predicated on a substratum of two larger goals: the restoration and maintenance of regional stability through the reestablishment of a regional balance of power and the successful definition of a leadership role for the United States in the post–Cold War global order.

The realization of the first of these two foundation goals was dependent on the removal of Saddam Hussein's regime from power, to secure an Iraqi government which would not pursue a revanchist policy. The achievement of the second was in some significant degree dependent on the accomplishment of the first. Defining victory in the context of these several and, to some extent, interlocking goals was possible, and the administration, at least inferentially, did so: the evacuation of Kuwait by Iraq with the consequent restoration of the Al Sabah family and, ultimately, a formal Iraqi undertaking to recognize the pre-August 1990 borders; the destruction not only of Iraq's chemical, biological, and nuclear stockpiles, production, research, and development facilities, but also of its offensive-capable conventional forces, such as the Republican Guard, which had conducted the August 2, 1990 invasion; and, finally, the removal by internal action of Saddam Hussein and the Revolutionary Council as well as core components of the regime, such as the internal security police, leading to the establishment of a broadbased and nonadventurist government.

The problem came, not in establishing goals or in defining victory in a way which was internally coherent and relevant to the realities on the ground, but in developing and applying an appropriate theory of victory. Whatever theory of victory might be finally developed and employed by the administration, whether or not it was fully articulated, would in largest measure depend on the conduct of offensive ground operations. With the commencement of the air campaign, two factors became apparent immediately: The air effort alone would not cause a collapse of Iraqi political will, and the commencement of the Scud attacks placed a greater importance on a rapid ground campaign which would, at the least, lead to a cease-fire before either the Israelis slipped the American leash or the pampered elites of Saudi Arabia and the United Arab Emirates forced hesitation on their respective governments, with results which would desperately impair the U.S. and Coalition efforts.

Whether or not the administration ever actually believed that the air campaign would constitute a suitable theory of victory cannot yet be determined with accuracy; but, if it had ever entertained such thoughts, they must have vanished as casualties of the first Scud strikes. Although the air effort was an important preliminary and complement to the ground offensive, it never did, nor could, cause a collapse of either the ability of the Iraqi government to maintain control of its forces and destiny or the political will of the Iraqi public. The lessons of history regarding strategic bombing in World War II, the Korean War, and the Vietnam War are identical. Strategic bombing does not fracture governments and populations; rather, the pressure applied by bombers, regardless of any specific successes against relevant military targets, consolidates the allegiance of populations to their government as well as popular political will. If the administration had ever placed its faith in bombing as a theory of victory, such was as misplaced as any confidence which might have been placed in economic sanctions. The only way in which any meaningful success might be achieved was through decisive ground action.

One reason which might have inclined the administration to have placed trust in airpower to provide an effective theory of victory was the same as propelled the Johnson administration to do the same twenty-five years earlier in Indochina: the manageability factor. By its nature, airpower is manageable and, to some extent, predictable, qualities which are high priorities to a national command authority. Although the "surgical strike" may, as a matter of practice, exist only in the minds of fantasy writers, compared to ground combat, air actions seem to be susceptible to a degree of control functionally the equivalent to that exercised by the surgeon over the knife. Ground combat, as every military philosopher and historian has agreed, is inherently messy from a policy management perspective. Ground actions develop a dynamic of their own, based on the legion of intangibles and irrational factors which constitute the well-known frictions and fog of war. As a result, administrations tend to abhor ground operations and, as was well illustrated by the U.S. experience in Vietnam, do not easily contemplate the employment of ground forces; nor do they do so until it is almost too late to think of the implications of their utilization. This appears to have been the case with the Bush administration, as it had been with that of Lyndon Johnson.

Considering the fixation of George Bush with the word *prudence* and the repeated use of the word to describe the policies and actions of his administration, it is not surprising that the virtue he so often celebrated is at the root of "The Hail Mary Play" coming to something less than the touchdown so ardently desired by president and theater commander alike. More accurately, the president was insufficiently prudent in the establishment of his goals or all too prudent in exercising the only theory of victory which had the chance to obtain them. Had the administration limited its goals to the restoration of the status quo ante, there would have been no need for ground operations to the banks of the Euphrates. As was demonstrated by the rapid progress of I MEF through the berm and into Kuwait City, the demoralized bullet catchers of the Iraqi forces were no match for the awesome ground and air firepower at the disposal of the U.S. forces. Although it would have been both necessary and desirable to use the XVIII Airborne and VII Armored Corps in an enveloping maneuver, such would not have needed either the depth or breadth of penetration during the exploitation and pursuit phase to assure the destruction of the Iraqi forces in Kuwait as well as to prevent the Iraqi mass of maneuver from any interference. There is strong reason to believe that had the political goal and definition of victory been limited to the ejection of the Iraqis from Kuwait, airpower could have been concentrated more completely on the Republican Guard units, with an outcome closely resembling that which did result from the ground offensive as executed. It is interesting to contemplate whether a focus on the limited goal might not have brought in the train of its accomplishment the others set forth or understood as predicates by the administration.

Had the Bush administration limited its goals to the restoration of the status quo ante bellum and the removal of Iraq's actual or potential capacity to use weapons of mass destruction, it is tenable to assert that a combination of ground offensive limited to the clearance of Kuwait in conjunction with the air campaign (particularly had special operations forces been employed more resolutely in direct action against those facilities associated with the production or development of chemical, biological, and nuclear weapons) would have been the most effective theory of victory. It might be unfortunate that the administration expanded the explicit goals to include the reduction of Iraq's conventional capacity to wage aggression, for desirable as such an outcome might have been, and agreeable as this might have been to the American public, it complicated the task of developing and implementing a proper theory of victory.

Ground combat is not only disorderly given the management imperative of administrations, but it has the real potential to pile American bodies in large and politically unattractive heaps. One of the highest, if not the single highest priority, for administrations facing war, from the administration of Franklin Roosevelt to that of George Bush, has been the reduction of American casualties to an absolute minimum. Undoubtedly, this priority was effectively transmitted to USCENTCOM. Since military commanders are rarely, if ever, indifferent to either the direct or indirect consequences of casualties, this guidance would have been scarcely necessary in the development of operational plans, particularly because the reduction of casualties was a primary consideration in the orientation of the AirLand battle concept to the use of maneuver and concentrated fire. However, to a prudent—perhaps overly prudent—president, the casualty reduction imperative would have loomed large as ground operations commenced.

As I MEF crossed the berm; as XVII Airborne Corps cranked up for an end run which would, in the case of the 24 Infantry (mechanized) lead to a 250-mile drive in barely four days; as the thousands of M1A1 Abrams and M2/M3 Bradleys of VII Armored Corps moved forward in the greatest concentration of armored power ever assembled, had the administration and its military advisers contemplated what came after the first battle concluded? Had the possibility been considered that the Republican Guard—the spine not only of the Iraqi army, the fist of Iraqi offensive capabilities, but also the ultimate maintainer of the regime—were not to be destroyed before the culminating point might be reached? Not to have done so would have been imprudent.

Possibly, it had been intimated to General Schwarzkopf that there would be only one chance to accomplish the destruction not only of the forces in

Kuwait but also of the Republican Guard, and as a result the attack was undertaken, even though some must have suspected that it would stretch soldiers, equipment, and logistics support to, and perhaps over, the limits. Perhaps, having had no experience with the AirLand concept in combat and pulled by the powerful attraction of an enemy in flight, the operational and tactical commanders, heeding the guidance of AirLand-based doctrine, with an abundance of enthusiasm took effective control of the battle and willingly sought to push the edge. Regardless of the reason or mix of reasons, by late on February 26, American forces with their British, French, and Arab partners seemed to be on the verge of completing the encirclement of the Iraqi Army and Republican Guard.

This was the critical moment in the offensive. The location of Coalition units was favorable for effecting encirclement, with the 101st Air Assault near the Euphrates southeast of As Samawah; the 24th Infantry pushing between Tallil and Jallibah, thus also threatening the main line of communication between Basra and Baghdad; and the 1st and 3rd U.S. armored, the 1st British armored, and the 1st U.S. Infantry driving on Safwan while JFC-N, I MEF, and JFC-E were pressing to and beyond Kuwait City. Clearly, the rapid tempo of movement and combat alike as well as the lengthening lines of communication were taking their toll despite the foresight of operational commanders, exemplified by the 24th division commander, Major General Barry McCaffrey, who had arranged for his unit not only to have a logistics train with 2.5 million gallons of fuel and 17,000 tons of ammunition but also had loaded his combat units with an additional 1.2 million gallons of the liquid, without which maneuver was impossible. Human weakness was also appearing because, as the Germans had discovered in August 1914, even the finest troops are subject to the depredations of physical and mental stress. There was a powerful injunction operating on commanders at all levels to take cognizance of the emerging encirclement and turn a Nelsonian eye to the unpleasant emerging reality of human and material limitations. That imperative was the AirLand concept, which stated that "an encirclement resulting from a pursuit can completely destroy an enemy force."[17] The destruction of the enemy's force in the field, the battle of annihilation, has been considered in the West to be the highest goal of generalship since Alexander the Great was a private.

Taking counsel of fears is never considered a military virtue; being aware of impending weakness is, or should be, because the failure to do so invites failure even on the verge of great success. The act of pressing on is not only deeply rooted in the military, but it has often been the sole key to success. In this case it represented a gamble, but a gamble well worth taking if CENTCOM had already been made aware of an impending administration decision not to allow a second offensive battle and if the alternatives to continuing the encirclement effort had been considered and found wanting.

For the Iraqis as well, the night of February 26 represented a critical point in the battle. Saddam Hussein and the Revolutionary Command Council must have realized that they had not only lost Kuwait and the overwhelming majority of their forces there, but were also in imminent danger of losing all the Republican Guard as well. The VII Corps units had already destroyed the Guard's Tawakalna mechanized infantry division and an attached regular army armored division and had mangled the Medinah armored division. The remnants of the Republican Guard, as well as at least a small fraction of the other units, could be salvaged, provided that they were withdrawn without delay to Basra, taking advantage of the fact that their opponent's armored units were coming in such close proximity that care would have to be taken lest fratricidal actions result. For the Iraqi regime, there were no alternatives; even that long-practiced survivor, Saddam Hussein, must have felt he was finally staring into the pit of hell.

Consider the Falaise Pocket, where the Allies and Germans faced a situation not unlike that which existed the night of February 26. At that time, complete encirclement had not been effected, with the result that airpower had been used to seal the gap. Despite great losses, the Germans had been able to reconstitute many of their badly shattered units, thus denying the Western Allies a decisive victory. Although the Iraqis were not the Germans and Coalition airpower was orders of magnitude superior to that which had been available in 1944, there were meaningful doubts about the efficacy of the air option. These were magnified by the reality that there existed another priority target for air attack: the Iraqis withdrawing from Kuwait City along the Basra highway. Additionally, it was necessary to have sufficient air forces to ensure that no Iraqi units could be moved south along the Euphrates, which would gravely danger the friendly forces facing its banks. Finally, the Scud hunt had to continue, as well as did strikes against various strategic targets which had not yet been destroyed with certainty. Simply put, even the large air force available might not be sufficient to seal the Basra pocket given its conflicting missions. On this ground alone, if there had been no commitment by the U.S. national command authority to the mounting of a second offensive, a continuation of the battle of encirclement was a justifiable gamble.

Had there been fresh, follow-on forces available to continue the attack through the line of contact which existed on the night of February 26, there would have been no gamble or risk involved, but there were no armored and mechanized divisions littering the sand dunes looking for work. Although the AirLand-based doctrine assumed that such divisions would be normally available, and there might well have been in the European venue for which the doctrine had been developed, reality, as is so often the case, caught up with assumption. If the essential definition of victory—the destruction of the offensive and regime maintenance forces of the Republican Guard—was to be realized, the attack would have to continue. It did, with a vengeance, with the 1st Brigade of the 24th Infantry racing 100 kilometers down the Basra highway, while the rest of the division destroyed an estimated six battalions of the Hammurabi Republican Guards armored division, and the 2nd Brigade of the 1st British armored division destroyed another 100 tanks and armored personnel carriers of the Medinah division. It was not enough. The United States and thus the Coalition accepted an Iraqi offer of cease-fire, allowing the balance of the Republican Guard to withdraw into Basra, taking with it the survival of the regime. The United States had failed to achieve victory or the complex interlocking system of goals in pursuit of which war had been waged. As a limited war in support of policy, the war was arguably too limited.

The Bush administration could adduce one reason with two components in support of the decision to accept the cease-fire and not renew the offensive after the inevitable period of rest and refit. Neither the reason nor the components had any relationship to the stated motivation: a fear of public revulsion should graphic footage or photographs of the appalling destruction wreaked on the retreating Iraqis north from Kuwait City be broadcast. The actual reason was prudence, and the components were time and lives. Time was critical on several grounds: An escalation of Scud attacks either in numbers or in the use of chemical payloads became more, rather than less, likely over time, bringing with it the enhanced potential of losing control of the Israelis as well as the potential collapse of the threatened Saudi and United Arab Emirate urban elites; the fault lines within the Coalition became more strained with every passing day, particularly because the Iraqis had not proven themselves inept in the use of war damage inflicted on civilian targets by Coalition air strikes as propaganda within the Arab and Moslem states, with the primary target population being the fellahin; and, finally, the political stance of the American public was that a quick and apparently decisive victory was more important than a palpably decisive victory delayed, even by a matter of days. Even more important was the probable loss of American lives should the offensive be renewed either into Basra or up the Euphrates toward Baghdad. Should either axis of attack (or both) be attempted, the advantages of maneuver and firepower which had brought U.S. forces and their partners such breathtaking success would be nullified by terrain. Entering Basra meant undertaking combat in an urban environment, which, as the Israelis had found in the course of their Lebanese incursion a decade earlier, was a deadly proposition. Moving toward Baghdad implied entrance on terrain far less favorable to envelopment and flank actions, greatly lengthening the lines of supply as well as solidifying Iraqi resistance. Either movement would not only translate into conflict protraction, it would also place more Americans into body bags, a proposition which no prudent administration could contemplate with equanimity. Far better to accept the cease-fire and place faith in the continued pressure of economic sanctions and diplomatic isolation as well as whatever other stresses might be invented and applied than to risk the enervation of domestic political will and support. In this the administration read the will of "We the People," the domestic political culture of the United States, accurately.

Although half a victory might be better than none, in this case the acceptance of the half victory, the partially accomplished goals, ignored the advice of Machiavelli never to leave in place a wounded enemy. In this case, the enemy was both wounded and humiliated, leaving Iraq in place to redevelop a capacity for the making of regional, and global, mischief. Although the Bush administration might well have been completely justified in its exercise of prudence on February 27, 1991, given that both components—time and lives—would have been expended without any certainty of a more desirable outcome, the same may not be said about the earlier articulation of goals and definition of victory or about the approval of the initial offensive without a full consideration of the next battle or, in the alternative, the necessary consequences of ending the war with the basis of the regime's power still fundamentally intact. This is the critical juncture at which the promise of AirLand doctrine could not be fully realized and, arguably, it is at this nexus—and not in the Iraqi desert on the night of February 26—that the "culminating point" might best be located.

Given that accomplishment of the several interlocking American goals depended on the removal of Saddam Hussein's regime from power, and given further that too much of the American definition of victory was attached to the same personality and the same outcome, any result other than the collapse of the Iraqi dictator as an outcome of the ground campaign was not acceptable. The administration, after developing goals and defining victory in a way that could not realistically be accomplished by a single, low-cost ground campaign and after not having considered the implications, had several options: Reduce expectations by focusing less on the prompt and complete removal of Iraq as a potential aggressor, thus devaluing Saddam Hussein; postpone the ground attack until follow-on forces could be deployed; or prepare domestic and international public opinion and governmental understanding for conflict protraction and an increased cost in lives. None of these were done, with the result that General Schwarzkopf, whether he knew it or not, had one opportunity for a touchdown; he threw the "Hail Mary."

NOTES

1. See also FM 100-5, *Field Service Regulations: Operations* (Washington, D.C.: Department of the Army, 1939, 1944, 1954, 1962, 1974).

2. Larry Cable, *Unholy Grail: The United States and the Wars in Vietnam, 1965–1968* (New York and London: Routledge, 1991), 34–38, including notes.

3. See, as an example, FM 100-5, *Operations* (Washington, D.C.: Department of the Army, 1986), 11–12.

4. Ibid., especially chaps. 3 and 4.
5. Ibid., 5, 13, 14, 25, 26.
6. W. Lance Bennett and David L. Paletz, eds., *Taken by Storm: The Media, Public Opinion and U.S. Foreign Policy in the Gulf War* (Chicago: University of Chicago Press, 1994).
7. FM 100-5, *Operations* (1986), 46–47.
8. Ibid., 120–21.
9. Bruce Watson et al., *Military Lessons of the Gulf War* (London: Greenhill, 1993), 146–55.
10. See Anthony H. Cordesman and Abraham R. Wagner, *The Lessons of Modern War*, Volume 2, *The Iran–Iraq War* (Boulder, Colo.: Westview, 1990).
11. FM 100-5, *Operations* (1986), 101.
12. Ibid., 106.
13. Ibid., 109.
14. Ibid., 117.
15. Ibid., 119–20.
16. Watson, *Military Lessons of the Gulf War*, 94.
17. FM 100-5, *Operations* (1986), 120.

9

U.S. Marine Operations in the Persian Gulf War, 1990–1991

John T. Quinn and Jack Shulimson

INTRODUCTION

Popular accounts of the Gulf War have tended to focus on the decisions of the Coalition high command and the marvel of modern technology. Stirring titles such as "Storm Over Iraq," "Crusade," and "Certain Victory" seem to suggest that the enemy faced by U.S. forces in the Gulf in early 1991 was of little or no consequence and that the issue was never in doubt. This is not the way the Gulf War should be remembered. So many things about the Coalition experience in the Gulf War need to be recalled clearly and in the proper context. Much of the war had a "North Africa circa 1942" feel about it, with the harsh desert environment, sparse population, and incredible logistical lifelines through the vast empty expanse. In sharp contrast, the Coalition's rear areas in Saudi Arabia featured some of the most extraordinary military infrastructure on the face of the planet. The threat to the peace and stability of the region posed by the Iraqi invasion of Kuwait should not be dismissed lightly, although President Bush's comparison of Saddam Hussein with Adolf Hitler invited such a response.

Aside from fielding one of the largest armies in the world, Iraq had the distinction of possessing recent experience in the use of battlefield chemical weapons and the employment of massed field artillery. Although they did not display a high degree of martial virtuosity in their eight years of war with Iran, the Iraqis had managed to survive and overcome a long war of attrition with a determined and often fanatical foe. Not only did they survive, but they visibly learned from early mistakes and adjusted tactics and operations accordingly. It is in this context that we must write the history of the Gulf War, not just in the context of "smart" bombs and Patriot missile "best hits" videos.

The Marine Corps experience in the Gulf is a significant chapter in military history for several reasons. As a relatively small, self-contained force based on the sea, its prewar planning and preparation for such a conflict provide an interesting contrast with the U.S. Army's. Its employment as a separate maneuver corps well inland from the sea severely challenged its traditional expeditionary logistics structure. Finally, its unique views on the efficacy and appropriate uses of airpower placed it in opposition to those of the U.S Air Force's—under whose aegis Marine aviation would have to fight the war.

PREPARATIONS FOR WAR

On the eve of the Iraqi invasion of Kuwait in the summer of 1990, the Marine Corps stood at a crossroads. As a result of the demise of the Cold War, there loomed the prospect of dramatic cuts in defense spending, which were sure to affect all of the Services. The Marine Corps not only faced this uncertain budgetary future but also braced to weather an event that seemed to follow every American postwar downsizing of the past century: questions about the Marine Corps's relevance to the national defense and its status as a separate Service.

Responding to the more immediate budgetary threat, the Corps targeted armor, artillery, engineers, and motor transport units for reduction and slated older, single-mission aircraft types for elimination from the inventory at an accelerated rate to save on maintenance and personnel costs. Although not scheduled to begin in earnest until fiscal year 1991, some units and equipment began to be disbanded and retired a few months early. Included in this group were the Corps's sole tactical photo reconnaissance squadron—flying the RF-4B Phantom II—and its heaviest artillery batteries equipped with the M-110 175-mm (8-inch) self-propelled howitzer. Already, notable shortfalls existed in other equipment, including an aging medium-lift transport helicopter fleet (the CH-46E "Sea Knight"), an outdated main battle tank (the M-60A1), and similarly limited communications gear.

The United States Marine Corps of 1990, nevertheless, remained a formidable fighting force. It had an active duty strength of 190,000 men and women—supplemented by over 40,000 members of the Selected Marine Corps Reserve (SMCR)—and retained a high level of combat effectiveness. Its Fleet Marine Forces (FMF), the Marine combat arm nearly 120,000 strong, consisted of three division-wing combined arms teams, designated

Marine Expeditionary Forces or MEFs. Each 40,000 person MEF could be further broken down into 16,500-person Marine Expeditionary Brigades (MEBs) or 2,000-man Marine Expeditionary Units (MEUs) as circumstances required. Embarked on forward-deployed Navy ships, several MEUs normally stood ready to meet challenges to the peace almost anywhere in the world.

OPERATION DESERT SHIELD

The events of August 2, 1990 found Marine units scattered around the globe involved in their traditional forward presence activities. Two MEUs were on station with the country's overseas numbered fleets, the 6th in the Mediterranean Sea and 7th in the Western Pacific. The 13th MEU (SOC), an element of the 7th Fleet, was in port in the Philippines after conducting disaster relief operations in northern Luzon. The 22d MEU (SOC), an element of the 6th Fleet, was on station off the coast of Liberia assisting in the evacuation of U.S. citizens and those of friendly governments from that civil–war-torn West African country.[1]

On opposite coasts of the continental United States, two of the five standing MEB headquarters—the 4th, located at Little Creek, Virginia, and the 7th, at Twenty-nine Palms, California—were in preparation for upcoming deployments to NATO exercises on the northern and southern flanks of Western Europe. Neither of the MEB headquarters "owned" the subordinate reinforced regiment, composite aircraft group, and combat service support group that made up a notional MEB. Rather, each of these elements were "chopped" from their parent division, aircraft wing, and force service support group (FSSG) by the MEF commander to the MEB as the situation required.

The 4th MEB, commanded by Major General Harry W. Jenkins, Jr., constituted the Atlantic Fleet's and II MEF's ready amphibious brigade. The MEB was normally assigned a reinforced infantry regiment (the 2d Marines, with various combat support detachments), a composite aircraft group (MAG-40, which included both fixed- and rotary-wing aircraft squadrons), and a brigade service support group (BSSG-4). In early August, the 4th MEB was in the midst of preparations for the NATO exercise Teamwork/Boldguard scheduled for September in Norway. The fleet had also alerted Jenkins and the MEB for a possible noncombatant evacuation operation in Liberia. With the Iraqi invasion of Kuwait, the MEB received new orders to deploy to Southwest Asia. What followed during the next two weeks was the traditional short-notice mount-out of thousands of Marines and many tons of materiel on board amphibious ships of the U.S. Atlantic Fleet for foreign shores.

The 7th MEB, in the high desert of the Mojave in southern California, was the headquarters of an as yet untried deployment concept. Conceived in the late 1970s as part of the Carter administration's effort to form a rapid deployment force to defend the Middle East oil fields, it involved the marriage of in-theater prepositioned afloat war materiel with airlifted Marines and their individual weapons and equipment. By the mid-1980s, the United States had deployed the equipment sets of three MEBs on board a total of thirteen military sealift command-chartered vessels near regional "hot spots." These vessels, known collectively as the Maritime Prepositioned Force (MPF), were divided into three squadrons of four or five Maritime Prepositioned Ships (MPS). The MPS squadrons (MPSRons) were based at Diego Garcia in the Indian Ocean, Guam, and the Azores in the mid-Atlantic Ocean.

At Diego Garcia on August 2 lay three (of the five) ships of MPSRon-2. A fourth ship was in a scheduled biannual maintenance period at the main MPF facility at Blount Island, Florida, and the fifth was off the west coast of Africa en route to Florida. The squadron's ships were loaded with (among other things) two companies of M-60 tanks, a battalion of towed and a battery of self-propelled artillery, many tons of aviation ordnance and fuel, and thirty days' supply of general support items for a 13,500-man MEB. The most readily available U.S. combat equipment set near the unfolding contingency (quickly labeled Operation Desert Shield), MPSRon-2 did not receive orders until August 7 to sail for the Persian Gulf. Much of the Marine establishment viewed this unexplained delay—despite the reported urging by Marine Commandant General Al Gray for the early dispatch of the squadron—with suspicion, coming at a time of intensifying competition between the Services for contingency roles.[2]

On August 8, Major General John I. Hopkins, the 7th MEB commander, received word to prepare his brigade for deployment to Saudi Arabia as part of the contingency operation. Having already anticipated the call by a few days, Hopkins and his staff had completed their preliminary planning. Although the doctrinal employment of the MPS called for the early deployment of detachments from the MEB to survey the offload site and help prepare the stored equipment for offloading, the severely compressed timeline of the unfolding contingency did not allow for this. Thus, these detachments would have to meet the ships pierside in Saudi Arabia and would have only hours to start removing and issuing equipment to arriving units.[3]

That same day, Lieutenant General Walter E. Boomer assumed command of I MEF. With those duties came the title of Commander, U.S. Marine Forces, Central Command (ComUSMarCent, more commonly MARCENT), which meant that Boomer was to coordinate the Marine buildup in the Gulf region and command Marine operations ashore. He reported immediately to General H. Norman Schwarzkopf, the Commander in Chief of the U.S. Central Command (CINCCENT), who instructed him to "heavy up" the 7th MEB's ground combat force for its deployment to the Gulf.

Acting on orders from Boomer, Brigadier General James M. "Mike" Myatt, the new commanding general of the 1st Marine Division, formed a reinforced regimental combat team (RCT) centered on the Twenty-nine Palms–based 7th Marines and "chopped" it to Hopkins's brigade. While Boomer headed to Rihyad, Saudi Arabia to coordinate with the CENTCOM forward headquarters, Hopkins marshalled his brigade's elements and began to push them out the door as airlift became available.

Starting on August 15 with the 1st Battalion, 5th Marines (1/5), the 7th Marines, commanded by Colonel Carlton W. Fulford, began deployment to Saudi Arabia. Following quickly behind 1/5 were the 1st and 2d Battalions, 7th Marines (1/7 and 2/7), and the 3d Battalion, 9th Marines (3/9). The 3d Battalion, 11th Marines (3/11), a towed artillery battalion augmented by a provisional battery of self-propelled howitzers, arrived within days. Instead of the standard company-sized engineer and armor attachments, the 1st Marine Division dispatched under strength battalions of tanks, assault amphibian vehicles (AAVs), and engineers. The RCT was rounded out by a reconnaissance company and two companies of the 3d Light Armored Infantry Battalion (3d LAI Bn) equipped with light armored vehicles (LAVs). All these elements were in place by August 21.

The 7th MEB's aviation combat element—Marine Aircraft Group 70 (MAG-70)—was a task-organized team consisting of a variety of aircraft squadrons. Beginning on August 17 with 14 AH-1W "Cobras" and 10 UH-1N "Hueys" of Marine Light Attack Helicopter Squadron 369 (HMLA-369), aircraft from stations around the Corps converged on Southwest Asia to join up with MAG-70. Competing air refueling priorities with Air Force units arriving in theater delayed the movement of Marine squadrons for several days. By the beginning of September, nevertheless, MAG-70 was in place in Bahrain and eastern Saudi Arabia and operating every type of tactical aircraft in the Marine Corps active inventory save one. The MAG-70 fixed-wing aircraft inventory included four squadrons (forty-eight aircraft) of F/A-18 Hornets, two squadrons (forty aircraft) of AV-8B "Harrier IIs," nine A-6E "Intruders," twelve EA-6B "Prowlers," and six KC-130 "Hercules." The MAG's helicopter detachment included forty AH-1W "Super Cobras," eighteen UH-1N "Hueys," twenty-four CH-46E "Sea Knights," eighteen CH-53D "Sea Stallions," and fourteen CH-53E "Super Stallions." The missing aircraft type—the OV-10A/D "Bronco," which lacked air-to-air refueling capability—did not arrive until mid-September after flying halfway around the world in a series of short hops between air bases.

To support and sustain this force, Brigade Service Support Group 7 mustered nearly 2,800 Marines and sailors in its maintenance, supply, motor transport, engineer support, landing support, medical, and dental detachments. Virtually the entire equipment set was off loaded from MPSRon-2 within days of its August 15 arrival at Jubayl. From the start of the deployment, BSSG-7 supplied the 7th MEB with the full range (including fuel) of essential combat service support. It was the early presence of his critical logistics "tail" that, as much as any other factor, allowed General Hopkins to declare the 7th MEB combat ready on August 25 and to assume the mission of the defense of the greater Jubayl area from XVIII Airborne Corps's forward elements.

The deployment of Marines to Saudi Arabia continued unabated with the arrival of a second MPS squadron, the Guam-based MPSRon-3, and most of the Marines of its paired MEB, the 1st, out of Hawaii. Arriving at Jubayl starting on August 26, this second wave of Marines included a reinforced infantry regiment (the 3d Marines), BSSG-1, and additional F/A-18 Hornet and medium- and heavy-lift helicopter squadrons. With the continuing air deployment of combat and combat support units from California, by September 3 General Boomer combined the existing 7th MEB with those units from Hawaii into an understrength MEF of nearly 18,000 Marines and sailors. He now had the better part of Myatt's 1st Marine Division, the 3d Marine Aircraft Wing (3d MAW) under Major General Royal N. Moore, and the 1st Force Service Support Group (1st FSSG) under Brigadier General James A. Brabham in eastern Saudi Arabia and Bahrain.[4]

The arrival by sea in mid-September of III MEF units from Okinawa, Japan further strengthened I MEF. The latter units, designated Amphibious Ready Group Bravo (ARG Bravo) when embarked on board ships of Amphibious Group One, included a regimental headquarters (the 4th Marines), the 1st Battalion, the 6th Marines (1/6), an additional artillery battery, and tank, AAVs, and combat engineer companies.

By late September, I MEF/MARCENT had amassed nearly 30,000 Marines in Saudi Arabia and Bahrain. The ground combat element of the force—the 1st Marine Division—included seven infantry, three artillery, and two tank battalions, as well as a battalion each of light armored infantry, combat engineers, and reconnaissance.[5] The 3d MAW's tactical aircraft inventory numbered 126 fixed-wing jets and turboprops and 116 helicopters.[6] Another 10,000 Marines and sailors were afloat in the Arabian Sea as of mid-September with the arrival of the 4th MEB and 13th MEU (SOC) under the command of Seventh Fleet/Naval Forces Central Command (NAVCENT).[7] General Schwarzkopf, in early October, capped Marine end strength in the Gulf (both ashore and afloat) at 42,500 Marines. With only 31,000 Marines and sailors ashore under his command, General Boomer protested against this ceiling, but to no avail, leaving I MEF with a host of manpower deficiencies.[8]

For the first several months, the I MEF mission remained that of defending the Jubayl critical area from Iraqi attack, but it was prepared to conduct offensive operations on order. While General Myatt's 1st Marine Division settled into a series of defensive positions well north of Jubayl, General

Moore's 3d MAW patrolled the skies above the northern Gulf and regularly practiced high-tempo offensive air support operations with the division. The 3d MAW's pilots and air controllers also regularly participated in training for joint air operations. With Lieutenant General Charles A. Horner, the commander of the 9th Air Force/U.S. Air Forces Central Command (CENTAF), designated by General Schwarzkopf as the Joint Forces Air Component Commander (JFACC), Marine tactical aviation fell under the authority of the theater air commander from the start. In accordance with the 1986 Omnibus Agreement between the Marine Corps and the Air Force, the wing would provide a portion of its sorties in support of the CINC's "big picture" air campaign under Horner's direction.

The framers of the Goldwater–Nichols Act of 1986 granted broad authority to the position of JFACC in a unified and subunified command, but in translating this authority into practical details, much had been left to the discretion of the CINC and his JFACC. This was of constant concern to the Corps, because it feared that its tactical aviation, if tied too closely to the Air Force's theater-wide air command and control system, would lose its highly valued responsiveness and flexibility to the MEF and its divisions. Marines had seen this happen before in both the Korean and Vietnam Wars, when in their view a high degree of centralization under Air Force control had resulted in a marked reduction in the effectiveness of close air support (CAS) provided to its own forces.[9] To prevent this situation in the Gulf, I MEF sought to "fence off" certain aircraft from JFACC control—most notably the AV-8B Harrier II and all of its helicopters—while apportioning its F/A-18, A-6E, and EA-6B sorties to the JFACC on a percentage basis.

Generals Boomer and Moore also sought an airspace "box" over I MEF's ground area of responsibility in which Marine tactical air operations and direct air support centers would take care of all Coalition aircraft and, under the aegis of the 3d MAW Tactical Air Command Center (TACC), execute the JFACC's "big picture" directives. Although General Horner did not initially agree to this level of decentralization, he did allow the 3d MAW reasonable autonomy and did not interfere with internal I MEF air control procedures. The wing's Tactical Air Operations Center (TAOC) at Jubayl served as a sector antiair warfare commander (SAAWC) under the combined 9th Air Force/Saudi Arabian Control and Reporting Center (CRC) for the eastern air defense area at Dhahran, Saudi Arabia. Marine F/A-18s based out of Bahrain were assigned combat air patrol (CAP) stations over the 7th Fleet's AOR in the northern Persian Gulf.[10]

As September became October, I MEF worked to improve the disposition of its tactical units and to integrate into the nascent Third U.S. Army theater logistics system after living off its MPS stocks for more than a month. CENTCOM assigned the United Kingdom's famed 7th Armored Brigade to I MEF as it flowed into Jubayl throughout the month. Marines quickly proceeded to form a close and satisfying relationship with their British counterparts. They developed gunnery and maneuver ranges out in the desert expanses after much prodding of the Saudi Arabian government. While maintaining their defensive posture, Marines and British soldiers began to bore sight their tank guns and focus on the future.[11]

The early November announcement by the Bush administration of the planned deployment of an additional 200,000 American troops resulted in a renewed burst of activity in the I MEF area of operations. The Marines' share of this massive reinforcement would consist mainly of II MEF's 2d Marine Division, a full helicopter group, and additional fixed-wing squadrons from its partnered 2d Marine Aircraft Wing. It also included the bulk of the 2d Force Service Support Group and an additional amphibious MEB (the 5th) from the West Coast. The 7th Armored Brigade would be joined by the 4th Infantry Brigade to form the 1st (U.K.) Armored Division. With the British forces already amply equipped with armor and combat engineers and the two Marine divisions "meched up" for desert warfare, I MEF would be well prepared for its assigned combat role. By Thanksgiving, this role had evolved to the task of supporting the Third U.S. Army's main attack to the west. The Marines would strike at and fix in place Iraqi forces in Kuwait, isolate the capital, and prepare to continue the attack northward.[12]

To make room for its reinforcing units, in early December I MEF moved the 1st Marine Division out of the Jubayl approaches north to a support area along the coast 120 kilometers from the Kuwaiti border. At Saudi insistence, the division's forward elements kept back from the border area. The 3d Marine Aircraft Wing headquarters displaced from Bahrain to Jubayl just before Christmas, and shortly thereafter the I MEF Main Command Post relocated to the coastal town of Safinaya, well forward of most of its ground units. As the 2d Marine Division and the 2d Force Service Support Group flowed into Jubayl by air, their battalions met up with equipment off MPSRon-1 and other chartered shipping and quickly deployed northward. At year's end, the 3d MAW's second helicopter group, MAG-26, headed up the Saudi coast and began to take up residence at an airfield near the town of Mishab, only 50 kilometers from the Kuwaiti border.

A vital element in the reinforcement of I MEF during December was the mobilization and deployment of much of the Selected Marine Corps Reserve (SMCR) and the Individual Ready Reserve (IRR). Starting in mid-November, the Marine Corps activated its first Reservists to support the buildup in the Gulf. Infantry, artillery, and armor battalions from around the country reported to Camp Lejeune and Camp Pendleton for last-minute training with their active-duty counterparts. Neighboring air stations played host to Reserve helicopter and fixed-wing squadrons destined for overseas service. Among the first SMCR units to ship out for the Gulf were several helicopter squadrons, which departed Southern California on December 1 with the 5th MEB on board thirteen ships of Amphibious Group Three. Nearly 900 of the MEB's 7,100 personnel were Marine Reservists.[13]

The 2d Marine Division, short one infantry regiment, one artillery battalion, and numerous smaller detachments with the 4th MEB, received the lion's share of SMCR units. The division eventually deployed to the Gulf from North Carolina in late December and early January with four regular and two Reserve infantry battalions, one active and one Reserve tank battalion, and numerous Reserve light armored infantry, artillery, and engineer companies and batteries. The 2d FSSG likewise joined many Reservists, and the 2d MAW's MAG-26 deployed to Saudi Arabia with four Reserve helicopter squadrons out of its complement of eight. Perhaps the true strength of the Marine Reserve lay in its versatility. Besides the thousands of Reservists with I MEF and the 5th MEB, several Reserve infantry battalions and aircraft squadrons took the place of regular III MEF units forward based in Okinawa and Japan, while the SMCR's 2d MEB marshalled at Camp Lejeune to take part in NATO's exercise Battle Griffin '91 in Norway during March.[14]

On December 17, General Schwarzkopf informed General Boomer that he was transferring the 1st (U.K.) Armored Division from I MEF's operational control to VII Corps's control in order to strengthen CENTCOM's main attack. As partial compensation, Schwarzkopf offered I MEF the U.S. Army's 1st Brigade (nicknamed the Tiger Brigade) of the 2d Armored Division. With the 2d Armored in the process of disbanding in August 1990, the Tiger Brigade had been grafted to the 1st Cavalry Division in place of its "round out" National Guard brigade. Although not nearly the size and strength of the British division he had just lost, Boomer welcomed the Tiger Brigade to the force and assigned it to Major General William Keys's 2d Marine Division, which was short one infantry regiment. The brigade, with 118 M1A1 Abrams tanks, sixty-one M2A2 Bradley Infantry Fighting Vehicles, twenty-five M109A3 Paladin 155-mm self-propelled howitzers, and ten MLRS units, reported to the division a few weeks later.[15]

With this sizable force of Marines, soldiers, and sailors, Boomer sought to craft an offensive plan that rapidly and effectively would accomplish the CINC's objectives for the supporting attack yet keep casualties among his men to the absolute minimum. After receiving CENTCOM's written guidance, Boomer, on January 1, issued a plan that envisioned a 1st Marine Division assault and breach of the Iraqi lines between the Al Wafra oil field complex and the coast on a narrow front. After forcing breaches in the Iraqi line, Myatt's division would hold open the gaps for Keys's 2d Marine Division, which would rapidly pass through and plunge into the Iraqi rear. The 2d Marine Division would then link up with lead elements of the 4th and 5th MEBs as they drove inland after conducting an amphibious assault on the port of Ash Shu'aybah, which lay 25 kilometers south of Kuwait City. The combined force would then sweep around to the west of the capital and seize key terrain south of Al Jahra that would effectively isolate the city. That done, the force would prevent the escape of Iraqi forces and, if required, assist the Arab forces drive on the city.[16]

DESERT STORM

By mid-January 1991, the bulk of I MEF was in place and awaiting the deadline of the 15th set by the UN Security Council for Iraqi forces to quit Kuwait. Elements of the 3d MAW continued to shift northward as its second helicopter group, MAG-16, moved into position at the Arabian American Oil Company (ARAMCO) airfield at Tanagib after the Kingdom of Saudi Arabia relented on earlier objections to its use. General Boomer, surveying the Iraqi defenses arrayed against his forces, on January 16 decided to shift his planned breach of the enemy's lines away from the coast to the western edge of the southern border. The attack would still be spearheaded by the 1st Marine Division, with the 2d Marine Division and the attached Tiger Brigade then passing through and seizing the aforementioned key terrain to the west of Kuwait City. At this time, the likelihood of the employment of an amphibious assault by NAVCENT began to fade as the threat to Allied ships posed by mines and antiship missiles—combined with the fear of high casualties on the beach—made this option look unacceptably risky to both Schwarzkopf and his naval commander.

With the start of the air campaign of Operation Desert Storm on January 17, Marine fixed-wing aviation flew air strike missions for the first time since the end of the Marines' involvement in the Vietnam War.* By the start of the war, the 3d MAW had on hand 194 fixed- and 178 rotary-wing aircraft and over 14,500 personnel, with more of both on the way. The F/A-18 "Hornets," A-6E "Intruders," and EA-6B "Prowlers" of MAG-11 joined coalition strikes on key targets in Iraq, while AV-8B Harriers from MAG-13 (forward) pounded Iraqi army positions in the Kuwaiti theater of operations (KTO). This effort continued around the clock through the end of January and early February. Like most of the Coalition air effort, Marine aircraft initially operated over hostile territory with near immunity. In the first ten days of the war, 3d MAW lost only one aircraft due to enemy action—an OV-10 "Bronco." However, as the focus of effort shifted from strategic targets to Iraqi Army formations in the field, the enemy began to exact a higher toll on the 3d MAW. AV-8B Harriers were lost over Kuwait on January 28 and February 9.

Poor weather during the first week hampered "the full prosecution of the air campaign" on the part of the wing. As January turned to February, the weather cleared but shortages of certain air ordnance stocks—in par-

---

*A Marine F/A-18 squadron was on board the USS *Coral Sea* (CV-42) during its participation in the retaliatory strike (Operation El Dorado Canyon) against Libya in 1986, but it flew only defensive air cover missions.

ticular, MK-80 series "dumb" bombs—restricted the 3d MAW from reaching its maximum sustained sortie rate. Complicating this for General Moore was the JFACC's continued call for the 3d MAW's full apportionment of its daily F/A-18 sorties (seventy-two plus). Moore and his staff had designed a conservative sustained-rate sortie schedule in order to preserve Marine air assets and ordnance for the "battlefield preparation" of Phase III and especially Phase IV, the air support for the ground offensive. The call for Marine air to fill the gaps in the air war caused by the great Scud hunt threatened to leave little for its "bread and butter" mission: close air support for Marine ground forces.[17]

On the ground in northeastern Saudi Arabia, the 1st and 2d Marine Divisions conducted artillery raids along the Kuwaiti border both to test Iraqi strength and reaction and to cover the creation of a major logistics base some 70 kilometers inland at Kibrit. The focus of the raids were Iraqi-occupied Kuwaiti police posts scattered along the southern and southwestern border. They went off generally without incident, and they served to perfect control and coordination and raise the confidence of the forces as they readied for the ground offensive.

The end of January witnessed a multipronged spoiling attack by elements of the Iraqi III Corps into northern Saudi Arabia. Although the media focused on the temporary seizure of the long-evacuated border town of Khafji, smaller columns also crossed the border at the midpoint and the western part of the southern Kuwaiti border area opposite Marine positions. Quickly repulsed, the Iraqis retreated with heavy losses. During a night melee at the western part of the border, the 1st Marine Division suffered its first combat casualties. An errant Maverick missile from an Air Force A-10 struck one light armored vehicle while a Marine TOW missile destroyed another. Friendly KIA from these two incidents totaled eleven Marines, whereas losses by the Iraqis were estimated to number in the hundreds.[18]

In the wake of this attack, Boomer and his lieutenants revisited their plans for the offensive into Kuwait. The original plan—to attack in echelon across the coastal half of the southern Kuwaiti border—seemed to be the best option given I MEF's limited combat engineering capabilities, especially in the wake of I MEF's loss of the 1st U.K. Armored Division. Attacking in echelon, however, would require a complex and difficult divisional passage of lines under potentially heavy artillery fire.

The arrival of additional combat engineering equipment in late January led General Keys to believe that his division could conduct a separate breach of Iraqi lines instead of the initial plan to follow in the wake of Myatt's 1st Marine Division assault. On February 1, Keys presented his plan for a second breach further to the west to General Boomer during the latter's visit to the 2d Marine Division. Boomer listened to Keys's assessment and concurred, giving him the go-ahead for further planning. The only decision that remained concerned the location of the second breach. The area around the Umm Gudair oil field looked promising to Keys's staff for two reasons: its proximity to Al Jahra, one of I MEF's key objectives, and the shorter distance (4 to 6 kilometers versus 20 at the original breach) between the two main obstacle belts. This shorter distance translated into shorter exposure time for Marine units in the expected Iraqi artillery "kill box."[19]

Placing the 2d Marine Division on the left offered the additional advantage to Boomer of having his more heavily armored force—the division having four tank battalions with a total of 194 M1A1 tanks and sixty-six M60A1s after the addition of the Tiger Brigade's two battalions—on the flank that faced the major Iraqi armor reserve. This had particular validity because General Boomer could not be certain that the neighboring Allied force on I MEF's western flank—the mixed Egyptian and Syrian divisions of the Joint Forces Command–North (JFC-N)—would remain apace of the I MEF and VII Corps advance. Such a lag would result in a gap between the two U.S. formations that could be exploited to a devastating effect by a competent foe.[20]

With a basic requirement that the two division assaults be within mutually supporting distance in terms of logistics, the only workable solution was to shift the 1st Marine Division's breach around the corner of the southwestern border—the so-called "heel"—while locating the 2d Marine Division's breach about halfway between the "heel" and the "elbow," where the border again switched from its general north–south orientation back to an east–west one. This shift in breach points, however, would have a significant impact on the force's logistics posture. The main I MEF combat service support area at Kibrit, which was nearly complete, was too far from the new breach points to support readily both divisions once they broke through the Iraqi defensive works.

After consulting with his staff and subordinate commanders, Boomer turned to his senior logistician, Brigadier General James A. Brabham, and the commanding general of the force's direct support command, Brigadier General Charles C. Krulak, about the feasibility of executing the new plan. Krulak felt that it was supportable, but not from his location at Kibrit. After a quick meeting with his staff, Krulak identified a better combat service support area: a gravel plain only 16 miles to the west of the Kuwaiti "heel." With only a few weeks before the anticipated ground offensive, Krulak knew it would require an unprecedented effort to reposition his 7,500-man group, but he felt that his Marines were up to the task.[21]

General Boomer agreed and, after checking with the CINC, gave his subordinates the go-ahead on February 6. Further complicating this huge displacement was the need to reposition one of the 3d MAW's two helicopter groups in order to support more effectively the offensive with transport and attack helicopters. Thus, MAG-26, only recently settled in at

Mishab on the coast, joined the westward mass migration of forces around the bottom of Kuwait. This site, dubbed "Al Khanjar" (roughly a short sword or dagger in Arabic) by Krulak's Marines, went from barren wasteland to a fully functioning combat service support area in less than two weeks. This move taxed to the limit the MEF's organic motor transport capabilities. A unique mix of active and Reserve Marines and third-party nationals served to operate a steady stream of military and leased commercial trucks on the road between Al Khanjar and Jubayl. Luckily, vast quantities of water did not have to be transported to Al Khanjar because of the February 17 discovery of an abandoned well head near this site that soon yielded much of I MEF's needs.[22]

While the air campaign slowly shifted its emphasis from strategic targets in Iraq to Iraqi formations in the Kuwaiti theater of operations, the two Marine divisions slid westward. With a small deception task force from the 1st Marine Division screening I MEF's westward shift, the remainder moved into its assembly areas below the edge of the Kuwaiti "heel" during the second week of February. General Keys's 2d Marine Division followed between the 12th and 20th, settling into positions north of their sister division. Keys's 2d Light Armored Infantry Battalion led the way and screened the division as it arrived in its assembly area.

In the skies above southern Kuwait, Marine F/A-18 "Hornets," A6E "Intruders," and AV-8B Harriers shifted their attention to enemy battlefield weapons, in particular the Iraqi Army's much vaunted artillery. A complex combination of remotely piloted vehicles (RPVs), forward air controllers (FACs) in OV-10 Broncos, and so-called fast FACs in the Corps's new two-seat F/A-18D "Hornet" guided attack aircraft to their targets.*

After mid-February, the wing's aviation ordnance stocks increased with the arrival of additional bombs and the release of some of NAVCENT's reserve of MK-20 "Rockeyes." Airspace command and control remained a delicate issue, with I MEF controlling the skies above its AOR but not those above its area of interest in southern Kuwait. This airspace box or "kill zone," known as high-density air control zones (HIDACZ) 8 thru 10, stretched between the southern border and just north of Kuwait City. Both Boomer and Moore viewed effective air control over this space as critical. To ensure the best possible air support operations, the 3d MAW's airborne direct air support center (DASC) was aloft for twelve hours a day and worked deep air support operations in conjunction with the Air Force's airborne command, control, and communications (ABCCC) aircraft, which served as the JFACC's executive agency for that area. In addition to those in its own DASC, experienced Marine air control and air support personnel helped man the ABCCC.[23]

---

*The Corps's only operational F/A-18D squadron—VMFA(AW)-121—was flown in from California in late January just for this purpose, and it proved highly effective in its assigned role.

By February 20, the last of I MEF's forces were in their assembly areas awaiting the order to begin the assault. As last-minute diplomatic maneuvering on the part of the Soviet Union threatened to upset the timing of the ground war, units throughout the force readied for the fight. The Iraqi Army earlier began to destroy Kuwaiti oil fields as part of an apparent scorched-earth policy. This yielded precious little military advantage for the Iraqis, but it soon transformed the short winter days into a perpetual twilight for those units downwind from the conflagration. By the end of the operation, those who fought in the shadow of this massive cloud of soot would look as if they had just completed a long shift deep in the bowels of a coal mine.

Early on February 23, General Myatt on the right flank ordered two of his division's regimental task forces, Taro (the 3d Marines, commanded by Colonel John H. Admire) and Grizzly (the 4th Marines, commanded by Colonel James A. Fulks), to cross into Kuwait and begin the infiltration of the area up to the first Iraqi defensive belt. Cautioned by General Boomer not to do anything irreversible prior to the 24th because of President Bush's ultimatum to the Iraqis, Myatt saw this employment of a tactic—used with great effectiveness by the German Army during World War I—as being vital to unhinge the Iraqi defenses and secure the breach at its most vulnerable point. Throughout the day and in occasional contact with the enemy, the infiltrating task forces crept into the no-man's land separating the border and the first Iraqi defensive belt while select teams of reconnaissance Marines carefully mapped out paths through the often poorly maintained mine fields. Just to the west of the border, the 1st Marine Division's mechanized task forces—Ripper (the 7th Marines, under Colonel Carlton W. Fulford), Papa Bear (the 1st Marines, under Colonel Richard W. Hodory), and Sheppard (the 1st LAI Bn)—moved into final attack positions. Colonel Patrick G. Howard, the commander of the 11th Marines, distributed his direct support artillery throughout the division but stood by to recentralize divisional fire missions if necessary.[24]

Just a few miles to the northeast, General Keys's 2d Marine Division completed similar preparations, although H-hour (actual moment of attack) for his division would be one and a half hours after Myatt's to steer any Iraqi reaction away from the main attack by Keys's Marines. The first of the division's regiments into the breach would be Colonel Lawrence H. Livingston's 6th Marines, followed closely by Colonel John B. Sylvester's Tiger Brigade and Colonel Larry S. Schmidt's 8th Marines. In division reserve would be the 2d Tank Battalion, newly equipped with M1A1 Abrams tanks on loan from the U.S. Army, while the massed artillery of the 10th Marines under Colonel Leslie M. Palm prepared to smother their Iraqi opponents.

At 0400 on February 24, I MEF launched its attack into Kuwait. On the right, the 1st Marine Division's two foot-borne regimental task forces

Figure 9.1
Map Showing the Order of Battle, February 23, 1991

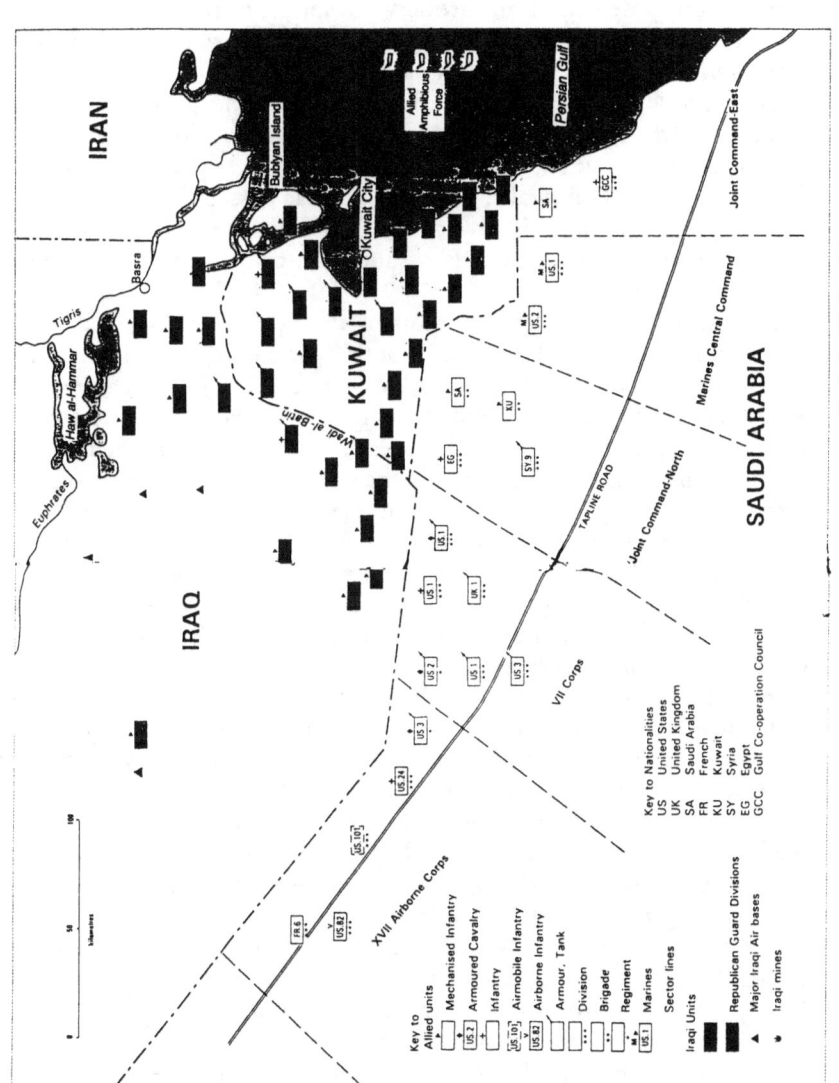

The Order of Battle: 23 February 1991

quickly succeeded in infiltrating the first obstacle belt and securing its flanks. The division's two mechanized task forces—Ripper (7th Marines) and Papa Bear (1st Marines)—plowed through the first belt and then rapidly breached the second by day's end. Counterbattery fire and air strikes quickly suppressed the Iraqi artillery. Despite occasional setbacks in the breaching operations, the division made extraordinary progress by evening while suffering only a handful of casualties.[25]

The experience was the same for the 2d Marine Division on the left flank. The 6th Marines literally plowed through both Iraqi belts within a matter of hours after encountering unexpectedly light resistance and taking few casualties. In their wake, the Tiger Brigade passed through the belts by midafternoon and moved forward on the left flank of the division's zone. The 8th Marines remained on the Saudi side of the breach until the next morning.

The much-feared use by the Iraqis of chemical weapons failed to materialize during the assault, although both divisions reported numerous but unsubstantiated indications of possible chemical weapons. As a precaution, assaulting units went into combat wearing their chemical protective overgarments, except for masks and gloves, which could be donned quickly if required. In the heat of the summer, the wear of the overgarments for more than a few hours would have been intolerable and would have likely resulted in numerous heat casualties; but the cool, wet weather of late February made continued wear of the overgarments bearable.

Well ahead of schedule, both Marine divisions slowed their advance during nightfall as concerns over fratricide and mine fields tempered thoughts of continuing the blitzkrieg-like advance. Even so, the tremendous headway gained during the day prompted General Schwarzkopf to move up the time of his main attack further to the west by more than 12 hours to 1500 on February 24. During that night of February 24 and the following morning, the divisions weathered a variety of local counterattacks and disjointed fire fights as Iraqi formations struggled to avoid annihilation or capture. In one well-publicized action, a Marine Reserve tank company from Yakima, Washington attached to a battalion of the 8th Marines helped to defeat decisively a battalion's worth of Iraqi armor.

For the Marine forces afloat under the 7th Fleet, the decision not to launch an amphibious assault was a bittersweet one. With some elements having been away from home for over eight months, the disappointment upon learning that they would not participate in the attack ashore was great. This was mitigated, however, by the knowledge that such an assault could have proved costly. The mining of the USS *Princeton* (CG-59) and USS *Tripoli* (LPH-10) a few days before the ground assault dramatically drove home this point. While the 4th MEB and 13th MEU (SOC) were relegated to feints and seizures of Kuwait's offshore islands, the 5th MEB was ordered ashore on February 23 to serve as the I MEF reserve. The threat of amphibious assault was taken seriously by the Iraqis, and it was later estimated that six of approximately eleven Iraqi divisions in southern Kuwait were deployed along the coast to guard against the threat from the sea.[26]

Beginning at 0600 on February 23 (G − 1), the 3d MAW surged its aircraft sortie rate in support of the Marine ground offensive. For the next five days, it averaged a section (two aircraft) of close air support every 6.5 minutes over southern Kuwait. Between February 24 and 28, the wing generated over 2,500 sorties, in spite of poor weather and limited visibility due to the smoking inferno of Kuwait's oil fields. This surge had its price: Two Harriers and a Bronco from 3d MAW and a Harrier from NAVCENT were lost over southern Kuwait. Two of the wing's F/A-18s suffered serious battle damage but were quickly repaired.[27]

On February 25 (G + 1), I MEF continued its northward assault, meeting what it later characterized as "varied amounts of uncoordinated and ineffective opposition" along the way.[28] In the 1st Division zone, General Myatt's forward command post repulsed an attack by elements of what was determined to be an Iraqi armored brigade. Coming from out of the inferno of the Burqan oil field, the attack was defeated with the invaluable assistance of Marine AH-1W "SuperCobra" attack helicopters from the 3d MAW. As the rest of the division bypassed Al Jaber Air Base, Task Force Grizzly commenced an attack to seize and clear it of the enemy, as Boomer planned to use the base for a forward aviation and logistics site. The operation continued into the next day, and by midafternoon on February 26 Al Jaber was declared secure—the first major I MEF objective to fall.

The 2d Division, after fighting off residual scattered counterattacks from the night before, likewise continued its advance. This was slowed somewhat as Keys waited for the 8th Marines (including the 3d Battalion, 23d Marines—a Reserve unit), which at daybreak on February 25 began moving to the right flank from its assembly areas on the other side of the obstacle belts. The 6th Marines fought off a battalion-sized armored force aiming for its logistics trains. Throughout the morning, the division's artillery regiment, the 10th Marines, engaged in ongoing counterbattery duels against Iraqi artillery units. In a rare event, the entire regiment—five battalions worth—conducted a synchronized "zone and sweep" fire mission against an Iraqi artillery concentration that resulted in the latter's destruction.

In the early afternoon of February 25, after marshalling its regiments on line, the 2d Marine Division attacked through 11 kilometers to Phase Line Red (the first phase goal of the ground offensive) north of Al Jaber in just shy of two hours, destroying all Iraqi equipment in the zone in the process. With visibility ranging between 200 and 500 meters by late afternoon, Keys chose to cease temporarily the advance and have his units consolidate just north of Phase Line Red for the night. Besides the obscuring of the battlefield from the hundreds of burning well heads, the operations of both divisions were increasingly hampered by the thousands of enemy prisoners of war (EPWs) being collected throughout their zones. Even with the creation prior to the ground offensive of specialized EPW-handling task forces, the requirement to transport them out of the battle area placed enormous strain on front-line units.[29]

I MEF continued the assault on the morning of February 26 (G + 2), with the 2d Marine Division striking for Al Jahra and the Mutla Ridge area west of Kuwait City. The 1st Marine Division attacked toward the international airport on the southern outskirts of the capital. That morning, General Boomer, operating from his small mobile command post right behind his divisions in Kuwait, instructed his subordinate commanders to press home their attacks. In the wake of intelligence reports that detected the beginnings of a wholesale Iraqi retreat from Kuwait City, he wanted to cut off their escape as quickly as possible.[30]

The 1st Marine Division pressed toward the airport throughout the day with its two heavy mechanized task forces, while its light armor task force—Sheppard—screened the division's open eastern flank. In the evening, task force Papa Bear (the 1st Marines) engaged and defeated a large Iraqi armored force just south of the airport in what has since been billed as the largest Marine tank battle in history. General Myatt assigned the actual capture of the objective to task force Sheppard, which did so early the next morning.[31]

In preparation for the 2d division attack, General Keys shifted his light armor screen from east to west to cover his still-exposed flank. Being careful to avoid interfering with Myatt's division on the right, Keys placed his two Marine regiments in the right and center sectors of his zone while directing the Tiger Brigade on the left to attack and seize the crucial high ground necessary to cut off the Iraqi Army's escape. Kicking off at 1200, the assault made good progress. The 6th and 8th Marines swept up to the western edge of the city, routing the enemy when it attempted to resist and destroyed its equipment. The Tiger Brigade did the same throughout its sector, rapidly breaching an unexpected mine field on the way to its objective. Seizing the high ground within the hour, the brigade's lead battalion, the 3d of the 67th Armor (3-67 Armor), completed the destruction of fleeing columns of Iraqis started earlier in the day by Marine and Air Force deep air strikes. By 1700, the division had seized all of its objectives, thereby isolating Kuwait City.[32]

While the 1st Marine Division finished clearing the Kuwait International Airport on February 27, the 2d Division coordinated the passage of lines near Al Jahra of an Egyptian brigade from JFC-N that was ordered to assist in the clearing of the capital. The divisions spent the remainder of the day clearing their respective zones of bypassed enemy pockets and prisoners. Late on February 27, CENTCOM passed word to I MEF of the impending unilateral cease-fire scheduled for 0800 on February 28, but for the Marines ashore, the "100 Hour War" was essentially over a day early.

CONCLUSION

As I MEF consolidated its positions in Kuwait, it took stock of its losses and breathed a collective sigh of relief. As compared to the earlier forecasted figure of nearly 10,000 Marines killed and wounded in a week's worth of fighting, the cost of Desert Storm seemed miraculously small: twenty-three dead and ninety-two wounded. Of course, the cost, as always, was very high to those few who gave their lives and their loved ones, who had to come to terms with their loss. Over 22,000 Iraqi soldiers were taken prisoner by I MEF during the same period. The cost to Iraq in terms of their killed and wounded soldiers in the Marine area was not determined, but a minimum figure of several thousand killed would not be an unreasonable guess.[33]

The performance of the Marine Corps in Operations Desert Shield and Desert Storm was noteworthy in many respects. At the outset of the crisis, the Marines' institutional emphasis on being the nation's force-in-readiness ensured that the Fleet Marine Force was able to pack up and leave home on short notice. Its adoption of the Maritime Prepositioned Force concept in the 1980s capitalized on its readiness by enabling the 7th MEB to arrive in theater early in the crisis with a credible combined arms force. Its inherent flexibility allowed for the quick integration of its assorted ground and aviation units into a cohesive force.

As the buildup in the Gulf progressed and the theater changed from its "expeditionary" nature to a "mature" one with a fully developed military infrastructure, the Corps was able to adjust roles from that of a "fire brigade" to a significant maneuver element. Often presented to the public by its detractors as a "light" force, I MEF, already wielding a strong right arm in the form of its aircraft wing, developed highly mechanized and armored divisions to suit the mission at hand. In perhaps the most unheralded aspect of the war, Marine combat service support proved extraordinarily adaptable and effective despite operating far from the sea.

During Desert Storm, the Marine Corps demonstrated that its unique air–ground team provided a powerful kind of synergy at the operational level of war. While not as spectacular as the Third U.S. Army's dash across the open desert, the two Marine divisions demonstrated their ability to maneuver with agility and fight on a hellish battlefield cluttered with manmade obstacles. The 3d MAW kept apace of events on the ground and responded quickly to calls for air support despite often poor visibility. Battlefield logistics support was also pushed well forward to front-line units, thus sustaining the high tempo of the Marine assault. The effective use of the Marine Reserve—including its combat units—in the liberation of Kuwait was a testament to the Corps's faith in its reserve establishment.

As with all military operations, the friction of war served to uncover problems both of organization and execution. Marines were the first to feel the sting of fratricide, and the lack of an effective Allied solution interjected a high level of caution and conservatism during the ground war. This was compounded by the relatively limited amount of night vision equipment within the force. The lack of organic dedicated airborne photographic reconnaissance assets was keenly felt by Boomer and his generals throughout the conflict. The MEF's communications and intelligence capabilities required extensive augmentation from outside the Corps to fight on such a large scale. The decision by General Schwarzkopf not to employ a large-scale amphibious assault—completely justified by the outcome of the ground campaign—underscored many of the problems confronting this hallmark Marine mission.

On balance, the Marine Corps made a sizable contribution to the war's successful outcome. Its strategic vision of its unique service role, operational air–ground cohesion, and tactical prowess made it an effective member of the joint and combined war-fighting team. Despite fighting on an unexpected scale far from the sea, the Marine Corps in Desert Storm proved itself to be the perfect strong right jab to Schwarzkopf's famous Third Army left hook.

NOTES

The basis for this chapter has been official Marine Corps command chronologies (COMDC) on file at the Marine Corps Historical Center (MCHC), Washington Navy Yard, Washington, D.C. Unless otherwise noted, the facts, figures, and descriptions of unit actions are based on descriptions in these files.

1. "Marines See Action: Middle East and Africa," *Marine Corps Gazette* September 1990, 4.
2. Editorial, *Marine Corps Gazette,* October 1990, 2. See also "Special Trust and Confidence Among the Trail-breakers," interview with Lieutenant General W. E. Boomer, *Naval Institute Proceedings,* November 1991, 48.
3. 7th MEB COMDC 1 Jul–3 Sep 90 (MCHC, Washington, D.C.).
4. 7th MEB COMDC 1 Jul–3 Sep 90 (MCHC, Washington, D.C.).
5. 1st Mar Div COMDC Sep 90 (MCHC, Washington, D.C.).
6. 3d MAW COMDC Sep 90 (MCHC, Washington, D.C.).
7. 4th MEB COMDC 1 Jul–31 Oct 90 (MCHC, Washington, D.C.). The MEB totaled nearly 8,000 Marines, and the 13th MEU (SOC) had another 2,300.
8. I MEF COMDC Oct 90 (MCHC, Washington, D.C.), 7.
9. For a particularly good account of the Korean War air issues from the Marine perspective, see Allan R. Millet's *Semper Fidelis: The Story of the United States Marine Corps* (New York: Macmillan, 1980), 502–5.
10. See "Marine Air: There When Needed," interview with Lieutenant General Royal N. Moore, Jr., USMC in *Naval Institute Proceedings,* November 1991, 66.

11. I MEF COMDC Oct 90 (MCHC, Washington, D.C.).
12. I MEF COMDC Nov 90 (MCHC, Washington, D.C.), 5.
13. 5th MEB COMDC 1 Jul–31 Dec 90 (MCHC, Washington, D.C.).
14. See 2d Mar Div, 3d MAW COMDCs 1 Jan–28 Feb 91 (MCHC, Washington, D.C.).
15. 2d Mar Div COMDC 1 Jan–13 Apr 91 (MCHC, Washington, D.C.), I-9.
16. I MEF COMDC Dec 90 (MCHC, Washington, D.C.), 5–7.
17. 3d MAW COMDC Jan–Feb 91 (MCHC, Washington, D.C.), 43–45.
18. I MEF COMDC 1 Jan–28 Feb 91 (MCHC, Washington, D.C.), 18–19.
19. 2d Mar Div COMDC 1 Jan–13 Apr 91 (MCHC, Washington, D.C.), II-6.
20. 2d Mar Div COMDC 1 Jan–13 Apr 91 (MCHC, Washington, D.C.), I-9, II-7.
21. DSC COMDC 16 Feb–13 Apr 91 (MCHC, Washington, D.C.). See also "A War of Logistics," interview with Brigadier General Charles C. Krulak, USMC in *Naval Institute Proceedings,* November 1991, 55–57.
22. DSC COMDC 16 Feb–13 Apr 91 (MCHC, Washington, D.C.).
23. MACG-38 COMDC Feb 91 (MCHC, Washington, D.C.).
24. 1st Mar Div COMDC 1 Jan–28 Feb 91 (MCHC, Washington, D.C.), 2–5.
25. I MEF COMDC 1 Jan–28 Feb 91 (MCHC, Washington, D.C.), 9. The Center for Naval Analysis estimated "a total of 9,667 direct combat casualties and 10,552 overall for a seven day campaign."
26. "The 1st Marine Division in the Attack," interview with Major General James M. Myatt, USMC in *Naval Institute Proceedings,* November 1991, 76.
27. 3d MAW COMDC 1 Jan–28 Feb 91 (MCHC, Washington, D.C.), 21, 47–49.
28. I MEF COMDC 1 Jan–28 Feb 91 (MCHC, Washington, D.C.), 24.
29. 2d Mar Div COMDC 1 Jan–13 Apr 91 (MCHC, Washington, D.C.), II-18.
30. I MEF COMDC 1 Jan–28 Feb 91 (MCHC, Washington, D.C.), 24.
31. 1st Mar Div COMDC 1 Jan–28 Feb 91 (MCHC, Washington, D.C.), 2–5.
32. 2d Mar Div COMDC 1 Jan–13 Apr 91 (MCHC, Washington, D.C.), II-21.
33. I MEF COMDC 1 Jan–28 Feb 91 (MCHC, Washington, D.C.).

Part V

THE NAVY'S ROLE IN THE GULF WAR

Even fewer people and scholars are aware of the details of the U.S. Navy's role in Operations Desert Shield/Storm than they are of the highly visible Air Force and Army role and even the less glamorous Marine Corps's role. The popular perception of the Navy's role in the Persian Gulf War is as a sort of cab service which shuttled ground troops and their supplies to the theater of operations and then took them home afterwards. To be sure the national media paid very little attention to the Navy's operations which flanked Iraq with ships in the Persian Gulf and the Mediterranean Sea. Nor did they cover the Navy's rapid response, its important sealift operations which underwrote Desert Shield, or the important role carrier based aircraft played in the high profile air campaign.

As Robert J. Schneller, Jr., suggests in his chapter "On the Storm's Outer Edge: U.S. Navy Operations in the Persian Gulf War," perhaps the Navy's role was not so secondary; maybe it was simply a matter of public relations. To be sure Schneller's piece decries the aforementioned oversights and seeks to enlighten the reader regarding the important part the Navy did play in the Gulf War.

Norman Friedman's chapter "Sailing in the Sand: The U.S. Navy's Role in the Gulf War," while predictably more critical of the institutional execution of the Navy's assignments, also demonstrates the significance of the Navy in the war especially regarding the sealift aspects of Desert Shield. Together these chapters remind us that without the Navy's support neither the ground war nor the air war would have been as successful. In the end, Schneller and Friedman's chapters, like many of the others in this book, demonstrate that no operations in this post–Cold War era can, with certainty, be successful without the concept of jointness. In this case, both authors make a strong case that the Gulf War most certainly could not have been won without the joint efforts of all the services including its seaborne component.

—William Head

10

On the Storm's Outer Edge: U.S. Navy Operations in the Persian Gulf War

Robert J. Schneller, Jr.

The United States Navy's ability to control the sea and project power ashore proved critical to the success of Desert Shield, and its war-fighting capabilities played a key role in the Coalition's victory over Iraq during Desert Storm.[1]

Because forward-deployed ships had formed the first line of defense for U.S. interests in the Persian Gulf region since the establishment of the Middle East Force in 1949, naval forces were on hand to respond immediately to Iraq's invasion of Kuwait on August 2, 1990. That day, the eight ships of the Joint Task Force Middle East, then operating in the Persian Gulf and North Arabian Sea, went on alert. Within one hour of the invasion, the Joint Chiefs of Staff (JCS) ordered the *Independence* battle group, then cruising in the Indian Ocean, to proceed at top speed to the Gulf of Oman, and the *Dwight D. Eisenhower* carrier battle group, then steaming in the central Mediterranean, to take up position in the Red Sea. By August 5, the *Independence* had reached a point from which its aircraft could strike Saddam's tank columns. *Dwight D. Eisenhower* drew within striking range shortly afterward.[2]

On August 4, President George Bush; Defense Secretary Richard Cheney; General Colin Powell, Chairman of the JCS; and General H. Norman Schwarzkopf, Jr., Commander in Chief of Central Command (CENTCOM), the U.S. unified command charged with the defense of American interests in Southwest Asia, met at Camp David to discuss the crisis. The prospect of Iraqi dictator Saddam Hussein establishing hegemony over the oil-rich nations on the Arabian Peninsula was frightening. As Bush later remarked, "Our jobs, our way of life, our own freedom, and the freedom of friendly countries around the world would all suffer if control of the world's great oil reserves fell into the hands of that one man."[3] After reviewing his options, Bush concluded that military power offered the best hope of deterring or halting further Iraqi aggression. On August 6, at the invitation of Saudi King Abdul Aziz ibn Fahd, Bush ordered American forces to Saudi Arabia. Operation Desert Shield had begun.[4]

Although not initially so conceived, Desert Shield unfolded in two phases. The first—a defensive phase—extended from August to October 31, 1990. The second—preparation for an offensive—lasted from November 1, 1990 to January 16, 1991, the eve of Desert Storm. Ultimately, the United States found itself at the helm of a Coalition of nearly thirty-five countries dedicated to reversing Saddam's invasion of Kuwait.

CENTCOM's Operation Plan (OPLAN) 1002-90, the latest in a series of U.S. war plans for the defense of the Gulf region, guided the buildup of U.S. forces in the theater and the defense of Saudi Arabia during the first phase. With the fall of communism in the Soviet Union and the end of the Cold War, the concomitant shift in U.S. strategic focus from global war to regional conflict, and the emergence of Iraq as the preeminent military power in the Gulf, Department of Defense and CENTCOM planners had predicated 1002-90 on the assumption of an Iraqi attack down the Arabian Peninsula. The plan called for the deployment of three aircraft carrier battle groups, one surface action group, a Marine expeditionary force, an Army airborne corps, various special operations forces, and nine Air Force (USAF) wings. First, light airborne, infantry, and special warfare forces would secure critical ports and airfields to enable the buildup in Saudi Arabia of heavier ground units, land-based air forces, materiel, and munitions. Then armored forces would beef up defenses on the likeliest avenues of approach for an enemy attack. A strong mechanized reserve would also enable CENTCOM to counterattack an invading Iraqi Army.[5]

American air and ground forces began arriving in the desert kingdom on August 7. In general, soldiers, Marines, aircrews, and naval reservists reached the theater by air, whereas more than 90 percent of their equipment and supplies came by sea. Regular naval personnel deployed on board their ships. CENTCOM's naval component, U.S. Naval Forces, Central Command (NAVCENT), controlled all naval forces assigned to CENTCOM's area of responsibility. On August 16, Vice Admiral Henry J. Mauz, Jr., Commander 7th Fleet, took command of NAVCENT.[6]

The first U.S. forces to arrive faced an Iraqi army in Kuwait that, by late August, numbered an estimated 265,000 troops. The Iraqi air force's 950 aircraft threatened not only the Coalition's forces, but also its supply line, as did the Iraqi navy's shore-based Silkworm antiship missiles and fleet of some 165 vessels, particularly its thirteen missile boats.[7]

General Schwarzkopf believed that an armored force more powerful than originally planned would be necessary to defeat a determined Iraqi drive on Saudi Arabia. However, shortages of fast sealift vessels with a roll-on/roll-off capability (RO/RO), crucial to unloading armored vehicles quickly, prevented him from deploying heavy forces as fast as he would have liked. Coalition commanders dubbed the weeks that passed until the armor arrived the "window of vulnerability" for Allied forces in Saudi Arabia and the "window of opportunity" for Saddam.[8]

Meanwhile, naval forces secured the sea lines of communication with the theater. The presence of U.S. and NATO naval forces in the Mediterranean, Red Sea, North Arabian Sea, and Persian Gulf restrained Saddam's supporters from aiding Iraq and might have deterred potential attacks on Allied shipping. Naval forces also defended the ports of Jubayl and Dammam in Saudi Arabia and Mina Sulman in Bahrain. The bulk of Central Command's supplies and equipment passed through these ports, which, at first, were vulnerable to assault by mine-laying boats, explosives-laden swimmers, missile-armed fast attack craft, or terrorists. The loss of any one would, at the minimum, have slowed down the buildup of Coalition forces and provided Saddam with extra time to shore up his own defenses or to negotiate a settlement. Accordingly, NAVCENT assigned Navy special warfare and Coast Guard units to each harbor for port security and harbor defense.[9]

From mid-August to early September, naval forces afloat and ashore comprised the bulk of allied military power facing Saddam Hussein. By September 1, the Navy had assembled a powerful armada in the Persian Gulf, the North Arabian Sea, and the Red Sea, including three carriers, one battleship, six cruisers, five destroyers, and eight frigates. Allied navies also dispatched ships to the region.

On August 15, the first three ships of Maritime Prepositioning Ship (MPS) Squadron 2 reached Jubayl. MPS 2 carried the equipment and thirty days of supplies for the 7th Marine Expeditionary Brigade (MEB). The 7th MEB's Marines, who had begun to arrive at Jubayl's air facilities on August 14, soon "married up" with their ship-delivered equipment. On August 25, the 7th MEB stood ready for combat.[10]

The success of Desert Shield depended on the United States' ability to move quickly hundreds of thousands of military personnel and millions of tons of equipment and supplies almost halfway around the globe. This task fell to the U.S. Transportation Command (TRANSCOM) under General Hansford T. Johnson, USAF and his three major components, the Air Force's Military Airlift Command (MAC), the Army's Military Traffic Management Command (MTMC), and the Navy's Military Sealift Command (MSC).

The Military Sealift Command, led by Vice Admiral Francis R. Donovan, controlled the twenty-five ships of the Afloat Prepositioning Force[11], eight SL-7 fast sealift ships, and hospital ships *Comfort* and *Mercy*. If necessary, MSC could also activate the ninety-six Ready Reserve Force (RRF) ships maintained by the Department of Transportation's Maritime Administration and charter merchantmen owned by U.S. and foreign commercial firms.

Admiral Donovan activated forty-four Ready Reserve Force (RRF) ships during Phase I, but only twelve of them were ready for operations on schedule. Delays in the activation of the others resulted largely from inadequate maintenance due to lack of funds. But once activated and turned over to Military Sealift Command, the RRF ships delivered about 22 percent of the unit equipment and related support in Phase I. RO/ROs carried nearly twice as much combat and support equipment in Phase I as all other ship types combined. MSC's seven operational SL-7 fast sealift ships with RO/RO capability delivered almost 20 percent of Central Command's unit equipment and related support during the first phase. To alleviate shortages of RO/ROs and other merchantmen, MSC chartered numerous U.S.- and foreign-flag ships. Chartered ships carried some 34 percent of the combat and support equipment during Phase I.

During the first phase of Desert Shield, MSC delivered 1,034,900 tons of equipment, 135,100 tons of supplies, and 1,800,000 tons of petroleum products to the Persian Gulf region. Of the 173 ships involved, 124 were U.S.-flag vessels, and these accounted for 85 percent of the tonnage. Even though Phase I ended formally on December 5, virtually all of Schwarzkopf's planned requirements had been satisfied by November 11.

General Johnson attributed much of the success of his operation to Saudi Arabia's ultramodern ports, airfields, and assistance; the international support for the military buildup in the Gulf; and Saddam's decisions not to attack Coalition maritime traffic or the ports of Saudi Arabia.[12]

During Desert Shield's first phase, the United States deployed over sixty naval vessels, an amphibious task force, more than 1,000 ground-based aircraft, and some 240,000 military men and women.[13] On November 1, Powell reported to the president that "Schwarzkopf . . . had the combat capability in place, in the region, to successfully defend against any Iraqi attack."[14]

Meanwhile, the UN instituted an embargo of all Iraqi overseas trade. On August 6, the UN Security Council passed Resolution 661, which prohibited trade and financial transactions with Iraq. The embargo had two goals: to degrade Iraq's military capabilities by denying the country access to vital foreign-produced supplies, spare parts, and equipment; and, more ambitiously, to compel Saddam to withdraw his forces from Kuwait.

To enforce the embargo, the U.S. Navy took the lead in a multinational blockade of Iraq. At the behest of President Bush, the U.S. Navy began maritime interception force (MIF) operations on August 17.[15] Eight days later, the UN Security Council passed Resolution 665, which authorized Coalition naval units to employ force to uphold the embargo and invited all UN member nations to participate in the blockade. Eventually, sixty warships from Argentina, Australia, Belgium, Canada, Denmark, France, Greece, Italy, the Netherlands, Norway, Spain, and the United Kingdom took part in MIF operations. GCC navies patrolled inshore waters to prevent merchantmen from evading the interception force. Maritime interception operations went on throughout the war and are still going on at this writing.[16]

Since the UN lacked a permanent military organization and staff, the U.S. Navy provided centralized direction of MIF operations. Admiral Mauz appointed Rear Admiral William M. Fogarty commander of the U.S. Maritime Interception Force (COMUSMIF). The senior naval officer present in each patrol sector coordinated combined operations in that sector. A U.S. carrier battle group commander was usually responsible for overall coordination of the patrols in the northern Red Sea, Persian Gulf, and northern Arabian Sea. The carrier battle group commander generally delegated MIF responsibility to the commander of his destroyer escort squadron. Eventually, the destroyer squadron commanders carried out independent interception operations and reported directly to Admiral Fogarty.[17]

Under the guidelines set forth in UN Security Council Resolutions 661 and 665, Coalition naval forces intercepted merchant ships bound to and from Iraq, Kuwait, and the Jordanian port of Aqabah, except those transporting medicines. Al Aqabah was included because King Hussein's government permitted overland transshipment of cargo to Iraq from that port.

Although each naval contingent followed rules of engagement laid down by their home government, Allied navies used common procedures. Maritime patrol aircraft kept watch over the waters surrounding the Arabian Peninsula, reported sightings of merchant ships, and directed Coalition warships to them. Normally, two Coalition combatants operated together. After intercepting a merchantman, the warships requested the ship's identity, point of origin, destination, and cargo. If the vessel proved not to be heading to or from a port in Iraq, Kuwait, or Jordan, the intercepting force allowed the ship to proceed unhindered. Suspicious merchantmen were directed to stop for inspection. The Coalition patrol would then dispatch a boarding party to the ship. The U.S. boarding parties normally consisted of Coast Guard law enforcement detachments and Navy personnel. If a merchantman refused to stop, the intercepting vessels inserted armed teams by helicopter to take temporary control of the ship.[18] Despite several tense moments, most MIF operations involved routine interceptions of hundreds of merchantmen from many nations innocently plying their trade in Middle Eastern waters.

By the start of Desert Storm, the maritime interception force in the Red

Sea was making fifty at-sea contacts each day, down from a total of 200 a day in August 1990. During the same period, the number of merchantmen entering or leaving the Jordanian port of Aqaba fell from thirty to fifty ships each day to three or four ships each day. As of September 26, 1994, Coalition forces had intercepted 21,427 ships, boarded 9,727, and turned 499 away from their intended destinations.[19] The embargo not only demonstrated Iraq's international isolation, but also denied Saddam access to world markets, eliminated his main source of income (oil exports), and stopped the resupply of his war machine.[20]

Throughout the fall of 1990, while Allied ships conducted MIF operations and troops and equipment streamed into the Kuwaiti theater of operations (KTO), leaders in Washington grappled with various measures to induce Saddam to relinquish his hold on Kuwait. President Bush had annunciated America's political goals on August 8, 1990: the immediate, unconditional, and complete withdrawal of all Iraqi forces from Kuwait; the restoration of Kuwait's legitimate government; the maintenance of security and stability in the Persian Gulf; and the protection of the lives of American citizens abroad.[21] Saddam's responses to UN political initiatives during the summer and fall of 1990 made it increasingly clear that an offensive operation would be necessary to achieve these goals. In August, USAF and CENTCOM planners worked up the first draft of a plan for a four-phase air, land, and sea campaign to eject Iraqi forces from Kuwait, code named Desert Storm. Early versions of the land phase envisioned an offensive by the single available Army corps, the XVIII Corps. In October, General Schwarzkopf concluded that a two-corps offensive stood a better chance of success and would produce far fewer casualties. President Bush agreed. On October 31, he decided to deploy an additional 200,000 troops to the KTO. The reinforcements would include three more carrier battle groups and another battleship from the Navy, the Marine Corps's II Marine Expeditionary Force and 5th MEB (embarked in the ships of Amphibious Group 3), 410 USAF planes, and the Army's VII Corps and 1st Infantry Division.[22]

Most U.S. air and naval forces deployed during Phase II arrived in the theater by mid-January. As in Phase I, most of the people came by air and most of the cargo by sea. During Phase II, MSC controlled some 220 ships, which delivered 1,270,300 short tons of equipment, 235,400 more than in the earlier effort. The 404,700 tons of supplies delivered in Phase II almost tripled that of Phase I. Finally, MSC delivered to theater forces 3,500,000 short tons of fuel, 1,700,000 more than in Phase I.[23]

While merchantmen delivered supplies and unit equipment, combatants prepared for war. On December 1, 1990, Vice Admiral Stanley Arthur replaced Vice Admiral Mauz as Commander 7th Fleet and COMUSNAVCENT in a routine turnover. Arthur organized his command into nine task forces or task groups (see Table 10.1). He divided the carrier battle groups

Table 10.1
NAVCENT Command Structure (December 26 onward)

Commander Naval Forces, U.S. Central Command (CTF 150)
  Vice Admiral Stanley R. Arthur
Commander Middle East Force (CTF 151)
  Rear Admiral William M. Fogarty
Commander Maritime Interception Force (CTF 152)
  Rear Admiral Fogarty
Commander Naval Logistics Support Force (CTG 150.3)
  Rear Admiral Robert Sutton
Commander Battle Force Zulu (CTF 154)
  Rear Admiral Daniel P. March
Commander Battle Force Yankee (CTF 155)*
  Rear Admiral Riley D. Mixson
Commander Amphibious Task Force (CTF 156)
  Rear Admiral John B. LaPlante
Commander Landing Force (CTF 158)
  Major General Harry W. Jenkins, USMC
Commander Mediterranean Strike Group (CTG 150.9)
  Rear Admiral Riley D. Mixson

*Rear Admiral George N. Gee became CTF 155 whenever Rear Admiral Mixson's flagship, the carrier *Saratoga*, posted to the Mediterranean.

Source: Michael Shepko, Sandra Newett, and Rhonda M. Alexander, *Maritime Interception Operations* (Alexandria, Va.: Center for Naval Analyses, 1991), 6.

into two battle forces, designated Zulu and Yankee, which operated, respectively, in the Persian Gulf and Red Sea. Naval air wings rehearsed strike operations at Fallon, Nevada before departing for the theater. Battle Force Yankee conducted "mirror-image" strike exercises with USAF units. Other naval units conducted combat search and rescue, surface warfare, antiair warfare, gunfire support, amphibious maneuvers, and a wide variety of other exercises.[24]

Even as Coalition forces prepared for war, the Allies sought a peaceful exit for the Iraqi Army in Kuwait. But when Saddam rebuffed initiative after initiative, the Coalition decided to launch Operation Desert Storm on January 17, 1991. On that day, two massive opponents squared off for control of Kuwait. Although the total Iraqi strength in the theater probably numbered less than 400,000, the Defense Intelligence Agency estimated that Saddam Hussein had deployed 540,000 troops arrayed in forty-three divisions, with 4,280 tanks, more than 2,800 armored personnel carriers, and approximately 3,100 artillery pieces. Twenty-five of these divisions hunkered down in two major defensive belts built by Iraqi engineers along the Kuwait–Saudi border. The remaining eighteen divisions stood by in reserve, including eight Republican Guard Forces Command divisions positioned north and west of Kuwait. Iraq's 950 aircraft were spread out among its twenty-four main operating bases and thirty dispersal bases. The Iraqi navy's missile boats sat in their bases and along the Kuwaiti coast.[25]

On the Coalition side, seven U.S. Army divisions, the two Marine Corps divisions comprising the I Marine Expeditionary Force, a British armored division, a French light armored division, and the equivalent of more than four Arab divisions stood ready for action. More than 2,400 fixed-wing aircraft from twelve Coalition countries flew from bases and aircraft carriers throughout the theater and around the world. In all, more than 600,000 men and women from thirty-one Allied nations prepared to liberate Kuwait.[26]

The Coalition naval armada numbered more than 150 ships from fourteen Allied nations. The U.S. Navy contributed 108 of these ships, including five carrier battle groups, two battleships, thirteen submarines, and the largest amphibious force mustered since the Korean War, carrying nearly 17,000 Marines. The *John F. Kennedy, Saratoga,* and *America* battle groups operated in the Red Sea while the *Ranger* and *Midway* battle groups steamed in the Persian Gulf. The *Theodore Roosevelt* battle group arrived on station in the Gulf on January 21. The naval array also included special warfare forces, naval construction battalions, medical units, cargo handlers, logistics ships and aircraft, explosive ordnance disposal units, mine countermeasures (MCM) ships, salvage and repair units, and harbor defense forces.[27]

CENTCOM's four-phase theater campaign plan for Operation Desert Storm sought to expel the Iraqi Army from Kuwait and to destroy Iraq's offensive capabilities in order to prevent future aggression. Phase I was a strategic air campaign aimed at decapitating Saddam's military power by rendering his forces blind, deaf, and immobile while leaving the basic economic and industrial infrastructure of Iraq intact. To accomplish these goals, Allied warplanes would strike twelve strategic target sets: leadership; command, control, and communications facilities; air defense systems; military depots and storage locations; nuclear, biological, and chemical weapons and production facilities; airfields; railroads and bridges; Scud missiles; oil refineries; electrical production; naval facilities; and the Republican Guard.[28]

In Phase II, Allied forces would establish air superiority in the KTO. In Phase III, air- and naval power would prepare the battlefield by isolating and reducing enemy forces in the theater. Phases I through III of the theater plan—strategic attack, air supremacy, and battlefield preparation—comprised the air campaign. If Saddam refused to capitulate during Phases I through III, the Coalition would launch Phase IV, a ground offensive aimed at ejecting the Iraqis from Kuwait.

Naval forces had two primary missions in Desert Storm: to support the air campaign, and to convince Saddam that the Allies intended to launch an amphibious assault on his left flank.[29] U.S. leaders had considered making a Navy–Marine amphibious landing in Kuwait or southern Iraq in support of the main ground thrust, but staff studies and simulations run in the fall of 1990 raised the specter of heavy casualties and a possible debacle because of the perceived complexity and extent of enemy beach defenses and sea mine fields. Therefore, Schwarzkopf never seriously considered a major amphibious landing on the Iraqi-held shore. But rather than disembark the amphibious forces, he decided to use them for deception operations, including a raid on Faylaka Island. Even if he had no intention of mounting a major assault, a credible amphibious threat might pin substantial Iraqi forces to the coast.[30]

The responsibility for coordinated employment of all U.S. and Allied air forces fell to General Schwarzkopf's Joint Forces Air Component Commander (JFACC), Lieutenant General Charles Horner, Commander U.S. Central Command Air Forces (COMUSCENTAF). Horner's primary instrument for planning air strikes was the air tasking order (ATO) system.

The Navy adapted its blue water "composite warfare" doctrine to the littoral nature of the theater campaign. The Navy strike warfare commanders supported General Horner and followed his air tasking order for CENTCOM air operations in Iraq and Kuwait. The antiair and antisurface warfare commanders concerned themselves with fleet defense. Battle Force Zulu's antisurface warfare commander also helped set the stage for the amphibious deception.[31]

During the first two days of Desert Storm, Navy aircraft hit strategic targets throughout the theater, including Iraqi airfields, port facilities, naval installations, and air defenses. In the first forty-eight hours, naval aviators accounted for 60 percent of the Coalition's suppression of enemy air defense (SEAD) sorties. Naval aircraft also conducted defensive air operations and flew combat air patrol and fighter sweep missions, while Tomahawk land attack missiles fired from surface ships and submarines struck oil, electric, and leadership targets. Two F/A-18 pilots from *Saratoga*'s VFA-81 shot down two Iraqi MiG-21s. By the end of the second day, Navy warships had fired a total of 216 Tomahawks while aircraft from Battle Forces Yankee and Zulu had flown 1,135 combat sorties.[32]

Ultimately, the air campaign emerged as a stunning testament to America's military prowess. However, on the road to victory, numerous problems arose in planning and execution. At first, many naval officers were reluctant to place carriers under the JFACC and had doubts about the efficacy of the ATO system. Incompatible doctrines and communications systems also created difficulties. Disseminating the daily air tasking orders to the fleet proved difficult. None of the carriers had the computer aided flight management system (CAFMS), which would have enabled the ships to receive the voluminous document electronically.[33] Instead of transmitting the tasking order through compatible computer systems, the fleet employed a "pony express" of aircraft to fly hard copies of the ATO out to each carrier every day.³⁴

Battle Forces Yankee and Zulu had different experiences in adapting to the ATO system. Because the Red Sea naval air forces had participated extensively in Desert Shield's "mirror-image" strike rehearsals under the JFACC, they had little trouble flying under the ATO system during the war. Battle Force Zulu's accommodation to the ATO system proved more difficult. Neither *Midway, Ranger,* nor *Theodore Roosevelt* exercised much with CENTAF or the ATO system before the war began. Because of this lack of prewar joint training, neither Battle Force Zulu nor CENTAF was familiar with the other's operational requirements and procedures when the shooting started. This mutual lack of familiarity bred bitter disputes over the legitimacy of allocating aircraft for fleet defense and concerns about striking maritime targets or targets of importance to the Amphibious Task Force.³⁵

To resolve these interservice disputes, General Horner allotted a portion of the Navy's daily sorties to fleet defense and maritime strike missions. This enabled Battle Force Zulu to plan and conduct these missions outside the air tasking order process, within the composite warfare framework. Thus, JFACC controlled air operations over land while Battle Force Zulu controlled air operations over the Persian Gulf.³⁶

The Gulf was the Coalition's right flank. Early in the war, Iraq's air and naval forces, particularly Exocet-armed aircraft and missile boats, had the potential to mount attacks against Allied ships and ports. Coalition naval forces put up a formidable antiair umbrella against these threats. Fighters and early warning aircraft from both battle forces flew combat air patrol missions and provided radar coverage. Many of the surface ships operating in the Persian Gulf also performed antiair duties. By mid-February, for example, twenty-one of the ships operating in the Persian Gulf, excluding the carriers, were partially or totally devoted to antiair warfare. The disposition of these ships provided the fleet with effective air control and overlapping radar coverage over most of the Gulf.³⁷

In the first few days of Desert Storm, the Allied aerial armada won air superiority and fragmented Saddam's strategic air defenses and command, control, and communications network. For the rest of January, the Coalition focused the bulk of its airpower against strategic targets. On January 27, Schwarzkopf announced that the Coalition had won air supremacy over Iraq and Kuwait. Iraqi air defenses retained the ability to react piecemeal to Allied strikes but could no longer coordinate defensive actions.³⁸

Although Phase I operations continued throughout the war, by early February the weight of the Allied air attack had shifted from strategic targets in Iraq to Phase III targets—Iraqi ground forces—in the KTO. From Schwarzkopf's perspective, this phase was intended to soften enemy ground forces in preparation for Phase IV, the ground offensive. The plan for the final assault envisioned a main attack as a "left hook" by armor-heavy forces, wheeling around the enemy right flank, cutting off Iraqi forces in Kuwait, and destroying the Republican Guard. The amphibious deception operations were designed to divert Iraqi attention from the main thrust and to pin Iraqi units to the coast. Supporting attacks by I MEF and Arab units along the Kuwait–Saudi border would fix and destroy Iraqi forces in Kuwait.[39]

During the battlefield preparation phase, Navy, Marine, and Air Force aviators along with Coalition European and Arab aircrews mounted round-the-clock strikes against Iraqi Army and Republican Guard units. Phase III aerial attacks fell roughly into two categories: interdiction missions against enemy lines of supply and direct strikes against enemy units. Naval aviators flew both types of missions.

Iraqi forces in the KTO were almost totally dependent on outside sources for supplies, including food and water. Aerial interdiction operations aimed to cut the flow of supplies to the KTO and to stop the movement of enemy forces within the theater. Interdiction missions struck bridges spanning the Tigris and Euphrates rivers, railroad marshaling yards, fuel depots, supply concentration areas, and highway interchanges. In addition, strike aircraft flew armed reconnaissance missions along sections of the main highways leading into the KTO, seeking and destroying truck convoys. By February 4, intelligence estimates indicated that the amount of supplies reaching Iraqi forces in the KTO was below the level needed to sustain combat operations.[40]

For direct attacks on enemy ground forces, air planners devised a "kill box" system. A "kill box" was a geographical area measuring 30 nautical miles by 30 nautical miles, subdivided into four quadrants 15 nautical miles square. The air tasking order assigned a flight of aircraft to each quadrant for a specified period of time. The Coalition expended more ordnance against kill box targets than any other kind. The Persian Gulf carriers launched their first kill box mission on January 25, followed four days later by the flattops in the Red Sea. Navy aviators operated in kill boxes in and around Kuwait.[41]

Whereas Battle Force Yankee operated from the same area throughout the war, Battle Force Zulu moved farther north as the campaign progressed. On February 14, the Gulf carriers reached a position 80 nautical miles north–northeast of Bahrain and 185 nautical miles southeast of Kuwait City, where they remained for the rest of the war. On February 8, Admiral Arthur ordered the *America* battle group to join Battle Force Zulu in order to concentrate more naval firepower in the KTO. The *America* battle group steamed approximately 2,000 miles in six days, taking up station in the Persian Gulf late in the afternoon of February 14. *America* commenced strike operations in the KTO early the next morning.[42]

Navy and Marine Corps aviation proved essential to the success of the forty-three–day air campaign, during which Allied air forces flew more than 100,000 sorties at an average of 2,500 sorties per day.[43] The 600 aircraft contributed by these naval services accounted for 28 percent of the Coalition's 2,300-plane armada and flew an average of 650 sorties per day.[44]

Despite fundamental differences in basic concepts of operations, procedures, and equipment between the Navy and USAF, however, "there were no show stoppers," as the Air Force liaison officer to the COMUSNAVCENT staff put it, "and the joint air campaign was conducted to exceptional effect."[45] While naval air forces did their part to rid the sky of Iraq's air force and dismantle the infrastructure of its war machine, Admiral Arthur carried out his mission of convincing Saddam that the Allies intended to launch an amphibious assault on Iraq's left flank. To pull off this deception, Arthur planned a two-stage maritime campaign: (1) Enable Coalition naval forces to operate in the northern Gulf by establishing air and sea control; and (2) conduct inshore operations in the northern Gulf—mine countermeasures, naval gunfire, and special warfare—to permit the Coalition to mount or to threaten a seaborne invasion of Kuwait, or to conduct amphibious raids.[46]

The first stage involved clearing a path to the coast of Kuwait along Saddam Hussein's seaward flank. The obstacles included the Iraqi Navy and enemy troops posted on oil platforms and islands in the northern Gulf. Rear Admiral Ronald J. "Zap" Zlatoper, Commander Carrier Group Seven and antisurface warfare commander in the Gulf, devised an aggressive "rollback" concept to neutralize Iraqi naval vessels and troops posted on oil platforms and islands. He aimed not only to defend the fleet from attack—standard antisurface warfare doctrine—but to seek out and destroy enemy naval forces at sea, along inland waterways, and in port.[47]

In Admiral Zlatoper's offensive antisurface warfare scheme, U.S. and British maritime patrol aircraft flew round-the-clock search patterns over the northern Gulf, Kuwaiti coastline, and Iraqi ports, on the lookout for enemy warships. Carrier-based fixed-wing aircraft cruised at low altitudes on armed surface reconnaissance and armed scout missions to search for and engage Iraqi units. Ship-based U.S. Navy Light Airborne Multi-Purpose System (LAMPS) III and Royal Navy Lynx helicopters also formed "hunter/killer" teams for antisurface missions. A LAMPS helicopter would sweep the waters with its long-range sensors to locate a target and then call in a Lynx to attack with its two Sea Skua air-to-surface missiles. U.S. Army Helicopter Improvement Program (AHIP) helicopters armed with Hellfire missiles also operated with the LAMPS units in hunter/killer teams. Cruisers and destroyers assigned to antiair warfare duty coordinated the operations.

A typical antisurface engagement began when the sensors on board a patrol aircraft detected a vessel and reported the contact to an air controller, who then vectored in aircraft flying antisurface missions in the area to identify the contact visually. When aloft antisurface aircraft were unavailable, low on fuel, or out of weapons, or when the situation warranted extra force, aircraft standing by on carriers were launched, or planes were diverted from fleet defense or strike missions. When the naval command determined a contact to be hostile, Allied aircraft attacked. At that point, the enemy was practically helpless, for Iraqi naval personnel lacked combat training and their defensive systems proved woefully inadequate. Although helicopter-launched missiles lacked the explosive punch to sink a larger vessel, follow-on attack jets had no difficulty finishing the job with cluster bombs.[48]

From January 22 through the end of the month, Allied aircraft flying offensive antisurface missions engaged Iraqi port facilities, Silkworm missile sites, or naval craft on a daily basis. On January 30, in what became known as the "Battle of Bubiyan Channel" or the "Bubiyan Turkey Shoot," a large force of Iraqi combatants based at the Az-Zubayr and Umm Qasr naval bases sortied on a high-speed dash for Iran. Saddam himself issued the sailing orders, hoping to preserve the boats for the postwar era. Coalition forces detected the movement and attacked the fleeing vessels for the next thirteen hours. In twenty-one separate engagements, Coalition naval aircraft destroyed or damaged seven missile boats, three amphibious ships, a minesweeper, and nine other Iraqi vessels in the shallow waters between Bubiyan Island and the Shatt-Al-Arab marshlands. Only one missile boat and one amphibious ship, both shot up, made it to Iranian waters. The Iranians promptly seized the remains of Saddam's navy, as they had his air force.[49]

By February 2, Coalition forces had destroyed or disabled all thirteen enemy missile boats and many other less-threatening combatants. Although the Navy conducted antisurface missions for the rest of the war, the principal surface threat to the Coalition was eliminated. On February 8, Admiral Arthur declared that the Coalition had established sea control in the northern Persian Gulf.[50] The successful conclusion of the Coalition's offensive antisurface operation made it possible for the second stage of the maritime campaign to begin. While Coalition ground forces set up the left hook, naval forces feigned with the right. Although Schwarzkopf had decided against launching a major assault from the sea, NAVCENT continued to prepare for one in order to lend credibility to the amphibious deception.[51]

Allied naval forces faced several layers of enemy defenses built during Desert Shield, including a sophisticated coastal defensive system and sea mine fields. Since early fall, NAVCENT had been receiving reports that the Iraqis were placing mines in Kuwaiti and northern Gulf waters. Unfortunately, the Navy could do little to monitor the situation, because General Schwarzkopf had prohibited Allied aircraft from flying north of 27 degrees 45 minutes N latitude and naval forces from steaming north of 27 degrees

30 minutes N latitude, fearing that reconnaissance operations closer to occupied Kuwait might trigger a war prematurely.[52]

In stage 2 of the maritime campaign, mine countermeasures (MCM) forces were to clear gunfire support areas and amphibious assault lanes to the Kuwaiti coast. Then battleships would move in to bombard Iraqi positions ashore and the Amphibious Task Force would feign assaults or conduct raids. The amphibious forces would launch a full-scale landing only if the ground offensive bogged down.

On February 13, a combined MCM/Naval Gunfire Support (NGFS) task force steamed into the northern Gulf. Designated Task Group 151.11, the force consisted of *Tripoli*, battleships *Wisconsin* and *Missouri*, thirteen U.S., British, and Saudi MCM vessels, and fifteen U.S. and British cruisers, destroyers, frigates, and support ships. *Tripoli* was the flagship for the task group as well as for the MCM group. To support the Amphibious Task Force, Battle Force Zulu conducted air strikes and provided antiair protection. SEALs reconnoitered Kuwaiti beaches.[53]

MCM operations commenced on February 16. U.S. MCM forces consisted of the newly commissioned minehunter *Avenger,* three forty-year-old minesweepers, and six MH-53E helicopters based on *Tripoli*. The Royal Navy deployed five *Hunt*-class MCM ships. The *Hunt*s were the most sophisticated MCM ships in the world. Because NATO had developed the mine warfare concept that the Allies employed in the Gulf for a European war in which western European navies would assume responsibility for MCM, the Navy accorded mine warfare a low priority for thirty years before the invasion of Kuwait. As a result, in both training and equipment, the U.S. MCM forces lagged far behind the British. Because of the relative inferiority of the U.S. MCM flotilla, the *Hunt*s led the way during Desert Storm MCM operations, while U.S. ships worked in areas already swept at least once by British *Hunt*s or by helicopters.[54]

As a result of Schwarzkopf's restrictions on reconnaissance missions in the northern Gulf during Desert Shield, Allied naval forces could only guess at the location of Iraqi mine fields. The initial intelligence assessment, based on limited information, led the MCM staff to believe that the mine fields lay much closer to the coast than they actually did.

The MCM ships began operations at a point they believed to be outside the Iraqi mine fields, but they actually passed through the main fields before turning on their equipment. Their initial mission was to clear a 15-mile-long, 1,000-yard–wide path to a 10-mile by 3.5-mile fire support area south of Faylaka Island.[55]

On February 18, the Aegis cruiser *Princeton* and the *Tripoli* both struck mines. No one died as a result, but both ships received extensive damage. Nevertheless, the Coalition got off relatively lightly in Saddam's mine fields. Prior to the mine strikes, several different Allied warships had also been operating unknowingly in mined waters. If *Tripoli* and *Princeton* had not struck mines, the rest of Task Group 151.11 would have steamed westward into mine-infested waters. Fortunately, many of the Iraqi mines had been improperly deployed, rendering many of them ineffective. Nevertheless, the recently discovered mine fields led Schwarzkopf to cancel the Faylaka Island raid and reinforced his decision not to launch a major amphibious assault.[56]

After leading the rest of Task Group 151.11 east of mined waters, the MCM group resumed channel clearing operations from a point farther out to sea, beyond the mine fields, and worked westward. By the evening of February 23, the MCM group had cleared a narrow, 1,000- to 2,000-yard-wide, 31-mile-long swath of water, enabling *Missouri,* the task group's new flagship, to commence bombardment of enemy positions ashore. From February 24 to 28, MCM forces worked to clear a channel to the Kuwaiti port of Ash Shuaybah.[57]

On February 9, Cheney and Powell met with Schwarzkopf and his senior commanders to discuss Phase IV. Even though Phase III was steadily reducing the combat potential of his army, Saddam showed no sign of capitulation. Schwarzkopf decided to launch the ground offensive on February 24.

On the eve of the final assault, Coalition forces lay coiled along a line stretching from the Persian Gulf 300 miles west into the desert, arrayed in four major formations. The Army's XVIII Airborne Corps and VII Corps held the westernmost position and would launch the main attack. The Joint Forces Command–North (JFC-N), consisting of Egyptian, Syrian, Saudi, and Kuwaiti forces, occupied the center of the line. To their right stood the I Marine Expeditionary Force, poised to drive into the heart of Kuwait. The Joint Forces Command–East (JFC-E), consisting of units from all six GCC states, anchored the Coalition line on the coast. Out in the Persian Gulf, the 4th and 5th Marine Expeditionary Brigades (MEBs) remained embarked in the thirty-one ships of Amphibious Group Two and Amphibious Group Three, ready to launch or to feign landings as necessary.

Naval bombardments proved critical to the Navy's mission. They not only softened enemy defenses, but they also lent credibility to deception operations by simulating preparatory fire. Unfortunately, the shallow water depths along the Kuwaiti coast did not permit ships to close within 5-inch gun range of targets ashore, limiting NGFS operations to the 20-mile range of the 16-inchers on board *Missouri* and *Wisconsin.* Nevertheless, both amphibious and ground forces benefited from naval gunfire support. During Desert Storm, the battleships' 2,700-pound 16-inch shells fell on four major target areas: the Kuwait–Saudi border, the vicinity of Ras Al Qulayah, the area north of Ash Shuaybah, and Faylaka Island.[58]

At 0800 on February 23, *Wisconsin* commenced shelling targets in Kuwait just north of the border to support the Joint Forces Command–East, which would begin its attack the next day. *Wisconsin's* projectiles rained down on Iraqi artillery and infantry positions, ammunition storage facilities, and logistics sites. At 2315, *Missouri* began shelling Faylaka Island to create the impression that a full-scale landing was coming in order to freeze Iraqi mobile reserves in position. That same night, SEALs created a similar impression with a mock attack on the Kuwaiti coast near Mina Saud.[59]

The ground assault to liberate Kuwait, which lasted a mere 100 hours, began at 0400 on February 24. The I Marine Expeditionary Force thrust directly toward its ultimate objective, Al-Mutl'a Pass and the roads leading from Kuwait City. Over the next four days, the Marines breached both Iraqi defensive belts in Kuwait, fought their way through pockets of stiff enemy resistance, and fended off several armored counterattacks on their drive north. The Army's XVIII and VII Corps executed their massive envelopment maneuver, rumbling north into Iraq and then east to attack the Republican Guard units arrayed north of Kuwait. By 0800 on February 28, Army units had won several fierce tank battles and had reached a position 30 miles west of Basra. Meanwhile, Arab forces of the Joint Commands North and East has secured most of their objectives in Kuwait and had liberated the Kuwaiti capital.[60]

Central Command dedicated numerous aircraft sorties to support the ground offensive. Although no U.S. Navy or non-U.S. Coalition fixed-wing aircraft participated in close air support, they did fly interdiction missions during the ground campaign. At first, interdiction missions aimed at disrupting counterattacks on Allied ground forces. Later, the focus shifted to destruction of a fleeing enemy. By the end of the first forty-eight hours, the front lines had moved so far north that Navy pilots shifted their attacks to Iraqi forces north of Kuwait City. Aircraft from Battle Force Zulu also struck targets on Faylaka Island to support amphibious deception operations. Bad weather and smoke hindered all air operations during the ground campaign.[61]

The Joint Forces Command–East attacked north along the coast road toward Kuwait City. Navy and Marine aircraft and naval gunfire support from *Wisconsin* supported its advance. The Joint Forces Command–East encountered no resistance until they moved beyond the range of *Wisconsin*'s 16-inch guns. The battleship's preparatory fire seemed to have driven the enemy away from the area. The I Marine Expeditionary Force and Amphibious Task Force also received naval gunfire support during the final assault, but during the initial stages, the I MEF fought outside the maximum range of *Missouri*'s 16-inch guns.[62]

Although naval gunfire doctrine considered calls from ground forces to be critical, direct support accounted for only 6 percent of the missions fired during Desert Storm. The rapid Allied advance and lack of determined Iraqi resistance accounted for part of the problem, but the battleships' dearth of direct support fire resulted primarily from their inability to operate close to shore, which, in turn, resulted from the limited water depths in the area and the Navy's incapacity to eliminate the mine threat in a timely manner. The Marines were disappointed that *Missouri* and *Wisconsin* remained out of range for most of their fight.[63]

On February 25, the Amphibious Task Force conducted a feint just north of the Kuwaiti port of Ash Shuaybah to pin down enemy forces to the beach. At 0300, *Missouri* opened fire on military targets near Ash Shuaybah. Iraqi targeting radars frequently painted *Missouri* and its escorts—the frigate *Jarrett* and the British destroyers *London* and *Gloucester*—prompting concern about potential missile and chemical attacks. At about 0400, ten helicopters of the 13th Marine Expeditionary Unit (MEU) took off from *Okinawa* and headed for Al Fintas, a Kuwaiti coastal town just north of Ash Shuaybah. Fifty minutes later, the helicopters arrived at a point roughly 3 miles from the beach and then turned around and flew back to the ship. Meanwhile, SEALs detonated charges along beaches south of Ash Shuaybah.[64]

At 0452, an Iraqi Silkworm battery near Al Fintas fired two missiles at the bombardment group. One of the Silkworms splashed down between *Missouri* and *Jarrett*, possibly as a result of countermeasures taken by the ships. *Gloucester* shot down the second Silkworm with two Sea Dart missiles. The bombardment group reported the incident to naval air forces, which destroyed the Silkworm launch site with Rockeye cluster bombs.[65]

On February 26, the Amphibious Task Force launched amphibious feints on Bubiyan and Faylaka Islands. As before, Arthur's intent was to fix enemy forces on the beach by simulating a helicopter-borne assault. Before dawn, seventeen helicopters took off from amphibious ships *Nassau*, *Guam*, and *Iwo Jima* and headed for Bubiyan Island, while six additional helicopters flew from *Nassau* for Faylaka Island. Navy Intruders and EA-6B Prowlers winged in support. The helicopters cruised within sight of defenders on the islands, fired rockets and machine guns, and then turned away. Harriers and Intruders attacked antiaircraft artillery which opened fire on Allied aircraft.[66]

Early in the morning of February 26, Central Command received reports of an Iraqi withdrawal from Kuwait City. CENTCOM launched Navy, USAF, and Marine aircraft to attack enemy forces retreating along the road from the Kuwaiti capital to Basrah. This stretch of superhighway lay within the kill box assigned to *Ranger's* air wing. Responding to the call, A-6E crewmen from VA-155 found themselves overlooking "an attack pilot's dreamscape." Hundreds of military and civilian vehicles of all descriptions laden with goods looted from Kuwaiti homes clogged the pavement in a pell mell bid to escape. Instead of fighting the mother of all battles, Saddam Hussein's army had become "the mother of all target opportunities," as one pilot put it.[67] The first attacks bottled up the main route with aerial mines, which forced many Iraqi convoys off the superhighway into the soft desert sand, where they bogged down. Aircraft attacked vehicles throughout the day and into the evening, despite a 10,000-foot cloud deck and thick black smoke. The aerial attack destroyed, damaged, or caused the abandonment of hundreds of vehicles along the road from Kuwait City to Basrah, which reporters later dubbed the "Highway of Death" or "Highway to Hell." Despite the ominous-sounding moniker, however, many more Iraqi soldiers fled on foot into the desert or joined the ever-growing army of prisoners than were killed by U.S. bombs. Analysis of photos of the area taken on March 1 indicates that Allied air forces destroyed some 1,400 vehicles, with only fourteen tanks and fourteen other armored vehicles among them. Journalists counted only 200 to 300 dead Iraqis at the scene.[68]

By daybreak on February 27, the I Marine Expeditionary Force had secured all of its objectives. Leathernecks consolidated their positions and began to mop up the last pockets of enemy resistance. Organized Iraqi action within Kuwait City ceased. Arab forces passed through Marine lines to liberate Kuwait City. While Kuwaiti citizens celebrated their liberation, Special Forces teams searched government buildings for remaining enemy soldiers. I MEF commander Lieutenant General Walter E. Boomer and his staff found a veritable gold mine in one building. An elaborate sand table stood in the middle of one room. It contained a relief map of Kuwait in full color, showing the position of Iraqi forces along the coast prior to the final assault. Large red arrows pointing from the sea indicated where the enemy had expected an amphibious attack. The Iraqis had positioned their defenses accordingly.[69]

The amphibious deception had worked. All told, Central Command estimated that the demonstrations against Ash Shuaybah and Bubiyan and Faylaka Islands pinned down 70,000 to 80,000 Iraqi troops—more than six divisions—to the Kuwaiti coast.[70] On the afternoon of February 27, General Powell briefed President Bush in the Oval Office on the military situation in the KTO. Essentially, the Coalition had achieved its military and political objectives. Bush ordered the cessation of offensive operations on 0800 on February 28, 1991 (Persian Gulf time)—exactly 100 hours after the final assault had begun.[71]

Coalition forces ceased offensive military operations at the appointed hour, but stood by to resume the attack if necessary. At this time, Central Command and the Defense Intelligence Agency assessed thirty-three Iraqi divisions as combat ineffective. Most Iraqi Army units had surrendered, had been destroyed, or were in flight. U.S. losses were miraculously few. In all, between August 3, 1990 and December 15, 1991, the United States lost 390 dead as a result of Operations Desert Shield and Desert Storm. Of these, the Navy lost fifty-six dead. In return for their sacrifice, the Coalition had won one of the most decisive victories in military history.[72]

CONCLUSION

The defense of Saudi Arabia hinged on America's ability to deploy military forces rapidly. Carriers and surface vessels operating in or near the region enabled the United States to respond immediately to the Iraqi invasion of Kuwait, presenting Saddam with the specter of war with the United States if he pressed on southward. Moreover, maritime prepositioning ships put ashore CENTCOM's first credible deterrent on the ground.

Rapid deployment of large forces capable of sustained combat operations depended on advanced planning, control of the sea lines of communication with the theater, and adequate sealift. Responsibility for the latter two fell to the Navy. On the down side, the shortage of RO/ROs and inadequate maintenance of RRF vessels slowed the pace of deployment. These deficiencies in America's sealift capability might have resulted in a much longer and bloodier campaign had Saddam invaded Saudi Arabia. Nevertheless, TRANSCOM, CENTCOM, and MSC conducted one of the largest sealifts in history in a relatively short period of time. Fortunately, neither Saddam nor his supporters attempted to interfere with the buildup.

The extent to which the blockade of Iraq degraded Saddam's military capabilities cannot be determined without access to Iraqi documents. Although the embargo did not by itself compel Saddam to withdraw from Kuwait, the multinational nature of the blockade reflected the solidarity of the Coalition in achieving this goal.

The Navy's problems in operating under the JFACC-ATO system during Desert Storm stemmed principally from inattention to jointness before the war. Fortunately, they did not present a serious obstacle to operational success. Participation in the prewar mirror-image strike rehearsals eased Battle Force Yankee's integration into the JFACC-ATO system. Furthermore, the relative lack of air and surface threats to the fleet in the Red Sea necessitated fewer fleet defense sorties and permitted fuller participation in the strategic campaign. On the other side of the Arabian Peninsula, Battle Force Zulu and the Air Force's mutual unfamiliarity with each other's operational requirements and procedures accounted for most of the interservice disputes and operational problems in the Gulf. The solution—to divide the Services' responsibilities geographically, with the Navy controlling air operations over Gulf waters and the USAF controlling operations over land—resembled Vietnam era "route packages." Since the war, however, the Services have ironed out these difficulties. During Operation Southern Watch, for example, Navy aircraft enforcing the no-fly zone over southern Iraq operated under the JFACC-ATO system as a matter of routine. Furthermore, aircraft carriers now have CAFMS equipment for electronic transmission of the ATO. These developments, as well as the strategic vision articulated in the Navy–Marine Corps White Paper "From the Sea," represent steps toward solving some of the problems that arose during the war.

Similarly, problems that arose in the battle of the northern Gulf did not adversely affect the outcome of the maritime campaign. The Navy's adaptation of composite warfare to littoral operations demonstrated the flexibility of naval doctrine. The amphibious feints worked exactly as intended, causing Saddam to commit enormous resources to the defense of his maritime flank and diverting his attention from Schwarzkopf's left hook. Because of Schwarzkopf's proscription of reconnaissance missions in the northern Gulf and the Navy's shortcomings in countermine warfare, MCM proved the weak link. As a result, Iraqi mine fields prevented the Coalition from launching amphibious assaults. The fact that the Navy would have sustained greater losses had the Iraqis deployed their mines properly will not be lost on future opponents of the United States. The Iraqi mine fields also prevented the battleships from steaming closer to shore to support the I MEF. Nevertheless, *Missouri* and *Wisconsin's* gunfire facilitated the advance of Arab ground units and enhanced the credibility of the amphibious deception. Since the war, the Navy has decommissioned all of its battleships and has yet to fill the resultant gap in its gunfire support capability.

In sum, as in two previous post-1945 wars on the Eurasian land mass, the United States Navy played a vital role in the Gulf War. The Navy's early fleet presence, rapid deployment, securing of sea lanes of communication, protection of ports, embargo patrol, and sealift of equipment and supplies ensured the success of Desert Shield. During Desert Storm, naval theater and maritime strike, defense of the Allied right flank, gunfire support, and amphibious deception operations played a key role in the Coalition's victory.

NOTES

1. This chapter is based on Edward J. Marolda and Robert J. Schneller, Jr., *Shield and Sword: The U.S. Navy in the Persian Gulf War* (Washington, D.C.: Naval Historical Center, 1996). The opinions and conclusions expressed in this chapter are solely those of the author and do not reflect the views of the Department of the Navy or any other agency of the U.S. government.

2. U.S. Department of Defense, *Conduct of the Persian Gulf War: Final Report to Congress,* 3 vols. (Washington, D.C.: USGPO, 1992), 1: 22, 2: E-24; U.S. Department of the Navy, *The United States Navy in "Desert Shield" "Desert Storm"* (Washington, D.C.: Office of the Chief of Naval Operations, 1991), 11–12.

3. George Bush, "Remarks to Department of Defense Employees," August 15, 1990, *Weekly Compilation of Presidential Documents* 26 (August 20, 1990): 1256.

4. Michael A. Palmer, *Guardians of the Gulf: A History of America's Expanding Role in the Persian Gulf, 1833–1992* (New York: The Free Press, 1992), 164–69.

5. *Conduct of the Persian Gulf War,* 1: 40–43, 2: D-4–D-8; Michael A. Palmer,

On Course to Desert Storm: The United States Navy and the Persian Gulf (Washington, D.C.: Naval Historical Center, 1992), 107.

6. *The United States Navy in "Desert Shield" "Desert Storm,"* vi.

7. *Conduct of the Persian Gulf War*, 1: 257–59; Richard P. Hallion, *Storm over Iraq: Air Power and the Gulf War* (Washington, D.C.: Smithsonian Institution Press, 1992), 146–47.

8. *Conduct of the Persian Gulf War*, 1: 46–47.

9. Lee Bosco, "Making Things Happen in the Persian Gulf: Logistics Command Proves No Desert Storm Puzzle Is Too Tough," *All Hands* 68 (June 1991): 34–35; Lee Bosco, "Port Harbor Security: Interservice Coalition Kept Ships Safe," *All Hands* 68 (August 1991): 25–26; COMUSNAVCENT *Command History, 1990*, 7–8, Operational Archives Branch, Naval Historical Center, Washington, D.C. (hereafter OA); *Conduct of the Persian Gulf War*, 2: F-10, J-2–J-10; Norman Friedman, *Desert Victory: The War for Kuwait* (Annapolis: Naval Institute Press, 1991), 104–5; Edward J. Marolda, "A Host of Nations: Coalition Naval Operations in the Persian Gulf War," in *Perspectives on Warfighting: Selected Papers From the 1992 Meeting of the Society of Military History*, vol. 3 (Quantico, Va.: Marine Corps University, 1994), 6; U.S. Coast Guard, "Desert Shield/Desert Storm Chronology," June 19, 1992, U.S. Coast Guard Historian's Office; *The United States Navy in "Desert Shield" "Desert Storm,"* 42.

10. Palmer, *Guardians of the Gulf*, 171; Edwin H. Simmons, "Getting Marines to the Gulf," *Proceedings* 117 (May 1991): 53–54; *The United States Navy in "Desert Shield" "Desert Storm,"* 28, B-2–B-5.

11. Twelve cargo ships or tankers carrying Air Force and Army material and thirteen maritime prepositioning ships.

12. *Conduct of the Persian Gulf War*, 1: 59, 2: E-11–E-13; Hansford T. Johnson, "Presentation to the Committee on Merchant Marine Fisheries, Subcommittee on Merchant Marine, U.S. House of Representatives" April 23, 1991; James K. Matthews and Cora J. Holt, *United States Transportation Command History: Desert Shield/Desert Storm*, Vol. I, 7 August 1990–10 March 1991 (Scott AFB, Ill: USTRANSCOM Office of History, 1992), 41–49; Douglas M. Norton, "Sealift: Keystone of Support," *Proceedings* 117 (May 1991): 42–46; Ronald F. Rost, John F. Addams, and John J. Nelson, *Sealift in Operation Desert Shield/Desert Storm: 7 August 1990 to 17 February 1991* (Alexandria, Va.: Center for Naval Analyses, 1991), 3–5, 8–13, 22–31; John Verrico, "Getting It There Vital to Victory," *Surface Warfare* 16 (May/June 1991): 6.

13. *Conduct of the Persian Gulf War*, 2: E-17–E-25.

14. U.S. Congress, Senate, Committee on Armed Services, *Crisis in the Persian Gulf Region: U.S. Policy Options and Implications*, Senate Hearing 101-1071, 101st Congress, 2nd session, 1990, 661.

15. A number of non-U.S. sources consider MIF as an abbreviation for multinational interception force.

16. Steven R. Bowman, *Persian Gulf War: Summary of U.S. and Non-U.S. Forces* (Washington: Congressional Research Service, Library of Congress, 1991); compilation, "Iraq Invasion of Kuwait and OP. Desert Shield," August 22, 1990; *Conduct of the Persian Gulf War*, 1: 23, 62–64; Peter P. Perla, *Desert Storm Reconstruction Report Volume I: Summary* (Alexandria, Va.: Center for Naval Anal-

yses, 1991), 3; *The United States Navy in "Desert Shield" "Desert Storm,"* 20–21, A-3, C-2.

17. Timothy J. Carroll, *Desert Storm Reconstruction Report Volume VII: Maritime Interception Force Operations* (Alexandria, Va.: Center for Naval Analyses, 1991), 13, 25–29; *Conduct of the Persian Gulf War,* 1: 64–66; Tom Delery, "Away, the Boarding Party!" *Proceedings* 117 (May 1991): 66; Michael Shepko, Sandra Newett, and Rhonda M. Alexander, *Maritime Interception Operations* (Alexandria, Va.: Center for Naval Analyses, 1991), 1; *The United States Navy in "Desert Shield" "Desert Storm,"* 20–23.

18. Rick Burgess, "Orions of Arabia: Patrol Squadrons in Desert Shield/Storm," *Naval Aviation News* 73 (September–October 1991): 15; *Conduct of the Persian Gulf War,* 1: 61–72, 80, 2: C-4–C-5, I-25; Carroll, *Maritime Force Interception Operations,* 13; Delery, "Away, the Boarding Party!" 67; Friedman, *Desert Victory,* 206; Richard H. Gimblett, "Preliminary Research Results: Canadian Naval Operations in the Persian Gulf, 1990–1991," March 5, 1992, 4; Andrew Vallance, "Royal Air Force Operations in the Gulf War," *Air Power History* (Fall 1991): 35.

19. *Conduct of the Persian Gulf War,* 1: 68–76, 2: I-22; CENTCOM PAO, telephone conversation with the author, September 29, 1994.

20. Palmer, *Guardians of the Gulf,* 175; U.S. Congress, House, Committee on Armed Services, *Crisis in the Persian Gulf War: Sanctions, Diplomacy, and War,* House Armed Services Committee 101-57, 101st Congress, 2nd session, 1990, 856; U.S. Congress, Senate, Committee on Armed Services, *Operation Desert Shield/Desert Storm,* Senate Hearing 102-326, 102nd Congress, 1st session, 1991, 180.

21. George Bush, "Address to the Nation Announcing the Deployment of United States Armed Forces to Saudi Arabia," August 8, 1990, *Weekly Compilation of Presidential Documents* 26 (August 13, 1990), 1216–18; George Bush, "The President's News Conference," August 8, 1990, *Weekly Compilation of Presidential Documents* 26 (August 13, 1990): 1223.

22. *Conduct of the Persian Gulf War,* 1: 83–116, 2: E-25–E-26; Thomas A. Keaney and Eliot A. Cohen, *Gulf War Air Power Survey Summary Report* (Washington, D.C.: Department of the Air Force, 1993), 27–53 (hereafter *GWAPS Summary Report*).

23. Rost et al., *Sealift,* 3; Francis R. Donovan, "Logistics and Sealift in Multinational Cooperation," in John B. Hattendorf, ed., *Eleventh International Seapower Symposium: Report of the Proceedings of the Conference* (Newport, R.I.: Naval War College Press, 1992), 69; *The United States Navy in "Desert Shield" "Desert Storm,"* 29.

24. Alan Brown, Lester Gibson, and Alan Marcus, *Desert Storm Reconstruction Report Volume XIII: Training* (Alexandria, Va.: Center for Naval Analyses, 1991).

25. John D. Heidenrich, "The Gulf War: How Many Iraqis Died?" *Foreign Policy* 90 (Spring 1993): 114; *Conduct of the Persian Gulf War,* 1: 113–14, 349–53; U.S. Department of the Air Force, *Reaching Globally, Reaching Powerfully: The United States Air Force in the Gulf War* (Washington, D.C.: Department of the Air Force, 1991), 5.

26. *Conduct of the Persian Gulf War,* 1: 114, 141, 2: E-17, E-25, I-19.

27. *Conduct of the Persian Gulf War,* 1: 114; Friedman, *Desert Victory;* Robert J. Schneller, Jr., "Persian Gulf Turkey Shoot: The Destruction of Iraqi Naval Forces during Operation Desert Storm," paper presented at the Society for Military His-

tory conference in Kingston, Ontario, Canada, May 1993; *The United States Navy in "Desert Shield" "Desert Storm,"* A-13–A-18.

28. John G. Humphries, "Operations Law and the Rules of Engagement in Operations Desert Shield and Desert Storm," *Airpower Journal* 6 (Fall 1992): 31.

29. *Conduct of the Persian Gulf War,* 1: 101, 255–57.

30. Peter de la Billiere, *Storm Command: A Personal Account of the Gulf War* (London: Harper Collins, 1992), 84; *Conduct of the Persian Gulf War,* 1: 294; Lieutenant Colonel Joseph N. Purvis, USA, interview by Edward J. Marolda, August 19, 1991, OA; H. Norman Schwarzkopf, Jr., *It Doesn't Take a Hero,* with Peter Petre (New York: Bantam Books, 1992), 356–61.

31. *Conduct of the Persian Gulf War,* 1: 253–54; Jeffrey Lutz et al., *Desert Storm Reconstruction Report,* Vol. 6, *Antisurface Warfare* (Alexandria, Va.: Center for Naval Analyses, 1991), 5-1; Frank Schwamb et al., *Desert Storm Reconstruction Report Volume II: Strike Warfare* (Alexandria, Va.: Center for Naval Analyses, 1991), 1–36; Robert W. Ward et al., *Desert Storm Reconstruction Report,* Vol. 8 *C3/Space and Electronic Warfare* (Alexandria, Va.: Center for Naval Analyses, 1992), 1–12.

32. *Conduct of the Persian Gulf War,* 1: 118–19, 152–67; Hallion, *Storm over Iraq,* 166, 173; Riley D. Mixson, "Where We Must Do Better," *Proceedings* 118 (August 1991): 38; *Operation Desert Shield/Desert Storm,* 261–62; Dirk T. Rose, "Saratoga MiG Killers: Hollywood Need Not Apply," *Naval Aviation News* 73 (May–June 1991): 13–14; Schwamb et al., *Strike Warfare,* 1–42, 1–43, 1–52, D-2.

33. Even though the 9th Air Force developed the ATO system, there were other Air Force commands that also lacked the appropriate equipment to use it.

34. Lyle G. Bien, "From the Strike Cell," *Proceedings* 117 (June 1991): 59; Eliot A. Cohen, "The Mystique of U.S. Air Power," *Foreign Affairs* 73 (January–February 1994): 117; Perla, *Summary,* 52, 55; Steven U. Ramsdell to Dean C. Allard, "Trip Report," 14 May 1991, OA; Schwamb et al., *Strike Warfare,* 2–11 through 2–12; msg., Colonel Brian E. Wages to COMUSNAVCENT, "End of Tour Report as Air Force Liaison Officer to COMUSNAVCENT for Operations Desert Shield/Storm," March 5, 1991, 3.

35. Msg., COMCARGRUFIVE to COMUSNAVCENT, February 21, 1991, "Miscellaneous DESERT SHIELD/DESERT STORM Working Papers from VADM Arthur's Personal Files," acc. 49 002812.00, Center for Naval Analyses, Alexandria, Virginia (hereafter CNA); Wages, "End of Tour Report;" Daniel J. Muir, "A View from the Black Hole," *Proceedings* 117 (October 1991): 86; Schwamb et al., *Strike Warfare,* 1: 10, 2: 28–30, 9: 6; *The United States Navy in "Desert Shield" "Desert Storm,"* A-13 through A-32.

36. *Conduct of the Persian Gulf War,* 1: 137; Hallion, *Storm over Iraq,* 155; Wages, "End of Tour Report."

37. Charles E. Chambers et al., *Desert Storm Reconstruction Report Volume III: Antiair Warfare* (Alexandria, Va.: Center for Naval Analyses, 1991), 1–1, 2–16; *Conduct of the Persian Gulf War,* 1: 269–73; Larry DiRita, "Exocets, Air Traffic, & the Air Tasking Order," *Proceedings* 118 (August 1992): 60–61; Dennis Palzkill, "Making Interoperability Work," *Proceedings* 118 (September 1991), 50–51; Perla, *Summary,* 86.

38. *Conduct of the Persian Gulf War*, 1: 119, 163–64; Schwamb et al., *Strike Warfare*, 4–11.

39. *Conduct of the Persian Gulf War*, 1: 100; Hallion, *Storm over Iraq*, 209.

40. *Conduct of the Persian Gulf War*, 1: 119, 178–79, 182, 190; *GWAPS Summary Report*, 97–98.

41. *Conduct of the Persian Gulf War*, 1: 180; *GWAPS Summary Report*, 52; Brian W. Jones, "Close Air Support: A Doctrinal Disconnect," *Airpower Journal* 6 (Winter 1992): 63; *Reaching Globally, Reaching Powerfully*, 37–38; Schwamb et al., *Strike Warfare*, 6–9, 6–14, 6–16, 6–18, 6–20.

42. *Operation Desert Shield/Storm*, 213; Schwamb et al., *Strike Warfare*, 1–46, 1–51.

43. Schwamb et al., *Strike Warfare*, 2–7.

44. By far the largest contingent was that of the U.S. Air Force, whose 1,100 planes represented almost half of the Coalition's total. The Navy contributed 400 aircraft, the Marines 200, and Allied air forces 600. The Navy averaged approximately 400 sorties per day, the Marines about 250, and the Air Force about 1,500.

45. Wages, "End of Tour Report."

46. *Conduct of the Persian Gulf War*, 1: 255–57.

47. COMCARGRUSEVEN, *Command History 1991*, OA; *Conduct of the Persian Gulf War*, 1: 259–64; Lutz et al., *Antisurface Warfare*, v; George Rodrique and Robert Ruby, "Taking Down the Oil Platforms," *Proceedings* 117 (April 1991): 53; Schwamb et al., *Strike Warfare*, 1–34.

48. Kay Atwal, "Through Sea, Sand, and Storm," *Defence* 22 (September 1991): 17; Chambers et al., *Antiair Warfare*, 1–1; *Conduct of the Persian Gulf War*, 1: 260–62, 270–71; Anthony H. Cordesman and Abraham R. Wagner, *The Lessons of Modern War*, vol. 2, *The Iran–Iraq War* (Boulder, Colo.: Westview Press, 1990), 102, 532; C. J. S. Craig, "Gulf War: The Maritime Campaign," *RUSI Journal* 137 (August 1992): 12–14; Friedman, *Desert Victory*, 209, 361; Marc E. Liebman, "We Need Armed Helos," *Proceedings* 118 (August 1991): 84–85; Lutz, *Antisurface Warfare*, 3–1, 3–10, 3–12, 4–14; Stuart Slade, "The FAC's End Approaches," *Naval Forces* 12 (November 1991), 12–13; *The United States Navy in "Desert Shield" "Desert Storm,"* A–18 through A–25; Bruce Watson et al., *Military Lessons of the Gulf War* (Novato, Calif.: Greenhill Press, 1991), 128; Ronald J. Zlatoper, "The War at Sea during Desert Storm," *The Hook* 19 (Fall 1991): 2.

49. Billeire, *Storm Command*, 255; COMCARGRUSEVEN, *Command History 1991*, OA; *Conduct of the Persian Gulf War*, 1: 264–67; Zlatoper, "The War at Sea," 2.

50. *Conduct of the Persian Gulf War*, 1: 267.

51. *Operation Desert Shield/Desert Storm*, 206.

52. *Conduct of the Persian Gulf War*, 1: 259, 273–76, 294–95; Joe Gawlowicz, "Mine Countermeasures in the Gulf," *All Hands* 68 (July 1991): 23; Murray Hammick, "Iraqi Obstacles and Defensive Positions," *International Defense Review* 24 (September 1991): 989; *Operation Desert Shield/Desert Storm*, 207; Bruce Watson, ed., *Military Lessons of the Gulf War*, 92.

53. *Conduct of the Persian Gulf War*, 1: 299; Henry S. Griffis et al., *Desert Storm Reconstruction Report*, Vol. 5, *Amphibious Operations* (Alexandria, Va.: Center for Naval Analyses, 1991), 27; *Operation Desert Shield/Desert Storm*, 382–85; msg., COMDESRON TWO to USCINCCENT, March 4, 1991, Desert Storm

Engagement Message File, acc. 57, 050399.00, CNA; Ralph Passarelli et al., *Desert Storm Reconstruction Report,* Vol. 4, *Mine Countermeasures* (Alexandria, Va.: Center for Naval Analyses, 1991), 7–1; Schwarzkopf, *It Doesn't Take a Hero,* 437.

54. Denise L. Almond et al., eds., *Desert Score: U.S. Gulf Weapons* (Washington, D.C.: Carroll Publishing Co., 1991), 263–65; *Conduct of the Persian Gulf War,* 1: 277–78; Fursdon, "Iraqi Mines Know no Ceasefire," *Navy International* 96 (May 1991): 142–46; Passarelli et al., *Mine Countermeasures,* 2–2, 2–5, 2–6; Rear Admiral Raynor A. K. Taylor, USN (ret.), interview by Edward J. Marolda and Robert J. Schneller, Jr., August 2–3, 1991.

55. *Conduct of the Persian Gulf War,* 1: 277–78, 284; map showing early February 1991 intelligence estimate of Iraqi mine fields and postwar map showing actual location of the mine fields, R.A.K. Taylor Papers, OA.

56. Passarelli et al., *Mine Countermeasures,* 5-14–5-15; Schwarzkopf, *It Doesn't Take a Hero,* 446; Taylor interview.

57. *Conduct of the Persian Gulf War,* 1: 273–88; msg., COMDESRON TWO to USCINCCENT, March 4, 1991, Desert Storm Engagement Message File, acc. 57 050399.00, CNA.

58. *Conduct of the Persian Gulf War,* 1: 287–88.

59. Robert S. Bell, *Desert Storm Reconstruction Report Volume XII: Naval Special Warfare* (Alexandria, Va.: Center for Naval Analyses, 1991), 20; *Conduct of the Persian Gulf War,* 1: 289–302; Gary E. Horne et al., *Desert Storm Reconstruction Report,* Vol. 14, *Naval Gunfire Support* (Alexandria, Va.: Center for Naval Analyses, 1991).

60. *Conduct of the Persian Gulf War,* 1: 358–411.

61. *Conduct of the Persian Gulf War,* 1: 194–95, 372–73; Williamson Murray, *Gulf War Air Power Survey,* Vol. 2, Pt. I, *Operations Report* (Washington, D.C.: USGPO, 1993), 296, 301–2, 310–13, 322 (hereafter *GWAPS Operations Report*); *Operation Desert Shield/Desert Storm,* 213–14; *The United States Navy in "Desert Shield" "Desert Storm,"* 38, H–5; Barry D. Watts and Thomas A. Keaney, *Gulf War Air Power Survey,* Vol. 2, Part II, *Effects and Effectiveness Report* (Washington, D.C.: USGPO, 1993), 231–33, 242 (hereafter *GWAPS Effectiveness Report*).

62. *Conduct of the Persian Gulf War,* 1: 286–93, 373; msg., Commanding Officer 1st ANGLICO to Commanding Officer 1st SRIG, "After Action Report, Liberation of Kuwait, February 21 to March 1, 1991," October 1, 1991; Captain Douglas Kleinsmith, USMC, interview by Edward J. Marolda and Robert J. Schneller, Jr., September 15, 1992, OA; Horne et al., *Naval Gunfire Support,* 1–2; 1st ANGLICO, "Operation Desert Storm: Naval Gunfire Lessons Learned: Communications," undated 1st ANGLICO document, OA; Charles J. Quilter II, *U.S. Marines in the Persian Gulf, 1990–1991: With the I Marine Expeditionary Force in Desert Shield and Desert Storm* (Washington, D.C.: History and Museums Division, Headquarters, U.S. Marine Corps, 1993), 86.

63. Lieutenant Colonel Charles H. Cureton, USMC, interview by Robert J. Schneller, Jr., 10 August 1992, OA; *Conduct of the Persian Gulf War,* 1: 273–93; Kleinsmith interview; Andrew F. Mazzara, "Supporting Arms in the Storm,"*Proceedings* 117 (November 1991): 44–45; Operation Desert Storm: Naval Gunfire Lessons Learned: Communications; Quilter, *With the I Marine Expeditionary Force,* 83–88.

64. Craig, "The Maritime Campaign," 14; Griffis et al., *Amphibious Operations,*

32–33; *Conduct of the Persian Gulf War*, 1: 273, 286–304, 375; USS *Missouri* (BB 63) Command History, 1991, *Missouri* source file, Ships History Branch, Naval Historical Center; "Victory at Sea," *All Hands* 68 (Desert Storm Special Issue): 23; Ward et al., *C3/Space and Electronic Warfare*, 4–6.

65. Msg., COMDESRON 22 to USCINCCENT, March 4, 1991, Desert Storm Engagement Message File, acc. 57 050399.00, Naval Forces Central Command Papers, CNA; msg., CTU 151.11.2 to CTF 151, February 25, 1991, OA; Billiere, *Storm Command*, 290; *Conduct of the Persian Gulf War*, 1: 273, 375; Griffis et al., *Amphibious Operations*, 32–33; USS *Missouri* (BB 63) Command History, 1991; Ward et al., *C3/Space and Electronic Warfare*, 4–6–4–10.

66. *Conduct of the Persian Gulf War*, 1: 304; Friedman, *Desert Victory*, 232; "DESRON-22: Messages on Desert Saber, Slash, Dagger, Storm, 1991," Post 1990 Command Files, OA; *Operation Desert Shield/Desert Storm*, 199.

67. Donald M. Lionetti, "Air Defense: No 'Road to Basra,'" *Army* 41 (July 1991): 16.

68. Steve Coll and William Branigin, "U.S. Scrambled to Shape View of Highway of Death," in Hedrick Smith, ed., *The Media and the Gulf War: The Press and Democracy in Wartime* (Washington, D.C.: Seven Locks Press, 1992), 205; COMCARGRUSEVEN, *Command History 1991*, OA; *Conduct of the Persian Gulf War*, 1: 397; *GWAPS Effectiveness Report*, 254; Quilter, *With the I Marine Expeditionary Force*, 97–98; *The U.S. Navy in Desert Shield/Desert Storm*, A–41.

69. *Conduct of the Persian Gulf War*, 1: 406–7; J. M. Shotwell, "The Ride into Kuwait City," *Leatherneck* 74 (May 1991): 21.

70. *Operation Desert Shield/Desert Storm*, 202–3; "Greater Gators: Amphibious Forces Kept Saddam Guessing," *All Hands* 68 (Desert Storm Special Issue): 33.

71. Bard E. O'Neill and Ilana Kass, "The Persian Gulf War: A Political–Military Assessment," *Comparative Strategy* 11 (April–June 1992): 224; Schwarzkopf, *It Doesn't Take a Hero*, 468–69.

72. *Conduct of the Persian Gulf War*, 1: 399, 2: A-1–A-13.

11

Sailing in the Sand: The U.S. Navy's Role in the Gulf War
Norman Friedman

The naval role in the Gulf War exemplified the uniquely naval virtue of sustained tactical and strategic mobility, with some important post–Cold War features. Only naval forces carry with them the means for sustained operation or combat. Thus they can often operate freely, in international waters, without local permission. Moreover, they offer an enduring presence. Other types of forces are indeed mobile, but only on a short-term basis. They cannot remain long in a distant theater, unbidden by local governments. Rather, they must either strike instantly or remain outside the theater, influencing events only by a perceived capability.

In the case of the Gulf War, it may have been decisive that U.S. carrier battle groups could appear in (and remain in) the theater without local permission, protecting Saudi Arabia whatever the Saudi government chose to do. Clearly, the Saudi government had a strong interest in preventing Iraqi forces from overrunning its borders. However, equally clearly, it faced major political dangers if it invited a Western country to defend it. To the extent that the United States could (and did) provide an important portion of that defense *without* Saudi permission, the Saudi government could ask for the rest.[1]

On the other hand, naval forces cannot carry the mountains of supplies which can be amassed at a fixed base ashore, so unassisted they cannot sustain combat for as long as, say, an air base, which has been built up over many months or years. Sustained naval operations require periodic resupply (sustained presence generally requires far less).[2]

Historically, naval mobility explains much of the strategic and tactical efficacy of naval forces. Although relatively few in number, by their mobility ships usually confront an enemy with a variety of possible threats. To the extent that the ships are difficult to detect and track far from shore, the enemy must deploy ground forces (which are ultimately far less mobile) to meet all plausible contingencies. The more mobile the naval force, the wider the range of threats, and the greater the effect on dispositions ashore. Much often also depends on the apparent invisibility of the naval force, at least when it is beyond the horizon of continuously operating shore-based surveillance. These mobility effects are, unfortunately, difficult to quantify, but they are apparent.

Conversely, a naval force intended to meet another seaborne force (e.g., in a blockade) must, in theory, itself cover a very wide variety of possibilities. Reconnaissance and surveillance (as well as countersurveillance measures) become extremely important. Blockade has become more difficult as the sheer number of ships has declined, due to rising unit cost. The Gulf crisis was the first demonstration of a new U.S. technological approach to solving this problem.

Because naval forces must be capable of operating autonomously, carrier air wings have to be self-sufficient. When war broke out in the Persian Gulf, the carriers provided only a fraction of fighters and bombers—but a dominant proportion of such supporting services as photo and electronic reconnaissance, as well as many defense-suppression aircraft.[3] Moreover, because the total number of aircraft on board a carrier is very limited, many of them must be capable of fulfilling multiple roles. For example, F/A-18s were used both for defense suppression and for attack. Once Iraqi air defenses had been neutralized, these aircraft could swing from one role to the other, greatly increasing the weight of attack a single carrier could impose.

The United States is fundamentally an insular power, capable of projecting power abroad and often granted base rights abroad. Since no base rights had been granted in the Gulf region, success there depended on U.S. success in rapidly projecting sufficient power to contain the problem while forces sufficient to defeat Iraq were built up. Ultimately, the bulk of the forces which actually ejected Iraq from Kuwait were ground-based aircraft and troops, but much of the enabling force which guaranteed them access was naval. Before 1914, a prominent British Admiral, Sir John Fisher, liked to say that the British Army was a projectile fired into enemy territory by the Royal Navy. The Gulf War fell into this category.

The great bulk (in this case, 85 percent) of the mass of vehicles and other military materiel needed for the battles in Saudi Arabia and Kuwait had to come by sea. Even fuel oil had to come by sea, since the only jet fuel refineries in the region were in Iraqi hands. It is still the case that, although personnel generally come by air, only a few heavy items can do so. It would have been deceptive to think only of combat, which was largely conducted by ground forces; to fight halfway around the world, U.S. and Allied forces had to come largely by sea.

One great problem in dealing with a distant emergency is that movement by sea is relatively slow. The operation in the Gulf benefited enormously from Central Command's efforts to build up a floating reserve in the Indian Ocean region, consisting of prepositioned Marine Corps vehicles and weapons and stocks of munitions for the Air Force. All were in ships operating from Diego Garcia, a relatively nearby island in the Indian Ocean. The Marines, in particular, found it easy to fly troops into Saudi Arabia to marry up with equipment coming from Diego Garcia. Unfortunately for the United States, Southwest Asia was and is unique in being thus prepared for an emergency. Saudi Arabia was also fortunate in having built up extremely good seaport facilities, so it was relatively easy to build up powerful ground forces once the holding force was in place.[4]

Events since 1991 make the interrelationship of ground and naval forces clearer. The 1991 victory was not, and for political reasons could not be, decisive. Saddam Hussein was left in control of Iraq, and his army retained much of its armor. Moreover, Saddam's financial problems, which caused him to attack Kuwait in the first place, not only remained but were exacerbated by the postwar UN embargo. By 1994, Saddam knew that several of the major powers, such as France and Russia, badly wanted the embargo lifted so that they could resume trade. Saddam decided to threaten Kuwait again, presumably expecting his friends on the UN Security Council to support his demand for normalization.

Saddam's new threat demonstrated the fragility of a ground-based regional deterrent. For some years, the United States had pressed Saudi Arabia to maintain stocks of ground equipment on its territory. Given such stocks, troops could easily fly in and mate up with their materiel. Only stocks in Saudi Arabia would have been both close enough to the border to be useful in combat, yet far enough back not to have been seized in the first day or so of a new Iraqi invasion. The U.S. position was apparently that the Saudis should pay both to amass and to maintain this materiel, and that rapid-reinforcement exercises, similar in concept to the old NATO reforgers, should be held.[5] Saudi Arabia would conclude a formal security agreement with the United States. Surely the Gulf War had demonstrated that it would take a substantial ground force in place to deal with an Iraqi attack.

As it happened, in 1994 enough materiel remained in Kuwait to equip the relatively small ground force the United States flew in. However, most observers were uncomfortably aware that this force could not have sufficed to stop, let alone repel, an Iraqi invasion. Moreover, even a small deployment carried enormous costs for the U.S. government. On the eve of the

1994 U.S. election, President Clinton announced major troop withdrawals from Kuwait, reportedly in hopes of gaining popularity at home. He was learning that sustained overseas troop deployments were difficult at best, and that any interventionist U.S. foreign policy might well demand significant simultaneous deployments on an embarrassing scale (troops were also called home from Haiti).

The Saudis were skittish, just as they had been in August 1990. They wanted security, but almost certainly they felt they were choosing between two threats, not simply between safety and danger. Any formal arrangement with the United States would enrage a conservative segment of the Saudi clergy, and that in turn might endanger the Saudi state. Indeed, any sustained foreign presence not entirely beholden to the Saudi government might well be considered dangerous.

That left the U.S. government with only two options, in the event of a new crisis. One would be a proactive strike on Iraq, using long-range bombers and missiles. The aircraft could probably fly from U.S. bases, though foreign acquiescence might be required for the tankers they would need. Above all, the strike would have to be so effective that it would stop the Iraqi army in its tracks—almost certainly without using nuclear weapons. Aside from its practical aspects, preemption of this sort raises enormous moral and political questions. Any evidence of Iraqi plans to invade Kuwait is likely to be ambiguous. Our Allies may well refuse to accept the U.S. warning of an Iraqi attack against Kuwait. A preemptive U.S. strike might well split the anti-Iraqi Coalition so badly that Saddam would indeed be able to demand normalization—even reparations for what he could present as unprovoked U.S. aggression.

For his part, Saddam presumably discovered that by making a relatively inexpensive gesture, he could force the United States to make costly deployments. Cycling his threat up and down would eventually cost the United States so much that deployments, even the small ones involved in the 1994 crisis, would become impractical. For its part, the United States decided to press for a new UN exclusion zone around Kuwait, which would reduce the threat Saddam could present. However, it is probably unrealistic to imagine that any ground-force exclusion zone can be very effective. Ground forces are just too ambiguous in character (e.g., When do police forces shade over into military formations?). The main U.S. hope must be that Saddam is now so desperate, due to a deteriorating economic situation, that he cannot afford to play a waiting game. The reader must decide how realistic that hope is.

The U.S. alternative has been to maintain significant U.S. forces in the region *not* subject to Saudi veto and, if possible, at a relatively low cost. That has meant warships carrying tactical aircraft, missiles, and Marines. Clearly, the threat they pose to Iraq is not anything like that used during the Gulf War; again we are back to forces which can hope to hold a line while heavy ground-based forces deploy. The hope must be that the sustained offshore presence so raises the cost of any Iraqi attack that Saddam will prefer to avoid mounting one.

This choice has not been clear-cut (partly, one suspects, due to interservice politics), but it is likely to become more obvious if Saddam does survive, and thus if the United States must face the probability of further Kuwait or Saudi crises.

The events of 1994 illuminate those of 1990. The Iraqi invasion of August 1990 presented the United States with two distinct problems. First, American forces in the area were clearly insufficient to stop any further Iraqi thrust into Saudi Arabia, not to mention liberating Kuwait. Second, it was by no means clear that the Saudi government felt strong enough to welcome large contingents of U.S. troops, which it might fear would destabilize it merely by their presence. The U.S. government feared that the Iraqis would continue on into Saudi Arabia. Iraqi control of the entire Gulf would be intolerable.

The only defensive forces which could move rapidly into the area without Saudi consent were U.S. carriers. Iraqi propaganda sought to preclude any Saudi request for U.S. protection. Because the naval forces provided that protection without Saudi consent, the Saudis could reasonably say that it was not for them to decide whether to accept outside help in their defense. They could therefore open their country to Western troops and aircrews.

The carriers had definite limitations. They probably could not have blunted a determined Iraqi move south, but at the least they could have slowed one while ground troops and ground air bases were built up. Given later evidence of the quality of the Iraqi ground forces, it is possible that even limited attacks by the carrier aircraft could have stopped an Iraqi advance into Saudi Arabia.

U.S. ground-based fighters were soon flown into Saudi Arabia, but because as yet they had no logistical base, they could not have mounted many combat sorties. As for ground troops, Marines and light army formations were soon flown in. The Marines had the major advantage that for some years they had maintained a floating reserve of equipment, including tanks, at Diego Garcia in the Indian Ocean. Like the carriers, this reserve quickly steamed to Saudi Arabia. Without these cargoes, the Marines would have amounted to little more than armed tourists, incapable of resisting any further Iraqi attack. The Marines, in effect, bought time to mass and load heavy equipment, first for the big blocking force and then for the heavy European-based armored units which smashed the Iraqi defenses of Kuwait. Again, most of the materiel necessarily arrived by sea.

As it turned out, the movement of the heavy materiel was largely a matter of securing sufficient strategic sealift. However, at the time there was a real question of whether some attack might be mounted as the ships passed through the Mediterranean and the Suez Canal. Saddam was by no means universally detested; Colonel Qadaffi was clearly a sympathizer. Mobile naval forces monitored Libya to detect any indication of impending attack. It seems likely that the presence of strong U.S. naval strike forces in the Mediterranean also helped deter interference with the Iraqi buildup; presumably Colonel Qadaffi did not want a repetition of the 1986 carrier air strikes. Similarly, NATO mine countermeasures craft were assigned to help keep the entrance to the Suez Canal clear.

There was also some question about whether Saddam might use irregular forces to attack ships as they arrived in Saudi ports. In retrospect, it seems clear that any sustained blockage would have made it very difficult to form the Allied ground force early enough to allow it to exercise to the point of its great efficiency once the ground war began. Saddam seems to have missed this opportunity. Special U.S. Coast Guard reserve units were activated to maintain port security in Saudi Arabia.

Naval forces also performed a useful prehostilities role in the form of a blockade. Between August 1990 and January 1991, the anti-Saddam Coalition had to be seen to be doing something about the problem. The chosen measure, and probably the only practical one, was an embargo. Although in retrospect it seems unlikely that any nonmilitary pressure could have forced Saddam out of Kuwait, the embargo was an extremely useful way of maintaining the Coalition's momentum.

Perhaps as important, because the embargo was a measure short of war, it was immediately acceptable to many in the West. Experience of previous conflicts shows that it often takes some time for people to accept that a problem cannot be resolved short of military action. For example, in 1939 many Americans considered participation in World War II entirely unjustified. Many fewer held that view by the fall of 1941. The embargo bought both buildup time and acceptance.

Technically, the blockade was not easy to implement. A small number of Allied warships had to stop and check merchant ships, which might be taking a wide variety of paths into Iraq or Jordan (from which cargoes were transshipped to Iraq). In an important sense, enforcing the blockade was not different from the problem of engaging an enemy's warships well beyond a ship's horizon (the decision to intercept a particular ship must be made well before the interceptor can possibly detect the approaching ship; otherwise an impractical number of interceptors is needed).

As it turned out, the U.S. Navy had been studying this problem for well over a decade, since it had decided to buy the antiship version of the Tomahawk cruise missile. By the time this weapon had been bought, the Russians had had a somewhat comparable missile, Shaddock (SS-N-3), in service for about a decade. As might have been expected, they found it difficult and expensive to keep track of potential naval targets. Not only were the targets highly mobile, but they were also embedded in a mass of nontargets. The Russians combined passive tracking (ashore, afloat, and eventually from space) with specialized active radar platforms, mainly reconnaissance bombers (e.g., Bear Ds). Their technique was expensive and could handle only a limited number of targets simultaneously. Moreover, a likely victim would be alerted by the approach of platforms needed to confirm the target's nature, position, course, and speed.[6]

The U.S. Navy wanted to minimize any additional expenditure associated with Tomahawk. It had numerous sources of information on ship movements, but they reported on an intermittent basis. Given such data plus information on likely ship performance, however, a powerful computer could build up a continuous picture of the probable positions of ships at sea. The picture was likely to be accurate enough for missile targeting. It had two important features: First, it showed virtually all shipping, not only a few warships of interest; and second, it did not require any particular sensor to focus on a ship of particular interest.

This technique proved extremely well adapted to blockade operations.[7] Information was provided by sources ranging from shipping agents to P-3s fitted with imaging radars. The key was sheer computer power, both ashore and on board the ships on blockade duty. The U.S. system turned out to be easy to spread within the Coalition as a whole, because the necessary software ran on standard computer workstations. The workstations could be provided virtually off the shelf, and the software was easy to reproduce. This experience suggests that the economics of military systems may be changing radically.[8]

In a larger sense, the blockade may have pointed the way toward a change in warfare, in which better use of available information makes possible massive economies in force (in this case, it made possible operations which the force on the spot otherwise could not have conducted). Of course, it did matter that Saddam's blockade-runners were unaware of the technique being used to stop them. They did not maneuver evasively, so it was relatively easy to project their movements ahead of time. Nor did Saddam's shipping controllers seek to confuse the system by having ships take crossing courses. Such countermeasures would presumably be obvious to any future Saddam aware of how the blockade had been conducted.

Once the offensive was mounted, the Allies derived important benefits from the ability to operate relatively freely in the waters around Kuwait and Saudi Arabia. Although Iraq itself had only a short coastline, naval forces were able to move into positions to attack the Iraqi defenses, both air and ground, from axes unavailable to the Allied forces massed on the ground in Saudi Arabia. This indirect sort of impact is typical of naval forces.

During the air attack phase, carrier aircraft attacked from both the Red Sea and the Persian Gulf. Most of the land-based aircraft flew directly north over the Saudi border. In theory, this sort of multiaxis attack should have helped saturate the Iraqi national air defense system. As it happened, the system was recovered.[9] The six carriers contributed about 23 percent of all Coalition aircraft, and at least a similar proportion of combat sorties.[10] The naval contribution was somewhat limited because prewar naval policy had limited purchases of laser-guided bomb kits and hard-target penetrators.[11]

Similarly, Tomahawk land-attack cruise missiles were fired from the Eastern Mediterranean as well as from the Red Sea and the Gulf. Shots from the Mediterranean could reach areas of western Iraq denied to other Tomahawk shooters (maximum missile range was about 675 miles). Tomahawk offered a much more important advantage. Rules of engagement limited aircraft to clear-air conditions, whereas Tomahawk was considered accurate even when weather was poor. Using it, the attackers could maintain constant pressure on Iraq.[12]

Once the war was over, Tomahawks offered a valuable means of maintaining pressure on Iraq. Compared to aircraft, the missiles had two great advantages. First, no missile attack exposed a pilot to capture or death. Second, the missile platform was much less expensive to operate (i.e., to maintain in theater) than a carrier. Tomahawks were used to retaliate after an Iraqi attempt to kill ex-President George Bush in 1993. No aircraft have been used in such a role, mainly because without a major attack on the Iraqi national air defense system, it would be impossible to guarantee that an airplane flying over a defended area would be safe. On the other hand, the missile carries a far smaller warhead than an airplane's bomb load, so it is likely to be far less destructive.

Naval forces must include powerful self-contained air defense, including both high-capacity radars and the means to track hundreds of air targets. Antiaircraft ships in the northern Gulf were used to help sort out the air picture there. In particular, it turned out that Aegis ships equipped with the SPY-1 phased-array radar could detect approaching Scud missiles, although they could not engage these targets. Presumably, they were able to contribute to warnings which cued Patriot radars in Saudi Arabia. This experience probably fed into postwar interest in naval forms of tactical ballistic missile defense, using variants of the Aegis missile (SM-2 Block IVA and beyond).

The amphibious feint made a much greater use of the inherent flexibility of naval forces. Although Kuwait had a short coastline, in the presence of strong amphibious forces, Saddam had to divert considerable ground forces to protect it. The concentration of these forces substantially reduced Iraqi presence on the long Kuwaiti land border. Moreover, the amphibious presence probably helped convince Saddam that ground forces would not risk moving through the trackless desert (he seems not to have appreciated the effect of global positioning satellites). The evidence for Saddam's thinking is a sand table recovered after Kuwait fell; it shows expected lines of Coalition advance.

To make the amphibious threat effective, the Coalition had to seize and maintain control over the northern end of the Gulf. It had to destroy the small Iraqi fleet, which was armed with antiship missiles, and neutralize the mine fields laid prewar by Iraqi ships and craft.

Destruction of the Iraqi fleet turned out to be relatively easy. Despite much prewar advertising, the small Iraqi missile boats were unable to shoot down the helicopters which destroyed them.[13]

Mine clearance proved far more difficult. Although the Coalition watched the Iraqis mine the northern Gulf, the position of the fields was only imperfectly known. One problem was that the Iraqis used numerous landing craft and seized pleasure craft to lay mines. It was difficult for observers to be sure of which sorties were for mine laying, and which for logistics (e.g., to transport booty out of Kuwait). Reportedly, sorties by all but the known Iraqi mine layers (two ex-Soviet ships) were classified as logistical. If this was true, in retrospect it was a remarkable failure of imagination, particularly after the Iranians had laid so many mines from small boats a few years earlier.

It was well known that mine neutralization would be lengthy and difficult. That made reconnaissance vital: Ships could, in theory, be sent to places which the Iraqis had failed to mine. The failure of mine surveillance was therefore a serious problem; it led to the mining of two U.S. ships, the amphibious carrier *Tripoli* (which was headquarters ship for mine clearance) and the cruiser *Princeton*. In the absence of reliable mine reconnaissance, the Coalition had to rely on standard techniques of mine clearance, which were slow. It seems arguable that quicker clearance, at least close inshore, would have been necessary for any landing to have achieved much surprise.[14]

Mine clearance presented another issue: protection against air attack. Modern minecraft are inherently expensive and cannot, therefore, be particularly numerous. Nor can they have much in the way of antiaircraft armament.[15] They are, therefore, valuable yet vulnerable units. High-performance missile ships, such as *Princeton*, had to be assigned to the northern Gulf to protect the mine clearance operation—hence their special vulnerability to mining.

The minecraft did have some air defense, in the form of hand-held missiles (such as Stingers), but it was not tied into any sort of large-scale air defense system and thus could not be controlled in a dense air environment. Many Coalition aircraft flew home via the Gulf; the only way to avoid shooting down friendlies was to prohibit surface shooters from engaging them. In retrospect, it would seem likely that, had the Iraqis tried to abort the clearance operation in the Gulf by firing (say) a missile at a mine hunter, the prohibition would have broken down and the Coalition would have lost some aircraft, possibly with enormous political consequences.

The Marine amphibious ships offshore did make a direct contribution.

Harriers (AV-8Bs) offshore helped attack Iraqi troops near the Kuwaiti coast, and at least some Marines went ashore by helicopter. On the other hand, no classical over-the-beach operation was attempted (although the feint was kept up by staging a highly publicized exercise landing before the war began). The experience might be read as suggesting that future landings should be made primarily by air (e.g., by V22) from amphibious carriers, but the Marines point out that, as in transportation to the theater of operations, heavy equipment and other materiel must come across the beach, by sea.

In the end, the naval contribution was invaluable, but once combat had been joined, ground-based forces provided far more weight. What happens the next time? The ground-based forces were in theater because the Saudis welcomed them and because Saudi Arabia provided perhaps a unique form of infrastructure. Not only is it not certain that this sort of welcome will come again, but some countries may not even welcome the sort of forward deployment ships the Marines used so successfully (as of this writing, Thailand had recently rejected a proposal to base such ships on its coast, for fear of infuriating China).

One conclusion may be that in future the United States will have to choose between relatively short-run, all-American, hit-and-run operations (ranging from presence to air raids to Marine landings) and larger wars in which Coalition partners would not merely play, but might have a deciding voice. The former would be mounted from the sea, with all the advantages of purely American control and all the disadvantages of limited scope and duration. For the latter, a U.S. capacity to operate freely from the sea may be decisive in forming and maintaining coalitions, since the United States will generally be able to offer either to act unilaterally or to veto further operations by withdrawing an essential element, with capacities our Allies may not share.

NOTES

Dr. Norman Friedman is the author of *Desert Victory: The War for Kuwait* (Annapolis: Naval Institute Press, 1992). Both this chapter and the book reflect the author's views and should not be taken as representative of the views of the U.S. Navy or of any other organization with which the author has been associated.

1. The writer is well aware of the long-standing U.S.–Saudi defense relationship and of the consultation with the Saudi government beginning virtually at the moment Kuwait was invaded. However, readers will also be aware of Saudi skittishness, both at the time of the invasion and more recently. The Saudi monarchy must always reckon with the force of Arab/Moslem nationalism (the two are not the same) and with strong underlying xenophobia. It would have been in the monarchy's interest to be seen as bowing to an inevitable U.S. presence rather than to be inviting one. For a recent view of the fragile nature of the current Saudi state, see

A. Cockburn and C. Cockburn, "Royal Mess," *New Yorker,* November 28, 1994, 54–72.

2. This is not to suggest that presence operations are cost free. If U.S. policy demands sustained presence on a year-in, year-out basis, then several ships will have to be maintained to keep one always in position. The Persian Gulf station is particularly difficult because it is so far from U.S. ports. Much depends on the definition of sustained presence. At one time, for example, a carrier in the Arabian Sea was considered on station only if it was always within twenty-four hours of a designated launch point. As soon as the carrier left the box thus defined, it was no longer considered available. It might require five or six carriers to sustain this kind of presence, but only three to keep a carrier continuously somewhere in the Arabian or Indian Ocean within (say) a week of any specific launch spot. On the other hand, a fixed base cannot easily or cheaply be relocated in accord with changes in national policy. The post–Cold War world is likely to be particularly turbulent and hence to require particularly frequent relocation of U.S. forces. The same ships which maintain presence off, say, the Persian Gulf can do the same job off, say, Korea. The demands set by the Arabian Sea station are taken from interviews with naval officers involved in force planning during the late 1970s and early 1980s.

3. Because the Air Force is organized in single-purpose squadrons, moving a few special-purpose aircraft into a theater can be difficult logistically. One lesson the Air Force drew from the war was that it should organize composite wings similar in concept to carrier air wings, providing all functions in a single unit. However, it is not clear to what extent maintenance of such a unit could be simplified, since the aircraft would all be of dissimilar types.

4. Contingencies elsewhere might present much worse logistical problems. Nor is it clear that the floating reserve at Diego Garcia has been entirely restored to its pre–Gulf War strength. The logistical situation in Southwest Asia was good because the United States had built up Central Command (previously the Rapid Reaction Force) precisely to fight in this area from 1979 on, although the usual scenario for its employment had been a Soviet descent into Iran or Pakistan. There is no comparable organization or floating reserve for any other part of the world.

5. In a reforger, troops flew in to marry up with stored Prepositioning of Material Configured to Unit Sets (POMCUS) equipment. POMCUS stocks were built up so that Soviet submarines could not entirely neutralize U.S. reinforcement of NATO. Opponents of the idea pointed out that West Germany was riddled with spies and that POMCUS stocks would be even easier than reinforcing ships to destroy. The idea in Saudi Arabia was different; it was that ships might arrive far too slowly. The Saudis apparently feared that some would see the stocks as the opening wedge of a U.S. protectorate (e.g., troops might be brought in to guard the stocks of weapons, particularly if some instability seemed to be coming).

6. For details of the Soviet Ocean Surveillance System (SOSS), see Norman Friedman, *Naval Institute Guide to World Naval Weapons Systems, 1991–1992* (Annapolis, Md.: Naval Institute Press, 1993), 4–5, 13 [hereafter *Naval Institute Guide*]. The U.S. Navy called the Russian system the SOSS. Its logic was that likely targets would have to emit characteristic signals, mainly from their radars and long-haul radio sets. Initially, then, the Russians relied on shore-based high-frequency radio direction-finders (HFDFs) for initial detection. Once a target had been identified, bombers could fly out to verify its location. Sometimes ships could be as-

signed not only to trail the target formation, but also to indicate which ship in the formation was the target. Presumably Russian successes in breaking U.S. naval codes (with the help of the Walker spy ring) helped materially. As U.S. long-haul communications shifted to satellites, the fixed HFDF net became less available. The Soviets began to use space-based passive satellites (which could pick up short-wavelength line-of-sight emissions, including those of characteristic radars). Their ultimate plan was apparently to shift from Bear Ds to space-based radars (on Recoverable Orbital Satellites [RORSATs]), but the radar satellite program was among the first to die as the Soviet defense economy collapsed. It was generally assumed within the U.S. Navy that the appearance of radar-equipped reconnaissance aircraft would foreshadow an attack: "two Bears in the morning, missiles in the afternoon." Several elements of U.S. naval policy of the 1970s and 1980s were designed to overload the limited target-handling capability of the SOSS.

7. This technique was probably also used to enforce the arms embargo in the Adriatic. In November 1994, Congress voted to deny any funds used to maintain an embargo against Bosnia; the European NATO Allies demanded that the embargo continue. Newspaper reports suggested that they were extremely angry not only because U.S. ships would be withdrawn, but because U.S. intelligence would no longer be available. Almost certainly the intelligence involved is the sort of surface shipping picture used to such effect before and during the Gulf War; probably none of the Allies can generate a similar picture.

8. At one time, most investment went into platforms, such as ships and aircraft. Then it shifted to the electronics and weapons the platforms carry, so that, for example, the proportion of system cost allocated to a shipyard is often no more than half. It was still the case that two ships or two aircraft cost about twice as much as one (although learning-curve savings would be felt in long production runs). Now, however, much of the cost of the weapon system is software. In theory, software can be reproduced cheaply (just how cheaply depends on licensing arrangements with the producer). If software accounts for, say, 80 percent of the cost of a system (like the one used to conduct the blockade), then two such systems will not cost too much more than one, since only hardware costs will have to be borne twice over. In theory, the use of standard digital hardware ought to make upgrades relatively inexpensive, since much of the cost of upgrading will be better software. The blockade system, JOTS (Joint Operational Tactical System), would seem to point the way toward this sort of development. Other techniques intended to overcome Iraqi air defenses may have materially reduced Coalition sortie rates. The air tasking order (ATO) seems to have been designed to concentrate aircraft on targets without any apparent concentration en route; aircraft followed pseudorandom paths. That such coordination could be achieved was a major technical triumph. However, it took time to put together each day's pattern, and apparently the Iraqis could reduce damage to mobile targets by moving within the ATO time cycle. Moreover, the ATO seems to have enforced a degree of rigidity which would not have suited a more fluid war. The carriers turned out to be ill equipped to receive the ATO, possibly because naval doctrine envisaged something closer to stream attacks. Ironically, once the Iraqi national air defense organization had been destroyed, there was little point in anything as elaborate as the ATO. Many accounts of the ATO describe it as an alternative to the Vietnam era "route package," in which specific target sets were assigned to specific services. See, for example, Rich-

ard P. Hallion, *Storm over Iraq: Air Power and the Gulf War* (Washington, D.C.: Smithsonian Institution Press, 1992), 143. Hallion fails to explain why it was so important to intermingle forces that rigidity precluded quick reattacks. Interviewed postwar, Navy pilots who fought in the Gulf were, however, very impressed with the degree to which the ATO avoided interference among the numerous aircraft operating over Iraq. The contention in this note is based on this author's experience of air attack tactical development during the 1980s.

9. It was never clear why the Iraqi national air defense system did not recover; U.S. air operations seem to have been designed on the assumption that at least partial recovery would occur within a few days. Possible reasons include the loss of foreign technicians due to the embargo (and, in particular, due to Soviet cooperation with the Coalition) and the sheer strain of maintaining a varied system. Reportedly, the Iraqis had maintained the system by ordering replacement parts as they were needed; this sort of practice would have been impossible during the war. The inference about U.S. expectations is based on continuing use of strike packages with substantial antiair defense components, as reported at the time and immediately postwar. Soon after the war, *U.S. News & World Report* claimed that the Iraqi defense system had been deliberately disabled by a computer virus in a console shipped to Iraq in 1990, but that seems unlikely. In particular, had the Allies had such an assurance, they would not have made the massive attack on the air defense system which was so widely reported just after hostilities began.

10. The sortie question is vexed. Carrier combat air patrol sorties probably were not counted, yet they would have been important had the Iraqis tried to penetrate the Gulf. Nor is it clear that sorties designed to block any sortie by Iraqi aircraft in Iran were counted as combatant. In addition, naval attack groups had a higher proportion of attacking aircraft than corresponding Air Force "packages," which included numerous defense-suppression aircraft through most or all of the war (some of the naval defense-suppression aircraft, F/A-18s, could serve as bombers as soon as the Iraqi air defense threat subsided; equivalent Air Force "Wild Weasels" were single purpose).

11. The Navy had ordered relatively few laser-guided bomb kits because aircraft often had to jettison their weapons to land back aboard carriers; it would have been expensive to dispose of numerous laser bombs that way. Much reliance was, therefore, placed on a new generation of aircraft fire control systems (e.g., in the F/A-18 Hornet). They did provide good accuracy, but not enough for bridge- or bunker-busting. Ironically, Navy A-6Es provided a large fraction of the designators available in the theater. As for hard-target penetrators, the Navy traditionally emphasized ground support rather than deep attacks against fixed targets such as aircraft hangarettes. Neither U.S. Service had shown any prewar interest in weapons capable of dealing with Iraqi command bunkers; the GBU-28 (dropped from F-111Fs on two bunkers at the end of the war) was improvised in wartime. For details of U.S. Gulf War bombs and bomb loads (including the development of the GBU-28), see Friedman, *Naval Institute Guide,* 162, 166–67, 194, 196–99, 812–13, 834. Early in 1992, then Chief of Naval Operations, Admiral Frank Kelso, announced that the Navy would buy GBU-24 hard-target penetrators. Information on Gulf War bomb loads was based on contemporary news accounts, particularly in *Aviation Week* and *Space Technology,* and on interviews with NAVAIR officers (con-

ducted for the book *Desert Victory*); the GBU-28 story was taken from its developer, Lockheed.

12. Tomahawk did have some major limitations. Its guidance system was based on terrain mapping; before the outbreak of war the Defense Mapping Agency had to work all-out to prepare sufficient maps. Defining missile paths was time-consuming and involved computers in the United States (mission profiles could be modified at sea, but entirely new ones could not be constructed). During and after the war, it was sometimes necessary to run multiple missiles through similar paths, and alerted Iraqi defenses certainly shot some down. Both limitations are being dealt with. Tomahawks are now being fitted with GPS guidance, which requires no precise ground map (except to tell the missile to avoid rises in the ground), and more powerful computers (moved to sea) make mission planning quicker and far easier. Tomahawk data were derived from interviews with representatives of McDonnell-Douglas, the missile's manufacturer. The Joint Project Office for cruise missiles, which is responsible for Tomahawk, produced a chart showing the growing percentage of missions for which digital mapping data were available as war approached in 1991.

13. The boats, mainly ex-Kuwaiti, were all equipped with radar-directed gun systems. One explanation of their failure is that their hulls vibrated too badly at high speed for the systems to maintain lock-on. Another is that the departing Kuwaitis managed to remove key software. That is less credible, simply because without the necessary software the guns probably would not have worked at all. The failure to stay locked on was clear in television footage of the attack on the boats shown during the Gulf War. Radar warning receivers in British Lynx helicopters attacking the boats visibly lit up as the boats' radars locked on, and then became dark as the helicopter maneuvered slightly to break those locks. See S. Slade, "Fast Attack Craft," in Norman Friedman, ed., *Navies in the Nuclear Age* (London: Conway Maritime Press, 1993; Annapolis, Md.: Naval Institute Press, 1994) [hereafter *Navies*].

14. For a discussion of mine countermeasures, see G. K. Hartman, *Weapons the Wait* (Annapolis, Md.: Naval Institute Press, 1979), 121–61. For a catalog of current mines and mine countermeasures, see Friedman, *Naval Institute Guide,* 733–84. No full account of mine countermeasures in the Gulf War has yet been published. The standard technique common to all Western navies is for a mine hunter to examine the bottom in detail using a high-definition sonar. Mine-like objects are examined by a higher definition set, and they may be attacked by a remotely controlled submersible laying a charge. Because the charge is likely to destroy the fuzing mechanism, but *not* the mine casing, the mine hunter must plot the position of the neutralized object, preferably on an electronic chart which other mine hunters can share. The technique is slow because the hunter has to stop before examining the mine (otherwise it may run over the mine) and because there cannot be many hunters (they are expensive, partly because they have to be acoustically and magnetically silenced). Mine countermeasure helicopters sweep an area before the hunters go in, in hopes of triggering any mines sensitive enough to detect and destroy a hunter. However, modern mines can generally be set to ignore a given number of ships before they go off, and an acoustic mine might easily be set to go off upon hearing a hunter's characteristic sonar. Wartime trials of laser mine detectors (particularly "Magic Lantern") suggested that some change in this situation might be

coming. Another important development was the use of mine-evasion sonars by combatant ships such as frigates. In theory, such devices might allow a ship to evade mines without sweeping them. They would be modern equivalents of the classic paravane of the past.

15. See D. K. Brown, "Mine Countermeasures Craft," in Friedman, *Navies*. The hunters are expensive because (1) they must be silenced acoustically and magnetically and (2) they require elaborate combat systems to locate mines precisely. Precise location is needed for the reason given in the previous note. The combination brings a mine hunter into the Corvette cost category. In contrast, World War II sweepers were numerous because they required little in the way of silencing (acoustic and magnetic mines were set coarsely, precisely to avoid attacking sweepers). Precise navigation was not an issue because mines were swept (destroyed) en masse, either by having their mooring wires cut or by being stimulated by decoy signatures produced by the sweeper. The advent of pressure mines, which could not be decoyed, made hunting essential.

Part VI

REEXAMINING THE ALLIED "VICTORY" IN THE GULF WAR

The U.S. Air Force is a victim of its history. The study of history is more than pride in the past, the exploits of heroes, and the pursuit of heritage as revealed in the symbolism of squadron patches and decorations. From the early 1920s until the USAF gained its separate service status in 1947, American airpower enthusiasts within the Army, although well intentioned, engaged in subterfuge to promote an independent service. This has left the U.S. Air Force with something of an identity crisis. Like an illegitimate child at a family reunion, the Air Force is uncomfortable with its origins precisely because its primary reason for being is based on the still unproven doctrine of strategic bombing now touted as the strategic air campaign.

At its essence, doctrine is based on history and not on the promise of technology. Airpower doctrine, unlike land and sea doctrine, is based on the prophecies of Giulio Douhet and Billy Mitchell and, to a lesser extent, on minor prophets like Alexander de Seversky, Curtis E. LeMay, and John A. Warden III. So far, the prophesy and the prophets have been unfulfilled. The major tenets of the faith, grounded in the promise that strategic bombing can strike at the enemy's vital center to break the opposing side's will while crippling or destroying its war-making capability, has not been realized. Airpower, while occasionally pivotal in warfare and often useful as a support for ground and sea operations, has never been decisive. The historically proven decisive instruments of warfare remain land and sea forces.

Historians have an advantage over theologians in that history is based on fact and theology is based on what the Apostle Paul described as "things unseen." Historians can agree on a reliable set of facts about battles like Gettysburg or Trafalgar. Reasonable scholars may have substantial disagreements about the interpretation of those facts and can argue their implications. Generally, the pursuit of truth is strengthened by the dialogue, and the military doctrine that results from that process is stronger and more useful. Airpower doctrine, however, because it is based on prophesy, demands a religious-like faith in that which is unseen—and unprovable. For airpower true believers, those who argue with the tenets of the faith or who criticize the institutionally sanctioned interpretations are heretics. Their ideas are not welcomed; there is no growth by debate. For airpower theory, there is no room for the dialectic.

This commitment to orthodoxy discourages criticism among those who write Air Force history, thus frustrating efforts at heuristic or interpretive writing. At its best, history is critical. Indeed, without that critical element, what one has is not history but propaganda. Airpower enthusiasts have, at best, a selective memory, and they seem ever in search of facts to support the institutional mythology necessary to support their assertions of decisive victory through airpower. History suffers as a result.

Both Michael T. Corgan and Caroline F. Ziemke seek, in their chapters, to reexamine the Allied efforts in the Gulf War and determine exactly what was won. Corgan, using a Clausewitzian paradigm, analyzes all of the aspects of the war from diplomatic maneuvers to the implementation of ground, sea, and air forces in terms of the great master's tried and true theories and appraisal of war. He does not attempt to force his conclusions on the reader as much as he points them to the facts and asks them to draw their own conclusions.

Ziemke, on the other hand, makes a frontal attack. She clearly does not believe that the Allies won a great military victory in the classic sense of the word. She thus demands that the reader, and fellow analysts, take a hard second look at this so-called victory and determine not only if the Allies won anything of value, but if there are any real military lessons to be learned. Indeed, she would say no to both of these.

In the final analysis, institutions and nations which confuse history with propaganda have no history. Like Nazi Germany and the Soviet Union, nations which based their understanding of the past on myth and ideology not only have no history, they have no future either.

—Earl H. Tilford, Jr.

12

Clausewitz's *On War* and the Gulf War
Michael T. Corgan

A number of recent studies of war and strategic thinking dismiss the relevance of Clausewitz. Technological change, nuclear weapons, or the electronic battlefield, it is said, have made *On War* essentially obsolete. But profound thinking on war, whatever its date, is still essential, and the Gulf War is no exception. Other studies have already given the major events of the conflict; time and declassification will provide missing details for more thorough operational analysis.[1]

This analysis takes a Clausewitzian perspective on the context and political conduct of the war. By this I mean those overarching and systematizing ideas on the phenomenon of war. I especially want to distinguish those ideas from Clausewitz's writing on operational principles—that is, warfare. Both topics are found intermingled in *On War,* but it is his writing on the phenomenon of war itself that can help provide insight into the larger questions of why the countries involved in the Gulf War chose to make war and what they expected to achieve.

I mean to include the whole body of *On War* and not just epigrams of Clausewitz to illustrate this or that point the author wished to make. Quoting selectively from this or that authority on strategy, whether Sun Tzu or whatever pro football coach is in vogue at the moment, is a perilous venture if the writer's framework does not closely correspond to that of the authority invoked. Confusion will likely result. Without a clearly understood and articulated overall framework, Clausewitz warned, a student of war will not be able to distinguish trivial from essential ideas. Inevitably, then, the student will not be able to gain insight into all the phenomena that need to be studied and the relationships of these phenomena to one another (*OW*, 578).[2] The framework for this study, the prism through which to view events, is Clausewitz's thought on the phenomenon of war itself.

Using a Clausewitzian framework can help accomplish several crucial tasks. Among the most important are deciding what the war is to accomplish, making the initial ends/means or benefit/cost assessment on the efficacy of war, and keeping strategy properly subordinated to policy. Similarly, this framework can provide a guide to assessing what an adversary's calculations are and what he or she may be planning.

A careful reading of *On War* shows that the author started out to provide a series of aphorisms after the manner of Montesquieu but surrendered to a more analytical approach in order to produce, like Thucydides, a book that would transcend its immediate times. This spirit of analysis led to the larger conceptual framework in which thinking on the principles of war fighting—warfare—were subordinated to what became a philosophical treatise on the essence of the phenomenon of war. War, as Clausewitz discussed it, is that political activity, with violent means added to other means, practiced by the nation-state for political objects. The famous modern military historian John Keegan certainly agrees with his analysis of Clausewitzian theory. Too many writers ignore Clausewitz's shift in emphasis and treat his work as the series of aphorisms he started to produce.[3] The following set of ideas on Clausewitz's contribution to military–political thinking has been influenced by Michael Howard's writings and lectures and further developed by teaching Clausewitz at the Naval War College and conducting advanced seminars on his thinking at the Massachusetts Institute of Technology (MIT) over a number of years.

The analysis will consider the approach to, conduct of, and conclusion to the Gulf War from the viewpoint of Iraq and the opposing Coalition. In practice, this will usually mean for Iraq what Saddam Hussein was up to, since only rarely did his underlings have much influence on events and decisions. For the Coalition side, it will largely be what Washington and the Bush administration intended since the American presence was the sine qua non of the Coalition. The aim of this theoretical approach is to reify Clausewitz's observation that a theory is an a priori condition or at least a guide to anyone who would attempt to learn about war from books (*OW*, 141).

The starting point for any Clausewitzian inquiry is the body of ideas on the relation of war and politics, specifically the political object of the war entered into and the ensuing and necessary relation of the war's strategy to the policy goal. A related question is what type of war will be fought, limited or unlimited in the sense that Clausewitz used these terms. Next, the "remarkable trinity" concept that Clausewitz introduced but never really developed will illustrate the relation of the states' leaders to their military leaders, on the one hand, and their populace, on the other. In the spirit of Clausewitz's own stated intent, I will consider those ideas from *On War* that do not fall into the categories of the commonplace and the obvious (though Clausewitz did write about such to some degree). These ideas are *suspension of action, friction, center of gravity,* and *the culminating point of victory.*

WAR: A CONTINUATION OF POLITICS *WITH THE ADDITION OF OTHER MEANS* (ORIGINAL EMPHASIS—*OW, 605*)

The question of Saddam Hussein's goals in taking Kuwait is too easily dismissed as simple territorial and self-aggrandizement. His miscalculation of starting a war he was bound to lose was simply the product of an irrational actor, insufficiently familiar with his possible adversaries, surrounded by sycophants, and deluded about the costs of war based on experience with an adversary that was not well organized. Events leading up to the invasion of Kuwait through to the present isolation of Iraq point to the need for a deeper explanation.[4] Two related questions suggest themselves: did Saddam think he would get away with such a blatant territorial grab? If it should happen that Saddam is challenged, who would challenge him?

Saddam did not travel in the West, but he was certainly in frequent and intimate contact with those who had and knew Western leaders. Moreover, there were visits to Baghdad by those seeking to incline him to a more stabilizing role in the Middle East, including the now notorious visit of American members of Congress. He was surrounded by sycophants. However, even with his reputation for ruthlessness toward those who opposed him, it was widely known that Saddam listened to reasoned advice and put his senior military officers in charge of strategy after he had demonstrated his shortcomings in that area against Iran. He had no way of appreciating the effects of not having control of the air in modern warfare. On the other hand, he had a good idea of what casualties he could take and a reasonable idea of how Americans responded to casualties of their own. Nor was it certain from his perspective that the response to his invasion of Kuwait would be war. He was familiar with the withdrawal of American Marines from Beirut in 1983 after fewer casualties than some Iraqi intraparty struggles.

Clausewitz's exhortation to conduct a means/ends assessment suggests that leaders should put themselves in their adversary's position to determine what the adversary's value system might be. The question to ask is, based on the adversary's value system, is there a political goal worth the risk of a military response, including all-out war, to the action the adversary has taken or is about to take? A broadly shared and essentially unexamined American assumption of Saddam's intentions prior to the actual invasion of Kuwait was that he could not and therefore would not risk provoking the United States into a war. Accordingly, there was virtually no high-level questioning of what Saddam's problems, other than regime survival against coup attempts, might be. Rather than conclude that there was nothing Saddam wanted that was worth risking a war for, it might have been better to assume that he *would* risk a war and then try to ascertain what benefit was worth that cost.

According to Clausewitz, "No one starts a war—or rather no one in his senses ought to do so—without first being clear in his mind what he intends to achieve by that war and how he intends to conduct it" (*OW*, 579). Assuming a Saddam in his senses, what did he mean to achieve? We must remember that his actions occurred in the context of the just ended and notably unsuccessful war with Iran. Explanations for the move into Kuwait, many given by Saddam himself, abound: a historically justified claim to the so-called Province 19, better Iraqi access to the sea, Kuwaiti perfidy in illegally siphoning oil from the Rumaila oil fields, and, later, an attempt to bring to a head all outstanding territorial issues (read Palestinian) in the region. But none of these justifications was heard so persistently before the invasion as were Iraq's attempts to gain some sort of restructuring or outright forgiveness of the overwhelming debt exacerbated by the recent war.[5] Kuwait, in particular, was a focus of Iraqi pressure. With OPEC in disarray and several nations, including Kuwait, underselling Iraqi oil prices, no amelioration of Iraq's financial situation from the one cash commodity Iraq possessed was likely.

A cost/benefit analysis done from an Iraqi viewpoint would have noted the intensification of the many problems with which Saddam had to deal. Domestically, the failed war could not add to Saddam's regime stability. There was Kurdish separatism, a largely Sunni majority without access to real power, popular discontent with the seemingly pointless war, incessant threats from within the ruling elite to Saddam's rule, and so forth. Internationally, the collapse of other regimes brought problems for Iraq, too. The collapse of potential supporters (actual, when it came to weapons) in Eastern Europe was a new calculus. But there was one problem above all others that joined the two foreign and domestic spheres—money.

Iraq, with its essentially "single crop" oil economy, faced a rapidly deteriorating situation for which no ready solution short of total dependence on foreign grants seemed possible. But Iraq could solve its most pressing domestic and international problem, simple liquidity, by eliminating at one stroke a major creditor, a major competitor on the oil market, a putative poacher of Iraqi oil resources, and an obstacle to its access to the sea. Under the circumstances, these were considerable benefits.

What were the costs likely to be from a "rational" (value-maximizing)

Iraqi viewpoint? There would be outcry and denunciation, but what serious concrete opposition was likely? Certainly the Kuwaiti forces offered no obstacle; nor, for that matter, did Saudi Arabia's forces by themselves or even any likely combination of forces from neighboring states (an Arab–Iranian alliance was and yet remains unlikely). Although eight years of war had taken their toll, Iraq retained the only modern, battle-tested army in the region capable of projecting power beyond its borders. As events in the war demonstrated, the ruling al-Sabah family in Kuwait enjoyed little sympathy in the world's regard, even among Kuwait's Arab neighbors.

Reaction in the West meant the United States. No other nation had the ability to deploy significant power outside its immediate region. What was there for Saddam to fear from America? On paper at least, American did have the capability to deploy significant forces overseas, but what evidence was there of will? Sitting in Baghdad, one could easily downplay or dismiss the two successful projections of American power in recent years, Granada and Panama. Both were carried out near home in the Caribbean against what were essentially small constabulary forces. The other two American interpositions of power to distant lands in the last generation—Vietnam and Lebanon—told quite a different story.

General Giap had pointed out over twenty years earlier, in his tract *Big Victory, Great Task,* that the U.S. people and their will were a "center of gravity" (a Clausewitzian concept to which we shall return) in U.S. military power: Americans would not suffer many casualties on faraway battlefields for obscure causes. More recently and closer to home, from Saddam's viewpoint, an example of characteristic irresolution was the American retreat from Beirut executed by the president for whom George Bush had been understudy. In these two cases, the advantage the United States had over virtually all other nations in the deployment of its power had also been shown to be a means of how that same power could be withdrawn when domestic pressure to do so raised the political costs of a military operation beyond any likely benefit. Both of these examples—U.S. forces deployed at a distance against a determined adversary and the failure of those forces—could strike any detached observer as more relevant than the two backyard operations that succeeded. For someone to whom such an assessment would be extraordinarily convenient and not patently irrational, the temptation to take it as fact must have been overwhelming.

Even if the Americans should want to intervene militarily on behalf of the Kuwaitis, they would still need an unlikely combination of Allies who possessed essential political and military resources. Britain and France had Security Council votes that must be affirmative, Russia had to join as well, and China had to be brought to acquiescence. To this mix there had to be added key Moslem states. Operating bases in either Saudi Arabia or Turkey, more likely in both, were essential to any military response. Saddam can be forgiven if he did not foresee the Coalition that was to be formed against him, unprecedented in its diversity and durability. As it became clear that such a Coalition was, however improbably, forming, there was a potential weapon to vitiate the power of any Western-based, anti-Iraq Coalition. If Saddam could link whatever he did to the Palestinian question and thereby force the West to stand with Israel, he could sow enough doubt to prevail. Even a modest attempt to "eat up half of Israel with fire" would almost certainly see an Arab–Western Coalition go up in smoke. American response to provocation might be problematic; Israel's was not likely to be so. Israel had always responded to attacks or perceived threats (as the ruins of Iraq's Osiraq nascent nuclear facility testified). Finally, if worst came to worst, Saddam could console himself with the thought that no Arab regime that had stood up to the Americans had lost power, regardless of the result.

Of course, it is easy to dismiss all this as post facto arguing from effect to cause. It is true that this is only one of many possible assessments of what Iraq was up to. But it is an assessment that does take into account the benefit—a solution to Iraq's most pressing problem—and weigh against it the likely cost—a small chance of military response against Iraq after a *fait accompli* and a much smaller chance that such a response would be effective. If this seems obvious now, it is notable that there seems to have been nothing like such an assessment, from what we know of public comment or of early actions taken, made by Washington. Clausewitz's focus on ends and means encourages a view from the adversary's perspective.

Using the same sort of analysis on the Coalition powers, is somewhat easier because the purposes of a proposed war to liberate Kuwait and the means to accomplish them were debated in public and at length. The several UN Security Council resolutions, painstakingly developed by U.S. and British urgings, spelled out the political conditions which Saddam would have to meet in order to rejoin fully the community of nations. The withdrawal from Kuwait, renunciation of any future attempt to incorporate Kuwait into Iraq, reparations for damages, release of and accounting for prisoners—all these were reasoned and measurable conditions. A military strategy (the means) to accomplish these resolutions (the ends) could be logically worked out even if costs were to be high. But, of course, the actual agendas of the dominant Coalition partners were somewhat more ambitious than the explicit aims. This was to cause some problems. Among other things, war aims tell a combatant when the culminating point of victory has been reached. If the aims are not clear, neither can the definition of victory be clear; you will not know when to stop fighting. The proper culminating point may be overshot, and this is not only "useless" but "damaging" (*OW*, 570). We will return to this point later.

Throughout the countries of the Coalition, there were a number of tacit aims beyond those in the UN resolutions. The principal Western partners and Iraq's immediate neighbors wanted to be sure that Iraq would lose the capability for continuing attempts at power projection by military force in the region. Certain elements of the U.S. decision-making elite (Britain's too) also wanted to see Saddam himself removed from office. This last was not, nor could it have been, an official UN or Coalition aim. But President Bush made strong enough statements to that effect, most notably his February 15 remarks inviting the Iraqi people to make Saddam "step aside." This seemed to be at least a possible goal for the ground campaign, once that had begun.[6] The role that such a possible expansion of aims had toward encouraging popular support for the war will be considered later.

The uncertainty introduced by statements of Bush and other officials could and did lead to confusion in the popular mind, and among some military as well, about when to end the fighting and how to estimate its results. Nonetheless, there was an essential clarity in the Coalition's explicit war aims—liberate Kuwait and make Iraq account for and compensate victims for Iraqi's transgressions—that aided immensely in both prosecuting the war and holding the Coalition together. These resolutions provided a minimalized set of goals for the war (adherence to them may well have established a precedent for future uses of force under the UN aegis). Expansion of war aims because of military successes, such as occurred in Korea, is something Clausewitz warns about: "The most far-reaching act of judgment that the statesman and commander have to make is to establish ... the kind of war on which they are embarking; neither mistaking it for, nor turning it into, something that is alien to its nature" (OW, 88).

LIMITED AND UNLIMITED WAR

Clausewitz distinguishes between unlimited war—war for a government's overthrow—and limited war—all other cases of war (OW, 75).[7] In the only two instances that the UN has authorized members to conduct large-scale military operations (Korea and now the Gulf), the Security Council has enumerated goals that did not include elimination of the aggressor regime. These precedents make it more likely that only limited wars will be sanctioned by the UN, especially if the aggressor is a significant military power. Unlimited wars for regime change, on the other hand, like the case of Haiti, would be likely only if the UN could muster overwhelming force or perform expertly in the area of diplomacy. Of course, this would work best only with the clear and present threat of military force behind it. The likely problem for future multinational collective security actions by democratic states will come from the strictures of limited war aims. Can governments sensitive to popular pressures sustain wars that are manifestly not crusades?

According to Clausewitz, "The degree of force that must be used against the enemy depends on the scale of political demands on either side. These demands . . . show what efforts each must make" (OW, 585). Of course, these demands are, as Clausewitz noted, never fully known, even for one's own side. If a war is to be limited, in Clausewitz's sense—something less than an effort to defeat the enemy completely—a measured and possibly limited effort is required (OW, 611 and especially 94). This calculated restraint on the use of force will inevitably be subject to countervailing pressures in a participatory society when a populace is aroused for war and demands a conclusive "victory" or, in American rhetoric, "unconditional surrender." This sort of pressure showed up in the Gulf War in the "no blood for oil" critiques leveled particularly at the U.S. administration by its domestic critics.

Given the fact of Kuwait's occupation, the emerging Coalition had first to define the political object, limited or unlimited, that would determine the kind of war to be fought between Iraq and forces ranged against it. Iraq's war against Kuwait, hardly a war at all, had been unlimited since the complete dissolution of the Kuwaiti state was sought and, temporarily at least, achieved, by Saddam. But any war he could fight, with the possible exception of Saudi Arabia and the United Arab Emirates, would have to be a limited war. He had just demonstrated conclusively his inability to project power beyond his borders, let alone overthrow a government. Thus, Saddam was in the position of preparing for a limited war (i.e., merely defending his regime) with the implications that this has for limiting the level of effort, even if that war was to be for his own survival. Saddam did attempt to link his war with the Palestinian question, and he did call for a holy war against Western powers, but these calls amounted to little more than rhetorical flourishes. Saddam could not fight an unlimited war.

The question of limited or unlimited war, then, rested mostly on the side of the Alliance. Unlimited war would mean the complete overthrow of the Iraqi government and, by that, Saddam Hussein's rule. To some degree, that question was settled by the UN Security Council resolutions, which did not call for or sanction such action. Moreover, there was the widely reported reluctance of Iraq's neighbors to see a political vacuum on their borders. Not only was there the problem of an incipient Kurdistan movement, but Sunni-Shia tensions could flare up among Iraqis, spill over into neighboring countries, and be turned into a regional war by Iran. Finally, unlimited war to overthrow an Arab government, no matter how much disliked by other Arab elites, could have a destructive impact—by turning the war into another West versus Arab struggle—on the remarkable Coalition that was essential to success in even a limited war.

Thus, both sides faced the likelihood that if war were chosen, it would be a limited war, one which did not seek the overthrow of any state (assuming that the Kuwaiti invasion would be undone). But political objectives decide the scale of effort, the culminating point of victory, and, overall, the cost/benefit calculus that determines when to fight and when to stop. For a limited war, both sides needed to prepare publics for considerable efforts that would, if successful, produce less than dramatic results.

Clausewitz was arguably the first military theoretician to appreciate the significance of fighting a war for limited aims in the modern state, one that now had an increasing degree of popular participation in political power. His inklings of what this might mean are contained in an idea he never lived to develop fully—the "remarkable trinity": "As a total phenomenon its dominant tendencies always make war a remarkable trinity—composed of primordial violence, hatred, and enmity . . . ; the creative spirit; and subordination [of the creative spirit to] policy [and] . . . reason alone" (*OW*, 89). Clausewitz assigns primordial violence to the people, the creative spirit to the commander and his army, and rational element to the government.

Clausewitz was the first theoretician to recognize that passion in the populace and not just in the army is an essential ingredient of modern war (*OW*, 88). It is no longer merely the sport of kings. The challenge, then, for both the commander and the government is to engage these primordial passions to garner support for what may often be less than inspiring political goals.

Saddam Hussein was and remains the undisputed leader of his nation and the source of real political power. Even so, he needed some degree of popular acquiescence to further sacrifices after the long war with Iran, which had produced little political result (and which exigencies of the new confrontation soon forced him to give away). Clausewitz summarizes his notion of the "remarkable trinity" by proclaiming that his goal is to develop a theory that "maintains a balance between these three tendencies" (*OW*, 88) (popular passion, governmental policy, and the commander's creativity). For Saddam, who essentially embodied two of these aspects, the challenge of finding a balance was thereby easier, but he still needed to keep the popular passion satisfied. This necessity circumscribed the amount of political maneuvering he could afford once he realized that the occupation of Kuwait was something that George Bush, for one, would not let stand. Reminiscent of Napoleon's complaint to Metternich, Saddam had to keep winning or appearing to win in order to maintain his legitimacy. There were few face- (and regime)-saving ways he could extricate himself from Kuwait. One possibility he did try, though unsuccessfully: linking a withdrawal from Kuwait to a Coalition promise to consider the Palestinian question.

The problem President Bush and the other Coalition leaders faced was orders of magnitude more complicated. Each of the states had its own political agenda, and each had its own populace with particular "passions" that had to be aroused, appeased, or otherwise manipulated. First, the Western Allies had to convince skeptical publics that a shooting war might be worthwhile or even necessary. This had to be done in such a way that it did not collide with the passions of the Arab states' publics about Western and infidel colonialism and imposition of alien ways (like the boundaries of the Arab states in question, as Saddam was wont to remind them).

Then, of course, the Russian public, newly involved in the political process, had to be convinced that their leaders were going along out of something other than abject surrender to a triumphalist capitalist world. China had its own way of dealing with popular sentiments.

In the domestic rhetoric and reportage of the Coalition participants, virtually every variety of competing popular passion—this nation's interest against that nation's—was raised. In this light, the restraint and simplicity of the UN-endorsed political objectives for "any measures necessary" seem all the more appropriate. A Coalition overthrow of the Iraqi regime or elimination of Saddam, an "unlimited war," may not have led to disaster, but the cautionary tone of Clausewitz's writings about war aims and their deliberate, dispassionate formulation suggests that it may have. To repeat, the statesperson and commander must ensure that they do not, through inappropriate aims, try to turn a particular war into something that is alien to its nature.

SUSPENSION IN WAR

The period of Coalition buildup after the invasion and before the air strikes deserves some comment. Clausewitz has a good deal to say about the element of time in war necessarily only favoring one side (*OW*, Book I, Chap. 1; Book III, chap. 3). How did this factor play out in Desert Shield and Desert Storm? Nearly eight months elapsed between the time Iraqi tanks rolled across the border into Kuwait and Coalition air strikes began on Baghdad. On whose "side" was time during this period? According to Clausewitz, because each side has differing and conflicting political purposes, a standstill which favors both sides is a logical impossibility (*OW*, 216). Since an aggressor necessarily has a positive (if not good) aim, positive action is proper to him, *whereas* the defender must try to stop the ongoing actions of the aggressor. Applied to the actions of Saddam in taking Kuwait, this means that suspension of action on his part marks the farthest extent of what he will accomplish through military means. Clausewitz's analysis holds that delay can only favor one side, usually the defender. If we assume that Saddam was behaving rationally throughout (i.e., value maximizing), then his actions of stopping with the occupation of Kuwait make more sense and, retrospectively, we can see what his principal aim may have been.

One of the early questions about Saddam's action is why he did not have his forces continue to the then vulnerable oil fields of Saudi Arabia and then withdraw after damaging them to limit their output and drive up the price of oil—his included—because of the specific action and nervousness about supplies in general. A merely punitive war to punish Iraq for such a raid would be hard to imagine. If, however, Saddam's aim was to solve an immediate and overwhelming liquidity problem, then the taking of Kuwait and Kuwait alone is rational. For afterward, as he indeed did, he may shift to a defensive posture and use the captured territory as a bargaining issue. Clausewitz observes that

> once . . . the political object has been achieved; there is no need to do more. . . . If the other state is ready to accept the situation, it should sue for peace. If not, it must do something; and if it thinks it will be better organized for action [later] it clearly has an adequate reason for not taking action at once.
> But *from that moment on* [the later moment when it is better organized] logic would seem to call for action by the other side. (*OW*, 82–83, emphasis added)

This seems to be a point on which all can agree. Saddam, though behaving rationally, miscalculated.[8] He had not planned enough moves ahead to deal effectively with a Coalition against him if one should emerge. This can be understood if he thought the odds of an effective one forming were slight, but it has the aura of wishing one's problems away, and wishful thinking does not accord with Saddam's previous record of political maneuvering.

As noted earlier, there were efforts by Saddam to take action after the Coalition began to form. These actions of expanding war aims, and perhaps adding allies or at least detaching some countries from the Coalition, all had an improvisatory nature that belied careful *planning*. Or Saddam simply could have miscalculated. He seems to have earlier underestimated the nature of the task in his attack on Iran. Clausewitz concludes the previously cited passage (*OW*, 82–83) by noting that his assumption is that both sides understand the situation perfectly. In life, as in chess, there are penalties for those who do not or cannot afford to think several moves ahead. Whatever Saddam's reasons for military action, the capture of Kuwait marked the limit of what he could conceivably accomplish through that special kind of politics, "politics, with the addition of other means." He now had to wait for reaction.

From the Coalition viewpoint, time was a factor as well. President Bush and others clearly took the view that time was working against the Coalition. First, there was concern because of the time it would take to get anything more than a tripwire force in place to protect Saudi oil fields. Once a credible defense was in place, time remained a negative factor for the Allies since it was they who now had the requirement for action to undo what Saddam had done. The approach of Ramadan and the intense heat of summer were certainly spurs to an early resolution of issues. The European Clausewitz, even though he had been on Kutuzov's retreat into Russia in 1812, thought that weather, with the exception of actual and not metaphoric fog, was rarely a factor in war. The biggest argument for resolution of the matter sooner rather than later, however, was the fragility of the Coalition. It was unprecedented Arab–Western, U.S.–Russian, cooperation, and no one could be sure how long it would last. Time, in terms of suspension of action, favored the Allies in the short run but favored Saddam in the long run. The Coalition powers' actions showed that its leaders thought this way—thus the "artificial" pressure of Security Council Resolution deadlines.

This notion of suspension favoring only one side clearly counters modern crisis resolution methods and is one of the reasons Clausewitz tends to drift out of fashion. *On War,* taken as a whole, is cautionary about using military force because this is the chanciest of all ways of achieving political goals. Clausewitz, who admired Machiavelli for calling things by their proper names, was determined to dispel illusions that suspension of action can work to both sides' benefit.[9]

FRICTION

Once the brief war had concluded, it was easy and somewhat commonplace to observe in retrospect that there was really no military challenge for the Coalition. But the Allies were right to be wary of an easy victory, even through airpower. Most of the Western commanders were versed in some of the basic Clausewitzian precepts; these had become a staple in greater or lesser detail in virtually all higher military educational institutions.[10] One of the most important contributions in the area of operations was Clausewitz's elaboration on the concept he called "friction." Things not only can go wrong; they must necessarily do so to some degree, for this is the nature of the phenomenon of actual war. Only in a Kantian or Platonic world of ideal forms is there perfection; the world of reality is a world of accidents, not essences. If Clausewitz's grounding in Greek philosophy led him to no other contributions to the study of war, this one might have been enough. Again, this may seem an obvious point; Murphy's law is common military lore. But post-Clausewitzian war making, from the Schlieffen Plan to some of the more enthusiastic press briefings for this or that system, suggests that there persists a large body of those who believe that this time everything will go right.

The bulk of what Clausewitz referred to in his concept of friction with its four constituents—danger, physical effort, intelligence (or its absence), and chance—has to do with operational matters, dealt with in other accounts.[11] But one aspect of friction—intelligence (or its absence, "uncertainty," as Clausewitz puts it)—clearly permeates all activities of war right up to the strategy/policy level. In the Gulf War, the lack of intelligence, which includes every sort of information about the enemy and its country, played a significant part in decisions for going to war and estimates about the way the war would be best fought (*OW,* 117).

On the Iraqi side, there were at least four major areas of intelligence shortcoming for Saddam. He had no personal knowledge of the West, which meant that, among other things, he was unlikely to appreciate where

Iraq and its activities stood on the list of the Bush administration's concerns. He took an accommodationist U.S. policy bred of preoccupation with events in Eastern Europe and the Soviet Union for a tacit recognition of his strength. The breakup of the Soviet empire meant to him largely the loss of weaponry and support. He could little be expected to see it in terms of a paradigm shift in international relations that would claim Washington's major attention—that would lead, for instance, to a search for a "new world order." The dissolution of the second world also had another impact on Saddam in the area of intelligence. He no longer had the sources about what was going on in the West that he once did.

The third intelligence failure was an even more dangerous one in that Saddam seemed to think he knew something that was not so. He had just fought an adversary with modern equipment but without real airpower. He had not, however, fought a first-class adversary with airpower. He had the makings of a modern Soviet equipped air defense system but no real experience in using it—he would have to get it right the first time against the most modern air force in the world.

Finally, there is the intelligence failure that should have been the least likely to happen. Even to the surprise of many in the West, Saddam's calls for terrorist campaigns and/or *jihad* fell flat. Perhaps he knew this would be so and was taking a course of desperation, hoping something might happen. But the failure of any significant response worked against him because it only served to highlight his isolation.

The Coalition had problems with friction in its intelligence, too. Saddam misread the strength of his appeal to Arab militants and Arab mass anti-Western sentiments, but his Arab neighbors were guilty of an even greater misestimate of what Saddam had in mind. Gaining objective intelligence assessments that are free of the self-imposed constraints of providing what political authorities want to hear is hard enough when only one country is involved. The problem compounds when countries of diverse outlooks, not completely trusting one another, attempt to share and integrate assessments. If the United States had misread Saddam's true nature, so had neighbors, who, by affinity, propinquity, and necessity, ought to have been much more attuned to what Baghdad was up to.

Intelligence problems even at the operational level had political ramifications. The Scud missiles launched at Israel turned out to be one of Saddam's potentially most powerful weapons. Yet even with complete control of the air and the United States' vaunted "national technical means of verification," it is still not certain whether any mobile Scud launchers were successfully located and destroyed. Compliance inspections conducted by UN teams after the war also indicate that much of Iraq's nuclear materials production capacity remained undetected. This is not to fault Coalition intelligence efforts, which were better than in previous wars, but it does reinforce the Clausewitzian notion of the inevitability of friction—that is, things that will not be known, regardless of technological development. Even when information is known, there remains the friction problem of disseminating intelligence to field commanders in a timely enough fashion to be useful in ongoing operations.

One other aspect of the problem of friction deserves mention: the problem of friendly fire casualties. Although Clausewitz does not mention this problem specifically—it would take too many volumes, says Clausewitz, to cover all the difficulties that the rubric of friction encompasses—it is clearly an inevitable consequence of war. This problem was exacerbated by real-time reportage of events (if usually in a narrowly limited portion of the action, with little or no context). Tabloid-style interviews with grieving relatives brought into everyone's home this saddest of the mischances of war. Clausewitz may have foreseen such possibilities of modern media when he noted that "every fault . . . is instantly exposed in war" (*OW*, 119). America's own history of war is replete with examples of self-inflicted casualties; two of the three American lieutenant generals killed in action, Stonewall Jackson and Leslie J. McNair, were killed by their own side, and one out of nine U.S. subs sunk in the Pacific in World War II were sunk by American torpedoes (two by their own). It is one of the ironies of modern superaccurate weapons that since they so often hit what they are aimed at, even if equally sophisticated systems are available to distinguish friend from foe, the incidence of friendly fire accidents persists. Precision-guided munitions and the electronic battlefield have not eliminated friction.

Although Clausewitz's concept of friction holds that lack of intelligence is inevitable, deciding what constitutes the heart of the enemy's ability to wage war is still a task that must be performed using what information is available. Since war is an act of force to compel the enemy to do your will, the force must somehow be made manifest to that enemy to achieve its effect. Thus, a nation's center of gravity must at some point make itself known in the act of entering on military operations, despite feints and misdirections. Mistakes in determining a center of gravity thus are likely to come from misassessment of the facts one has rather than from ignorance of facts one does not have.

CENTER OF GRAVITY

One of the more important contributions of Clausewitz to thinking on war grows from his emphasis on the importance of political objectives dictating military means. To achieve victory in war is to remove the particular "other means" which the adversary has added to its repertoire of political activity and return interstate relations to nonviolent politics. In the modern state, war was no longer a game to be played for a sovereign's reputation or other intangibles, although it could still wrongly revert to such a thing. One thinks of the attempt to capture capital cities by Napoleon in 1812 and both sides in the American Civil War. War was merely the means to get the enemy to do your will (or prevent the enemy from doing its will). The best way to do this was to destroy the enemy's ability to use these other or violent means in its politics. Clausewitz again borrowed a physics metaphor and likened this ability of the enemy to use force to a center of gravity on which all movement and power depended. It is against such a center of gravity that "all our energies should be directed" (OW, 595–96). This center is usually (but not always, as we shall see) the army of the adversary. In the Gulf War, then, what were these centers of gravity?

Since Iraq was in the war on its own, its center of gravity was clearly its military forces. But further examination of so obvious a point is necessary. One of the first issues was whether or not Saddam Hussein was the real center of gravity. Certainly, many advanced the notion that to eliminate him was to eliminate the source of his problems—public speculation on this point even cost one general officer his career. But was this true? We cannot know for sure, but if Saddam were removed, the capability for mischief from Iraq, as well as most of the conditions that prompted that mischief, remain. A Saddam successor would inevitably come from Saddam's coterie. Why should such a person be much different from Saddam? That regional stability would likely improve is a view that the Iranian revolution in 1978, if nothing else, should have discouraged.

If it is not Saddam Hussein, then is the Iraqi military the center of gravity for Iraq? This, indeed, is the center of gravity, but it is not the military as a whole. Rather, it is those aspects of the military that gave Iraq an opportunity to cause problems for its neighbors: its power projection capability that constitute the center of gravity. Much of the Iraqi military's efforts, after all, were involved with trying to establish internal order in various fractious regions of Iraq. Two parts of the army did represent real threats to neighboring states, however: the elite Republican Guard divisions and the Scud missile batteries. An Iraq unable to bring power to bear beyond its borders is no longer an imminent threat.

Certainly, Coalition leaders recognized the importance of these parts of Saddam's military: The air campaigns before and during the ground action were, ultimately, focused on these targets. But both proved, in the end, hard to isolate and destroy. The problem of the Scud launchers was one that caused redirection of air sorties away from army units, including the Republican Guard. During the ground campaign, that same Guard which had deployed behind the conscript troops (whether to be a strategic reserve or to be better positioned for escape, we cannot know for sure) did avoid the kind of decimation visited on other Iraqi units.

I do not mean to suggest that the Allies failed to defeat militarily the Iraqi forces. But the survival of these two forces, or centers of gravity, for so long under the most adverse conditions may provide part of the explanation for why Saddam was able to survive politically. In this respect, it is helpful to keep in mind one of Clausewitz's first dicta, that no result in war is ever final: "The defeated state often considers the outcome merely as a transitory evil, for which a remedy may still be found in political conditions at some later date" (*OW*, 80). Finally, regarding the Iraqi center of gravity, it must be remembered that UN sanctions have been largely transferred to the Iraqi civilian public. The Scuds are gone (we think), but the Republican Guard retains more of its capabilities than it is comfortable to think.

On the Allied side, it seems obvious that the center of gravity was the overwhelming and modern force ranged against Iraq. But this was not necessarily so. If it had been, only a madman would have thought to fight against it. If the center of gravity were something else, more susceptible to the power Saddam did have, then his resistance to Coalition pressure to withdraw from Kuwait looks like a shrewder move than he was given credit for. Here Clausewitz has an observation that is uncannily apposite: "Among alliances, it [the center of gravity] lies in the community of interest" (*OW*, 596). If this is correct, then Saddam did not have to achieve a military defeat of the Alliance. Rather, he had to divide the Alliance's community of interest. That is precisely what he tried to do with his calls to make the war a Moslem–Christian holy war, or a West and Israel versus Arab war with the Palestinian issue at the center. As noted earlier, however, he did not seem to put the care into developing this effort that it would have warranted—another fortunate miscalculation for the Coalition. The rewards to Saddam for more preparation and perhaps conciliation could have been considerable.

The "remarkable trinity" (*OW*, 89) of war includes the notion that the passions of the people are as integral to the element of violent means in war as is the leadership's rational calculation to the political object. If the popular "passion" is dampened or turned against the war effort, as with the United States in Vietnam, or directed by members of a Coalition against each other, then a key aspect of military power is lost. When Clausewitz speaks of destroying the enemy's forces, he takes pains to emphasize that he is not limiting this idea to physical forces; "the moral element must also be considered" (*OW*, 97). Suppose that skillful anti-Western propaganda had forced either Turkey's or Saudi Arabia's government to refuse permission for use of their bases for operation against Iraq. Even if it had been the lesser problem of Turkey denying use of the Incirlik base, Iraq would not have had a two-front war and two possible domestic insurrections to worry about and could have made more effective force deployments. The absence of Saudi bases would have made a ground campaign all but impossible, except for amphibious assault at an obvious location. The "community of interests" among Coalition members, however fragile, was clearly a center of gravity. Any weakening or obfuscation of the several UN resolutions that did allow military measures would have made U.S.

action much more difficult to sell to the Congress or the American people. There is a lesson here for future aggressors, perhaps even Saddam at some later date, on where to focus efforts.

CULMINATING POINT OF VICTORY

The next question became when to stop the shooting. As Clausewitz suggests, there is not always an obvious answer. The concept of a point beyond which the commander should not press his attack, even though it is successful, is introduced in Book 4, Chapter 7 and Book 7, Chapter 5 as an operational principle; but by Chapter 22 of the latter book, Clausewitz has raised the culminating point of victory to a principle of war itself (*OW*, 570). Not to overshoot the target is the responsibility of the commander and political leaders in war. This idea is fully in accord with Clausewitz's admonitions to keep military action always at the service of political goals. Moreover, Clausewitz speculated that most future wars would be limited. A culminating point in victory would naturally recur in "every future war." In future wars, though—which Clausewitz seems to think would be like the unprecedentedly large-scale wars in which he had fought—the destruction of the enemy would probably not be the military aim. Limited aims would be necessary to maintain political coherence in the bloodier wars he foresaw.

Saddam did stop his forces after they had occupied Kuwait, though nearby Saudi oil fields remained vulnerable for many weeks thereafter. Was this, as earlier statements had suggested, his culminating point of victory? Perhaps in the short term it was, but in retrospect it seems that he could have accomplished much of what he sought, not by continuing to occupy Kuwait, but by establishing a compliant or puppet regime and withdrawing Iraqi forces. Again, as with his calls to expand war aims, Saddam made a half-hearted effort to establish such a regime, but it amounted to little. By remaining in place in Kuwait, Saddam's forces presented a clear target for focusing political reaction. As Clausewitz notes, "Experience goes to show that such reactions [to insufficient or unculminated uses of force] have completely disproportionate effects" (*OW*, 570). The likelihood that the force of reaction will be an increase over that force to which it responds is a point made elsewhere in the notion of war tending to extremes (*OW*, 77). Saddam did not withdraw, and thus there was the problem of determining the culminating point of victory for the Coalition forces in the ensuing war.

The Coalition had two political goals—liberate Kuwait and reduce Iraq's capability for power projection, including the ability to make weapons of mass destruction. The first was relatively easy and measurable; the second goal proved somewhat more problematic. The final chapter about the controversies surrounding the endgame of Desert Storm is still to be written— American pilots refusing to fly missions of aerial slaughter along the "highway of death" leading out of Kuwait, the escape of Republican Guard units, General Schwarzkopf's admission of being fooled by the Iraqis on the use of helicopters, the decision to halt fighting after exactly 100 hours of ground war, and so on.

The point is that the second goal, eliminating the ability to make weapons of mass destruction, was less official and less measurable than the first and almost certain to lead to confusion about what the culminating point of victory should be. This is precisely why Clausewitz insists that political goals should be as clear as circumstances permit, should be dominant over operational concerns, and should not be changed, especially in the "fog of war." It is not that there was a better time or better circumstance under which to conclude military operations. There may have been, but any conclusion short of destruction of Iraq as a political entity was bound to leave loose ends. Especially for Americans, more comfortable with goals of "unconditional surrender" of enemies, the inescapable messiness of concluding a limited war is a lesson still hard to learn.

CONCLUSION

Clausewitz was the first to say that principles and theories he put forth were no sure recipe for success in war. A cookbook approach or "war by geometry" was a chimera. His study and insights, however, were meant to educate the mind of the commander (who could be a singular or collective entity, but essentially an entity which embodies both strategic and political visions), or, more accurately, to guide the commander in self-education, "not to accompany him to the battlefield" (OW, 141). If a theory of war did no more than remind us of important elements, it would still be useful. If we piece together Clausewitz's theories about the phenomenon of war and its various components—that is, accept his general postulate about the relationship of war and politics and add his other pioneering insights—we have the best beginning of that education.

To begin, wars have, or should have, a clear political purpose, and that purpose subordinates all military considerations. From that purpose, a cost/benefit analysis can be made and used as a benchmark to measure the war's progress or lack of it. The "remarkable trinity" reminds us of the balance of reason, passion, and creativity that is necessary throughout the conduct of the war. This balancing of reason and passion is especially difficult when a war, as most wars in the nuclear age will be, is fought for limited political aims. Suspension or delay in taking action is a characteristic that will particularly beset coalition operations where the various members have different agendas, styles of action, and degrees of trusting one another. The concept of friction alone, if no other principle did so, ratifies Clausewitz's continuing relevance. A worldwide audience watching CNN's real-time reporting saw friction operating in the Gulf War (even if not at the Coalition press briefings). All the modern technologies and advances have only shifted the locus of its most irritating operation, not removed it. The concept of center of gravity is one of several areas we can regret that Clausewitz never developed at length. Yet even in this Clausewitz's basic observations are all too often overlooked, simple as they are.

Finally, knowing what is or ought to be the culminating point of victory may prove the hardest task of all. Ever since World War II, American political and military leaders have been faced with trying to cope with a world that is too dangerous to allow wars to be fought as crusades that end with triumphal marches through a defeated capital. Indeed, the Truman–MacArthur controversy over political aims, the subservience of strategy to policy in Korea, embodied this collision of the old order with the new. Edward Luttwak's *Strategy* highlights this Clausewitzian notion of reciprocal and paradoxical action.[12] The more dramatically a victory is proclaimed, the greater the impetus of the defeated to redress the result. As noted earlier, Clausewitz fully understood that results in war are never final.

There is much more in Clausewitz that can be applied profitably toward an understanding or analysis of the Gulf War. The whole area of military genius and the qualities and actions of the commanders are worth the considerable study that has already begun. The matter of subordination of strategy to policy (or competing policies) will certainly need greater examination, especially after more details become public. Nonetheless, the purpose of this chapter has been to demonstrate how the corpus of Clausewitzian thought can be used profitably to understand the phenomena that have occurred and, for future commanders and state leaders, to understand better what may occur. Emphasis must be placed on using Clausewitz, not for individual nuggets or aphorisms, but for his whole framework, a coherent and interrelated body of thought about the nature of war.

Bernard Brodie, in his essay "The Continuing Relevance of *On War*" in the Paret/Howard translation, makes two points about Clausewitz's work worth repeating (*OW*, 45–58). First, Clausewitz really did get down, as no one else had before, the fundamentals of war and its essence—namely, it is a violent act toward the accomplishment of political goals. No treatise on war in itself or on techniques of warfare is comparable. Second, no one since has supplanted or enlarged on Clausewitz's breadth and depth of understanding.

Too often, there is a temptation to hold *On War* so difficult and arcane as only to be mined for nuggets of insight. But, as, Clausewitz tells us in his comment on the genesis of *On War,* he developed an entire theory which, departing from the original intention to set forth a series of observations without a specific system or formal connections, would eventually draw together causal connections from Clausewitz's earlier works as well as later analyses (i.e., those in *On War*) into one conclusion, producing in the end "a reasonable whole" (*OW*, 63). Other works are certainly useful in shaping and filling in details that aid understanding of his work. But Clausewitz's thought on the nature of war, taken whole in his magnum opus, is the place to start. Perhaps because it is so cautionary when taken whole, *On War* is more favored in smaller doses by those who must rouse others to action.

Reviewing the few themes selected, it may seem simple (Clausewitz even tells us it will seem so) to apply these ideas to analysis, but evidence shows that all too often in the fog of crisis or actual war, this is not done—this or that factor is overlooked or dismissed. On recognition of this inevitable frictional tendency, forgetting under stress, the great strategist shall have the last word: "Everything in war is very simple, but the simplest thing is difficult" (*OW*, 119).

NOTES

1. Among the books worth noting are Colonel Harry G. Summers, Jr., *On Strategy II: A Critical Analysis of the Gulf War* (New York: Dell, 1992); Lawrence Freedman and Efraim Karsh, *The Gulf Conflict 1990–1991: Diplomacy and War in the New World Order* (Princeton, N.J.: Princeton University Press, 1993); and Rick Atkinson, *Crusade: The Untold Story of the Gulf War* (New York: Houghton Mifflin, 1993). Paul Wolfowitz's review of *Crusade*, "Victory Came Too Easily," *National Interest* 35 (Spring 1994), also provides an insider's viewpoint. Eliot Cohen's review essay on extant books on the Gulf War "Tales of the Desert," *Foreign Affairs* 73, no. 3 (May/June 1994), suggests that a forthcoming book by General Bernard Trainor will be an important addition to this literature.

2. Unless otherwise stated, all references to Clausewitz's thought and to *On War* (*OW*) are from Carl von Clausewitz, *On War*, eds. and trans. Michael Howard and Peter Paret (Princeton, N.J.: Princeton University Press, 1976).

3. But see also Michael I. Handel, *Sun Tzu and Clausewitz Compared* (Carlisle Barracks, Pa.: Strategic Studies Institute, 1991) for an alternative view on Clausewitz's level of analysis: "While Sun Tzu is, for the most part, concerned with the conduct of war on the highest strategic level, Clausewitz is primarily concerned with the lower strategic operational levels of warfare" (p. 10). There is much operational warfare analysis in *On War* (Books IV–VII), but, by his own account, that is not the gravamen Clausewitz intended in his magnum opus. Sun Tzu is enjoying something of a vogue, perhaps more than that, in military education circles. For instance, the Navy's new *Naval Doctrine Publication 1* (Washington, D.C., 1994) invokes Sun Tzu on the now preferred style of maneuver warfare. Clausewitz's work is mentioned only as a suggested follow-on reading. My contention is that Clausewitz deserves primary and continuing consideration because of his overall conception linking war and the modern state and the comprehensive, if unfinished, framework of his thinking.

4. The author has been political–military analyst for WHDH-TV (CBS) in Boston since 1989 and had daily access to press services from many countries concerning the events leading up to and including Desert Storm. The accuracy of any

press reports from the several countries of the Coalition, here and elsewhere referred to, is not argued. The mere fact that stories of varying motives and aims among the Coalition members circulated publicly created the atmosphere in which national leaders made decisions and sought public support.

5. See, especially, Freedman and Karsh, *Gulf Conflict,* chapters 2 and 3 on this point.

6. Ibid., 412.

7. The note Clausewitz wrote on revising his text is one of the clearer statements of the idea of the two kinds of war: limited and unlimited. Most of his explicit discussion of the two kinds of war occurring in the later portions of *On War* has to do with unlimited war (in terms of political object), but his observations elsewhere show he had both sides of this duality in mind. On Clausewitz's use of dualities, note the comments on his method, see *OW,* 517 and 523.

8. It is worth recalling that Clausewitz never pretends to offer a theory for eliminating miscalculation or simple mistake. Indeed, his friction metaphor asserts that such is inevitable.

9. Peter Paret and Daniel Moran, eds. and trans., *Carl von Clausewitz: Historical and Political Writings* (Princeton, N.J.: Princeton University Press, 1992). This work, along with Peter Paret, *Clausewitz and the State* (New York: Oxford University Press, 1976), is extremely useful for shedding light on Clausewitz's world and educational grounding and his other writings, which show the growth of ideas set forth in *On War.*

10. On the study of Clausewitz in the English-speaking world prior to World War II, see the excellent study by Christopher Bassford, *Clausewitz in English: The Reception of Clausewitz in Britain and America, 1815–1945* (New York: Oxford University Press, 1994).

11. The subject of friction is treated specifically in Book I, Chapters 4–7, but references to the working of this tendency are found throughout *On War.*

12. Edward Luttwak, *Strategy: The Logic of War and Peace* (Cambridge, Mass.: Belknap Press, 1987), emphasizes the idea of reciprocal action in war that Clausewitz introduces in Book I, Chapter 1, passim, and the paradox of success containing the seeds of failure. This latter point is in the spirit of the "culminating point of victory."

13

A New Covenant?: The Apostles of Douhet and the Persian Gulf War
Caroline F. Ziemke

The forty-three–day air campaign against Iraq during the Persian Gulf War of January–February 1991 came as close as any has to date to a textbook application of airpower in a non-nuclear conflict.[1] In its planning, if not always its execution, the military and civilian architects of the Persian Gulf air war conformed to most of the accepted principles of airpower. Although political constraints were certainly present (as they should have been), they were neither excessive nor capricious. Air forces from all Service branches operated under a single Joint Forces Air Component Commander (JFACC). The daily air tasking orders provided blueprints for air operations, which included most of the available air assets on any given day and ensured, at least, that the right hand knew what the left was doing. The net result was an air campaign that could concentrate air forces at the decisive point, focusing effort on strategic targets early in the war and shifting to preparing the battlefield as the ground campaign drew near. Airpower may not have operated as a seamless web, but the lines between tactical and strategic airpower blurred. Tactical aircraft flew strategic missions; strategic aircraft flew operational missions.

Nonetheless, airpower in the Gulf War was not sufficiently seamless to forestall continuing debate over the relative decisiveness of strategic versus tactical air operations. As has every U.S. air campaign since World War II, the air war against Iraq had several distinct aspects: the strategic air campaign, the air superiority campaign, degradation of the Republican Guard and Iraqi forces in the Kuwait theater of operations (KTO), and air support of the ground offensive. The first phase consisted of a strategic bombardment campaign conducted according to classic airpower theory, which targeted Iraq's national command authority; nuclear, biological, and chemical capabilities; fixed Scud missile sites; air bases; military storage and production facilities; and so forth. The three other phases consisted of operational and tactical strikes against Iraqi military forces in the KTO, reinforcements and lines of communication between Iraq and the KTO, and mobile Scud sites. For most of the war, the various phases of the air war operated concurrently, although the strategic phase dominated operations in the opening days of the war and gradually shifted toward increasing emphasis on battlefield preparation as the war progressed. On the first day of the air campaign, roughly 66 percent of "shooter" sorties were directed against strategic targets, largely outside the KTO. By G-Day (day 39 of the air campaign, day 1 of the ground campaign), the Coalition air campaign directed about 82 percent of sorties against operational targets within the KTO, flying only 12 percent of its missions against strategic targets deep in Iraq.[2]

During and immediately after the war, it looked to many military analysts as though the decades-long debate over the efficacy of strategic bombing theory might be over. Theory, it seemed, had met reality with stunning results. Never before has the United States, or any other power in modern times, secured so decisive a military defeat, so quickly, with so few casualties and so little collateral damage. Few would argue with the contention that airpower contributed mightily to that outcome. Among those analysts who come down on the side of revolution is a subgroup that sees the victory over Iraq as the ultimate vindication of concepts of air warfare that date back as far as the 1920s.

The airpower option had many outspoken advocates before the war. Most of these prewar advocates—including General Michael Dugan, whose public speculation concerning airpower's role in the war to come led to his firing as Air Force chief of staff in October 1990—were relatively temperate in their postwar pronouncement. Like Dugan, they generally warned that Desert Storm, while a triumph, was the "last war," the circumstances of which would never be repeated.[3] A few, however, offered a harder-line, more "Douhetan" assessment. One of the more outspoken of the new Douhetans has been Edward N. Luttwak, who suggested shortly after the war ended that Desert Storm demonstrated that air warfare had "finally recovered the lost qualities of Air Power that Douhet, Mitchell, Trenchard and the other theorists of the 1920s had taken for granted" and that, as a result, "the promise of 'victory through air power' was finally redeemed in the Iraq air war, after a 70-year detour through competitively increasing speeds, tentative acquisition and often gross imprecision in delivery."[4] Air Force Chief of Staff General Merrill A. McPeak declared at war's end that the Gulf War marked "the first time in history that a field army has been defeated by airpower."[5] Richard P. Hallion, Chief of the Office of Air Force History, put it most directly: "Simply (if boldly) stated, air power won the Gulf War."[6] In the wake of the Persian Gulf War, it seemed that a new set of apostles had emerged to declare that airpower had at last fulfilled its promise as an invincible tool of U.S. policy that could go anywhere to hit any target and against which there would be no defense.

This new promise of airpower was particularly reassuring in the wake of communism's collapse, as the United States began retreating from its Cold War network of forward military bases in Europe and the Pacific and set off on the long, painful process of military restructuring and downsizing. The Air Force embraced this new view of airpower's potential in a new strategic vision that then secretary of the Air Force labeled "Global Reach, Global Power": With enough B-2s, the current fleet of F-117s, and a few dozen F-22s a year, the Air Force could reach out and touch anyone, anywhere, anytime, without forward basing, and with minimal support from surface forces. For the Air Force, the Persian Gulf strategic bombing campaign fitted perfectly its image of conflict, the movies that run through airmen's minds when they think about war.[7] They became our movies too: daily video spectacles of PGMs flying into the front door of the Iraqi defense ministry and down the air shafts of hardened aircraft shelters. At the least, it seemed that airpower had achieved a new primacy as a result of a war that Luttwak characterized as "90 percent bombing and 10 percent ground combat."[8]

Three years later, the euphoria of the immediate postwar period seems almost naive. The outcome of the war looks more ambiguous: Saddam Hussein is still in power, and the United Nations is still battling to shut down Iraq's nuclear, biological, and chemical weapons programs. The role of airpower also seems less clear cut. Even the Department of the Air Force's own Gulf War Airpower Survey stopped short of declaring the first defeat of a ground army by air forces and relegated the strategic bombing campaign to a supporting, not a decisive, role. Regarding Douhet, the jury is still out. Rumors of the death of the Vietnam syndrome were also greatly exaggerated. Success in the Persian Gulf has not translated into greater flexibility in employing U.S. military force in crises abroad.

Airpower advocates have proven unable to translate their stunning success in the Gulf War into an advantage in the battle for shrinking defense resources. Predictions that the outcome of the Gulf War would bring an end to balanced forces and was the harbinger of an airpower–intensive twenty-first–century force structure and military strategy have not, thus far, proved accurate. Some analysts have seen that outcome as the product of institutional inertia and a general unwillingness in both military and civilian circles to challenge the status quo. Others see more sinister forces at work. Luttwak, for one, attributes the failure to restructure U.S. forces to a "sleight of hand" in which former Joint Chiefs of Staff Chairman General Colin Powell, and others, "evoke[d] the Gulf War . . . for realism" and then "quietly replaced[d] it with the planned war that was never fought, and base[d] the required forces on the latter rather than the former."[9]

Although institutional forces are clearly at work, the inability of airpower advocates to cash in the political capital of a popular and successful war and effect a dramatic realignment of U.S. military strategy and capabilities may be due, at least in part, to weaknesses that have plagued the airpower movement since its inception. The problem may be intellectual. From its earliest years, airpower has been less a capability than a concept. As a result, the debate over its relative decisiveness has always taken on the character of philosophical discourse, thinly disguised as operational analysis. In particular, the body of post–Desert Storm literature that falls under the general rubric of "Douhet was right after all" shares three important and potentially misleading characteristics with its World War II, Korean, and Vietnam predecessors. First, such assessments generally lack a sense of the historical context in which the airpower theorists emerged and thus fail to distinguish the meat of their theory from the political hyperbole. Second, those who declared after the Gulf War that airpower was either vindicated or on the verge of becoming so erred in underestimating the contribution of airpower to operational success in the past. It is not, after all, necessary that air forces *alone* win wars for them to be an indispensable and potentially decisive military instrument. Finally, in the escalating debates over its relative decisiveness, the term *airpower* is too often treated, by supporters and detractors alike, as synonymous with strategic bombardment. This is no accident; that airpower is indivisible, a seamless web, is a vital part of its theology. In the minds of its advocates, it is not possible to separate strategic bombing from airpower; all legitimate employments of offensive air forces (battlefield interdiction and offensive strike) are variations on strategic bombardment concepts. In a sense, the rhetorical inflexibility of most airpower advocates has undermined the credibility of their concepts. By allowing airpower to become synonymous with strategic bombing, they raise the stakes in the debate; either airpower wins wars and is thus decisive, or it does not and is not.

THE PROMISE OF AIRPOWER

The basic concepts of airpower theory have deep historical roots in military philosophy. In 500 B.C., the Chinese military philosopher Sun Tzu identified three key contributors to military success: concentration of force, swiftness, and flexibility. "Where he concentrates," Sun Tzu wrote, "prepare against him; where he is strong, avoid him. . . . Keep him under a strain and wear him down."[10] As if predicting the political and military pressures that drove campaign planning for the Persian Gulf War in 1991,

Sun Tzu warned that "victory is the main object of war. If this is long delayed, weapons are blunted and morale depressed." Military strategy should thus seek swift, decisive victory because "there has never been a protracted war from which a country has benefited."[11]

German military philosopher Carl von Clausewitz held that in warfare "the destruction of the enemy is always what matters most" and depends on the ability to identify and direct all energies against his "center of gravity": "the hub of all power and movement, on which everything depends," usually the army.[12] This concept of centers of gravity is an integral part of all airpower theory along with another of Clausewitz's central dicta: "Act with the utmost concentration . . . act with the utmost speed." Offensive war "requires above all a quick irresistible decision."[13] Before the age of the airplane, however, the ability to identify and reach the enemy centers of gravity was limited, too often forcing military commanders to accept that "when an objective was beyond one's strength in the first place, it will always remain so."[14] Airpower went far toward resolving the resulting dilemmas for military strategists by vastly expanding the range of objectives within realistic reach of military strength.

Clausewitz derived his theories of war from historical experience: the Napoleonic Wars of the early nineteenth century. The first-generation airpower theorists were similarly rooted in their recent past. World War I had brought the meliorism of the Age of Progress to a crashing and bloody halt.[15] The survivors of the Great War, civilian and military alike, vowed not to repeat the bloody attrition war that characterized combat in the trenches of 1914–1918. Some saw new military technology as the problem; others saw it as the potential savior. Politicians, motivated by a sincere, if naive, desire for peace, sought—through the League of Nations, disarmament treaties, and other international agreements—to eliminate the technology of violence, thus ensuring peace by removing the engine of war. The mainstream military—skeptical of humankind's ability successfully to outlaw war—focused on learning and incorporating the strategic and operational lessons of the last war to avoid repeating them in the next. Most U.S. and European military thinkers continued to focus on traditional concepts—infantry, ships of the line—but a few renegades sought solutions to static, attrition warfare in new technologies—aviation, submarines, tanks. No single group of technology advocates was more active, imaginative, or effective in capturing the popular imagination than the airpower theorists of the 1920s and 1930s.

Italian military theorist Guilio Douhet's *Command of the Air* (1923) was one of the earliest and most influential of the early airpower treatises. Douhet's central tenets were simple and straightforward. First, the introduction of aircraft had fundamentally altered the nature of warfare by allowing the space over the earth to decide the outcome of war on the surface. Second, victory in future wars would require acquisition of command of the air:

preventing the enemy air forces from flying while preserving for one's own forces the ability to do so freely. Third, there were two acceptable targets for offensive airpower: the enemy's air forces on the ground, and civilian morale and the enemy's will to resist. Fourth (to the detriment of Douhet's post–Battle of Britain credibility), there is no effective defense against a determined bomber offensive. Finally, air forces should be organizationally independent of ground and naval forces and armed, structured, and deployed for the decisive strategic role. In Douhet's mind, capabilities of air forces thus organized were limited only by the number of aircraft available: "Since a bombing unit is potentially able to destroy any target on a specified surface, a fully activated Air Force is potentially capable of demolishing as many such targets, or surfaces, as there are bombing units."[16] In short, airpower had solved the Clausewitzian dilemma of reaching an opponent's centers of gravity by allowing the nation that possessed a predominance of air force to "strike mortal blows into the heart of the enemy with lightening speed."[17]

The officer most responsible for formulating early strategic bombing concepts in the United States was Lieutenant Colonel Edgar S. Gorrell, who became the chief of the U.S. Army Air Service in late 1917. Both his Gorrell Plan for a preemptive strategic bombing campaign against Germany and his postwar analysis of the future strategic bombing predated Douhet's better-known theories by several years and anticipated many of his concepts. Gorrell was a Clausewitzian who saw military victory as the product of both material destruction of a large portion of the enemy's force and the psychological destruction of its hope for victory and will to resist. The great promise of airpower lay in its ability to affect both the material and moral state of the enemy: The best way to stop the opposing army at the front line was to use airpower to destroy factories that supply that army, shatter the morale of the working people, and undermine public support for the war.[18] Gorrell did not carry his argument to Douhet's apocalyptic extreme and maintained that the fate of the ground army, specifically the infantry, was still decisive: "The operations of bombardment squadrons cannot be entirely isolated from the remainder of the work in the air and are inseparable from the operations of the Army as a whole."[19]

In Gorrell's vision, airpower promised neither cheap, easy victory nor the obsolescence of infantry. He equated the nation at war with a drill: the point (the Army) endured the roughest treatment, but unless the shank (the nation) was strong, it would break under the strain of extended use. It was airpower's job to "break the shank of the drill or to so weaken it that the whole instrument will break."[20] Because of military and political skepticism concerning the promise of airpower, Gorrell's theories lay dormant through most of the interwar period. When the political environment for airpower eventually improved, his relatively low-key approach was overshadowed by the histrionics of later airpower theorists.

The best known of the American "apostles of airpower" was Brigadier General William ("Billy") Mitchell. As the U.S. air commander at St. Mihiel and the Meuse–Argonne, Mitchell had been responsible for innovations that enabled tactical aviation to help the Allies turn the tide in those battles. Mitchell returned from the war enthusiastic about tactical aviation and pioneered its development during the 1920s. Peacetime politics triggered a fundamental change in Mitchell's perspective that left him forever associated with the "Douhetan" school, despite his early tactical experience. Mitchell, like Douhet, came to believe that the advent of military aviation had fundamentally changed the concept of national defense: "The airplane is now the arbiter of a nation's destiny. There are no longer frontiers, in the old way. A nation's frontier is now a blanket of air ten miles thick, laid entirely over it."[21] Moreover, he held that advancements in military technology had rendered ground combat indecisive. Armies had become "holders of ground" that could not advance "with rapidity to the vital centers of an opposing nation and bring quick and decisive victory." Air forces, in contrast, could go "straight into the vital centers of the opposing side and paraly[ze] them," could do so while imposing less physical destruction than had land armies, and could—through future technological developments—do so with minimal risk to themselves.[22]

Mitchell became a crusader for airpower's liberation from the concepts of the Army and the Navy, neither of which were capable of thinking of airpower in any but an auxiliary role. Arguing that the making of war could no longer be gauged entirely by land and sea concepts, Mitchell asserted that "a new set of rules for the conduct of war will have to be devised and a whole new set of ideas of strategy learned by those charged with the conduct of war."[23] To allow airpower to remain in a subordinate role would, Mitchell believed, amount to a waste of a capability uniquely suited to American strategic and social realities. Two factors in particular made the United States the natural leader in airpower. First, a population imbued with a strong sense of patriotism and a large pool of educated and athletic young men gave America the raw human potential to build an efficient air force willing to take risks and pay a high price, if necessary, in wartime. Second, the United States enjoyed unique industrial strength, technological know-how, and all of the skilled labor and raw materials necessary to develop a thriving aviation industry.[24] Mitchell warned, however, that the United States' predominance among potential aviation powers, although natural, was not automatic. The nation would have to make a moral and material commitment to airpower and do so early. Airpower, more than any other kind of military force, required the victor to land the first punch; like Douhet, Mitchell was confident that "the nation that gets in the first great air blow amidst the enemy is the one that will win." Victory through airpower, then, depended on forces in being. The construction and development of aviation technology and techniques, however, takes years of preparation by knowledgeable people; "armies and navies," Mitchell warned, "are entirely incapable of either visioning what it is or carrying it out."[25]

Mitchell's court-martial in 1926 for insubordination and subsequent public crusade to promote strategic bombing had implications for the Air Corps, and later the USAF, beyond the predominance of strategic bombing in its doctrine. Mitchell alarmed the rest of the military establishment with claims for airpower potential couched in such intemperate rhetoric as his 1927 assertion that "we must relegate armies and navies to a place in the glass case of a dusty museum . . . we must not entrust our national defense to these honored but obsolete services, because they will surely bring us to the Scilla of the fixed and narrow routine of the armies, and the Carybdis of the 'brass hats' and organized buncombe of the navies."[26] As General Henry J. ("Hap") Arnold would later note, although Mitchell's doctrine was basically sound, his tactics were not shrewd: Instead of softening War Department resistance to the new airpower theories, the net result of "Mitchellism" was—and would continue to be—to cement skeptics more than ever against emerging airpower.[27]

The ultimate irony of Mitchell's career would be that the next generation of airpower visionaries would pay homage to his devotion to the cause but dismiss his doctrinal theory as "too tactical and thus obsolete" for the nuclear era.[28] The generation of airpower theorists that emerged from the mushroom clouds over Hiroshima and Nagasaki made Douhet and Mitchell look circumspect. The first major post–Word War II airpower apostle and publicist—and the only airpower theorist to have his ideas marketed by Book-of-the-Month Club and animated by Walt Disney Studios—was an expatriate Russian pilot, Major Alexander De Seversky. De Seversky drew a number of lessons from the early phases of the air war in Europe (1939–1942), which, he argued, collectively proved the primacy of the air weapon over all future forms of warfare. Some were reasonably conventional: that no land or sea operations are possible without first assuming control of the air; that in aerial warfare the factor of quality is more decisive than the factor of quantity; that the destruction of enemy morale from the air depends on the ability to conduct precision bombing; and that the principle of unity of command, long recognized on land and sea, is equally vital to forces in the air.[29]

De Seversky did not stop, however, with the conventional and the comfortable. Long before the atomic attacks on Japan, De Seversky painted an apocalyptic picture of airpower's future role. "The epoch of troop landing and war 'fronts' and struggles for a few miles of disputed soil has ended forever," he wrote in 1942; the key now "is no longer *occupation* but *destruction* . . . and the destruction is now systematic, scientific—the planned wrecking of a great nation."[30] De Seversky's word choice was key: Air forces cannot occupy, but they can certainly destroy. Airpower had, in

De Seversky's view, important advantages over land warfare. First, "by piercing vital organs and nerve centers," air attacks against enemy industrial power could incapacitate an entire nation.[31] Second, such large-scale demolition of the enemy's heartland, which would be considered horrible vandalism if produced by ground forces, "can be passed off as technical preparation or 'softening' when carried out by aerial bombing."[32]

The end of World War II and the dawn of the atomic age did not bring any moderation in De Seversky's views. The U.S. defeat of Japan, he asserted, canceled out for all time "the classic doctrine that a nation cannot be defeated while its army is intact." Ignoring two years of painstaking and bloody naval actions and amphibious advances across the Pacific that brought B-29s within range of the Japanese home islands and depleted Japan's military power to the breaking point, De Seversky posited that without airpower and the atomic bomb, the United States would likely have found itself in a war that was "protracted for tens and even scores of years, and most likely would have ended in stalemate." He dismissed moral misgivings over atomic weapons as sentimentalism; there were, he argued, "no visible effects different in nature from those caused by incendiary bombing," and "had Hiroshima and Nagasaki been modern concrete and steel cities, there would have been no wholesale collapse of houses, no bonfire, and no such tremendous loss of life."[33]

In 1954, De Seversky criticized the "balanced force" concept advocated by Army and USAF Tactical Air Command (TAC) leaders, charging that the Air Force's Strategic Air Command (SAC), although well led and well manned, was "puny," of "last war vintage," and amounted to a modern "Maginot Line." Scarce national defense resources would, he argued, be better invested in developing its most modern force: the air arm. The nation should devote at least two-thirds of its national defense effort to offensive and defensive airpower since, De Seversky argued, only an invincible SAC "can save America from atomic destruction."[34] De Seversky remained an outspoken and articulate advocate well into the 1950s, but by then he had taken a back seat to an even harder-line, and ultimately more influential, airpower apostle—SAC Commander General Curtis E. LeMay.

As Commander of the SAC during the era of "Massive Retaliation," General LeMay conveyed a message that resonated in a U.S. political establishment and public disillusionment due to a protracted and, some thought, unsuccessful war in Korea. The combination of airpower and nuclear weapons ended the era of such "limited wars." In the nuclear age, any war is potentially global in scope, and "only a foolhardy nation would ever base its prewar strategy upon the doubtful assumption that what started as a localized conflict would remain localized."[35] LeMay was vehement in opposing what he regarded as the artificial and dangerous division of U.S. airpower into "tactical" and "strategic" aviation establishments. In particular, he objected to "tying down" a substantial portion of USAF aviation to support of surface forces. In its showdown to the death with the Soviet Union, the United States could not "afford the luxury of devoting a substantial portion of our Air Force effort to support of ground forces." National policy, he felt, dictated that the first and only objective should be deterrence through a capability to "win"—not through ground skirmishes but via the airpower battle. LeMay advocated the unification of SAC and TAC into a single Air Offensive Command that would enable the Air Force to devote all of its resources to the same goal: "As a matter of top priority, for reasons of national survival, they must deter together through their ability to defeat Communist airpower together. Both TAC and SAC must plan to fight and win at the same time and in generally the same places, using every last element of their strength in the battle."[36] LeMay dismissed concerns—expressed by, among others, the commander of TAC, General Otto P. Weyland—that to place so great an emphasis on offensive strategic operations against the Soviet Union would leave USAF ill prepared for the demands of regional, "brushfire" wars. After all, LeMay argued, if you can lick the cat, you can lick the kitten.

Its strategic focus did not serve LeMay's Air Force well during the Vietnam War. The experience was so traumatic that it was over a decade before the Air Force fully regained its bearings and began institutionalizing the "lessons" of the Southeast Asian war. A third generation of airpower apostles eventually emerged with new theories of how airpower would win wars. The intellectual leader of the newest apostolic generation is Colonel John Warden, who, not coincidentally, was one of the most important architects of the strategic air campaign against Iraq. Colonel Warden characterized his 1989 monograph, *The Air Campaign,* as a score for the "orchestration of war" that reconciled traditional airpower concepts with some of the hard-learned lessons of the Vietnam era. Warden stopped short of predicting that airpower alone would win wars or declaring ground and naval forces strategically obsolete. In the post–Goldwater–Nichols spirit of "jointness," Warden pointed out that he did not conceive his air campaign as distinct from surface operations; rather, he suggests, his concepts proceed from the notion that "orchestration, not subordination or integration, is the *sine qua non* of modern warfare."[37]

While paying homage to the importance of the ground campaign, Warden followed in the tradition of denigrating the inability of surface warriors to think in three dimensions. In his view, U.S. military orthodoxy—as embodied in ground commanders from Ulysses S. Grant to George Marshall—adopted the "least attractive alternatives" in planning military campaigns: either a broad front approach that defeats concentric circles of enemy forces ("castles") in detail or an approach that reduces one or two "castles," ignores any others, and plunges through the gap to seize the capital. Both approaches share the risk of leaving both sides exhausted with no clear victor.[38] Airpower, Warden argued, presents a quicker and cheaper strategic option: "to figure out a way to avoid the castles entirely and go directly to the political center—the capital or the king."[39] As the chief air planner in Washington during the Gulf War, Warden proposed a strategic air campaign that aimed, first, at the innermost circle—the national command authority, including, many analysts have concluded, Saddam Hussein himself; command, control, communication, and intelligence capabilities; air defense networks—and only later at the outer rings (Military forces in transit or at the front). Mitchell and Douhet would have been proud. Warden did depart somewhat from airpower orthodoxy in his recognition that the air campaign could and should be tailored to the realities of the contingency—the nature of the enemy, the political and military objectives at stake, and the capabilities of U.S. forces in being—and that airpower may not always be the key force.

Warden's "principles for the orchestration of war" also bore the distinct imprint of the lessons of Vietnam, particularly regarding the issue of will. "Nobody gives up *everything* until further resistance becomes impossible physically, or futile" and "the degree of pain a state is willing to endure is related to what it is asked to give up." Warden concluded that the asymmetry of objectives in Southeast Asia undermined U.S. military success. In Vietnam, as in most wars, "beauty [was] in the eye of the beholder."[40] Whereas Vietnam was of little more than symbolic importance to the United States, to the Viet Cong and the North Vietnamese it was a "sparkling jewel" for which they were willing to fight to the death. Warden identified an important lesson here: Because "the intensity of the fight is established by the side that has the greatest interest and will, military objectives and campaign plans must be tied to political objectives as seen through the enemy's eyes, not one's own." When U.S. will is less resolute than that of its opponents (as was the case in both Korea and Vietnam and is likely to be the case in the vast majority of future crises), it is necessary to find a military instrument that can inflict maximum damage to enemy leadership while minimizing the kinds of military costs—specifically, American casualties—that have served in past wars to undermine U.S. political will. Except in those cases in which "time is of the essence, and it is agreed that ground action can lead to the political objective significantly faster than could air action" (counterguerrilla war, occupation of limited pieces of territory), Warden argued airpower would provide that decisive edge.[41]

STRATEGIC BOMBARDMENT IN PRACTICE

The first real operational test of airpower theory came in Europe during World War II. Historians of World War II airpower are still debating the degree to which strategic bombing contributed to Allied victories over Germany and Japan in World War II. Those most critical of the role of strategic bombing lie at the farthest extremes of the debate. On one flank stand those who argue that strategic bombing represented technology run amok and, worse, exacted enormous costs on both sides with little measurable strategic payoff.⁴² On the other are those who argue that strategic bombing was not decisive in Western Europe because it was ill employed by military and political leaders who did not understand its capabilities. Resulting political constraints on airpower's employment and the diversion of air assets to the conduct of "tactical" operations in the prelude to the Normandy invasion violated the central principle of concentration of force at the decisive point.

The United States Strategic Bombing Survey drew a set of tentative conclusions concerning the air war in Europe in 1945 that have withstood the test of time and subsequent scholarship fairly well. The logical focus of the Pacific survey effort on the effects of the atomic bomb leaves it with no similarly rewarding analysis of the efficacy of conventional bombardment of Japan. In particular, the European survey considered the effect of the strategic bombing campaign against Germany's "vital centers"—those nerve centers that strategic targeters before and since have considered essential to even the most basic function of the nation. It concluded that strategic bombing had a profound effect on the ability of the German nation to continue the war effort, but that that effect was far from immediate; in fact, it took years to develop. "The will to operate remained to the very end," the survey found, and "there always seemed to be a plentiful supply of pick-and-shovel labor." Over time, realization of the futility of repair efforts set in with a disheartening effect as the German people saw that their labors "failed to halt the decline in capacity, much less to secure any recuperation of more than minor duration."⁴³ Nonetheless, when the German Army finally surrendered in April 1945, the means still existed to continue the fight, although few could see the point.⁴⁴ The survey, furthermore, did not consider the contribution the Soviets made to the attrition of German military capability through Germany's long and bloody campaign in the East.

The survey's conclusions had a "good news, bad news" character about them. The good news was that "the German experience suggests that even a first class military power—rugged and resilient as Germany was—cannot live long under full scale and free exploitation of air weapons over the heart of the territory." The strategic bombing campaign had mortally wounded Germany. The bad news was that "Germany fought back, and did so for a very long time."⁴⁵ The worst news of all was that airpower was most decisive in preparing for and supporting the Allied reinvasion of the European mainland: a use of airpower that Air Force leaders in Europe—including 8th Air Force commander and future Air Force Chief of Staff Carl Spaatz—viewed as a dangerous diversion of resources away from their essential mission.⁴⁶

Germany and Japan were exactly the kinds of enemies against which

Douhet, Mitchell, and other interwar air theorists had designed their concepts: modern, industrialized societies with high labor and population concentrations in a relatively few urban areas, and with a complex and exposed economic infrastructure. In both Korea and Vietnam, attempts to apply those traditional concepts of airpower against very different kinds of enemies met with much less satisfying results. The Air Force in Korea stubbornly clung to its traditional concepts, directing the lion's share of its resources after April 1951 to a costly "strategic bombing" campaign against an enemy that presented precious few appropriate targets and a largely ineffective deep interdiction campaign ironically code-named "Operation Strangle." Airpower played a key role in the Korean War—in both its close air support and battlefield interdiction missions—but the potentially valuable lessons of those operations fell on deaf ears in an increasingly SAC-dominated Air Force.

The Korean War might have afforded the Air Force some useful hints for future limited wars against non-Europeans—that, for example, deep interdiction failed because the Chinese and Koreans were less dependent on their supply lines than Western armies and were, at any rate, extremely clever in sustaining supply lines in spite of the bombing.[47] Two factors prevented the Air Force from institutionalizing these lessons. First, at the highest levels of the Air Force, the dominant opinion both during and after the war was that Air Force assets should not have been employed in Korea at all, but should have been held in strategic reserve to fight the real war with the Soviets. Second, among those who bothered to think about Korea, the predominant lesson was that airpower could have "won" the Korean War if only it had been allowed (1) to strike targets across the Yalu into China, and (2) to employ nuclear weapons.[48] The ubiquity of such thinking demonstrated that the Air Force had missed the political–military lessons of the first limited war of the Cold War era: that the United States had achieved its original objectives in Korea and paid a high price for not sticking to them, and that limited war in an era of potentially explosive superpower tension presents more than just a weapons employment problem.

The Air Force was not alone in drawing the wrong lessons from Korea. President Eisenhower's "no more Koreas" pledge and "New Look" defense program enabled the Air Force to proceed boldly into the future without so much as a backward glance and impelled the other Services to do the same. Through the 1950s, the United States had only one enemy—the Soviet Union—and it was the right enemy for the favored weapon. It was Douhet's dream opponent: industrialized, somewhat urbanized, and devoted to an "evil" ideology that seemed to make mortal conflict with the leader of the capitalist world inevitable. Few questioned the morality of employing nuclear weapons against so dastardly a foe; and few envisioned the United States employing its military forces against any other. In the Air Force, even the Tactical Air Command—the sole sanctuary for limited war thinking in the Air Force—would devote the lion's share of its energy and resources to building a nuclear strike capability and becoming a sort of mini-SAC. The concept of limited war—in which political considerations would take predominance over targeting problems—would not resurface until the late 1950s. By then, procurement decisions and doctrinal hardening of the arteries had set airpower on an irreversible path to frustration in the next war.

The Air Force, and the national command authority that it served, entered the Vietnam War confident in the belief that superior U.S. military technology could solve any strategic problem. The air campaign failed against North Vietnam for two basic reasons. The first, stated by Lt. Col. Mark Clodfelter in *The Limits of Air Power,* was that "they never fully realized that airpower's political efficacy varies according to many diverse elements, and that no specific formula guarantees success."[49] The problem was more basic than that. As historian Earl H. Tilford, Jr., suggests, a second explanation follows from the first. The Air Force, according to Tilford, failed in Vietnam because it "did not—indeed, could not—develop a strategy appropriate to the war at hand" and, in fact, "failed to articulate any coherent strategy at all."[50] Airpower did not fail in Vietnam because of any lack of tactical or technological capabilities: Losses in the Rolling Thunder and Linebacker campaigns, although traumatic and often unnecessary, were not crippling, and U.S. airpower hit virtually every target it sought to destroy as it had in Korea. It is a fact that is, however, irrelevant.

This faith in technology, the tendency to focus on a weapon's lethality rather than on its political efficacy, led those who masterminded the strategic aspects of the Vietnam air war not to ask the important questions. Was the link between the Viet Cong and Hanoi strong enough that strategic bombing in the North could bring the desired results? Had strategic bombing sufficiently raised the threshold of pain in the North, could Hanoi—even if it wanted to—have forced an end to the Southern insurgency? What would be the political cost—both domestic and international—of inflicting such intense punishment on a nation against which the U.S. government had never declared war?[51] Given the nature of the fighting (sporadic) and the logistical requirements to keep the insurgents and, later, the North Vietnamese regulars fighting (in the pre-Tet years, about 34 tons of material daily, roughly seventeen standard U.S. army truckloads per day), could any amount of bombing have adequately interdicted the supplies moving from North to South?[52]

As in the case of the Korean air war, it is important to note that although airpower—and, in fact, U.S. military power in general—failed in Vietnam in its strategic mission, its performance in Southeast Asia was not without positive lessons. As historian Donald J. Mrozek argues convincingly, "Something worthwhile may yet be salvaged from the American enterprise in Southeast Asia.... Assessment of the Vietnam conflict may finally combine positive endorsements of some technical and tactical measures with broader cautions and criticisms in strategic matters."[53] It is far from clear, however, that airpower advocates have learned the right lessons from Vietnam. The ubiquitous contention that Linebacker II (the 1972 "Christmas bombings" that many believe forced the North Vietnamese back to the negotiating table and paved the way for the 1973 Peace Accords) redeemed the efficacy of strategic bombing reflects the same myopia that led De Seversky to ignore three and a half years of advances on the ground and sea and declare that the atomic attacks on Japan won World War II.

As both Clodfelter and Tilford point out, there is little sign that Vietnam undermined the Air Force's faith in technology or the conviction that its doctrine is appropriate to any conflict.[54] The more common view within the Air Force is that as good as technology was in Vietnam, it was not good enough and that future improvements "can help airpower compensate for the limitations imposed upon combat commanders by economic, geographical, and political considerations."[55] In fact, the Air Force—like the broader defense community—may have emerged from Vietnam with more myths than lessons: that Linebacker II won the war, and (somewhat paradoxically) that victory in Vietnam was prevented only by political constraints that kept us from winning. These two "lessons" of Vietnam would become the pillars of wisdom guiding the conception of the air campaign against Iraq in 1991.

THE NEED FOR A NEW COVENANT

The common thread that binds the apostles of airpower is their faith in the technological "silver bullet"—a breakthrough that will make airpower's performance match its theoretical promise. At a more basic level, however, the airpower thinkers from Douhet to Warden share a common aim with all military thinkers: the desire to avoid the often apparently futile carnage of previous wars. Few serious historians would take issue with Douhet's prediction that the introduction of the airplane into the military arsenal changed forever the character of warfare. Even fewer responsible military commanders—ground or naval—would choose to go to war without airpower were it available. The history of warfare since the 1920s proves beyond any reasonable doubt that airpower is a potentially decisive military instrument and that winning wars is very difficult (and usually impossible) without a predominance of it. So why the long, often acrimonious debate over the decisiveness of airpower? Why do its post–Persian Gulf War advocates even see a need for its "redemption"? Where did the apostles of airpower go wrong?

There are several answers. First, airpower theorists generally failed to anticipate the impact of nonaviation technologies on the theoretical capabilities of airpower. Improvements in armor and mechanization after World

War I meant armies no longer stood still, vastly complicating the job of hitting targets and distinguishing their targets from yours. In the Persian Gulf, Coalition air forces had little trouble striking entrenched Iraqi forces in the KTO. Yet the ineffectiveness of mobile SCUD hunting and the continuing problem of friendly fire casualties indicates that the challenges of mobility have not been answered. Even more troublesome has been the steady advance of defensive technologies. The bomber does not always get through—9,949 U.S. bombers did not in World War II, thirteen B-52s did not during Linebacker II—and against an opponent more competent than Iraq it would be foolhardy not to assume that at least a few would not today. Aspiring aggressors are no doubt already pondering how best to blunt the U.S. technological advantage. Present-day Stanley Baldwins take heed: better to undersell the capability and be pleasantly surprised than to become overconfident and be caught unawares by some future "son of People's War."[56]

A second mistake the airpower theorists made was to compress the time necessary for strategic bombardment to achieve its desired effects on enemy morale and capabilities. It turns out that most societies (including Iraq) can withstand much greater punishment than the airpower theorists thought. In spite of technological advancements in air and ground warfare, Clausewitz is still right: The key to military victory is the destruction of the enemy's army on the ground. In all probability, Saddam Hussein called his forces out of the KTO because he saw the prospect for rebuilding some of his former regional hegemony dwindling with each tank "plinked" and each division surrendered. In an effort to salvage as much of his military potential as possible from the meat grinder that CNN told him the KTO had become, he had to pull out when he did. One clear lesson of the Persian Gulf War is that although airpower provides the technological capability to bypass the castles, sooner or later you have to engage the enemy's army on the ground, whether with attack aircraft, tanks, artillery, infantry, or bows and arrows.

The third, and perhaps most debilitating, weakness of airpower theory was its failure to consider the effect of political and cultural differences among nations. The United States learned tough lessons about ethnocentric military strategies in Korea and Vietnam. De Seversky understood the mismatch between a strategy designed for warfare against modern, urban, industrialized societies (strategic bombardment) and less industrialized opponents. Where he went awry was in assuming that such opponents would not matter in the clash of titans that the Cold War became. There is an important message here for future military strategists. Iraq was unique less in the extent to which it adopted the trappings of European military power and infrastructure than in its doing so in a way that maximized its vulnerability to strategic bombing (centralized industry, communications, and military command and control) and minimized the relative advantages (operational and tactical flexibility, resilience, and military effectiveness). Iraq represents one type of Third World opponent, but it would be foolhardy to forget the other paradigm—the opponent who (like the North Koreans, Communist Chinese, Viet Cong, and North Vietnamese) played their unique cultural strengths to their advantage and significantly blunted the effect of Western technological superiority.

Strategic tunnel vision is a fourth weakness of traditional strategic bombing thinkers. By making airpower synonymous with strategic bombing, airpower advocates effectively excluded some of the most potentially decisive aspects of airpower from their own scale of effectiveness. This absolutist approach put the burden of proof on the strategic bombing advocates and left them prey to skeptics, who criticized their "pie in the sky by and by" zealotry. With the disappointing outcome of the air war in Vietnam, the rest of the airpower community began to assert itself. The dominance of tactical aviation—the rise of the "fighter mafia" in the early 1970s—was a function of the realization within the Air Force that the apostles had oversold the promise of strategic bombardment. As the debate over the B-2 illustrates, it is now the strategic elements of the Air Force that face charges of being unaffordable and largely irrelevant luxuries.

The final, and ultimately the greatest, weakness of the apostles of airpower has been their ahistoricism. In looking forward for solutions, airpower's prophets too often failed to learn the real lessons of past wars. Rather than forging positive lessons, successive generations of airpower theorists tended to dismiss as anomalous any disappointing experience and responded by ratcheting up their rhetoric another notch. The quest for technological solutions prevented successive generations of airpower theorists from learning the most important lesson of the airpower experience: that the human spirit is not logical, that societies do not operate according to cost–benefit principles, and that war is a political rather than a technological enterprise.

"Was Douhet right after all?" is probably not even the right question to ask in today's security environment. Although the Persian Gulf War may well have been a harbinger of the military–technical future, it is just as likely to have been the death rattle of an era. The inevitable process of revisionism has cast doubt on many of the early, optimistic assessments of what happened in the Hundred-Day War. Precision-guided munitions enabled air forces to operate with impressive accuracy, but they did not achieve one bomb, one target, one kill. The air campaign in and outside the KTO severely degraded Iraqi military effectiveness, but "decapitation" proved an elusive objective: Saddam Hussein still runs the show in Baghdad. The Gulf War turned out not to be as one dimensional as it looked on television, and the strategic outcome was less obviously successful. We may never know what the real effects of strategic bombardment were on Baghdad, but few still argue that it won the war.

Ultimately, what has most undermined the victory of airpower is not what happened in Iraq in 1991, but what has happened elsewhere since then. Subsequent events—in Somalia, Bosnia, Haiti, and Rwanda—make it impossible to ignore the unpleasant reality that the crises of the post–Cold War era are unlikely to lend themselves to tidy responses like strategic bombing. The Persian Gulf War is not proving a model easily transferable to most of the crises cropping up in today's world. Former Bush administration National Security Council staff member David Gompert voiced the kind of frustration that is likely to characterize force employment decisions for the foreseeable future: "Only massive Western intervention would have stopped and reversed Serbian aggression, not some smart bomb down the right Serbian chimney."[57] Airpower will certainly be a cornerstone of U.S. military operations in the future, but the conflicts ahead will offer few, if any, suitable targets for a Desert Storm–style air campaign.

Even in the realm of the major regional contingency (MRC) that is now the currency of U.S. military planners, arguments over whether Douhet was right after all are neither useful nor very interesting. As communication, industry, resources, and economies are becoming increasingly internationalized, vital centers are becoming more nebulous and targets more difficult to discern. If we thought it was tough to hit a ball bearing plant in Germany in 1943, we discovered it was even tougher to cut a fiber-optic cable in Baghdad in 1991. Over the long term, in a future in which a computer virus could shut down a nation's defense establishment, the prospect of manned bombers flying thousands of miles to drop explosives on buildings may become as anachronistic as the joust. Today, in a world in which crises seem most often to take on the character of mass terror conducted by low-ranking military personnel and political operatives resulting in mass starvation, disease, refugees, and, at the worst extreme, virtual genocide, the prospect of manned bombers flying thousands of miles to drop explosives on buildings is irrelevant.

NOTES

1. Portions of this chapter originally appeared in January 1992 as "Promises Fulfilled: The Prophets of Air Power in Desert Storm," commissioned by the Washington Strategy Seminar as a background paper for its series of seminars on "Air Power in the New Security Environment" held between May 1991 and August 1992 in Washington, D.C.

2. These figures are based on data found in James A. Winnefield, Preston Niblack, and Dana J. Johnson, *A League of Airmen: U.S. Airpower in the Gulf War* (Santa Monica, Calif.: RAND Corporation, 1994), 306, 313.

3. Michael Dugan, "First Lessons of Victory," *U.S. News & World Report*, March 18, 1991, 36.

4. Edward N. Luttwak, "Air Power in U.S. Military Strategy," in *The United States Air Force: Aerospace Challenges and Missions in the 1990s, Conference Pa-*

per Summaries (Cambridge, Mass.: The International Security Studies Program, The Fletcher School of Law and Diplomacy, Tufts University, April 3–4, 1991), 3–4.

5. "The Air Campaign: Part of the Combined Arms Operation," briefing presented by General Merrill A. McPeak, USAF, Washington, D.C., DOD, March 15, 1991.

6. Richard P. Hallion, *Storm over Iraq: Air Power and the Gulf War* (Washington, D.C.: Smithsonian Institution Press, 1992), 1.

7. Carl H. Builder, *The Masks of War: American Military Styles in Strategy and Analysis* (Baltimore: Johns Hopkins University Press, 1989), 115.

8. Edward Luttwak, "Washington's Biggest Scandal," *Commentary* (May 1994): 32.

9. Ibid., 32.

10. Sun Tzu, *The Art of War,* trans. by Samuel B. Griffith (New York: Oxford University Press, 1963), 67, 68.

11. Ibid., 73.

12. Carl von Clausewitz, *On War,* trans. by Peter Paret (Princeton, N.J.: Princeton University Press, 1976), 577, 595.

13. Ibid., 598, 617.

14. Ibid., 600.

15. For a thorough exposition of this lost innocence, see Paul Fussell, *The Great War and Modern Memory* (London: Oxford University Press, 1975), chap. 1.

16. Guilio Douhet, *Command of the Air,* trans. by Dino Ferrari (Washington, D.C.: Office of Air Force History, 1983) 50 [hereafter *Command of the Air*].

17. Ibid., 15.

18. Lieutenant Colonel E. S. Gorrell, "The Future Role of American Bombardment Aviation" [1918], United States Air Force Historical Research Agency, Maxwell AFB, Alabama, 248. 222–78, 14–16.

19. Ibid., 16.

20. Ibid.

21. General William Mitchell, "Airplanes in National Defense," *The Annals of the American Academy of Political and Social Science* 131, no. 220 (May 1927): 39 [hereafter "Airplanes in National Defense"].

22. Ibid., 39–40.

23. William Mitchell, *Winged Defense: The Development and Possibilities of Modern Air Power—Economic and Military* (New York: G. P. Putnam, 1925), 1–26.

24. Ibid., 26.

25. Mitchell, "Airplanes in National Defense," 41.

26. Ibid., 42.

27. Thomas H. Greer, *The Development of Air Doctrine in the Army Air Arm, 1917–1941* (Washington, D.C.: Office of Air Force History, 1985), 17.

28. Bernard Brodie, quoted in Douhet, *Command of the Air,* editor's intro., p. x.

29. Major Alexander P. De Seversky, *Victory through Air Power* (New York: Simon and Schuster, 1942).

30. Ibid., 11.

31. Ibid., 102.

32. Ibid., 104.

33. Alexander De Seversky, "Report to Secretary of War Robert Patterson on the Role of Air Power in the Victory over Japan," February 11, 1946, Papers of Carl Spaatz, Library of Congress—Manuscript Division, Washington, D.C., Box 255, "Air Power—U.S."

34. "Air Force Called 'Puny,' " *New York Times,* January 4, 1954; "De Seversky Prods U.S.," *New York Times,* February 3, 1954.

35. United States Congress, House, Committee on Un-American Activities, *Soviet Total War: Historic Mission of Violence and Deceit,* Vol. I, statement of General Curtis E. LeMay, "Strategic Air Command and World Peace," September 23, 1956.

36. Curtis LeMay, "Speech to Major USAF Commanders Conference, 28–30 January 1957," *History of the Strategic Air Command,* July 1–December 31, 1957, Vol. II, exhibit 2, Air Force Historical Research Agency, Maxwell AFB, Alabama.

37. Colonel John A. Warden III, *The Air Campaign: Planning for Air Combat* (Washington, D.C.: Pergamon–Brassey's, 1989), 124.

38. Ibid., 115.

39. Ibid., 139.

40. Ibid., 111.

41. Ibid., 123–27.

42. Michael Sherry, *The Rise of American Air Power: The Creation of Armageddon* (New Haven: Yale University Press, 1987); Ronald Schaffer, *Wings of Judgment: American Bombing in World War II* (New York: Oxford University Press, 1985).

43. United States Strategic Bombing Survey, *Overall Report (European War),* September 30, 1945, 64.

44. Ibid., 38.

45. Ibid., 107.

46. Ibid., on Spaatz's opposition to the diversion of air assets away from strategic attacks on the German heartland, see, for example, David Eisenhower, *Eisenhower at War, 1943–1945* (New York: Random House, 1986).

47. Earl H. Tilford, Jr., *Setup: What the Air Force Did in Vietnam and Why* (Maxwell AFB, Ala.: Air University Press, 1991), pp. 18–21 [hereafter *Setup*].

48. See, for example, Colonel Dale O. Smith and Major General John DeF. Barker, "Air Power Indivisible," *Air University Quarterly Review* 4, no. 2 (Fall 1950); General Frederic H. Smith, Jr., "Nuclear Weapons and Limited War," *Air University Quarterly Review* 12, no. 1 (Spring 1960); and Robert F. Futrell, *The United States Air Force in the Korean War* (Washington, D.C.: Office of Air Force History, 1983).

49. Mark Clodfelter, *The Limits of Air Power: The American Bombing of North Vietnam* (New York: Free Press, 1989), 203–4 [hereafter *Limits of Air Power*].

50. Tilford, *Setup,* xvi.

51. For the best recent attempt to answer these important questions, see Larry Cable, *Unholy Grail: The United States and the Wars in Vietnam, 1965–1968* (London: Routledge, 1991).

52. Ibid., 205.

53. Donald J. Mrozek, *Air Power and the Ground War in Vietnam* (Washington, D.C.: Pergamon–Brassey's, 1989), 155.

54. Clodfelter, *The Limits of Air Power,* 210.

55. General William W. Momyer, *Air Power in Three Wars* (Washington, D.C.: Office of Air Force History, 1978), 339.

56. British Prime Minister Stanley Baldwin warned, in 1932, that it was time for the "man in the street to realize there is no power on earth that can protect him from bombing, whatever people may tell him.... The bomber will always get through." Stanley Baldwin, "The Bomber Will Always Get Through," *New York Times,* November 11, 1932.

57. David Gompert, "How to Defeat Serbia," *Foreign Affairs* (July/August 1994): 41–42.

Selected Bibliography

The following is a composite of the major works and sources used by the various authors in their individual chapters.

PRIMARY SOURCES

Since most of the primary documents used to write these chapters are still very new, the vast majority are still found at their original sources. Among these sources are the Departments of State, Defense, Transportation, Commerce, and Labor. Other government records were gleaned from the U.S. Senate and House of Representatives, including the Committees on Foreign Affairs, Armed Services, and the various subcommittees. In addition, the immense numbers of military records have been derived from such agencies as the Departments of the Army, Navy, and Air Force as well as from the Joint Chiefs of Staff and their joint commands, specifically Central Command (CENTCOM), Southern Command (SOCOM), and Transportation Command (TRANSCOM). This was augmented by material from various Air Force, Army, Navy, and Marine Corps units and commands, such as the Air Force's Air Combat Command (formerly Tactical Air Command/Strategic Air Command), Air Mobility Command (formerly Military Air Command), U.S. Air Forces, Europe and Air Force Materiel Command (formerly Air Force Logistics Command/ Air Force Services Command). Other sources for documents included the National Archives in Washington, D.C., and East Point, Georgia; Reagan and Carter Presidential Libraries; Boston University Library; Harvard University Library; Georgia Institute of Technology Library; Mercer University Library; Army archival holdings at Carlislie Barracks, Pennsylvania, the Army's Center for Military History (CMH) in Washington, D.C. and Ft. Leavenworth, Kansas; Air Force archival holdings at the Air Force Historical Research Agency at Maxwell AFB, Alabama, Warner Robins Air Logistics Center History Office, Robins AFB, Georgia, Air Mobility Command History Office and TRANSCOM History Office both at Scott AFB, Illinois, Air Force Materiel Command History Office, Wright–Patterson AFB, Ohio, and the Air Force Office of History Archives at Bolling AFB, D.C.; and Navy, Marine, DOD, Congressional, and Central Intelligence Agency archives in Washington, D.C. In addition to these government items, papers were used from contractors, transportation industries, and private individuals. To this end, several personal meeting transcripts, telephone calls, telegrams, radio messages, and correspondence/interviews between key individuals and the authors were used to write these chapters. Last, but not least, many documents were used which were generated in the Kuwaiti and Iraqi theaters of operations both in the field and at headquarters.

Among the items used by the authors were situation reports; after-action reports; site team reports; mission reports from various military units; background reports; command, service, and secretary-level briefings; briefing slides; radio messages; telegraphic messages; secure-line messages; letters of various kinds; memos; memos for the record; official charts of various kinds; telephone transcripts; meeting minutes of various kinds; transcripts of on site media briefings; official tables of various kinds; point papers; bullet papers; talking papers; statements before Congress and other government agencies; public speeches, talks, lectures, and addresses made to civic groups, college classes, as well as Congress and other government agencies; fact sheets and press releases from official agencies; staff summary sheets; contracts; transcripts of congressional testimony; official biographies of senior government officials and military officers; information papers; Gulf War Air Power Survey "Black Hole" files; master attack plans; daily target charts; master target list; white papers; target attack charts; target planning worksheets; case studies; test results, reports, and studies; movies; tapes; and photographs. Finally, two authors have used personal copies of the Christian Bible and the *Qur'an*.

GOVERNMENT PUBLICATIONS

The following items are published report by government agencies or institution and individuals contracted by the government to publish reports and provide analyses for the U.S. government. This also includes published (internal or otherwise) interviews of key leaders. Also included are official histories, white papers, state publications, and publications from foreign governments.

Air Force Logistics Management Center (AFLMC). *Final Report LX912097, Air Force DESERT SHIELD/DESERT STORM Logistics Lessons Learned.* March 1992. Microfiche Reproduction.

Air Force Pamphlet (AFP) 200-18. *Target Intelligence Handbook, Targeting Principles.* October 1, 1990.

Air Force Pamphlet (AFP) 200-17. *An Introduction to Air Force Targeting.* June 23, 1989.

Barlow, Barry, Davis, Richard G., and Jamieson, Perry. Interview with Lieutenant General Charles A. Horner, Commander, 9th AF. March 4, 1992.

Bash, Brooks L. Research Report. "CRAF: The Persian Gulf War and Implications for the Future." Naval War College, June 19, 1992.

Belvoir Research. "Development & Engineering Center Report 2527, Performance of Fuels, Lubricants, and Associated Products Used During Operation DESERT SHIELD/STORM." August 1992. Microfiche Reproduction.

Broght, Carl T., and Hale, Sharon R. "Strategic Sealift for DESERT SHIELD Not a Blue Print for the Future." Naval War College, June 1991. Microfiche Reproduction.

Buchanan, Thomas H. *The Tactical Air Control System: Its Evolution and Its Need for Battle Managers*. Research Report No. AU-ARI-87-1. Air University, Maxwell AFB, Alabama, 1987.

Bush, President George. "Remarks to Department of Defense Employees." August 15, 1990. *Weekly Compilation of Presidential Documents*. August 20, 1990.

Bush, President George. "Address to the Nation Announcing the Deployment of United States Armed Forces to Saudi Arabia." August 8, 1990. *Weekly Compilation of Presidential Documents*. August 13, 1990.

Bush, President George. "The President's News Conference." August 8, 1990. *Weekly Compilation of Presidential Documents*. August 13, 1990.

Central Tactical Air Forces, Intelligence. "The TACC Targeting Process," in *Target Intelligence Standard Operating Procedures*. 1990/1991.

Chenoweth, Mary. *Rand Case Study N-2838-AF, the Civil Reserve Air Fleet: An Example of the Use of Commercial Assets to Expand Military Capabilities During Contingencies*. June 1990. Microfiche Reproduction.

Collins, John M. "High Command Arrangements Early in the Persian Gulf Crisis." CRS Report for Congress, 90-453 RCO. September 21, 1990.

COMUSNAVCENT Command History, 1990. Operational Archives Branch, Naval Historical Center, Washington, D.C., 1992.

Davey, Kim L. "C-130 War Readiness Spares Kit (WRSK) Resupply during Contingency Operations—A DESERT SHIELD/STORM Analysis." Master's Thesis, Air Force Institute of Technology, September 1991.

De Seversky, Alexander. "Report to Secretary of War Robert Patterson on the Role of Air Power in the Victory over Japan." February 11, 1946. Papers of Carl Spaatz, Library of Congress—Manuscript Division, Washington, D.C., Box 255, "Air Power—U.S."

Dees, W. Jack. "Gulf Security and the Gulf Arab Contribution." Naval War College, June 6, 1991. Microfiche Reproduction.

Defense Science Board (DSB). *Lessons Learned During Operations Desert Shield & Desert Storm*. Washington, D.C.: Department of Defense, May 1992.

Department of the Air Force, U.S. *Reaching Globally, Reaching Powerfully: The United States Air Force in the Gulf War*. Washington, D.C.: Department of the Air Force, 1991.

Department of Defense, U.S. *Soviet Military Power, Prospects for Change 1989*. 1989.

Department of Defense, U.S. *Conduct of the Persian Gulf War: Final Report to Congress*. 3 Volumes. Washington, D.C.: Government Printing Office, 1992.

Department of the Navy, U.S. *The United States Navy in "Desert Shield" "Desert Storm"*. Washington, D.C.: Office of the Chief of Naval Operations, 1991.

Englehardt, Joseph P. "Desert Shield and Desert Storm: A Chronology and Troop List for the 1990–1991 Persian Gulf Crisis." *SSI Special Report*. Carlisle, Pa.: Strategic Studies Institute, March 1991.

Field Manual No. 100-5. *Field Service Regulations: Operations*. Washington, D.C.: Department of the Army 1939, 1944, 1954, 1962, 1974.

Field Manual No. 100-5. *Operations*. Washington, D.C.: Department of the Army, 1986.

Foreign Broadcast Information Service (FBIS). Middle East (Jordan Television), Near East, Soviet Union (TASS, Moscow Domestic Service), and South Asia.

Gorrell, Lieutenant Colonel E. S. "The Future Role of American Bombardment Aviation" [1918]. United States Air Force Historical Research Agency, Maxwell AFB, Alabama, 248.222-78.

Gulf War Air Power Survey, Statistical Compendium. Table 185. "Strike Counts by Master Target List Categories." Table 186. "Daily Strikes by Master Target List Categories." 1991.

Hallion, Richard. "Reaching Globally, Reaching Powerfully: The United States Air Force in the Gulf War." USAF White Paper, September 1991.

———. "The Future of Air Power." Speech at Kelly AFB, Texas, 1994.

Harvard Study Team. *Harvard Study Team Report: Public Health in Iraq After the Gulf War*. May 1991.

Herring, George. "The Johnson Administration's Conduct of Limited War in Vietnam." Speech at U.S. Air Force Academy Harmon Memorial Lecture. October 14, 1990.

History (S/Decl OADR). *Military Airlift Command*. 1990. Information Used (U).

History (S/RD). *Strategic Air Command*. 1990 & 1991. Information Used (U).

Johnson, General Hansford T. CINCUSTRANSCOM/CINCMAC. Address to National Aviation Club, Washington, D.C. March 28, 1991.

Johnson, General Hansford T. "Presentation to the Committee on Merchant Marine Fisheries, Subcommittee on Merchant Marine, U.S. House of Representatives." April 23, 1991.

Joint Forces Air Combat Command. "Theater Air Campaign." Progress briefing to Secretary of Defense Richard Cheney and Chairman of the JCS, General Colin Powell, Riyadh, Saudi Arabia. February 8, 1991.

Lambert, Robert B. "Sealift In Operation DESERT SHIELD." U.S. Army War College, March 1991. Microfiche Reproduction.

Launius, Roger D., and Cross, Coy F., II. *MAC and the Legacy of the Berlin Airlift*, USAF Monograph. April 1989.

Leiser, Gary (22 AF). Interview with Brigadier General Edwin E. Tenoso, Commander, Airlift Forces (COMALF) in Saudi Arabia during Operation DESERT SHIELD/STORM. May 28, 1991.

Leland, J. W. MAC Office of History. Interview with Colonel D. J. Bottjer, MAC Senior CAT Director during DESERT SHIELD/STORM. September 9, 1992.

Leland, J. W. MAC Office of History. Interview with Major General V. J. Kondra, MAC Deputy Chief of Staff for Operations. May 14, 1991.

LeMay, General Curtis. "Speech to Major USAF Commanders Conference, 28–30 January 1957." *History of the Strategic Air Command*. July 1–December 31,

Selected Bibliography 315

1957. Vol. II, exhibit 2, Air Force Historical Research Agency, Maxwell AFB, Alabama.

McPeak, General Merrill A. "The Air Campaign: Part of the Combined Arms Operation." Briefing, Department of Defense, Washington, D.C., March 15, 1991.

Marolda, Edward, and Schneller, Robert J. Interview with Rear Admiral Raynor A. K. Taylor, USN (ret.). August 2–3, 1991.

Matthews, James K. Interview with Wallace T. Sanson, Deputy Commander, MSC, January 1993.

Matthews, James K. Command Historian, USTRANSCOM. Interview with former CAT Airlift Cell Members, USTRANSCOM, Air Force Lieutenant Colonel Taylor Huddleston, March 20, 1991, and Lieutenant Colonel Craig R. McCollor, April 28, 1993.

Matthews, James K., and Holt, Cora J. *1990 USTRANSCOM History, Volume I, Desert Shield/Desert Storm 7 August 1990–10 March 1991.* USAF Annual History. 1992.

Military Traffic Management Command, Transportation Engineering Agency Deployment Planning Guide. Appendix C—Strategic Movement Requirements. August 19, 1991.

Morse, John P. Research Report. "The RRF in Operation Desert Storm: A First Look." Naval War College, May 1991. Microfiche Reproduction.

Navy, U.S. *Naval Doctrine Publication 1.* Washington, D.C., 1994.

Nichols, Representative William (Democrat–Alabama). *House Armed Services Committee,* "Hearings on the Reorganization of the Department of Defense," February 19, 1986.

Raach, George T., et al. *Conduct of the Persian Gulf War, Final Report to Congress.* Three Volumes. U.S. Department of Defense, April 1992.

Russ, General Robert D. USAF (Commander of TAC). "Open Letter to the Field." *AirLand Bulletin 81-1.* Langley AFB, Virginia: TAC-TRADOC ALFA, March 31, 1988.

Schneller, Robert J., Jr. "Persian Gulf Turkey Shoot: The Destruction of Iraqi Naval Forces during Operation Desert Storm." Paper presented at the Society for Military History conference in Kingston, Ontario, Canada. May 1993.

Schwarzkopf, General H. Norman. Testimony before Congress, Senate Committee on Armed Services. *Threat Assessment; Military Strategy and Operational Requirements.* 101st Congress, 2nd session. February 8, 1990.

Sessons, William H., and Maxson, Thomas J. Research Report. "Civil Reserve Air Fleet: Looking from DESERT STORM to the Future." Army War College, April 1992.

Snedeker, Clayton H. (21st Air Force). "Excerpt from Interview with Lt. Gen. Vernon J. Kondra." August 24, 1990–May 31, 1991.

Tactical Air Command Manual (TACM) 2-1. *Aerospace Operational Doctrine: Tactical Air Operations.* April 15, 1978.

Terasawa, Katsuaki L., and Gates, William R. "Burden Sharing in the Persian Gulf War: Lessons Learned and Implications for the Future." Naval Postgraduate School, Monterey, California. August 1992.

Tiernan, Captain Harold S. "History of MSC during Operation Desert Shield/Desert Storm." July 16, 1991.

Title V Input (S-DECL OADR). U.S. Commander in Chief Transportation. *Title V, SECDEF Report to Congress on Desert Shield/Desert Storm.* April 1991.
Title V: Conduct of the Persian Gulf War. Washington, D.C.: USGPO, 1993.
U.S. Coast Guard History Office. *The United States Navy in "Desert Shield" "Desert Storm."* 1992.
U.S. Congress. House, Committee on Armed Services. *Crisis in the Persian Gulf War: Sanctions, Diplomacy, and War,* House Armed Services Committee. 101st Congress, 2nd session, 1990.
U.S. Congress. House, Committee on Un-American Activities. *Soviet Total War: Historic Mission of Violence and Deceit.* Volume I, Statement of General Curtis E. LeMay. "Strategic Air Command and World Peace." September 23, 1956.
U.S. Congress. Senate, Committee on Armed Services. *Crisis in the Persian Gulf Region: U.S. Policy Options and Implications.* Senate Hearings. 101st Congress, 2nd session, 1990.
U.S. Congress. Senate, Committee on Armed Services. *Operation Desert Shield/ Desert Storm,* Senate Hearings. 102nd Congress, 1st session, 1991. 180.
U.S. Strategic Bombing Survey. *Overall Report (European War).* September 30, 1945.
U.S. Transportation Command History Office & Military Airlift Command History Offices. *General Hansford T. Johnson, Commander in Chief, United States Transportation Command and Air Mobility Command, An Oral History.* December 1992.
Williams, Peter. Pentagon Spokesperson. Briefing Transcript for January 27, 1991. Section 1, p. 6.

SECONDARY SOURCES

The following are the journals, magazines, and newspapers, used by the authors in writing their chapters. For specific titles and publication information, see the Notes at the end of each author's chapter.

Magazines and Journals

Defense Issues, Government Executive, Airlift, Defense Transportation Journal, Defense 91, The MAC Forum, Air Force Magazine, Aviation Week & Space Technology, Journal of Commerce, Sea Power, Proceedings of the Marine Safety Council, Navy Times, Fortune Magazine, Daily Shipping News, Naval Institute Proceedings, Translog, The New Yorker, New York Review of Books, Time, Ethics and International Affairs, Army Magazine, Newsweek, Facts on File, U.S. News and World Report, Airman, Air Force Journal of Logistics, Air Power Journal, Naval War College Review, Foreign Affairs, The Washington Quarterly, Interfaces, Air University Quarterly, Foreign Policy, National Interest, Business Week, Jane's Defence Weekly, Security Studies, Air Power History, Public Administration Research and Theory, Military Logistics Forum, Government Executive, Armed Forces Journal International, Air Force Times, Commentary, Navy International, All Hands, International Defense Review, Inside the Army, Leatherneck, Army,

The Hook, RUSI Journal, Defence, Foreign Policy, The Annals of the American Academy of Political and Social Science, Naval Aviation News, Surface Warfare, Marine Corps Gazette, Naval Forces, and *Comparative Strategy.*

Newspapers

Al-Ahram, Al-Thawra (Baghdad), *Chicago Tribune, Dayton Daily News, Fairborn Daily Herald, Henderson Hall News, Izvestiya, Kelly Observer, The New York Times, Pravda, Rabita, USA TODAY, Wall Street Journal, Washington Post, The Washington Times.*

Books

The following are selected book-length works from the notes of the various authors. They are books directly or indirectly dealing with the Persian Gulf War, the military and its history, and/or America's presence in the Middle Eastern region. For other sources, see the Notes following each chapter.

al-Ahsan, Abdallah. *OIC: The Organization of the Islamic Conference.* Herndon, Va.: International Institute of Islamic Thought, 1988.
Almond, Denise L., et al., eds. *Desert Score: U.S. Gulf War Weapons.* Washington, D.C.: Carroll Publishing Co., 1991.
Atkinson, Rick. *Crusade: The Untold Story of the Persian Gulf War.* New York: Houghton Mifflin, 1993.
Baritz, Loren. *Backfire: A History of How American Culture Led Us into Vietnam and Made Us Fight the Way We Did.* New York: Ballantine, 1986.
Bassford, Christopher. *Clausewitz in English: The Reception of Clausewitz in Britain and America, 1815–1945.* New York: Oxford University Press, 1994.
Bell, Robert S. *Desert Storm Reconstruction Report.* Volume XII, *Naval Special Warfare.* Alexandria, Va.: Center for Naval Analyses, 1991.
Bengio, Ofra, ed. *Saddam Speaks on the Gulf Crisis: A Collection of Documents.* Tel Aviv: Tel Aviv University Press, 1992.
Bennett, W. Lance, and Paletz, David L., eds. *Taken by Storm: The Media, Public Opinion and U.S. Foreign Policy in the Gulf War.* Chicago: University of Chicago Press, 1994.
Berger, Carl, ed. *The United States Air Force in Southeast Asia, 1961–1973: An Illustrated Account.* Washington, D.C.: Office of Air Force History, 1984.
Berquist, Ronald E. *The Role of Air Power in the Iran–Iraq War.* Maxwell AFB, Ala.: Air University Press, 1988.
Bowers, Ray L. *The United States Air Force in Southeast Asia: Tactical Airlift.* Washington, D.C.: Office of Air Force History, 1983.
Bowman, Steven R. *Persian Gulf War: Summary of U.S. and Non-U.S. Forces.* Washington, D.C.: Congressional Research Service, Library of Congress, 1991.
Brown, Alan, Gibson, Lester, and Marcus, Alan. *Desert Storm Reconstruction Report.* Volume XIII, *Training.* Alexandria, Va.: Center for Naval Analyses, 1991.

Builder, Carl H. *The Masks of War: American Military Styles in Strategy and Analysis*. Baltimore: Johns Hopkins University Press, 1989.

Cable, Larry. *Unholy Grail: The United States and the Wars in Vietnam, 1965–1968*. New York and London: Routledge, 1991.

Carpenter, P. Mason. *Joint Operations in the Gulf War: An Allison Analysis*. School of Advanced Airpower Studies Thesis. Air University, Maxwell AFB, Alabama, June 1994.

Carroll, Timothy J. *Desert Storm Reconstruction Report*. Volume VII, *Maritime Interception Force Operations*. Alexandria, Va.: Center for Naval Analyses, 1991.

Carter, Ashton B., Perry, William J., and Steinbruner, John. *A New Concept of Cooperative Security, Brookings Occasional Papers*. Washington, D.C.: The Brookings Institute, 1992.

Chambers, Charles E., et al. *Desert Storm Reconstruction Report Volume III: Antiair Warfare*. Alexandria, Va.: Center for Naval Analyses, 1991.

Chanoff, David, and Van Toai Doan. *Portrait of the Enemy*. New York: Random House, 1986.

Chanoff, David, and Bui Diem. *In the Jaws of History*. Boston: Houghton Mifflin, 1987.

Clark, Teresa R., Gunkel, Richard A., Lausten, Lawrence L., Phillips, Barbara A., and Slate, Mitchell P. *Gulf War Air Power Survey*. Vol. IV, Part 2, *Space Operations*. Washington, D.C.: USGPO, 1993.

Clausewitz, Carl von. *On War*. Edited and translated by Michael Howard and Peter Paret. Princeton, N.J.: Princeton University Press, 1976.

Clodfelter, Lieutenant Colonel Mark. *The Limits of Air Power: The American Bombing of North Vietnam*. New York: The Free Press, 1989.

Cohen, Eliot A., et al. *Gulf War Air Power Survey*. Washington, D.C.: U.S. Air Force Office of History, 1993.

———. *Gulf War Air Power Survey. Volume 5, A Statistical Compendium and Chronology*. Washington, D.C.: USGPO, 1993.

Cohen, Eliot A., and Keaney, Thomas A. *Gulf War Air Power Survey Summary Report*. 11 vols. (10 unclassified). Washington, D.C.: USGPO, 1993.

Cohen, Roger, and Gatti, Claudio. *In the Eye of the Storm: The Life of General H. Norman Schwarzkopf*. New York: Farrar, Straus & Giroux, 1991.

Cordesman, Anthony H., and Wagner, Abraham R. *The Lessons of Modern War, Volume II: The Iran–Iraq War*. Boulder, Colo.: Westview, 1990.

Craven, Wesley Frank, and Cate, James Lea, eds. *The Army Air Forces in World War II*. 7 vols. Chicago: University of Chicago Press, 1955. New imprint, Washington, D.C.: Office of Air Force History, USGPO, 1983.

Davis, Richard G. *Carl A. Spaatz and the Air War in Europe*. Washington, D.C.: Center for Air Force History, 1983.

———. *The 31 Initiatives*. Washington, D.C.: Office of Air Force History, 1987.

de la Billiere, Peter. *Storm Command: A Personal Account of the Gulf War*. London: HarperCollins, 1992.

De Seversky, Major Alexander P. *Victory through Air Power*. New York: Simon & Schuster, 1942.

Selected Bibliography 319

Douhet, Guilio. *Command of the Air*. Translated by Dino Ferrari. Washington, D.C.: Office of Air Force History, 1983.
Eisenhower, David. *Eisenhower at War, 1943–1945*. New York: Random House, 1986.
Elshtain, Jean Bethke, et al., eds. *But Was It Just? Reflections on the Morality of the Persian Gulf War*. New York: Doubleday, 1992.
Eschmann, Karl J. *Linebacker, The Untold Story of the Air Raids Over North Vietnam*. New York: Ivy Books, 1989.
FitzGerald, Mary C. *The Impact of the Military–Technical Revolution on Russian Military Affairs*. Volume I. Washington, D.C.: Hudson Institute, 1993.
Foss, Christopher F., and Gander, Terry J., eds. *Jane's Military Vehicles and Logistics*. Couldson, Surrey, England: Jane's Information Group, 1991.
Freedman, Lawrence, and Karsh, Efraim. *The Gulf Conflict 1990–1991: Diplomacy and War in the New World Order*. Princeton, N.J.: Princeton University Press, 1993.
Friedman, Norman. *Desert Victory: The War for Kuwait*. Annapolis: Naval Institute Press, 1992.
———. *Naval Institute Guide to World Naval Weapons Systems, 1991–1992*. Annapolis, Md.: Naval Institute Press, 1993.
Friedman, Norman, ed. *Navies in the Nuclear Age*. London: Conway Maritime Press, 1993; Annapolis, Md.: Naval Institute Press, 1994.
Fussell, Paul. *The Great War and Modern Memory*. London: Oxford University Press, 1975.
Futrell, Robert F. *The United States Air Force in the Korean War*. Washington, D.C.: Office of Air Force History, 1983.
Greer, Thomas H. *The Development of Air Doctrine in the Army Air Arm, 1917–1941*. Washington, D.C.: Office of Air Force History, 1985.
Griffis, Henry S., et al. *Desert Storm Reconstruction Report Volume V: Amphibious Operations*. Alexandria, Va.: Center for Naval Analyses, 1991.
Hallion, Richard P. *Storm over Iraq: Air Power and the Gulf War*. Washington, D.C.: Smithsonian Institution Press, 1992.
Handel, Michael I. *Sun Tzu and Clausewitz Compared*. Carlisle Barracks, Pa.: Strategic Studies Institute, 1991.
Hansell, General Haywood S. *The Strategic Air War against Germany and Japan*. Washington, D.C.: USGPO, 1986.
Hart, B. H. Liddell. *Strategy* (rev. ed.). New York: Meridian, 1991.
Hartman, G. K. *Weapons the Wait*. Annapolis, Md.: Naval Institute Press, 1979.
Hattendorf, John B., ed. *Proceedings: Eleventh International Seapower Symposium: Report of the Proceedings of the Conference*. Newport, R.I.: Naval War College Press, 1992.
Herring, George. *America's Longest War*. New York: John Wiley & Sons, 1979.
Hill, Lewis D., Cook, Doris, and Pinker, Aron. *Gulf War Air Power Survey*. Vol. V, Part 1, *A Statistical Compendium*. Washington, D.C.: USGPO, 1993.
Hone, Thomas C., Mandeles, Mark D., and Terry, Sanford S. *Gulf War Air Power Survey*. Vol. I, Part 2, *Command and Control*. Washington, D.C.: USGPO, 1993.
Horne, Gary E., et al., *Desert Storm Reconstruction Report Volume XIV: Naval Gunfire Support*. Alexandria, Va.: Center for Naval Analyses, 1991.

International Institute for Strategic Studies. *The Military Balance, 1991–1992.* London: International Institute for Strategic Studies, 1991.
Joint Operational Interface of the Ground Attack Control Capability Study. Langley AFB, Va.: 1986.
Johnson, James T., and Kelsay, John, eds. *Cross, Crescent, and Sword.* Westport, Conn.: Greenwood Press, 1990.
Kemp, Anthony. *The Maginot Line, Myth and Reality.* New York: Military Heritage Press, 1988.
Kennett, Lee B. *A History of Strategic Bombing.* New York: Charles Scribner's Sons, 1982.
———. *The First Air War, 1914–1918.* New York: The Free Press, 1991.
Lamberth, Benjamin S. *DESERT STORM and Its Meaning, the View from Moscow.* Santa Monica: RAND Corporation, 1992.
Lund, John, et al. *An Assessment of Strategic Airlift Operational Efficiency.* Washington, D.C.: RAND Corporation, 1993.
Luttwak, Edward. *Strategy: The Logic of War and Peace.* Cambridge, Mass.: Belknap Press, 1987.
Lutz, Jeffrey, et al. *Desert Storm Reconstruction Report Volume VI: Antisurface Warfare.* Alexandria, Va.: Center for Naval Analyses, 1991.
MacIsaac, David. *Strategic Bombing in World War II: The Story of the United States Strategic Bombing Survey.* New York: Garland, 1976.
Mandeles, Mark D. *Understanding Command and Control in Complex Military Organizations.* Alexandria, Va.: The J. de Bloch Group, 1993.
Marshall, George Catlett. *Selected Speeches and Statements of General of the Army George C. Marshall.* Washington, D.C.: The Infantry Journal, 1945.
Middle East Watch. *Needless Deaths in the Gulf War.* Washington, D.C.: Middle East Watch, 1991.
Millet, Allan R. *Semper Fidelis: The Story of the United States Marine Corps.* New York: Macmillan, 1980.
Mitchell, Brigadier General William. *Winged Defense: The Development and Possibilities of Modern Air Power—Economic and Military.* New York: G. P. Putnam, 1925.
Momyer, General William W. *Air Power in Three Wars.* Washington, D.C.: Office of Air Force History, 1978.
Mrozek, Donald J. *Air Power and the Ground War in Vietnam.* Washington, D.C.: Pergamon-Brassey's, 1989.
Murray, Williamson. *Gulf War Air Power Survey, Vol. II, Part I, Operations Report.* Washington, D.C.: USGPO, 1993.
Pagonis, William G., and Cruikshank, Jeffrey L. *Moving Mountains: Lessons in Leadership and Logistics from the Gulf War.* Boston: Harvard Business School Press, 1992.
Palmer, Michael A. *Guardians of the Gulf: A History of America's Expanding Role in the Persian Gulf, 1833–1992.* New York: The Free Press, 1992.
———. *On Course to Desert Storm: The United States Navy and the Persian Gulf.* Washington, D.C.: Naval Historical Center, 1992.
Paret, Peter. *Clausewitz and the State.* New York: Oxford University Press, 1976.
Paret, Peter, ed. *Makers of Modern Strategy, from Machiavelli to the Nuclear Age.* Princeton, N.J.: Princeton University Press, 1986.

Selected Bibliography

Paret, Peter, and Moran, Daniel, eds. and trans. *Carl von Clausewitz: Historical and Political Writings*. Princeton, N.J.: Princeton University Press, 1992.
Passarelli, Ralph, et al. *Desert Storm Reconstruction Report Volume IV: Mine Countermeasures*. Alexandria, Va.: Center for Naval Analyses, 1991.
Pelletiere, Stephen, Johnson, Douglas V., II, and Rosenberger, Leif R. *Iraqi Power and U.S. Security in the Middle East*. Carlisle Barracks, Pa.: Strategic Studies Institute, U.S. Army War College, 1990.
Perla, Peter P. *Desert Storm Reconstruction Report Volume I: Summary*. Alexandria, Va.: Center for Naval Analyses, 1991.
Perspectives on Warfighting: Selected Papers from the 1992 Meeting of the Society of Military History. Vol. 3. Quantico, Va.: Marine Corps University, 1994.
Pike, Douglas. *Vietcong: The Organization and Techniques of the National Liberation Front of South Vietnam*. Cambridge, Mass.: MIT Press, 1966.
———. *PAVN: People's Army of Vietnam*. Novato, Calif.: Presidio Press, 1986.
Piscatori, James, ed. *Islamic Fundamentalisms and the Gulf War*. Chicago: American Academy of Arts and Sciences, 1991.
Proctor, J. Harris, ed. *Islam and International Relations*. New York: Praeger, 1965.
Quilter, Charles J., II. *U.S. Marines in the Persian Gulf, 1990-1991: With the I Marine Expeditionary Force in Desert Shield and Desert Storm*. Washington, D.C.: History and Museums Division, Headquarters, U.S. Marine Corps, 1993.
Rost, Ronald F., Addams, John F., and Nelson, John J. *Sealift in Operation Desert Shield/Desert Storm: 7 August 1990 to 17 February 1991*. Alexandria, Va.: Center for Naval Analyses, 1991.
Scales, Brigadier General Robert J., Jr., et al. *Certain Victory: The United States Army in the Gulf War*. Washington, D.C.: Office of the Chief of Staff, U.S. Army, 1993.
Schaffer, Ronald. *Wings of Judgment: American Bombing in World War II*. New York: Oxford University Press, 1985.
Schultz, Richard H., Jr., and Pfaltzgraff, Robert L., Jr., eds. *The Future of Air Power in the Aftermath of the Gulf War*. Maxwell AFB, Ala.: Air University Press, 1992.
Schwamb, Frank, et al. *Desert Storm Reconstruction Report Volume II: Strike Warfare*. Alexandria, Va.: Center for Naval Analyses, 1991.
Schwarzkopf, General H. Norman, with Petre, Peter. *It Doesn't Take a Hero*. New York: Henry Holt and Bantam Books, 1992.
Sharp, Admiral Ulysses Simpson Grant. *Strategy for Defeat: Vietnam in Retrospect*. Novato, Calif.: Presidio Press, 1986.
Shepko, Michael, Newett, Sandra, and Alexander, Rhonda M. *Maritime Interception Operations*. Alexandria, Va.: Center for Naval Analyses, 1991.
Sherry, Michael. *The Rise of American Air Power: The Creation of Armageddon*. New Haven, Conn.: Yale University Press, 1987.
Smith, Hedrick, ed. *The Media and the Gulf War: The Press and Democracy in Wartime*. Washington, D.C.: Seven Locks Press, 1992.
Smith, Jean Edward. *George Bush's War*. New York: Henry Holt, 1992.
Smock, David, ed. *Religious Perspectives on War*. Washington, D.C.: United States Institute of Peace, 1992.

Summers, Colonel Harry G., Jr. *On Strategy II: A Critical Analysis of the Gulf War.* New York: Dell Publishing, 1992.
Sun Tzu. *The Art of War.* Translated by Samuel B. Griffith. New York: Oxford University Press, 1963.
———. *The Art of War.* Translated by Samuel B. Griffith. New York: Oxford University Press, 1971.
The United States Air Force: Aerospace Challenges and Missions in the 1990s, Conference Paper Summaries. Cambridge, Mass.: The International Security Studies Program, The Fletcher School of Law and Diplomacy, Tufts University, 1991.
The United States Strategic Bombing Survey, Summary Report (European War) 1945. Reprinted in *The United States Strategic Bombing Surveys (European War) (Pacific War).* Maxwell AFB, Ala.: Air University Press, 1987.
Tilford, Earl H., Jr. *Setup: What the Air Force Did in Vietnam and Why.* Maxwell AFB, Ala.: Air University Press, 1991.
———. *Crosswinds: The Air Force's Setup in Vietnam.* College Station: Texas A&M University Press, 1993.
Trainer, Bernard, and Gordon, Michael. *The Generals' War: The Inside Story of the Conflict in the Gulf.* Boston: Little Brown Inc., 1995.
van Creveld, Martin. *Technology and War: From 2000 B.C. to the Present.* New York: The Free Press, 1989.
Ward, Robert W., et al. *Desert Storm Reconstruction Report Volume VIII: C3/ Space and Electronic Warfare.* Alexandria, Va.: Center for Naval Analyses, 1992.
Warden, Colonel John A. *The Air Campaign: Planning for Combat.* Washington, D.C.: National Defense University Press, 1988 and Pergamon–Brassey, 1989.
Watson, Bruce, et al. *Military Lessons of the Gulf War.* Novato, Calif. and London: Greenhill Press, 1991 and 1993.
Watts, Barry D., and Keaney, Thomas A. *Gulf War Air Power Survey.* Volume II, Part 2, *Effects and Effectiveness.* Washington, D.C.: USGPO, 1993.
Westenhoff, Charles M., ed. *Military Air Power: The CADRE Digest of Air Power Opinions and Thoughts.* Maxwell AFB, Ala.: Air University Press, 1990.
White, Lynne, Jr. *Medieval Technology and Social Change.* London: Oxford University Press, 1972.
Winnefeld, James A., Niblack, Preston, and Johnson, Dana J. *A League of Airmen: U.S. Air Power in the Gulf War.* Santa Monica, Calif.: RAND Corporation, 1994.
Woodward, Robert. *The Commanders.* New York: Simon & Schuster, 1991.

Index

A.A.R. Brooks & Perkins, 99
Abdul Aziz ibn Fahd, 28, 29, 31, 34, 35, 38, 226
Accuracy of bombing, 153 n.19
Ad Damman, Saudi Arabia, 74
Admire, John H., 214
Aegis system, 258
A-6E "Intruder," 205, 207, 210, 213, 241, 263 n.11
Afghanistan, 14 n.18, 25, 48
A-4 aircraft, 108
AH-1W "Cobra," 205, 217
Aimpoints, 143–45
Airborne command, control, and communications (ABCCC), 213
Air campaign, 107–9, 111–23, 189, 193–94, 195, 213; aspects, 290–91; and centers of gravity, 283; in Iraq, 5; Islamic response to, 60; and Marines, 210, 213; and Navy, 257–58; and parallel warfare, 128–52; strategy, 232; as term, 125 n.20. *See also* Airpower
Air command and control system, 142

Air conditioning, 92
Air Corps Tactical School (ACTS), 136
Aircraft Battle Damage Repair (ABDR), 93
Aircraft carrier, 226, 252, 255, 258, 261 n.2
Aircrew availability, 68
Air defense systems, 137, 143, 145, 295, 305; of Iraq, 281; naval, 258, 259; targets, 232, 233
Airfields as targets, 116, 117, 143, 145, 232, 233
Airflow, 73, 74
Air-ground cohesion, 219
AirLand Battle strategy, 88, 142, 177–78, 182–83, 191–92; and casualties, 195; and envelopment, 196; and fresh troops, 197; and Schwarzkopf, 187–89
Airlift, 65–66, 67–82, 226
Airlift Control Center, 78
Airlifters, 67
Airline industry (United States), 75–76
Air Logistics Center, 98

Air Mobility Command (AMC), 81
Airpower, 1, 4, 7, 11–12, 87, 280;
  basing, 255; Coalition, 187, 232;
  command and control, 157–69; cost,
  262 n.8; doctrine, 267–68, 293–304;
  and ground operations, 113, 141,
  194, 211; history of, 107–9, 293–
  304; Iraqi view of, 185; limitations,
  197; maintenance, 68, 94–95;
  Marine, 202, 207, 219, 220, 236;
  Navy, 235, 236, 240; role, 113,
  141–42, 155 n.42, 158, 177, 178,
  185, 267, 290–307; and Saddam,
  281; strategy, 127–52, 142; superiority, 88, 145, 232, 234; and surface
  forces, 295; traffic control, 158;
  trust in, 194. *See also* Air campaign;
  specific aircraft
Air refueling, 68, 80
Air Reserve Component (ARC), 76–77
Airspace limitations, 81
Air Tasking Order (ATO), 115, 142,
  147 n.33, 152 n.3, 158, 233; and
  battle groups, 234, 262 n.8; design,
  262 n.8; efficiency, 233
Air University, 136
Akham al-bughat (laws for rebellion),
  53, 56–57
Al-Azhar, 56, 57
Alexander the Great, 154 n.25
Algeria, 32
Al Jaber, 217
Al Jahra, Kuwait, 210, 212, 218
Alliances, 17–19
Allies at Falaise Pocket, 197
Al-Mutl'a Pass, 240
Al Wafra, 209
Amphibious assault, 210, 216–17, 220,
  234, 239, 260; and casualties, 232–
  33; effectiveness, 242, 244, 258–59;
  strategy, 235, 236, 237
Amphibious Group Three (USMC),
  208, 239
Amphibious Group Two (USMC), 239
Amphibious Ready Group Bravo
  (ARG) (USMC), 206
Amphibious Task Force, 238, 240, 241
Annihilation, 177, 196; and parallel
  warfare, 138–41, 146, 148, 149,
  150, 151, 154 n.25
Antiair command, 233
Antiaircraft artillery (AAA), 4–5
Antiair warfare, 234
Antisurface command, 233, 236
Antisurface warfare, 236–37
Antiwar movement, 4
Appeasement of Iraq, 23
Aqabah, Jordan, 229, 230
Arabian American Oil Company air-
  field, 210
Arabian Peninsula, 229
Arabian Sea, 261 n.2
Arab-Israeli Wars, 5, 48, 129, 135,
  137
Arab League, 31–32, 36
Arab nationalism, 260 n.1
Arab states, 27, 30–32, 34–35, 43–44,
  232, 273, 274
Arab unity, 36
Arab world, 18
Area defense targets, 130
Argentina, 14 n.18
Arkin, William, 121–22, 125 n.18
Army Helicopter Improvement Pro-
  gram (AHIP), 236
Arnold, Henry J. "Hap," 297
Arthur, Stanley, 230, 231, 236, 237,
  241
Artillery, 201
A-7 aircraft, 108
Ash Shuaybah, Kuwait, 209, 239, 241,
  242
A-6 aircraft, 108
Aspen Institute, 27–28
Assad, Hafaz, 31, 38, 43, 181
As Salman, 185
As Samawah, 196
Assault amphibian vehicle (AAV), 205
Assessment, 141–42, 145, 159, 270,
  271–72, 286; of airpower, 290–307;
  of airwar, 118–23; of bomb damage,
  167
Atkinson, Rick, 124 n.7
Attack flow plan, 154 n.32
Attrition, 138–41, 148, 149, 150, 151,
  201–2, 294

Index   325

Australia, 14 n.18, 33
Automated decision support systems, 158
Automatic Test Equipment (ATE), 94
AV-8B "Harrier II," 167, 205, 207, 210, 213, 241, 260
Avionics Intermediate Station (AIS), 98
Aziz, Tariq, 39
Azon bomb (VB-1), 137
Azores, 204
Az-Zubayr, Iraq, 237

Ba'ath party, 52, 56, 59
Badran, Mudar, 45 n.22
Baghdad, 117–18, 128, 139–40, 159–65, 196
Baghi (rebel), 56
Bahrain, 14 n.18, 32, 205, 207
Baker, James, III, 25, 29, 38–39, 43, 171 n.30
"Balanced force" concept, 298
Baldwin, Stanley, 305, 310 n.56
Balkans, 129
Baltic states, 39
Bandar bin Sultan (prince of Saudi Arabia), 29, 37, 39
Bangladesh, 14 n.18
Bare base assets, 93–94
Baritz, Loren, 9
Bartlett, Bruce, 39
Base Engineering Emergency Forces (Prime BEEF), 94
Base Level Self-Sufficiency Spares, 101 n.8
Bases: for air force, 69, 71, 72, 80–81, 88; bare assets, 93–94; closure, 69–70; forward, 88, 151; for ground force, 252, 255, 260; for Military Airlift Command, 71; naval role, 252, 253–55, 257; offshore, 254–55; operations, 68; political problems, 253–55; preparation, 89, 113; for radar, 261 n.6; in Saudi Arabia, 273, 284; sea, 252; for ships, 261 n.2; staging, 71, 72, 80–81; supply store, 93; in Turkey, 90, 273, 284; in U.K., 90

Basra, Iraq, 128, 138, 184, 185, 188, 196, 240
Basra highway, 197, 241–42, 285–86
Battle damage assessment (BDA), 141–42, 145, 159
Battlefield preparation, 115, 211, 232, 234–35, 291
Battle Griffin '91 exercise, 209
Battleships, 238, 239
Battlespace management, 149–50
Bear D aircraft, 257, 261 n.6
Belgium, 14 n.18, 187
Berlin Airlift, 67–68, 83 n.6
Bessmertnykh, Alexander, 171 n.30
B-52 aircraft, 108, 117, 127
B-52G aircraft, 95–96
"Big picture," 207
Billeting of Air Reserve Component, 77
Bingham, Price T., 11, 12
Biological weapons, 113, 114, 128, 193, 195, 232; destruction of, 120–21, 122; Iraqi use, 97; and U.S. public opinion, 184
Biscone, Greg, 127–28
Black Hole planners, 115, 124 n.8, 142–43
Blockade, 252
Blockade of Iraq, 243, 256–57, 262 n.8. *See also* Embargo
Blount Island, Fla., 204
Blue Ball Express, 92
Bombs, bombing, 153 n.19, 167, 239–40, 244, 263 n.11, 290–307; strategic, 111–23, 193, 290–307; Vietnam War, 193, 302, 303–4; World War II, 118, 123 n.2, 136–37, 193, 298, 300–302, 305, 307
Boomer, Walter E., 3–4, 205, 206, 207, 214, 218, 220, 242; and air control, 213; strategy, 209, 210, 211
Bosnia, 2, 48, 262 n.7, 307
Brabham, James A., 206, 212
Bracken, Paul, 171 n.34
Brady, Nicholas, 38
Breach points, 211–12
Bridges, 116

Brigade Service Support Group (BSSG), 203, 205–6
Britain. *See* United Kingdom
British Commonwealth, 42
Brodie, Bernard, 287
B-2 aircraft, 292, 306
Bubiyan, Kuwait, 185
Bubiyan Channel, battle of, 237
Bubiyan Island, 237, 241, 242
Bubiyan Turkeyshoot, 237
Buckingham, Fredric N., 78
Burden sharing, 102 n.13
Bureau of legal interpretation (Dar al-Ifta'), 57
Burqan oil field, 217
Bush, George, 3, 6, 12, 150, 195, 225–26; attack on, 258; and cease-fire, 198–99, 242; and China, 32; and Coalition, 43; commitment to Arabs, 34; diplomacy, 9, 17–18, 37–40; and embargo, 228–29; on ethics of war, 47; and ground war, 194; image, 18; and Israel, 190; and Mubarak, 31, 45 n.24; objectives, 27, 108, 112, 179, 180–81, 188, 192–93, 230, 270, 275; policy style, 8; and Reagan, 273; response to, 55; selling of Gulf War, 180–81; and Soviet Union, 25–26; and time element, 279; and Vietnam, 11

Cable, Larry E., 10, 12, 174, 323
Cable News Network (CNN), 1, 37, 47, 117, 286–87
Cairo West AB, Egypt, 72, 80
Camouflage, 92
Campaign Plans Division, 163n
Camp David, Md., 29
Camp Lejune, N.C., 208
Camp Pendeleton, Calif., 208
Canada, 14 n.18
Cannibalization of supplies, 96
Capability to fight, 129–30, 135
Cargo handling, 99
Carrier Group Seven, 236
Carter, Jimmy, 18, 29, 204
Castles model, 299–300, 305
Casualty rates, 129, 130, 150, 182, 198, 209, 211; and American policy, 195, 273; and amphibious assault, 210, 232–33; Coalition, 5, 242; Iraqi, 219, 242; Marine, 216, 219; in Vietnam, 303; Warden on, 300
Centers of gravity, 119, 134, 141, 143, 154 n.33, 185; and airpower, 111; Clausewitz on, 282–83, 287, 294; of Coalition, 284–85; Douhet on, 295; of Iraq, 113, 283–84; United States, 273
Central control of military, 166, 168–69, 170 n.11, 184, 207, 229
Central Intelligence Agency (CIA), 28, 183
C-5 aircraft, 71, 72–73, 77, 80, 108
C-5A aircraft, 77, 90
C-5B aircraft, 90
Change of Operational Control (CHOP), 79, 85 n.81
Charleston AFB, S.C., 73, 74, 77, 90
Checkmate, 113
Chemical and biological contamination, 97
Chemical warfare, 76, 92, 128, 184
Chemical weapons, 113, 114, 116, 193, 195, 232; destruction of, 120–21, 122, 128; Iraqi use, 97, 181, 201; and Israel, 190; precautions, 216
Cheney, Richard B., 28–29, 30, 31, 35, 38, 69, 225, 239
CH-46E "Sea Knight," 202, 205
CH-53D "Sea Stallion," 205
CH-53E "Super Stallion," 205
China. *See* People's Republic of China
Christianity, 49, 189, 190
Churchill, Winston, 88
Civil engineers, 94
Civilian suffering, 120
Civilian targets, 60
Civil Reserve Air Fleet (CRAF), 68, 75–76, 83 n.8, 90
Civil strife, 52, 53, 56–57, 61
Clausewitz, Karl von, 7–8, 9, 10, 121, 134, 153 n.8, 177; and Gorrell, 295; and Gulf War, 268, 269–88; principles, 270–71, 286–88, 294

Index   327

Clinton, Bill, 2, 254
Clodfelter, Mark, 13 n.5, 303, 304
Close air support (CAS), 207, 211
Clothing, protective, 216
Coalition, 4, 14 n.18, 21–46, 40, 174; air, land, sea campaign, 230; airpower, 87, 148 n.44, 187, 232, 236; casualty rates, 5, 242; centers of gravity, 284–85; cohesion, 174, 182; condemnation of, 58; creation of, 27–34, 273–74; diplomacy, 231; and embargo, 256; ethics of, 49; failures, 10, 192–99; finances, 21, 24–25, 33, 40; fragility, 279; goals, 274–75, 285–86; image, 175, 189; losses, 88; maritime campaign, 236–39, 244; military forces, 21, 232; military positions, 239; naval forces, 227, 229, 232; perspective, 270, 274–75; and preemptive strike, 254; problems in, 198; and public opinion, 277–78; solidarity, 243; strains on, 34–37; strategy, 186–89, 227, 234–35; success of, 159, 168, 267–68; and time element, 182. *See also individual members*
Coastal defensive systems, 237
Cohen, Eliot, 118
Cold War, 4, 226, 287
Collective security, 179
Collins, John M., 169
Colonialism, 18, 35–36, 50, 54, 58, 277
Combat Logistics Support Squadron (CLSS), 93
Combat Supply System (CSS), 96
Command, control, communications, intelligence (C4I), 148, 300
Command Analysis Group (CAG), 69, 77
Command and control, 118–19, 130, 143, 148, 166, 177, 182; airborne, 213; of air forces, 142, 157–69; antisurface, 233, 236; Iraqi, 140, 184–85, 234; and Marines, 213; organization, 168; problems, 157–69, 178; targets, 112, 113, 114, 116, 117, 128, 145, 158, 232, 300

Commander, U.S. Marine Forces, Central Command (MARCENT), 204, 206
Commander in Chief, Central Command (CINCENTCOM), 112, 142
Commander of Airlift Forces, 78
Command of joint forces, 150–51
Command structure, 81, 89, 113, 204, 230–31, 233
Commercial airlines, 69
Commercial Reserve Air Fleet (CRAF), 7, 75–76
Common support equipment (CSE), 94–95
Communications, 118–19, 128, 148, 182, 232, 300; Iraqi, 234; problems, 159, 166, 177, 178, 196; satellites, 261 n.6; sea lines, 227, 243; targets, 108, 114, 116, 117; technology, 109, 147
Community of interest, 284
Complexity of war, 166, 167
Composite warfare, 233, 244
Composite wings, 261 n.3
Computer aided flight management system (CAFMS), 233, 243
Computer assisted force management (CAFM), 142
Computers, 118–19, 257, 262 n.8, 263 n.9, 264 n.12
Concentric circles model, 299–300, 305
Concept of Operations (CONOPS), 141–45
Conduct of the Persian Gulf War, 118–22
C-141 aircraft, 71, 72–73, 77, 80, 89, 90, 108
C-130 aircraft, 68, 78, 79, 95, 98, 108
Conference on Security and Cooperation in Europe (CSCE), 33
Conferences on Islam and war, 48, 49
Constitution of Medina, 51
Containment, 179–80, 181–82
Contamination, 97–98
Context of Gulf War, 269
Control and Reporting Center (CRC), 207

Control as objective, 134, 135, 138–41, 143, 146
Control of forces, 134, 166, 168–69
Conventional Air-Launched Cruise Missiles (CALCM), 128
Conventional airpower, 112
Corgan, Michael T., 9–10, 12, 268, 323
Cost/benefit analysis, 270, 271–72, 286, 306
Cost of airpower, 262 n.8
Cost of computers, 262 n.8
Cost of sea war, 257
Cost of weaponry, 256–57, 262 n.8
Creation of Coalition, 27–34, 273–74
Creativity in Clausewitz, 277
Crimean War, 2
Crisis Action Team (CAT), 69, 70, 73
Cross section of aircraft, 137–38
Crusaders, 189
Cuba, 41
Culminating point of attack, 188, 191, 199, 274–75
Culminating point of victory, 285–86, 287
Culture and Coalition, 34–35, 159
Czechoslovakia, 14 n.18

Damage repair, 93
Dammam, Saudi Arabia, 227
Dar al-Ifta' (bureau of legal interpretation), 57
Decadence, 54
Decision-making process, 165–68
"Declaration of Mecca," 59
Decontamination, 97–98
Defection from Iraq, 189
Defense and C3, 178
Defense Intelligence Agency, 231
Defense Logistics Agency (DLA), 75, 89, 92, 99
Defense Personnel Support Center, 92
Defense Science Board, 165
Defense suppression aircraft, 137, 263 n.10
Defense targets, 130
Defensive systems, 130, 237, 305
Denmark, 14 n.18

Deployment of force, 147, 148, 151
Depots as targets, 232
Deptula, David A., 11, 109, 115–16, 163, 170 n.11, 323–24
Desert warfare, 88, 91–92
De Seversky, Alexander, 267, 297–98, 304, 305
Destruction as objective, 134, 135, 143, 145, 146, 177, 196; Clausewitz on, 284, 294; De Seversky on, 297; and effect, 138–41; Gorrell on, 295; of ground forces, 305
Al Dhafra, 160
Dhahran, Saudi Arabia, 72, 73, 74, 90, 207
Diego Garcia, 90, 91, 92, 127, 204, 253, 255, 261 n.4
Dimensions of war, 133–34
Diplomacy, 4, 9, 17–18, 37–40, 181, 231, 275
Direct Air Support Center (DASC), 213
Disease, 120
Donovan, Francis R., 228
Douhet, Giulio, 107, 108, 135, 136, 267, 291, 292, 301–2; principles, 294–95
Dover AFB, Del., 75, 76, 77
Dugan, Michael, 291
Dynamic planning of air campaign, 159–65

Early warning sites, 130
EA-6B "Prowler," 205, 207, 210, 241
Echelon formation, 211
EC-130E ABCCC aircraft, 158, 168–69
Economic activity, 21–44
Economic sanctions, 32, 41, 42, 198–99
Economics of weaponry, 256–57, 262 n.8
E-8A JSTARS aircraft, 158, 168–69
Effectiveness of force, 147
Effect of targeting, 138–41, 143, 145
EF-111 aircraft, 160
Egypt, 14 n.18, 51–52, 56, 190–91, 212, 218, 239; and air campaign,

60; and Coalition, 31, 40, 189–90; on ethics of war, 47; and fellahin, 190
XVIII Corps, U.S., 79, 190–91, 194, 206, 230, 239, 240
Eighth Air Force, 129, 130–31, 152 n.4
8th Marines, 214, 216, 217, 218
81st Tactical Fighter Wing (TFW), U.S., 98
82nd Airborne, U.S., 75, 191
86th Tactical Fighter Wing (TFW), U.S., 98
Eisenhower, Dwight David, 302
Electric circuit analogy, 130–31
Electric power targets, 113, 114, 116, 117, 119, 120, 128, 232; and control objective, 139–40, 143; and parallel warfare, 133, 136
Electromagnetic pulse (EMP) hardened, 125 n.18
Electronic battlefield, 269
Electronic countermeasures (ECM) testing, 98
Electronics contamination, 97–98
11th Marines, 205
Embargo of Bosnia, 262 n.7
Embargo of Iraq, 4, 24, 27, 125 n.26, 228–29, 243, 253, 256, 263 n.9
Ends/means analysis, 270
Enemy Prisoner of War (EPW), 218, 219, 242
Engineers, 94
Envelopment, 187–88, 191, 194, 196, 240
Environmental war, 60
Equipment problems, 157–58
Ethics, morality, 18, 47–63, 120, 179–80, 254, 298, 302
Ethnicity and nationalism, 51
Ethnocentrism, 305
E-3A AWACS aircraft, 158, 168–69
E-2C Hawkeye, 158
Euphrates River, 185, 196, 235
Europe, 51, 177
European Commonwealth, 42
Evolution of warfare, 129
Exclusion zone, 254

Execution of air war, 115–18
Exocet missiles, 234
Expansion of war, 285, 302
Exploitation and pursuit phase, 188, 191, 194

F/A-18 "Hornet," 205, 207, 210, 213, 252, 263 nn.10, 11
Falaise Pocket, France, 197
Falkenhayn, Erich von, 154 n.25
Fallon, Nevada, 231
Fatwas (juristic opinions), 48, 49
FAX systems, 109, 154 n.30
Faylaka Island, 233, 238, 239, 240, 241, 242
Fear, 190
Fellahin, 190, 198
F-15 aircraft, 98
F-15E aircraft, 128, 167
F-4G aircraft, 108, 160
Field Manual (FM) 100-5, 177
Field repair teams, 5
5th Marine Expeditionary Brigade (MEB), 208, 209, 216, 230, 239
5th Marines, 205
50th Tactical Fighter Wing (TFW), U.S., 98
Fighter interception, 158
Finances of Coalition, 21, 24–25, 33, 40
Al Fintas, Kuwait, 241
Al Firdos bunker, Baghdad, 117–18, 125 n.18
Firecontrol systems, 263 n.11
Firepower, 177
1st Armored, U.S., 196
1st Armored Division, U.K., 191, 196, 208, 209, 232
1st Brigade, 24th Infantry, U.S., 197–98, 209
1st Cavalry Division, U.S., 209
1st Force Service Support Group (FSSG), U.S., 203
1st Infantry Division, U.S., 196, 230
I Marine Expeditionary Force (MEF), U.S., 210, 219–20, 232; action, 240, 242; command of, 204; disposition, 190–91, 196; effectiveness, 194;

force strength, 209; main command post, 208; strategy, 235
1st Marine Division, U.S., 206, 208, 209, 210, 211, 214–16, 217, 218
1st Marine Expeditionary Brigade (MEB), U.S., 206
1st Marine task force, U.S., 214, 216, 218
Fisher, Sir John, 252
Fitna (civil strife), 52
Five-rings model, 108, 109, 112
Fleet Marine Force (FMF), 202–3
Flight time for airlift crews, 77
Fogarty, William M., 229, 231
Follow On Spares Kits (FOSK), 96, 98
F-111 aircraft, 96, 108, 159–65
F-111F aircraft, 167, 263 n.11
F-117 (stealth) aircraft, 117, 119, 127, 157, 165, 167, 292; development, 138; use of, 140, 141, 150, 152 n.23
Food distribution and parallel warfare, 136
Force, uses of, 134
Force package size, 137–38
Forces and ring model, 112
Force Service Support Group (FSSG), 203
4th Infantry Brigade, U.K., 208
4th Marine Expeditionary Brigade (MEB), U.S., 203, 206, 209, 216, 239
4th Marine task force, U.S., 214, 217
Fort Bragg, N.C., 75
Fort Dietrick, Md., 97
48th Tactical Fighter Wing (TFW), U.S., 98, 159–65
401st Tactical Fighter Wing (TFW), U.S., 98
463L pallets, straps, nets, 99, 105 n.33
4401st Munitions Maintenance Squadron, U.S., 95
14th Air Division (Provisional), U.S., 163n
France, 14 n.18, 28, 33, 38; and Coalition, 189; detention of citizens, 40; and embargo, 253; and Iraq, 88; military forces, 191, 232; and United States, 273; and Vietnam, 3; and World War II, 184–85, 187
Franco-Prussian War, 2
Frankfurt, Germany, 74
Free Kuwaiti Interim Government, 54
Friction in war, 280–82, 286
Friedman, Norman, 12, 223, 324
Friendly fire, 211, 216, 220, 259, 282, 305
"From the Sea" white paper, 243–44
Frontal attack, 187–88
F-16 aircraft, 159–65
F-22 aircraft, 165, 292
Fuel supply, 95, 104 n.24
Fulbright, J. William, 8
Fulda Gap, Iraq, 178
Fulford, Carlton W., 205, 214
Fulks, James A., 214

Gates, Robert, 39
GBU-27, 150
GBU-28, 263 n.11
General Secretariat of the People's Islamic Conference, 55
Germany, 14 n.18, 33, 38, 102 n.13, 295; and World War II, 7, 135, 187, 197, 300–301
Gettysburg, Battle of, 268
Al-Ghazali, 51
Giap Vo Nguyen (Vietnamese general), 273
Global economy, 307
Global Positioning System, 109, 258, 264 n.12
"Global Reach, Global Power," 292
Glosson, Buster C., 114, 115, 118, 124 n.8, 163, 164, 167
Goldwater-Nichols Act of 1986, 207, 299
Gompert, David, 307
Gorbachev, Mikhail, 33, 36–37, 38, 171 n.30, 180, 182
Gorrell, Edgar S., 295
Government center targets, 128, 143, 146
Granada, 82, 179
Grant, Ulysses S., 2, 154 n.25, 299
Gray, Al, 204

Greece, 14 n.18
Griffith, Tom, 126 n.27
Grizzly (4th U.S. Marine task force), 214, 217
Ground defense of Saudi Arabia, 112
Ground forces, 151, 177, 178, 194, 234–35; and airpower, 194, 211, 267, 305; De Seversky on, 298; destruction, 305; goals, 134; Gorrell on, 295; LeMay on, 299; logistics, 255; massed, 146–47; Mitchell on, 296; and Navy, 252, 260
Ground operations, 173–220, 195, 232, 260, 263 n.11, 291; and airpower, 111, 113, 141, 194; goals, 275; and navy, 253
Guam, 204
Guidance, Apportionment, and Targeting (GAT), 162–63, 167
Gulf Cooperation Council (GCC), 90, 239
Gulf of Oman, 225
Gulf of Tonkin resolution, 8
Gulf states, 102 n.13, 121
Gulf War Air Power Survey (GWAPS), 116, 118–22, 123 n.2, 159

Haifa, Israel, 190
"Hail Mary Play," 79, 187, 192, 194, 199
Haiti, 2, 254, 275, 307
Hallion, Richard P., 9, 10, 15 n.23, 124, 292
Hammurabi division, Iraq, 197–98
Handel, Michael I., 288 n.3
Hardened bunkers, 140
Hardened shelters, 292
Hard-target penetrators, 258, 263 n.11
Hart, B. H. Liddell, 153 n.8
Harvest Bare, 93
Harvest Eagle, 93
Harvest Falcon, 93–94
Hashmi, Sohail H., 9, 18, 324
Hassan II (king of Morocco), 31
Hastings, Battle of, 169 n.2
Haybannya oil facility, 128
Head, William, 324
Heat, coping with, 91–92

Heavy Operations Squadron team (HORSE), 94
Hellfire missiles, 236
Helsinki meeting, 33
Herring, George, 6
High-altitude airdrop training, 78–79
High density control zones (HDCZ), 213
High-frequency radio detection finder (HFDF), 261 n.6
High Priority Mission Support Kits (HPMSK), 96
"Highway of Death," 197, 241–42, 285–86
Hijra, 51
Hill AFB, Utah, 94
History and propaganda, 268
History of airpower, 107–9, 293–304
Hitler, Adolf, 6, 181, 184, 189, 201
HMS *Gloucester*, 241
HMS *Hunt*, 238
HMS *London*, 241
Ho Chi-minh, 6
Hodory, Richard W., 214
Holocaust, 190
Hopkins, John I., 204, 205, 206
Horner, Charles A., 78, 113, 165, 166–67, 207, 233, 234
Hospital ships, 228
Host Nation Support (HNS), 91
Howard, Michael, 270
Howard, Patrick G., 214
H-3 airfield (Iraq), 128
Humanitarian aid, 41
Hunt class ships, 238
Hussein, Saddam, 1, 2, 4, 6; and airpower, 281; and Ba'athist ideology, 52; as *baghi*, 56; call for terrorism, 281; as center of gravity, 283; command ability, 119; condemnation of, 56; image, reputation, 55, 56–57, 58, 59, 175; and intelligence, 280–81; and Iran, 279; and Islamic shrines, 55; isolation, 281; *jihad*, 281; and limited war, 276; maritime action, 228; mistakes, 40–41, 184, 279; as *mujahid*, 58; objectives, 179, 270, 271–74, 278–79; and Palesti-

nian conflict, 276, 277; and pan-Arabism, 54; peace agreement, 171 n.30; power, 12, 175–76, 292, 306; propaganda, 36; and public opinion, 277; removal of, 180, 192, 193, 275, 292, 306; renewed threat, 253; strategy, 6–7, 108, 184–85, 189–90, 216–17, 227, 231–32, 242, 258, 284; and subordinates, 271; support for, 62; and suspension, 278–79; as target, 300; victory, 285

Hussein I (king of Jordan), 28, 31, 39–40

Ibn Baz (Shaykh 'Abd al-'Aziz ibn Baz), 57, 60, 62
Ibn Siddiq (Shaykh 'Abd al-'Aziz ibn Saddiq), 61
Iceland, 33
Imam, 51
Imperialism, 54
Incirlik AFB, Turkey, 94, 284
Incrementalism, 112
Indian Ocean, 261 n.2
Industry, 133, 134, 136, 146, 305–6
Infant mortality, 120
Information problems, 157–58, 165–68
Information warfare, 149, 150
Infrastructure, 96, 114, 133, 146, 232, 302; of Iraq, 123, 184; in Middle East, 82, 90, 95; ring model, 112; of Saudi Arabia, 82, 90, 95, 201, 228, 253, 260
Initiative in war, 178
Instant Thunder, 112–14, 115, 142
Insurance and airlift, 75–76
Integrated air defense system (IADS), 116, 130
Intelligence, 145, 147, 148, 165, 280–82; and Bosnia, 262 n.7; failures, 183–84; on Iraq, 231–32; role of, 182–83; sea traffic, 257; and systems, 147; targets, 300
Interceptor operations center (IOC), 140–41
Interdiction operations, 108, 112, 235, 240, 302

Intermediate level maintenance (ILM), 98
International Court of Justice, 50
International Islamic Law Commission, 50
International law and Islam, 63
International Logistics Center (ILC), 89
International relations and Islam, 48, 49–53
In-theater airlift, 69, 77–78, 92
Invasion of Kuwait, 49, 54–60
Invasion of Saudi Arabia, 87–88, 158, 170 n.7
Iran, 18, 29, 43, 237, 261 n.4, 272, 273
Iran-Iraq War, 48, 55, 97, 121, 123, 201–2; and Saddam, 272, 279; tactics, 184, 185; U.S. support, 180–81
Iraq, 17, 18, 123, 180, 234; air defenses, 4–5, 140, 257–58, 263 n.9, 281; air forces, 88, 122, 185, 234; airspace limitations, 81; appeasement of, 23; and Arab League, 32; army, 1, 88, 108, 114, 121–22, 123, 129, 176, 189, 191, 226–27; biological weapons, 97, 113, 114, 120–21, 122, 128, 193, 195, 232; blockade of Iraq, 243, 256–57, 262 n.8; casualty rates, 219, 242; centers of gravity, 113, 283–84; chemical weapons, 97, 113, 114, 116, 120–21, 122, 128, 181, 193, 195, 201, 232; civil war, 61; command and control, 140, 184–85, 234; communications, 234; defection from, 189; diplomacy, 181; disposition of forces, 184–85, 231–32; economy, 254, 272; embargo of, 4, 24, 27, 125 n.26, 198–99, 228–29, 243, 253, 256, 263 n.9; and France, 88, 253; ground forces, 234–35; image, reputation, 30–31, 34, 41, 54–55, 180; infrastructure, 123, 184; intelligence on, 231–32; isolation, 25–26, 181–82, 198–99, 230, 281; and Kurds, 49, 58, 59, 61, 97, 122–23, 272, 276; logistics, 184; military, 108, 169, 176, 183, 184–85, 201–2; and

Index

nationalism, 51–52; navy, 234, 236, 259, 264 n.13; nuclear weapons, 113, 114, 116, 120–21, 122, 193, 195, 232, 274; objectives, 179, 271–74; and People's Islamic Conference, 58; ports, 237; postwar conditions, 122; public opinion, 272, 277; and rebellions, 49; Revolutionary Command Council, 54; role in Middle East, 226; scorched earth policy, 214; and Shi'ites, 49, 59, 61, 122–23, 276; and Soviet Union, 25–26, 88, 171 n.30, 184, 214; Sunni party, 272; as threat, 122; threats to, 272–73; training of forces, 189, 237, 244; and United Kingdom, 184; and United Nations, 274; viewpoint, 270; weaknesses, 184–85, 305–6
Irkutsk meeting, 25
Islam, 47–63
Islamic army, 57–58
Islamic resurgence, 49
Islamic shrines, 55–56
Isolation of Iraq, 25–26, 181–82, 198–99, 230, 281
Israel, 17–18, 35, 58, 59, 198, 274, 284; and Iraqi propaganda, 55; and Saddam's strategy, 190; and Scud attacks, 60, 121, 126 n.31, 190, 193; and United States, 35, 44 n.35
Italy, 14 n.18

Jabir al Achmed al Sabah, 37, 38
Jackson, Stonewall, 282
Jallibah, Iraq, 185, 191, 196
Japan, 21, 38, 135, 297, 300–301; financial role, 24, 33, 102 n.13
Jeddah New AB, Saudi Arabia, 72, 80
Jenkins, Harry W., 203, 231
Jet Engine Intermediate Maintenance (JEIM), 98
Jihad, 18, 36, 47–63, 281, 284
Johnson, Hansford T., 7, 68, 227, 228; and airlift, 69, 71, 76, 77, 80, 81
Johnson, Lyndon, 3, 6, 8, 194
Joint Chiefs of Staff, 188, 225
Joint Forces Air Component Commander (JFACC), 142, 149–50, 166–67, 207, 211, 233, 290
Joint Forces Command, East (JFC-E), 191, 196, 239, 240
Joint Forces Command, North (JFC-N), 191, 196, 212, 218, 239, 240
Jointness, 150, 178, 224, 253, 262 n.8, 299; Air Force and Army, 142; Air Force and Marines, 207; Air Force and Navy, 231, 233, 236, 243
Joint Task Force Middle East, 225
Jomini, Antoine Henri de, Baron, 2, 65, 177
Jordan, 31, 32, 39–40, 47, 256
Jubayl, Saudi Arabia, 74, 90, 206, 227
Julius Caesar, 154 n.25
Jus in bello and *jus ad bello*, 60–61
Justice and Islamic law, 53

Kant, Immanuel, 280
KC-10 aircraft, 7, 79–80, 90, 95–96
KC-130 "Hercules," 205
KC-135 aircraft, 80, 108
Keegan, John, 270
Kelso, Frank B., II, 3–4, 263 n.11
Kennedy, John F., 6
Keys, William, 209, 211–12, 213, 214
Khadduri, Majid, 49
Khafji, 189, 211
Al Kharj, Saudi Arabia, 95
Ibn Khaldun, 51
Kibrit, Saudi Arabia, 211, 212
Kill box system, 235
King Fahd International Airport, Saudi Arabia, 74–75
King Khalid Military City, 74–75, 90
Kondra, Vernon J., 71, 72, 73
Korea, 261 n.2
Korean War, 5, 12, 129, 175, 275; and ethnocentrism, 305, 306; and Gulf War, 179–80; and strategic bombing, 193, 302; and United Nations, 275
Krauthammer, Charles, 61
Krulak, Charles C., 212
Kuehl, Daniel T., 11, 108–9, 324–25
Kurds, 49, 58, 59, 97, 272, 276; rebellion, 61, 122–23

Kuwait, 2, 14 n.18, 18; border targets, 239; and burden sharing, 102 n.13; and Coalition finances, 40; coast, 236; defense of, 27; and embargo, 229; evacuation of, 193; importance of, 27; invasion of, 54–60; logistics, 184; military force, 189, 191, 239; occupation of, 122, 183; reoccupation, 151; reputation, 30, 34; and Saddam, 272; sea lanes, 257; theater of operations, 159; threat to, 253; threat to Iraq, 273
Kuwait City, 185, 196
Kuwait International Airport, 218

Lajes AB, Azores, 69
Langly AFB, Va., 96
Language differences, 81, 159, 182
Laos, 108
LaPlante, John B., 231
Laser-guided bombs (LGB), 108, 137, 258, 263 n.11
Laser mine detectors, 264 n.14
Leadership, 112, 113, 114, 116, 117, 119, 232; and Clausewitz, 270–71; control of, 134; and parallel warfare, 130, 133; and ring model, 112; and serial warfare, 130, 143
League of Nations, 294
Lebanon, 18, 34, 198
Lee, Robert E., 2
Legitimacy of Coalition, 23
Leland, John W., 11–12, 66, 325
LeMay, Curtis E., 267, 298–99
Levels of war, 133–34
Leverage ability, 147
Libya, 32, 135, 256
Light Airborne Multi-Purpose System (LAMPS) III, 236
Limited war, 6, 175, 270, 275–78, 285, 286; LeMay on, 298; problems, 302–3; and public opinion, 180
Linebacker air campaigns, 5, 13 n.6, 108, 303, 304
Linehaul operations, 92
Line Replacable Unit (LRU), 97, 98
Lithuania, 39
Little Creek, Va., 203

Littoral operations, 244
Livingston, Lawrence H., 214
Logistics, 11, 65–66, 113, 184, 201, 227–28; and Air Force, 87–100; and Bush, 181; Iraqi, 184; and Marines, 202, 205–6, 207, 210–11, 212, 217; and Navy, 226, 227–28, 230, 251–52, 255; problems, 196, 255. *See also* Maritime Prepositioned Force; Prepositioned materiel
Logistics airlift (LOGAIR), 98–99
Loose coupling organization, 168–69
Low altitude navigation target infrared radar for night (LANTIRN) tests, 98
Luftwaffe, 137
Luttwak, Edward, 287, 289 n.12, 291, 292–93
Luxembourg, 33
Lynx helicopter, 236, 264 n.13

Machiavelli, Niccolò, 152, 199, 280
Machine gun, 2
Magic Lantern, 264 n.14
Maginot Line, 3, 6, 185
Maintenance, 98, 261 n.3
Major Regional Contingency (MRC), 307
Management of Coalition, 37–43
Management of war, 166, 175, 194, 195
Mandeles, Mark D., 9–10, 11, 12, 109, 325
Maneuver. *See* Mobility
March, Daniel P., 231
Marine Aircraft Group (MAG) 11, 210
Marine Aircraft Group (MAG) 13, 210
Marine Aircraft Group (MAG) 26, 208, 209, 212–13
Marine Aircraft Group (MAG) 40, 203
Marine Aircraft Group (MAG) 70, 205
Marine Expeditionary Brigade (MEB), 203
Marine Expeditionary Force (MEF), 202–3
Marine Expeditionary Unit (MEU), 203
Marine Light Attack (MLA) Helicopter Squadron 369, 205

Index   335

Maritime campaign, 236–39, 244
Maritime Interception Force (MIF), U.S., 228–29
Maritime Prepositioned Force (MPF), U.S., 204, 219, 228, 243, 253, 255. See also Prepositioned materiel
Maritime Prepositioned Ship Squadron (MPSRon), U.S., 204, 208
Maritime Prepositioned Ship Squadron (MPSRon) 2, U.S., 91, 204, 227
Maritime Prepositioned Ship Squadron (MPSRon) 3, U.S., 206
Marshall, George C., 169, 299
Mass destruction, 61, 113, 122, 130, 181, 192, 195, 285, 286
Massed forces, 136–37, 146, 147, 148
"Massive Retaliation" concept, 298
Master Attack Plan (MAP), 115–16, 129, 133–34, 152 n.3, 154 n.32, 159–65, 170 n.11
Master Target List (MTL), 116, 138
Maurutania, 32
Mauz, Henry J., Jr., 226a, 229
Al Mawsil, Iraq, 128
Maxim, Hiram Stevens, Sir, 2–3
McCaffrey, Barry, 196
McDonald, Charles C., 89
McGuire AFB, N.J., 77
McNair, Leslie, 282
McPeak, Merrill A., 291
Means/ends analysis, 271–72
Mecca, Saudi Arabia, 55–56
Mechanicsburg, Pa., 75
Media, 1, 3–4, 37, 47, 54, 117, 263 n.9, 286–87
Medieval Islam, 50, 53
Medina, Saudi Arabia, 55–56
Medina division, Iraq, 197–98
Mediterranean Sea, 81, 223, 227, 255–56
Meuse-Argonne sector, France, 296
Microelectronics, 158
Middle East and Europeans, 51, 189
Military doctrine, 177–83, 192, 267
Military education, 280
Military forces, control of, 134, 166, 168–69

Military Sealift Command (MSC), 227–28, 230
Military support (MS) targets, 116, 117
Military Traffic Management Command (MTMC), 227
Mill, John Stuart, 11
Mina Sulman, Oman, 227, 240
Mine countermeasures (MCM), 238, 244, 256, 259, 264 nn.14, 15
Mine evasion sonar, 264 n.14
Mine fields, 216, 237–39, 244, 259
Mirror-image strike rehearsals, 234, 243
Mirror imaging, 185
Mishab, Saudi Arabia, 208
Mission Capable (MC) rates, 94
Mission Incapable Parts (MICAP), 96
Mitchell, William "Billy," 107, 135, 136, 267, 291, 296–97, 301–2
Mixson, Riley D., 231
Mobility, 88, 159, 177, 178, 251–52, 304–5
Mojave Desert, 203–4
M1A1 Abrams tank, 209, 212, 214
M109A3 Paladin howitzer, 209
M-110 howitzer batteries, 202
Montesquieu, Baron de la Brède et de, 270
Moore, Royal N., 206–7, 211, 213
Morale, 295, 297, 300
Morality. See Ethics, morality
Moran, Daniel, 289 n.9
Morocco, 14 n.18, 32
Mrozek, Donald J., 303–4
M-60A1 tank, 202, 212
M2A2 Bradley Infantry Fighting Vehicle, 209
Mubarak, Hossni, 28, 31, 45 n.24, 56
Mujahid (one who wages jihad), 58
Mulroney, Brian, 38
Multi-Man Intermittent Cooling System, 92
Multinational Interception Force (MIF), 245 n.15
Munitions supply, 95
Murphy's law, 280
Muslim nationalism, 51–52, 260 n.1

Muslim states, 50, 54, 189–90, 198, 273
Muslim World League, 56, 57
Mussolini, Benito, 6
Myatt, James M. "Mike," 205, 206, 214, 218

Napoleon I, 154 n.25, 177, 282
Napoleonic Wars, 294
Nasser, Gamal Abdal, 52
Nationalism, 51–52, 55, 260 n.1
Naval Gunfire Support (NGFS) force, 238, 239
Netherlands, 14 n.18
"New Look" defense program, 302
News media, 4
New Zealand, 14 n.18, 33
Niger, 14 n.18
Night vision equipment, 211
Ninth Air Force, U.S., 113, 147 n.33, 207
9th Marines, 205
Nitze, Paul, 147
Nixon, Richard, 3
Nonlethal weapons, 149, 150
Noriega, Manuel, 179
Normandy, invasion of, 189, 301
North Arabian Sea, 225, 227
North Atlantic Treaty Organization (NATO), 27, 33, 203, 209, 227, 256; and Bosnia, 262 n.7; and Soviet strategy, 261 n.5; strategy, 177
North Vietnam, 300
North Vietnamese Army (NVA), 6
Norway, 14 n.18
Nuclear, biological, chemical capability (NBC), 113, 114, 120–21, 122, 193, 195, 232. *See also* Biological weapons; Chemical weapons; Nuclear weapons
Nuclear weapons, 113, 114, 116, 193, 195, 232; and airpower, 117, 297–99; and Clausewitz, 269; destruction of, 120, 122, 123, 274
Nunn, Sam, 8

Objectives in war, 114–15, 141–48, 270, 302; annihilation, attrition, 138–41, 148, 149, 150, 151, 154 n.25; of Bush, 27, 108, 112, 179, 180–81, 188, 192–93, 230, 270, 275; control, 134, 135, 138–41, 143, 146; of Saddam, 179, 270, 271–74, 278–79
Occupation, 297
Offloading, 72–73, 99, 227
Oil fields, 214, 217
Oil platforms, 236
Oil supply, 17, 27, 60, 180, 204, 272; and Iraqi economy, 230; Saddam's view of, 54, 272; and Saudi Arabia, 91; targets, 114, 116, 128, 133; threat to, 225; value of, 230
Oman, 14 n.18, 32, 77, 191
Omnibus Agreement (1986), 207
101st Air Assault, U.S., 191, 196
Operational level in war, 133–34, 141–45, 154 n.33, 157, 280
Operational tempo, 178, 196, 219
Operation Desert Express, 73–74, 90–91
Operation Desert Shield, 17, 54–60, 67–82, 210–19, 226, 227–28, 230
Operation Desert Storm, 17, 60–61, 67–82, 203–10, 229–30, 231, 232–33
Operation European Desert Express, 73–74, 90–91
Operation Just Cause, 68, 70
Operation Plan (OPLAN) 1002-90, 29–30, 226
Operation Restore Hope, 80
Operations centers, 130
Operation Southern Watch, 243
Operation Strangle, 302
Orchestration of war, 141, 299, 300
Organization of military, 159, 165–69
Organization of Petroleum Exporting Countries (OPEC), 272
Organization of the Islamic Conference (OIC), 50, 54, 56, 57
Osiraq nuclear facility, Iraq, 274
Outsize cargo, 70, 84 n.21
OV-10A/D "Bronco," 205, 210, 213
Overhead imaging, 183–84

Oversize cargo, 70, 84 n.21
Ozal, Turgut, 38

Packaging Reconstitution/Augmentation Team (PAT), 93
Pagonis, William G., 89
Pakistan, 14 n.18, 189–90, 261 n.4
Palestine Liberation Organization (PLO), 32
Palestinian conflict, 59, 62, 272, 274, 276, 277, 284
Palm, Leslie M., 214
Panama, 68, 70, 82, 179
Pan-Arabism, 51–52, 54, 62, 63
Pan-Islamism, 51–52, 63
Papa Bear (1st U.S. Marine task force), 214, 216, 218
Papp, Daniel S., 9, 17–18, 325
Parallel warfare, 127–52
Paralysis of enemy, 146
Paret, Peter, 289 n.9
Passion, popular, 277, 284, 286
Patriot missiles, 258
Peace dividend, 179
Pearl Harbor attack, 135
Pentatomic division, 178
People's Army of North Vietnam, 5–6
People's Islamic Conference, 58
People's Republic of China, 4, 17, 18, 39, 260; and Coalition, 32–33; and ethnocentrism, 306; role of, 25; and United States, 273
Persian Gulf, 223, 225, 227, 231, 234, 237, 257
Phase Line Red, 217
Phenomenon of war, 269–70
Photo reconnaissance, 202, 220
Physical environment, 187, 188, 198, 201
Pike, Douglas, 5–6
Pilot augmentation, 71–72
Pilot pools, 72
Planning of air operations, 111–15
Plato, 280
Point defense targets, 130
Poland, 14 n.18
Policy and strategy, 270, 286

Political community of Islam. See Umma
Political purpose, 286, 287
Political will, 193–94
Politics, 17–19, 21–44, 269, 270, 271–75, 275–76, 303; and bases, 253–55
Politics and religion, 48
Pope AFB, N.C., 75
Populace, 112, 133, 134, 270–71
Popular passion, 277, 284, 286
Ports as targets, 114, 233
Positional warfare, 184–85
Post–Cold War military, 148, 149, 202, 261 n.2
Postcolonial regimes, 49
Powell, Colin, 3–4, 11, 28–29, 87, 188, 225, 239, 242, 293
Precise weapons delivery, 135, 136–37, 165
Precision bombing, 297
Precision-guided munitions (PGM), 108, 137, 138, 158, 292; effectiveness, 146, 157, 306; and Navy, 258, 263 n.11
Precision Measurement Equipment Laboratory (PMEL), 98
Preemptive strike, 254, 295
Preparations for Desert Storm, 226
Prepositioned materiel, 91, 93, 255. See also Maritime Prepositioned Force
Prepositioning of Materiel Configured to Unit Sets (POMCUS), 261 n.5
Presence operations, 261 n.2
Pressure mines, 264 n.15
Primakov, Yevgeny, 36, 171 n.30
Production and ring model, 112
Production targets, 114, 143
Programmed depot maintenance (PDM), 98
Projection of force, 147, 148, 252, 283, 285
Propaganda, 36, 48, 55, 59–60, 268, 284
Prophet Muhammad, 51, 57, 58
Protective aircraft, 137
Province 19, 272
Provisioning Coalition, 91

P-3 aircraft, 257
Public opinion, 4, 23, 180–81, 182, 184, 198, 256, 284; and Clausewitz, 270–71; and Coalition, 277–78; in Iraq, 272; and limited war, 276; and Saddam, 277; and victory, 275; will to fight, 295
Public relations, 180–81, 223
Purpose of war, 134

al-Qadaffi, Muammar, 255–56
Qarun (Qur'anic figure), 54
Qatar, 14 n.18, 32
Qian Qichen, 42–43
Quayle, Dan, 29
Queen Bee facilities, 98
Quinn, John T., 12–13, 174, 325
Qur'an, 51, 53, 56, 62

Rabitat al-'Alam al-Islami (Muslim World League), 56
Radar, 137–38, 143, 258, 261 n.6, 264 n.13; airborne, 158; posts in Iraq, 140; and sea targets, 256–57
RAF Upper Heyford, U.K., 69
Railroads, 116, 136
Ramadan, 279
Ramstein AB, Germany, 69
Rand, 72, 126 n.27
Range of power, 147
Rapid Area Distribution Support (RADS), 93
Rapid Engineer Deployable (RED) team, 94
Rapid Reaction Force, 261 n.4
Ras Al Qulayah, 239
Readiness, lack of, 165
Readiness in Base Services (Prime RIBS), 94
Ready Reserve Force (RRF) ships, 92, 228, 243
Reagan, Ronald, 18, 34, 178, 179, 273
Real-time control, 166–67
Reason in Clausewitz, 277, 286
Rebellion and Islam, 53
Reconnaissance, 183–84, 235, 244, 261 n.6; restricted, 237–38; at sea, 236, 252, 257, 259
Reconnaissance-strike complex, 158
Recoverable Orbital Satellite (RORSAT), 262 n.6
Red Sea, 225, 227, 231, 257
Reduction of Marine Corps, 202
Refueling aircraft, 67
Regimental Combat Team (RCT), 205
Regionalism, 17–19
Rehabilitation in Islamic law, 53
Reinforcement of Coalition, 75, 230
"Remarkable trinity," 270–71, 277, 284, 286
Remotely piloted vehicle (RPV), 213
Replacement supplies, 125 n.26, 263 n.9
Republican Guard, 114, 115, 116, 122, 126 n.34, 128, 191, 231–32; destruction of, 193, 195–96, 197–98; disposition, 185; envelopment of, 240; escape, 286; strategy concerning, 194–95; as threat, 283, 284; withdrawal of, 197
Requirements of airlift, 70–71
Requirements Validation Cell, 70
Reserve forces, 77, 93, 208–9
Resolutions. *See under* United Nations
Responsiveness of forces, 147
Resupply of forces, 75, 79, 96–97
Revolutionary Command Council, 54, 193
Revolution in Military Affairs (RMA), 109, 157–69
RF-4 Phantom, 108
RF-4B Phantom II, 202
Rhein-Main AB, Germany, 69, 73–74
Rice, Donald, 118
Ring model, 108, 109, 112
Ripper (7th U.S. Marine task force), 214, 216
Rivalry between services, 167, 176, 178, 204, 205, 243
Riyadh, Saudi Arabia, 73, 98
Rockeye cluster bomb, 241
Rollback of Iraq, 181–82
Rolling Thunder, 5, 112, 303

Roll-on/roll-off capability (RO/RO), 227, 243
Roosevelt, Franklin, 195
Rosenthal, Andrew, 171 n.30
Rota AB, Spain, 69
Route package system, 243, 262 n.8
Royal Navy, 241
Royal Navy, United Kingdom, 236, 238, 252
Rules of engagement, 229, 258
Rumaila oil fields, Iraq, 272
Russell, Richard B., 8
Rwanda, 307

Al-Sabah family, 37, 38, 55, 193
Sadat, Anwar, 56
Saddam Line, 185, 189, 190–91
Safety of aircrews, 71
Safiyana, Saudi Arabia, 208
Safwan, 185, 196
St. Mihiel, France, 296
Salah al-Din (Saladin), 58
San Antonio Air Logistics Center, 92
Sanitation, 120
Satellites, 258, 261 n.6
Saudi Arabia, 8, 14 n.18, 17, 18, 77; and air campaign, 60; airspace limitations, 81; bases, 273, 284; border targets, 239; and cease-fire, 198; clergy, 254; and Coalition, 29–30, 40, 91, 189–90, 193; defense of, 27, 113, 151, 226, 279; and fellahin, 190; and ground-based forces, 260; infrastructure, 82, 90, 95, 201, 228, 253, 260; invasion of, 87–88, 112, 243, 278; and Iraq, 56, 273; and Islamic shrines, 55–56; joint operations, 159; Marines in, 205; military force, 190–91, 239; military role, 24; and Muslim World League, 56; National Guard, 189; oil provisions, 91; and People's Islamic Conference, 58–59; politics, 253–55; port security, 256; and prepositioned materiel, 261 n.5; reaction to Gulf War, 260 n.1; and Scud missiles, 60, 121, 190; sea lanes, 257; and United States, 260 n.1; and U.S. Navy, 251; and Western forces, 55–56, 57; xenophobia, 260 n.1
Scheduling problems, 159
Schlieffen plan, 187, 280
Schmidt, Larry S., 214
Schneller, Robert J., 12, 223, 326
Schwarzkopf, H. Norman, 11, 28–29, 112, 113, 174, 209, 216, 225; and Al Firdos incident, 118; and casualty rates, 210; criticized, 10; failure of, 189; ground offensive, 239; "Hail Mary Play," 79, 187, 192, 194, 199; image, 3; and Marines, 206; and Republican Guard, 195–96; strategy, 7, 79, 186–89, 227, 233
Schweinfurt, Germany, 130–31
Scorched earth policy, 214
Scowcroft, Brent, 23, 32, 37
Scud missiles, 76, 145, 193, 197, 211, 283; and Islamic law, 60; and Israel, 35, 190; mobility, 305; political goal of, 189–90; and Saudi Arabia, 190; significance, 126 n.31, 183–84, 281; targeted, 113, 114, 116, 120, 121, 122, 128, 232, 284; and United Arab Emirates, 190
Sea control, 237
Sea Dart missile, 241
Sea forces, 151, 267
Sealift, 65–66, 92, 223, 226, 243, 255
Sea lines of communication, 227, 243
SEALs, 238, 240
2nd Brigade, 1st armored division, U.K., 197–98
2d Force Service Support Group (FSSG), 208, 209
II Egyptian Corps, 190–91
II Marine Expeditionary Force (MEF), 203, 230
2d Light Armored Infantry Battalion, USMC, 213
2d Marine Aircraft Wing (MAW), 208
2d Marine Division, 208–18 passim
2d Marine Expeditionary Brigade (MEB), 209
2d Marine Regiment, 203
2nd Armored Division, U.S., 209
2d Tank battalion, 214

Sector antiair warfare commander (SAAWC), 207
Sector operations center (SOC), 140–41
Secularism and Islam, 52
Secure Telephone Unit-III (STU-III), 166
Selected Marine Corps Reserve (SMCR), 202, 208–9, 219–20
Self-propelled howitzer, 205
Self-sufficiency, 252
Senegal, 14 n.18
Sensor technology, 158, 165, 166, 257
Serial (sequential) warfare, 130–33, 143
Service rivalry, 167, 176, 178, 204, 205, 243
7th Armored Brigade, U.K., 207–8
VII Corps, U.S., 74, 190–91, 194, 197, 209, 230, 239, 240
7th Marine Expeditionary Brigade (MEB), 203, 219, 227
7th Marines, 205
7th Marine task force, U.S., 214, 216
7th Marine Expeditionary Brigade (MEB), 91
7th Fleet, 203, 206, 207, 216, 230
Seymour Johnson AFB, N.C., 94
Shaddock (SS-N-3) missile, 256–57
Shah of Iran, 181
Shaibah airfield, Iraq, 128
Shari'a (Islamic law), 51
Sharp, Ulysses Simpson Grant, 13 n.2
Shatt-Al-Arab marshlands, 237
Shelter busting, 117
Shepherd (1st Marine Light Armored Infantry Battalion), 214, 218
Shevardnadze, Eduard, 25, 42–43
Shi'ites, 49, 59, 61, 122–23, 276
Ship cost, 262 n.8
Shoot, move, talk, 177
Shop Replacable Unit (SRU), 97
Shulimson, Jack, 12–13, 174, 326
Sigonella AB, Italy, 69
Silkworm missiles, 237, 241
Simultaneous (parallel) warfare, 130–34

1610th Airlift Division, Provisional, U.S., 78
6th Fleet, 203
6th Marines, 206, 214, 216, 217, 218
6th Light Armored, France, 191
Slot time, 73
SL-7 fast sealift ship, 228
Smoke on battlefield, 240
Software, 262 n.8, 264 n.13
Somalia, 2, 80, 129, 307
Sonar, 264 n.14
Sortie, 124 n.14, 158, 263 n.10, 291
South Korea, 14 n.18, 21
Southwest Asia, 93, 253, 261 n.4
Southwest Asia transport plan, 70
Soviet Ocean Surveillance System (SOSS), 261 n.6
Soviet Union, 4, 6, 7, 17, 18, 39, 226, 299; and Bush, 25–26; and Coalition, 32–33, 36–37, 263 n.9; collapse of, 49, 176, 179, 180, 281, 292; and embargo, 253; as enemy, 302; and Iraq, 25–26, 88, 171 n.30, 184, 214; public opinion, 278; role, 25; sea reconnaissance, 261 n.6; strategy, 151–52, 156 n.50, 261 n.4; submarines, 261 n.5; and United States, 273; weapons, 256–57; in World War II, 301
Space dimension of war, 133–34
Space systems, 147, 149, 166, 258
Spain, 14 n.18, 90
Spare parts, 73, 79, 96, 98
Spatz, Carl, 301
Special operations forces, 183–84, 195, 242
Special Planning Group, 124 n.8, 142–43
SPY-1 radar, 258
Stability of Middle East, 180, 192, 201, 230, 283
Stalin, Josef, 180
Standard Air Munitions Packages (STAMP), 89, 95
Standard munitions, 108
Standard Tank, Rack, Adapter, and Pylon Packages (STRAPP), 89, 96
State sovereignty, 50

Index

Static defense, 184–85
Static planning of air campaign, 159–65
Status quo ante bellum, 192, 194, 195
Stealth aircraft, 137–38, 165. *See also* F-117 aircraft
Stinger missile, 259
Stirrup, 169 n.2
Strategic air defenses (SAD), 116
Strategic airpower, 7, 69, 111–12, 113, 117, 298–99
Strategic bombing, 193, 300–304
Strategic level in war, 133–34, 157
Strategy, 142, 146, 148–49, 176, 270, 286; of air campaign, 111–23, 232; for AirLand Battle, 88, 142, 177–78, 182–83, 187–89, 191–92, 195, 196, 197; of airpower, 127–52; of amphibious assault, 235, 236, 237; of Boomer, 209, 210, 211; concerning Republican Guard, 194–95; European, 177; for ground war, 174, 175–99; and mass, 146, 148; modern, 177–79; and NATO, 177; of parallel warfare, 127–52; and policy, 270, 286; of Saddam, 6–7, 108, 184–85, 189–90, 231–32, 242, 258, 284; of Schwarzkopf, 7, 79, 186–89, 227, 233; of Soviet Union, 151–52, 156 n.50, 261 n.4; and technology, 148–49, 165; of United States, 2–13, 177–83, 226, 234–35, 261 n.5, 292–93, 294, 295–307, 299; in World War II, 177, 184–85, 187
Strengths in warfare, 183
Strike, 124 n.14, 170 n.8
Strike sortie, 158, 170 n.8
Stuttgart, Germany, 74
Sudan, 32
Suez Canal, 255–56
Suit, William, 11–12, 65, 326
Sullivan, Gordon, 156 n.50
Summer, Harry G., Jr., 10, 11, 12
Sunni party, 52, 272, 276
Sun Tzu, 139, 269, 293–94
Sununu, John, 29
Supplies, 65–66

Supply and Reconstitution/Augmentation Team (SAT), 93
Support aircraft, 137
Suppression of defenses, 252
Suppression of Enemy Air Defenses (SEAD), 137, 160, 162, 233, 263 n.10
Surface forces, 134, 146–47, 151, 295
Surface-to-air missile (SAM), 4, 116, 128, 129
Surgical strike, 194
Surveillance, 158, 159, 183–84, 252, 261 n.6
Suspension in war, 278–80, 286
Sutton, Robert, 231
Sylvester, John B., 214
Synchronization in war, 178
Synergy, 150
Syria, 14 n.18, 32, 40, 51–52, 189–90, 190; military forces, 190–91, 212, 239
Systems as targets, 135, 143, 145, 147, 154 nn.30, 33; for control, 134, 146, 148

Tactical Air Control Center (TACC), 158, 159
Tactical Air Control System (TACS), 141
Tactical air forces, 98, 298–99
Tactical Air Operations Center (TAOC), 207
Tactical ballistic missile defense, 258
Tactical Fighter Wing (TFW), 159, 167; and central planners, 158
Tactical level in war, 133–34, 157
Tactical Shelter Systems, 96
Taif AB, Saudi Arabia, 80, 160
Tallil, Iraq, 140, 160, 162, 185, 196
Tanagib, Saudi Arabia, 210
Tanker aircraft, 67, 80
Tanker Airlift Control Center, 81
Al Taqqadum airfield, Iraq, 128
Target coverage, 138
Targeting, 114–15, 143, 232, 233, 263 n.11, 295; of defenses, 130; of intelligence, 300; for interdiction, 232; in Internal Look 90, 112; of Iraq, 263

n.11; of military support, 116, 117; and naval bombardment, 239–40; of naval ports, 114, 223; and parallel warfare, 133; problems with, 234, 304–5; of production facilities, 114, 143; and radar, 158; of Saddam, 300; at sea, 256–57; of ships, 261 n.6; of systems, 134, 135, 143, 145, 146, 147, 148, 154 nn.30, 33; theory of, 127–52; Warden on, 299–300

Target Planning Worksheet (TPW), 161–62, 170 n.11

Taro (3rd U.S. Marine task force), 214

Task Group 151.11, 238–39

Tawakalna infantry division, Iraq, 197

Teamwork/Boldguard exercise, 203

Technology, 2, 5, 109, 124, 142, 147, 169 n.2; after World War I, 294; and airpower, 303, 304; and Clausewitz, 269; and modern strategy, 148–49, 165; nonaviation, 304–5; and parallel war, 135, 137–38, 145; and politics, 303; revolutionary aspects, 157; and sensors, 158, 165, 166, 257; significance of, 201, 202; success of, 175

Tedder, Arthur William, Baron, 135

Tel Aviv, Israel, 190

Telecommunications, 158

Tempo of battle, 178, 196, 219

Tenoso, Edwin E., 78, 79

10th Marines, 214, 217

Terminology of transport, 70

Terrain mapping guidance system, 264 n.12

Terrorism, 281

T-56 aircraft, 98

Thailand, 260

Thatcher, Margaret, 17, 27–28, 37, 42

Theater planning, 115

3rd Armored Division, U.S., 74

3d Battalion, 23d Marines, U.S., 217

3d Battalion, 67th Armor, USMC, 218

III Corps, Iraq, 211

III Marine Expeditionary Force (MEF), U.S., 206

3d Light Armored Infantry Battalion, USMC, 205

3d Marine Aircraft Wing (MAW), U.S., 206–7, 208, 210–11, 212, 213, 217, 219

3d Marine Division, U.S., 206

3d Marine Expeditionary Brigade (MEB), U.S., 206

3d Marine task force, U.S., 214

3rd Armored, U.S., 196

Third World, 3, 5, 12, 50

13th Marine Expeditionary Unit (MEU), 203, 241

13th Marine Expeditionary Unit (MEU) (SOC), 206

36th Tactical Fighter Wing (TFW), U.S., 98

363d Tactical Fighter Wing (TFW), U.S., 159–65

388th Tactical Fighter Wing (TFW), U.S., 94

Thucydides, 270

Thumrait, Oman, 96

Tiananmen Square massacre, 32

Tiger Brigade, U.S., 209, 210, 212, 214, 216, 218

Tigris River, 235

Tilford, Earl H., Jr., 13 n.5, 171 n.34, 303, 304, 326

Time dimension, 133–34, 145, 147, 151, 190, 251; and bombing, 301, 305; and cease-fire, 198; and Clausewitz, 278–80, 286; in Gulf War, 158, 181, 182, 227, 243, 278–80

Time-Phased Force Deployment Data (TPFDD), 70, 71

Tinker AFB, Okla., 75

Title XIII insurance, 75–76

Title V report, 118–22

Tolstoy, Leo, 168

Tomahawk Land Attack (Cruise) Missile (TLAM), 128, 150, 233, 256, 258, 264 n.12

Torrejon AB, Spain, 69

Total airlift system, 71

Total force policy, 68, 76–77

Tracking supplies, 97

Trafalgar, Battle of, 268

Training, 76, 78–79, 88, 89, 91; of Coalition forces, 81–82, 176, 182; of Iraqi forces, 189, 237, 244; jointness, 142, 231
Training and Doctrine Command (TRADOC), 142
Transportation, 93, 133, 134, 136
Trenchard, Hugh Montague Trenchard, 1st Viscount, 291
TR-1 ASARS aircraft, 158
Tufts University Institute for Foreign Policy, 107
Tunisia, 32
Turkey, 14 n.18, 33, 40, 81, 90, 273, 284
20th Tactical Fighter Wing (TFW), U.S., 98
24th Infantry (mechanized), U.S., 191, 196, 197–98
Twenty-nine Palms, Calif., 203
22nd Marine Expeditionary Unit (MEU), U.S., 203

UH-1N "Huey," 205
'Ulama, 18, 48–49
Umma (Muslim community), 48, 50–52
Umm Gudair oil field, 212
Umm Qasr, Iraq, 237
United Arab Emirates, 14 n.18, 32, 40, 77, 189–90, 190, 193, 198
United Kingdom, 14 n.18, 17, 18, 33, 54; airbase, 90; and Coalition, 189; detention of citizens, 40; and Iraq, 184; military force, 191; Royal Navy, 236, 238, 241, 252; and United States, 273; and World War II, 187
United Nations: and Bush, 9; embargo, 4, 24, 27, 125 n.26, 228–29, 243, 256, 263 n.9; exclusion zone, 254; image of, 63; and Muslim states, 50; postwar inspections, 120, 121, 123, 281, 292; resolutions, 32, 33, 39, 41–42, 43, 55, 229, 274, 280; role of, 179–80; Security Council, 2; use of economic sanctions, 42; use of military, 42; and war, 275

United States, 2–3, 14 n.18, 30, 58, 63, 283; and Arab states, 274; center of gravity, 273; and Coalition, 189; defense spending, 202, 292; ethics, morality, 179–81; force size in Gulf, 182; foreign policy, 254, 281; and France, 273; and intelligence, 281–82; and Israel, 35, 44 n.35, 190; leadership role, 37–43; military doctrine, strategy, 2–13, 177–83, 226, 292–93, 294, 295–307; military role, 24; post–Cold War role, 179–80, 181–82, 192, 261 n.2, 292; public opinion, 23, 40, 180–81, 184, 198, 256, 284; and Saudi Arabia, 253–54, 260 n.1, 261 n.5; and Soviet strategy, 261 n.5; and Soviet Union, 273; and United Kingdom, 273. See also individual services
United States Air Force (USAF), 67–82, 107–9, 111–23, 127–52, 157–69; doctrine, 267, 302; force size, 148 n.44; GWAPS report, 118–22; jointness, 142, 207, 231, 233, 236, 243; and Korean War, 302; logistics, 87–100, 261 n.3; and Marines, 207; and Mitchell, 297; mobility, 88; and Navy, 243; organizational structure, 166; origins, 267; planning, 112, 113; and reinforcements, 230; role, 176; and technology, 303, 304; training, 76, 78–79, 88, 89, 91, 142, 231. See also individual units
United States Air Force Logistics Command (AFLC), 89, 93
United States Air Force Logistics Information File (AFLIF), 97
United States Air Force Reserve (AFRES), 69, 77, 80
United States Air Force Strategic Air Command (SAC), 79–80, 90, 95–96, 113, 298, 299
United States Air Force Tactical Air Command (TAC), 93, 113, 298, 299, 302–3
United States Air Forces Europe (USAFE), 93

United States Air National Guard (ANG), 69, 77, 80
United States Army (USA), 89, 141–42, 155 n.42, 175–99, 226, 255; action, 192–99; disposition, 190–92; doctrine, 177–83; strategy, 187–89. *See also individual units*
United States Army Central Support Command, 89
United States Central Command Air Force (CENTAF), 67, 96–97, 112, 113, 142
United States Central Command (US-CENTCOM), 29–30, 90, 111–12, 191, 201, 226, 261 n.4
United States Coast Guard (USCG), 229, 256
United States Congress, 8, 9, 44 n.4
United States Department of Defense (DOD), 75, 118, 148
United States Department of Transportation, 228
United States Federal Aviation Administration (FAA), 75
United States Marine Corps (USMC), 74, 92, 173–74, 213, 232, 236; air force size, 148 n.44; commander, 204, 206; logistics, 202, 210–11, 212, 213, 217; prepositioning, 204, 205–6, 207–8, 219, 227, 228, 255, 258, 261 n.4; and reinforcements, 230; role, 176, 201–20, 226. *See also individual units*
United States Military Airlift Command (MAC), 67–82, 90, 227
United States Military Sealift Command (MSC), 90
United States National Guard, 93
United States National Security Council (NSC), 27, 28–29
United States Naval Forces Central Command (NAVCENT), 206, 210, 230
United States Navy (USN), 89, 148 n.44, 233–34, 243–44, 253, 262 n.8; and air campaign, 257–58; logistics, 226, 227–28, 230, 251–52, 255; mobility, 251–52; and reinforcements, 230; role, 176, 223–60. *See also individual units*
United States Pacific Air Forces (PACAF), 93
United States Strategic Bombing Survey (USSBS), 118, 123 n.2, 301
United States Transportation Command (USTRANSCOM), 7, 65, 68, 69–70, 89, 90, 227, 243
Unity of command, 297
Unlimited war, 270, 289 n.7
Urban combat, 198
U.S. News & World Report, 3–4, 263 n.9
USS *America*, 232, 235
USS *Avenger*, 232
USS *Comfort*, 228
USS *Dwight D. Eisenhower*, 31, 225
USS *Guam*, 241
USS *Independence*, 225
USS *Iwo Jima*, 241
USS *Jarrett*, 241
USS *John F. Kennedy*, 232
USS *Mercy*, 228
USS *Midway*, 232, 234
USS *Missouri*, 238, 239–40, 244
USS *Nassau*, 241
USS *Okinawa*, 241
USS *Princeton*, 216, 238–39, 259
USS *Ranger*, 232, 234, 241
USS *Saratoga*, 232, 233
USS *Theodore Roosevelt*, 232, 234
USS *Tripoli*, 216, 238–39, 259
USS *Wisconsin*, 238, 239–40, 244

VA-155, 241
Validation of transport needs, 70
Value system, 271–72
Vehicles in logistics, 94
Victory, 197–98, 274–75, 285, 287, 294; definition of, 181–82, 192, 193, 195, 285–86
Videotaping, 167
Viet Cong, 5–6, 192, 300, 303
Vietminh, 6
Vietnam: political structure, 303
Vietnam War, 1, 3–8, 11, 12, 113, 180, 184; and airpower, 82, 194,

299, 306; and ethnocentrism, 305, 306; and European strategy, 177; and force package, 137; and Horner, 129; legacy of, 175, 292; and Marines, 207; and morale, 300; and precision munitions, 108; and public opinion, 284; route package system, 243, 262 n.8; and strategic bombing, 193, 302, 303–4; and Tactical Air Control, 141, 142; and technology, 303, 305; U.S. failure, 192
Violence in Clausewitz, 277, 284, 286
Volunteer Army, 178
Vuono, Carl E., 3–4

Wadi Al Kirr airfield, 127
Walker spy ring, 261 n.6
Walzer, Michael, 48
Warden, John A., III, 107, 108, 112–13, 267, 299–300
Warfare, 270, 271–75, 289 n.7, 306; limited, 6, 175, 180, 270, 275–78, 285, 286, 289 n.7, 298, 302–3; parallel, 127–52; types, 270, 275–78, 289 n.7. *See also* Objectives in war
Wargames, 111, 123 n.1
War Powers Act, 7
War Readiness Spares Kits (WRSK), 89, 96, 98, 101 n.8
War Reserve Materiel (WRM), 94
Warsaw Pact, 87, 88, 89, 177, 178
Washington, George, 154 n.25
Waterloo, Battle of, 2
Weakness in warfare, 183
Weapons cost, 262 n.8
Weapons of mass destruction, 61, 113, 181, 192, 195, 285, 286, 292
Weapons technology, 148–49
Weather, 145, 183, 210–11, 240, 258, 279

Western alliance, 33–34, 43–44
Western culture, 34–35
Western European Union, 33
Western forces, Islamic response to, 57, 59–60
Western imperialism, 51
Weyland, Otto P., 299
Will to fight, 129–30, 135, 273, 295, 300, 301
Wimp factor, 18
Wisner, Frank, 31
Woodward, Robert, 8
World Airways, 75
World War I, 3, 129, 185, 187, 294, 295
World War II, 3, 5, 129, 135, 189, 197, 201; bombing, 118, 123 n.2, 136–37, 193, 298, 300–302, 305, 307; European theater size, 159; friendly fire, 282; and nuclear war, 297; and public opinion, 256; Russian strategy, 156 n.50; sea mines, 264 n.15; strategy, 177, 184–85, 187; targeting, 143; and technologies, 305

Xenophobia, 260 n.1

Yakima, Wash., 216
Yankee Battle Group, 231, 233, 234, 235, 243
Yemen, 32, 41

Zaragoza AB, Spain, 69
Ziemke, Caroline F., 9–10, 12, 268, 326
Zlatoper, Ronald J. "Zap," 236
Zulu Battle Group, 231, 233, 234, 235, 238, 240, 243

About the Editors and Contributors

LARRY E. CABLE is Associate Professor of History at the University of North Carolina at Wilmington. He served in Vietnam, and is now an acknowledged academic expert on Vietnam-era military intelligence and unconventional warfare. His recent books include *Conflict of Myths: The Development of American Counterinsurgency Doctrine and the Vietnam War* (1986) and *Unholy Grail: The United States and the Wars in Vietnam, 1965–1968* (1991).

MICHAEL T. CORGAN is a member of the Political Science faculty at Boston University, specializing in international security affairs and American political institutions. He also teaches an advanced course on Clausewitz and his impact at the Massachusetts Institute of Technology with David Ralston, of that school's History Department. A widely published author, Dr. Corgan has been a member of the National Security Decision Making faculty at the Naval War College and earlier, while on active duty in the Navy, taught in the Strategy Department.

COLONEL DAVID A. DEPTULA, USAF, is on detail to the Commission on Roles and Missions of the Armed Forces. He has earned an M.E. degree in systems engineering, from the University of Virginia, and an M.S. degree in national security strategy, from the National War College. He served in a variety of assignments, which gave him an opportunity to take part in air operations, planning, and joint war fighting at all levels. While working on the Air Staff for the Secretary of the Air Force, he developed concepts for the application of airpower; developed courses of action on force structure, combatant air forces, and long-range planning; and assisted on the white paper, *The Air Force and US National Security: Global Reach— Global Power*. In August 1990, he participated in the original design of the air campaign against Iraq. Detailed to Saudi Arabia, he became the principal offensive air campaign planner for the Joint Force Air Component Commander's director of campaign plans. During the war, he was the director of the Iraq Target Planning Cell. Colonel Deptula is a command pilot with over 2,000 hours in the F-15.

NORMAN FRIEDMAN is a defense analyst who has published nineteen books on naval and defense issues—including *Desert Victory: The War for Kuwait, Naval Institute Guide to World Naval Weapons Systems*, and *The U.S. Maritime Strategy*. As a staff member, and later Deputy Director of National Security Studies of the Hudson Institute (1973–1984), Dr. Friedman conducted or participated in numerous studies for government and industry. He also served as a consultant to the Department of the Navy. He received his Ph.D. in solid-state physics from Columbia University in 1974.

SOHAIL H. HASHMI is assistant professor of international relations at Mount Holyoke College. He received an M.A. in near eastern studies from Princeton and a Ph.D. in political science from Harvard. He is the author of several articles on Middle East politics and Islamic political thought in international relations. He is currently completing a book on the Islamic ethics of war and peace. The research for his contribution to this volume was supported by an SSRC–MacArthur Foundation Fellowship in International Peace and Security.

WILLIAM HEAD is Deputy Center Historian, Warner Robins ALC, Robins AFB, Georgia. He received his Ph.D. in U.S. Diplomatic History from Florida State University, 1980. His most recent publications include "Air Power in the Persian Gulf: An Initial Search for the Right Lessons," *The Air Force Journal of Logistics* (Winter 1992) (Outstanding Article for 1992); co-editorship of *Looking Back on the Vietnam War: A 1990s Perspective of Decisions, Combat, and Legacies* (Greenwood, 1993); and *Every Inch a Soldier: General Augustine Warner Robins and the Development of American Air Power Before World War II* (1995).

COLONEL DANIEL T. KUEHL, PH.D., USAF, Retired, teaches military strategy at the National Defense University's School of Information Warfare and Strategy. His twenty-two–year USAF career included assignments in missile operations, nuclear plans, and doctrine development. He was a member of the Checkmate planning group that developed the Instant Thunder strategic air campaign plan. He wrote "The Air Campaign" chapter in the DOD's official report *Conduct of the Persian Gulf War;* and as the head of the Air Staff element supporting the *Gulf War Air Power Survey (GWAPS),* he contributed to most of the Survey's products, including editing its *Statistical Compendium.* Dr. Kuehl holds a Ph.D. from Duke University and has published in a wide variety of military-related journals.

JOHN W. LELAND is senior Historian, Air Mobility Command. He received his Ph.D. from Ohio State University. He served as a civilian historian at Strategic Air Command for sixteen years. He is a specialist in humanitarian airlift and air mobility operations during the Persian Gulf War. His many publications include *Military Airlift Command and the Afghan Humanitarian Relief Program* (USAF Excellence in Monographs Award, 1990); *Humanitarian Airlift to Soviet Armenia* (1990); and *Operations Provide Hope: A Humanitarian Airlift to the States of the Former Soviet Union* (USAF Excellence in Historical Publications Award, 1993).

MARK D. MANDELES is a defense analyst who received a Ph.D. in political science from Indiana University. His most recent publications include "Between a Rock and a Hard Place: Implications for the U.S. of Third World Nuclear Weapon and Ballistic Missile Proliferation," *Security Studies* (Fall 1991), and co-authorship of the Department of the Air Force's *Gulf War Air Power Survey: Command & Organization* (Washington, D.C.: Office of Air Force History, 1993).

DANIEL S. PAPP is Professor of International Affairs and former Director of the School of Social Sciences at Georgia Tech. He has also served as Senior Research Fellow at the Center for Aerospace Doctrine, Research, and Education at Air University and as Research Professor at the Strategic Studies Institute of the U.S. Army War College. Dr. Papp received his Ph.D. in International Affairs from the University of Miami. His numerous book and article publications include *Soviet Perceptions of the Developing World During the 1980s: The Ideological Basis* (1985) and *The Political Economy of International Technology Transfer* (Greenwood, 1986).

MAJOR JOHN T. QUINN, USMC is a Historical Writer at the USMC Historical Center in Washington, D.C. He is working on histories of Marine communications and logistics in Operations Desert Shield and Desert Storm. During the war, he served as a communications officer with the 3d Marine Aircraft Wing in Saudi Arabia and Baharain. Major Quinn received his M.A. in National Security Affairs from the Naval Postgraduate School Monterey, California, 1993.

ROBERT J. SCHNELLER, JR., is a historian of Contemporary History at the Naval Historical Center in Washington, D.C. He received his Ph.D. in military history from Duke University in 1991. He has published several articles and is co-author of a forthcoming history of U.S. Navy operations during the Gulf War.

JACK SHULIMSON is Head, History Writing Unit, USMC Historical Center. He received his Ph.D. from the University of Maryland, College Park. He has written extensively on USMC history, including several volumes in the USMC official history of Vietnam. His most recent publication is *Marines' Search for a Mission, 1880–1898*.

WILLIAM SUIT is a historian for the USAF. He received his Ph.D. from Kent State University in 1988. He has delivered papers on USAF Logistics during Desert Storm and U.S. research and development during the war to several conferences. He has also published a myriad of articles, including an article for *Air Power History* on USAF logistics during Desert Storm.

EARL H. TILFORD, JR., is Director of Studies, the Strategic Studies Institute, U.S. Army War College, Carlisle, Pennsylvania. He earned his Ph.D. in American and European Military History from George Washington University. His many publications include *A History of U.S. Air Force Search and Rescue Operations in Southeast Asia, 1961–1975* and *Crosswinds: The Air Force's Setup in Vietnam* (1993).

CAROLINE F. ZIEMKE is a Research Staff Member at the Institute for Defense Analyses. She received her Ph.D. in Military History and Strategic Studies from Ohio State University. Her most recent publications include "Peace without Strings: Interwar Naval Arms Control Revisited," *Washington Quarterly* (Winter, 1992) and "Promises Fulfilled? The Prophets of Air Power and Desert," *Washington Strategy Seminar, 1992*.